Race,
Culture,
and the
Revolt
of the
Black
Athlete

Race, Culture, and the Revolt of the Black Athlete

THE 1968 OLYMPIC PROTESTS
AND THEIR AFTERMATH

Douglas Hartmann

THE UNIVERSITY OF CHICAGO PRESS
CHICAGO AND LONDON

Douglas Hartmann is associate professor of sociology at the University of Minnesota. He is coauthor of *Ethnicity and Race: Making Identities in a Changing World.*

The University of Chicago Press, Chicago 60637
The University of Chicago Press, Ltd., London
© 2003 by The University of Chicago
All rights reserved. Published 2003
Printed in the United States of America
12 11 10 09 08 07 06 05 04 03   1 2 3 4 5

ISBN: 0–226–31855–9 (cloth)
ISBN: 0–226–31856–7 (paper)

Library of Congress Cataloging-in-Publication Data

Hartmann, Douglas.
    Race, culture and the revolt of the black athlete : the 1968 Olympic protests and their aftermath / Douglas Hartmann.
        p.   cm.
    Includes bibliographical references and index.
    ISBN 0-226-31855-9 (cloth : alk. paper) — ISBN 0-226-31856-7 (pbk. : alk. paper)
    1. Olympic Games (19th : 1968 : Mexico City, Mexico).   2. African American athletes—Political activity—History—20th century.   3. United States—Race relations—History—20th century.   I. Title.

GV 722 1968 .H37 2003
796.48—dc21   2003010932

⊗ The paper used in this publication meets the minimum requirements of the American National Standard for Information Sciences—Permanence of Paper for Printed Library Materials, ANSI Z39.48–1992.

For my childhood friend,

William Cole
and
the alumni of the
Office of Special Programs
at the
University of Chicago

Contents

Illustrations

Preface: Sport, Race, and a Decade of Disruption

In 1963 one of the most prominent African American sports-writers of the day, A. C. "Doc" Young, published *Negro Firsts in Sports*. The book, written for a popular and presumably integrated audience, was divided into two parts. The first was a series of biographical sketches of selected "pioneer" black athletes (both well known and unknown), the second a lengthy appendix detailing the statistics, accomplishments, and awards of Negro athletes and athletic institutions across the country. The volume's primary purpose, as its title and structure suggest, was simply to compile and chronicle the individuals, incidents, and institutions that had "blazed the trail" to what Young called the "Golden Era" of Negro athletics in the United States. But Young's book, which was released by Johnson Publishing, the parent company of *Ebony* magazine, had a much larger, more ambitious motive: to demonstrate that sport was a leader—perhaps the leader—in the social advancement African Americans had made in the United States over the course of the twentieth century. Sport, Young proclaimed, was nothing less than "the door-breaker to progress [for] Americans of color [in all] walks of life" and the "proof to the world that democracy can work." It is a point he made no fewer than five times in the first fourteen pages of the book, going so far as to suggest—certainly for effect, but without any hint of irony—that Willie Mays was as important a figure for civil rights as Martin Luther King Jr. and that Jackie Robinson ranked next to Jesus Christ among the most important and honorable men ever to have walked the earth.

The notion that sport is a positive, progressive force for African Americans and race relations in general is an idea—or, in social scientific parlance, an "ideology"—that resonates deeply in contemporary American popular culture. A 1996 public opinion poll conducted for *U.S. News and World Report*, for example, found that 91 percent of Americans thought that "participation in sports" helps a "person's ability to . . . get along with different ethnic or racial groups." Seventy-eight percent of these respondents thought that sport had either a very positive (25 percent) or somewhat positive (53 percent) impact on society taken as a whole.[1] I myself grew up believing these ideas deeply and wholeheartedly—actually, they were for me a kind of cultural commonsense. To an idealist white kid raised in a medium-sized, very segregated town on the banks of the Mississippi River in southern Missouri, the prowess, prominence, and popularity of African American athletes in American popular culture seemed an unassailable rejoinder to the racist stereotypes and prejudices so otherwise prevalent. Before I entered high school, in fact, little league baseball and city-sponsored flag football leagues provided the only meaningful personal contact I had with African Americans (kids or adults), and these experiences were, at least for me, both eye-opening and almost uniformly positive. What was more, sport's ostensibly apolitical, color-blind meritocracy and its implicit melting-pot vision of American culture fit perfectly with my own optimistic republican individualism.

Thus, it was with great discomfort and trepidation that I realized, when taking my first college course on sport, that most of those whom I recognized as experts on the subject thought exactly the opposite: that since the 1960s a whole host of critics—journalists, coaches, a handful of athletes, and, most of all, scholars of sport—had been questioning the assumption that sport participation is inevitably connected with African American advancement. In stark contrast to the sport-as-positive-racial-force ideology to which I was accustomed, these critics were arguing that racial inequalities and injustice were not so much challenged and overcome in sport as they were reproduced there. Their arguments were based upon both solid evidence of the persistence of racism and discrimination in sport as well as an understanding of the subtler (and perhaps even more fundamental) ways in which African American athletic success served to both reinforce existing racial stereotypes and legitimate systemic racial inequalities.[2] The subtitle for one of the most prominent (and controversial) recent contributions to the literature boldly and succinctly states the dominant motif I was startled to find: "Sport Has Damaged Black America and Preserved the Myth of Race" (Hoberman 1997).

This radical disjuncture between the populist beliefs I grew up with and the expert critiques I learned about in school has motivated my research and writing on race and sport ever since. For reasons involving both my concern with theoretical parsimony and personal temperament, I have resisted the temptation to choose one side over the other. Instead, I have tried to see the contributions and insights of both and the ways in which they might complement each other. To capture and convey my thinking on the matter I have borrowed from Pierre Bourdieu (1988) and Stuart Hall (1981, 1996) to describe sport as a "contested racial terrain" (Hartmann 2000, 2002; see also Early 1998; V. Andrews 1996; Birrell 1989). At the core of this concept and vision is the notion that sport is a "double-edged sword" (Kellner 1996), not just a place (or variable) whereby racial interests and meanings are *either* inhibited *or* advanced but rather a site where racial formations are constantly—and very publicly—struggled on and over.[3] Douglas Kellner's discussion of Michael Jordan begins to capture and convey this more empirical, multifaceted way of thinking about the racial dynamics of sport:

> On the one hand, Michael Jordan is a spectacle of color who elevates difference to sublimity and who raises Blackness to dignity and respect. An icon of the sports spectacle, Michael Jordan is the Black superstar and his prominence in sports has made him a figure that corporate America can use to sell its products and its values. Yet, such are the negative representations and connotations of Blacks in American culture and such is the power of the media to define and refine images that even the greatest Black icons and spectacles can be denigrated to embody negative connotations . . . (f)igures of choice to represent social transgression and tabooed behavior. (1996, p. 465)

And this holds not just for the broad symbolic functions of sport but also for its concrete, on-the-ground practices and policies. The racial dynamics of sport are both positive and negative, progressive and conservative, determined in context and defined by both possibilities for agency and resistance as well as systems of constraint.

Thinking through all of this, I found myself continually coming back to a movement I first heard about in that same introductory sport studies course that had so radically disrupted my adolescent assumptions about sport's racial force and significance: the race-based athletic protest that had emerged in the United States in the late 1960s, the movement that has come to be called the "revolt of the black athlete" (Edwards 1969).

The more I read and learned about this movement, the more difficult it became to determine precisely how its participants understood the relationships between race and sport, and if (and how) their activities in the realm of sport made a productive contribution to the larger struggle for African American freedom and justice. As such, this movement seemed a perfect case by which to interrogate my essentially agnostic vision of sport as racially contested and conflicted. More than this, I came to see that this period of revolt marked the first serious and sustained public challenge to the ideology that sport is an inherently positive and progressive racial force. To be sure, such ideas had been put forward before and a great many racial battles had been fought (and won) in the sports arena. But never previously (and for that matter never since) had so many African American athletes felt the need to speak out, clearly and self-consciously, on issues of racial prejudice and discrimination both in sport and outside it. Never again would a sportswriter like "Doc" Young be able to assume that his ideas about the racial force of sport would go uncontested. Important in its own right, this very "revolt" was also instrumental in giving birth to the serious, sustained critical thinking about the racial forces and functions of sport that emerged in the United States in the 1970s.

Much of this revolt first came to life, as sports historian David K. Wiggins (1997) has described, in that pivotal year in American culture of 1968. It was in 1968 that Muhammad Ali's battles with the U.S. government and legal system regarding his conviction on charges of draft evasion and the subsequent stripping of his heavyweight title came to a head. It was also during this year that more than three dozen protests by black athletes on predominantly white college and university campuses emerged across the country (see also Wiggins 1988). In professional sports, racial tensions among members of the Cleveland Browns and the St. Louis Cardinals football teams captured headlines all over the country. The Major League Baseball season began with controversies over the scheduling of games in the wake of Martin Luther King Jr.'s assassination, saw African American athletes assume prominent roles on problems ranging from Vietnam to free agency, and culminated with the huge controversy over Jose Feliciano's blues-inspired rendition of the national anthem during that year's World Series and the subsequent hiring of Jesse Owens as a race relations "troubleshooter" for the American League (Briley 1989). But of all the activities and events of this "year of awakening," as Wiggins aptly calls it, none were more self-conscious, sustained, controversial, and consequential than those surrounding the 1968 Mexico City Olympic Games.

The 1968 African American Olympic Protest Movement

This is not a movement that most Americans know much about. In fact, to the extent that they "know" about it at all, they are likely to only recognize it in the form of a single and singularly powerful image: that of two African American athletes poised on an athletic victory podium, Olympic medals hanging around their necks and black-gloved fists raised high above lowered eyes and bowed heads. (See fig. 1.)

This image was the performative work of Tommie Smith and John Carlos, two American sprinters who had finished first and third respectively in a world-record-setting 200-meter dash at the 1968 Mexico City Olympic Games. The extended prologue that constitutes the first substantive chapter of this book is an analysis of the Olympic ritual system and tropes of representation that have made (and continue to make) this image a prominent and powerful public icon. Following anthropologist John

Fig. 1. Tommie Smith and John Carlos, on the victory stand in Mexico City, 1968. Photograph from AP/Wide World Photos.

MacAloon's path-breaking work on Olympic spectacle and ritual (1981, 1984, forthcoming), I argue that the enduring intrigue of the image Smith and Carlos produced can be traced to the way in which these athletes were able to interject "blackness"—in the form of their own black bodies—into a ceremonial system that quite literally had no place for nonnational identities such as race, class, religion, or (in a more complicated case) gender.

Working out this analysis not only foreshadows and frames many of the theoretical points about sport and race relations that appear throughout the book: it also—because Smith and Carlos's image so clearly transcends the world of sport—allows me to suggest the broad social and theoretical significance of this study and of the study of sport and race in general. I am speaking here primarily of the powerful and yet still underappreciated role that sport plays in constituting understandings of race, citizenship, and nation in the contemporary United States, as the work of scholars as diverse as C. L. Cole (1996), Henry Yu (2000), or Mark Dyreson (1998) has begun to illuminate. While a full treatment of their insights cannot be elaborated here, I want to mention three of the defining features of American sport that help account for its unique social and symbolic significance. One is sport's dramaturgical or "myth-making" qualities, its ability to produce cultural performances, personalities, and styles that are both widely seen and deeply felt. Connected with this is what might be called, following Clifford Geertz (1973), sport's paradoxical "deep play" character—the way in which it is understood and experienced as simultaneously serious and trivial (see also MacAloon 1988a). A third and final property of sport that helps us to explain its social force (and one that, to my mind, has not received the attention it deserves) has to do with the close semantic connections between American sport culture and melting-pot, meritocratic individualism. It is this association that helps explain why sport has so often been seen as both model of and metaphor for social life (and why social protests in sport are so controversial and deeply contested).[4]

But the grand theoretical points revealed in this introductory semiotic analysis only begin to capture the full sociohistorical significance of the image of Smith and Carlos. They say little or nothing about where this image and this gesture came from, why it proved to be so politically controversial, or how our memories of it (and the meanings and motives that have been attributed to it) have changed so dramatically over the years. To begin to address these questions and thus get to the deeper significance of this image and of sport itself as related to issues of race and nation, it is necessary to delve into the story that surrounds it. What is needed, in short, is a full-scale history.

And this *is* an image with a history. Despite what is often implied or assumed, Smith and Carlos's gesture was not the spontaneous act of two isolated, impetuous individuals. Quite the contrary, Tommie Smith and John Carlos were members of a small cadre of world-class athletes and nationally recognizable activists who, led by a young sociologist from San Jose State named Harry Edwards, tried to engineer an African American boycott of the 1968 Mexican Games under the banner "Olympic Project for Human Rights" (OPHR). Even though a boycott never did materialize, those associated with the OPHR participated in a broad, if somewhat haphazard, series of athletically based, racially oriented protest activities in the year leading up to the Games. These included a boycott of the New York Athletic Club's nationally televised indoor track meet, meetings on several dozen college campuses around the country, calls for the expulsion of South Africa from the Olympic movement, and an aborted effort to organize an alternative "Third World" Olympics.

These details constitute the backbone of the historical narrative that occupies the first half of this book. Chapter 2 introduces Tommie Smith and his teammates, outlines the rationale behind their proposal for a black Olympic boycott, and details Harry Edwards's role in helping to shape and define these ideas with the creation of the OPHR. Chapter 3 describes the individuals, interests, and ideals that stood in opposition to the OPHR and their boycott initiative from its initial public presentation in the fall of 1967 and onward. Chapters 4 and 5 detail, respectively, how the movement evolved and transformed itself in reaction to this opposition and how these struggles were played out in the year leading up to the 1968 Games and culminating in Smith and Carlos's dramatic victory-stand demonstration in Mexico City.

The basic outlines of this story are fairly well known to specialists in the field of sport studies. (The post-1968 aspects of the story, which constitutes the second half of this book, have received less attention.) There are works devoted to constructing the basic historiography of the episode (Harris 1995; Spivey 1984; Grundman 1979; Wiggins 1997), popularizing this history (cf. Ashe 1988, pp. 188–195; Baker 1982, pp. 290–295), or some combination thereof (Moore 1991a, 1991b; Cashmore 1982). In recent years this movement has been referenced or discussed in a number of different scholarly contexts—for example, in analyses of "black power" in American culture (Van Deburg 1992, pp. 104–121), African American cultural heroes (Van Deburg 1997, pp. 118–126), the paradoxical place of sport in American culture (MacAloon 1988a), "enlightened racism" (McKay 1995), and the emergence and changing consciousness of African American athletes (Harrison 2000; Harris 2000; Wiggins 1994). In an earlier paper, I myself used some of the material in this book to make an argument about the importance of "popular culture" in racial and ethnic relations (Hartmann 1996). But none of these treatments is anything near the full, book-length account this movement deserves, much less do they explore the broader relationships among race, sport, and culture that I believe are implicated and revealed therein.[5]

Perhaps the biggest and most basic problem with the existing historiography is that it has mainly understood this movement (and the image so closely identified with it) as an episode in the history of racism, and struggles against racism, in the world of sport. There are a number of limitations with this reading, not the least of which is that this is precisely *not* how Tommie Smith and his associates understood and portrayed their activism in the months leading up to the demonstration (as I will detail in Chapter 2). But perhaps the most serious problem with situating this movement strictly within the analytic confines of racism in sport is that this frame has made it easy (especially for people not interested in sport) to underestimate the broad social and theoretical significance of this episode and, in turn, of the role that sport plays in reproducing racial images, identities, and ideals in the United States and American nationalism itself. Too often instead the story of this movement has been ignored or dismissed as an interesting but basically unimportant bit of historical trivia. To give just one striking example: in all of the biographies of Martin Luther King Jr. that have been published, I have been able to find only one reference—a single sentence—to King's involvement with Smith and Carlos despite King's involvement with the OPHR and his appearance at a national press conference in support of their planned Olympic boycott in December of 1967.[6]

Simply put, the story of this movement is broader, more complicated, and much more revealing than standard accounts would suggest or imply. The public significance of this movement is (and was) signaled by the prominence of its participants, especially those from outside the world of sport. Nationally syndicated columnist Louis Lomax served as a formal adviser to the group, and African American activists as diverse as Martin Luther King Jr., Stokely Carmichael, and H. Rap Brown all made public appearances in support of the prospective boycott. On the other side, African American Olympic hero Jesse Owens, International Olympic Committee President Avery Brundage, and governor of California Ronald Reagan were all highly visible and intense public critics of the initiative. (Reagan, as we shall see, demanded the termination of Harry Edwards's teaching contract at San Jose State, claiming that the former athlete was "contributing nothing toward the harmony of the races"; Edwards, for his part, suggested that it was not he who needed to be relieved of his duties, calling the governor a "petrified pig, unfit to govern.") So intense and consequential were the struggles over the idea of an Olympic boycott that at one point Vice President Hubert Humphrey—in the middle of his own unsuccessful campaign for the White House—stepped in to try to mediate between the parties.

My overarching objective in undertaking this project, in fact, was to show that this is not just a story about racism in sport but is also a story about how sport is implicated in the history and structure of race and racism (and nationalism and liberalism) in contemporary, post–civil rights American culture. It is thus worth highlighting some of the other features of the narrative that follows—my version of the history—that make it unique and (hopefully) significant.

The Architecture of the Account That Follows

Perhaps the first and most basic feature of this telling of the story of the 1968 African American Olympic protests is that I have tried to situate this movement in its appropriate sociohistorical context. This serves two basic purposes: to illustrate the broader meaning and social significance of these events, and to show that this movement actually grew out of a broader social history and cultural circumstance—African American activism in the immediate, post–civil Rights period, and the broader, 1960s radicalization of American politics and culture. None of this is to suggest that racism and discrimination in sport had nothing to do with the OPHR. Rather, my goal (developed especially in Chapter 4, drawing upon the vast scholarly literatures on social movements and cultural resistance)[7] is to demonstrate that the movement is most accurately understood as a product of complicated and oftentimes contradictory activist interests and ideals. More specifically, the "movement" was an uneasy coalition of both moderate race-based protests against overt, old-line racist practices and policies in the world of sport as well as more radical, collectivist critiques of post–civil rights racial culture.

I do not mean to overemphasize (much less romanticize) 1960s movements and movement organizing. A second characteristic of the account that follows (and one that is arguably more important given prevailing public beliefs about the positive and progressive racial force of sport) is that I use the public response to the resistance of black athletes as a lens through which to view the social interests and ideological structures that complicate and constrain sport's impact on race relations. As is foreshadowed by my attention to Olympic symbology, I focus on the way in which sport's unique apolitical, color-blind ideology—the ideology that had for so long made it a genuinely progressive racial force—suddenly became an obstacle for activists who had achieved numerous formal, legal victories and yet still found themselves up against cultural and institutional inequalities that were both deeper and more persistent than they first imagined. I elaborate on this contribution in chapter 3, offering a close, critical analysis of the cultural rhetoric by which the idea of a boycott was condemned and rejected in the mainstream American mass media and public sphere. Key here are the deep ideological connections between sport culture and the particularly individualist-assimilationist conceptions of racial justice that define dominant American mores (not to mention much conventional social theory).

These deep and mutually supporting sociocultural structures—which I might call, following the sociologist Arthur Stinchcombe (1982), the "deep cultural structures" of sport, race, and American nationalism in the United States[8]—are foundational to my description and analysis of the entire Olympic protest movement and of the American race-sport nexus more generally. They also reveal a great deal, I believe, about American nationalism, the problems of race, and the otherwise hidden limits of color-blind, race-neutral liberalism. These ideas are informed and inspired by the large body of work produced by scholars of critical race theory (cf. Essed and Goldberg 2002) and critical whiteness studies (Roediger 1995 [1991], 2002; Lipsitz 1998; Doane 1997; Goldberg 1993; Frankenberg 1993; Morrison 1992). Central to these works is an understanding of the way that the dominant culture normalizes, naturalizes, and privileges the experiences and understandings of the white majority while constructing racial difference itself as problematic if not pathological— all within a universalist, color-blind language and discourse that obscures and denies these very cultural specificities and social foundations.[9] More than a mere theoretical perspective, critical race theories serve as a key methodological tool for the whole of this study. As the movement pushes up against these idealized structures (and tries to use them or challenge them), I am able to develop an ever more sophisticated understanding of the relationships among sport, race, and culture in contemporary American society, the possibilities they enable and the ultimate limits they present.[10]

This book is not just a historical rereading and theoretical reframing of existing accounts of the 1968 Olympic protest movement; it also contributes a substantial amount of original research to the subject. My analysis of the sociocultural structures that conspired against athletically based racial activism (chapter 3), for example, is based upon an extensive sample of public reactions to the boycott initiative recorded in mainstream national newspapers and periodicals that I collected, assembled, and analyzed. My account is further informed and supplemented by a thorough reading of six publications I defined as key sources "of record": the *New York Times*, the *Los Angeles Times*, the *Chicago Tribune*, the *San Jose Mercury News*, the *San Jose Spartan* (the student paper at Smith's alma mater), and *Track and Field News*. I also collected a vast array of materials—books, biographies, autobiographies, oral histories, video and film footage, and event programs—related in one way or another to this history from numerous research archives and libraries, and I conducted a series of interviews with people connected in one way or another with the incidents and events of the movement.[11]

These sources served not only as useful gauges of public reactions, posturing, and debate, they also revealed numerous previously unreported or improperly reported details about the movement. The centrality of my original research to this study is perhaps most obvious in the second half of the narrative, where I move beyond the "revolt" itself and examine the impacts and outcomes of this movement on sport and in American culture.

Beyond the "Revolt"

As with so much of the scholarly literature on social movements,[12] existing accounts of the 1968 Olympic protests pay little attention to what happened to the movement (and why), and what (if anything) came out of all this. It is almost as if everything ended the moment Smith and Carlos stepped off the victory podium in Mexico City. But of course this was not the case. The image their demonstration produced was not forgotten, and activist-athletes continued to press the American athletic establishment for change well into the 1970s. These athletes focused not only on race but also and increasingly on issues such as athletes' rights and gender equity. In combination with the public pressures for institutional reform that resulted from disappointments and controversies associated with the American performance in the 1972 Munich Games, this activism and unrest sparked a series of reforms and transformations that decisively reshaped the organizational structure of amateur athletics in the United States. The culmination of this era, and its most obvious historical legacy, is the 1978 federal Amateur Athletic Act, which not only marks the first time the federal government intervened in American amateur athletics but constitutes the organizational system still in place today (Chalip 1988). Thus it is that I think of the 1968 African American Olympic protest movement and the revolt of the black athlete more generally not just as a single year of awakening but as a whole decade of disruption.

This decade of continued resistance and resulting reform constitutes the focus of the second half of this study. Reminiscent of Bruce Kidd's (1995) important socio-institutional history of Canadian sport, I examine the evolution and impact of race-based activism on sport and in American culture in the years immediately following the rise and eventual collapse of black athletic resistance. These chapters begin with a brief discussion of what happened to Smith and Carlos and the image they produced in the years immediately following the 1968 Games, but their focus is more on the other struggles their demonstration helped to inspire and the impacts of these struggles. Chapter 6 traces the evolution of social protest in and around sport in the aftermath of 1968. In contrast to the period of boycott mobilization, the post-1968 struggles implicating race coalesced around full-blown charges of racial discrimination in sport itself and gave rise to a whole series of institutional responses and reforms. These charges were accompanied by the emergence of other forms of athletic activism and unrest that involved white athletes as well as black, and women as well as men. A movement in its own right, this broader "athletic revolution" (Scott 1971) persuaded many coaches, administrators, college presidents, and sports fans that the entire structure of amateur athletics in the United States was in danger of collapsing and also gave rise to the popular and scholarly critiques of sport that enabled this very study.

Chapter 7 focuses on what seems to have remained the most prominent and problematic aspect of athletic unrest: what I call the "racial crisis" in American athletics. Here I explain why race remained such a salient issue for the American sporting establishment, even after the decline and collapse of any meaningful athletic activism. More important, I detail how the American athletic establishment—represented here mainly by the organizations and elites of the U.S. Olympic Committee (USOC) and the National Collegiate Athletic Association (NCAA)—went about responding to the racial crisis in their midst. I argue and attempt to demonstrate that their collective response was an almost textbook example of the racial equilibrium model sketched out by Michael Omi and Howard Winant (1994). Once they realized that the charges of racism in and around sport would not quietly go away, sport leaders and elites went about insulating themselves and their institutions against the more radical charges while taking steps to reform established racial practices and policies to absorb the more moderate and publicly legitimate aspects of African American athletic activism. The cumulative effect of these responses was to reestablish—or "rearticulate"—a more stable, acceptable racial equilibrium in sport. The broad outlines and main institutional and cultural aspects of this racial order remain very much with us today.

Here some of the broader theoretical aims and objectives of this project begin to emerge more fully formed. A case study illustrating sport's contested terrain becomes a more historically nuanced analysis of how the institutional structures and cultural dynamics that constitute sport today actually emerged and took shape. Historical event thus becomes, in the more general terms used by scholars such as Marshall Sahlins (1985) or

William Sewell Jr. (1996a), a transformation of structure rather than just a mere illustration of it.

Chapter 8 then takes a step back to offer an assessment of some of the broader cultural consequences of this new, postprotest racial order in sport. Here my emphasis is less on the social and racial organization of sport per se and more on the symbolic role that sport plays in contemporary American culture, especially with respect to race and African American men. The empirical material on which this analysis is based comes from the 1984 Los Angeles Olympic Games that took place in the wake of the decade that is the focus of this study. The group that organized the Games, the Los Angeles Olympic Organizing Committee (LAOOC), proved to be an energetic and exemplary practitioner of the new approach to dealing with issues of race in the American athletic establishment. Even more important is the masterful way in which President Ronald Reagan put Olympic imagery and sporting tropes to use in articulating his ideals about race, culture, and American citizenship during his reelection campaign. Finally, the 1984 Games represent the historical moment and space where Tommie Smith, John Carlos, and their demonstration began to be rehabilitated, turned in the public memory into an example of civil rights heroism. An integrated treatment of all these factors reveals the ways in which sport, in this postprotest era, continues to be racially consequential and contested, but in much subtler ways than before—where the agency and impetus has shifted toward the institutions of the athletic establishment and their need to carefully interpret, convey, control, and contain mostly male African American athletes and the meanings they represent and embody in contemporary American culture. It is also in this chapter that the relationships among race, nation, sport, individualism, and masculinity take fuller shape.

Theoretically, these findings take us beyond both Omi and Winant's generative work (1994) and recent sociological studies of social movement outcomes to suggest the crucial role that popular cultural institutions, practices, and symbols such as those implicated in sport play when it comes to the politics of race in contemporary American society. In recent years scholars from disciplines and departments across the academy (including David Roediger, Robin Kelley, George Lipsitz, Lisa Lowe, Cornell West, David Theo Goldberg, Robyn Weigman, and Peggy MacIntosh) have produced a large and very impressive body of work exploring such ideas. Yet, despite their substantial analytical power, intellectual sophistication, and deep social significance, these works have had (with some notable exceptions) surprisingly little impact on either mainstream sociology or its relevant subfields of race and culture. The reasons for this are, as is so often the case, complicated and beyond the scope of this discussion.[13] But sport presents an exciting empirical site from which to continue and expand the exploration of the deep and consequential relationships among race, culture, and social change in contemporary American society. If this historical narrative serves to introduce and illustrate a more critical, cultural approach to race relations to a broader audience of sociologists and social scientists, it will have accomplished one of its most basic and important objectives.

Acknowledgments

Many people contributed greatly to the making of this book. At the top of the list are those athletes, activists, and others who took the time to talk, both on and off the record, to a naive, young graduate student about their recollections of African American athletic activism and their understandings of sport and race in the United States more generally: Arthur Ashe, Timuel Black, John Carlos, John Dobroth, Doug Gatlin, Anita DeFrantz, John Dobroth, Dick James, Roy Johnson, Fekrou Kidane, Richard Lapchick, John MacAloon, Kenny Moore, Mark Payodeski, Judith Pinero-Keiffer, Kenneth Reich, Chris Shenkel, Art Shinberg, Tommie Smith, Patty (Johnson) Van Wolvelaere, Jay Weiner, and Willie Whyte.

Librarians and staff at the following institutions provided essential materials, facilities, and assistance: the King Archives in Atlanta; the NCAA library (formally in Kansas City, Kansas); the Paul Ziffren Sports Resource Center of the Amateur Athletic Foundation in Los Angeles; the Avery Brundage Papers housed at the University of Illinois Department of Special Collections; the USOC Archive at the Olympic Training Center in Colorado Springs; the Hubert H. Humphrey papers collected at the Minnesota Historical Society in St. Paul; and the Olympic Studies Center in Lausanne, Switzerland.

The bulk of the first half of the book was written with the support of a dissertation writing fellowship from the Department of Sociology at the University of California, San Diego. I am indebted to my mentors and advisers at San Diego—Steve Cornell, Dick Madsen and Chandra Mukerji, Michael Schudson, and George Lipsitz—who not only supported my work but helped me develop the skills necessary to complete it.

Friends and colleagues at the University of Minnesota encouraged and inspired me to continue to make the project bigger and better. Ronald Aminzade, Liz Boyle, Rod Ferguson, Joe Galaskiewicz, Barbara Laslett, Mary Jo Kane, Larry May, Joel Nelson, Jennifer Pierce, Robin Stryker, and Chris Uggen all deserve special recognition for reading and commenting on versions of the manuscript at crucial moments. I also received generous support from the University of Minnesota Grant-in-Aid of Faculty Research and the Multicultural Initiative of the Vice President of Multicultural Affairs, and invaluable (and often unpaid) research assistance and intellectual stimulation from numerous Minnesota students, including Jordan

Barlett, Murat Ergin, Ben Fiest, John Gipson, Chad Pahl, Chris Phelps, Jeremy Staff, Maura Rosenthal, Melissa Weiner, and Darren Wheelock.

I have also benefited greatly by the ideas and support from communities of scholars from a wide range of disciplines and interests. The project was also enriched by audience response at presentations at the University of California, Santa Cruz (American Studies Department); the University of California, Riverside (Ethnic Studies Department); Loyola University, New Orleans (Sociology Department); the University of Minnesota (Sociology and American Studies Departments); and the annual meetings of the American Studies Association, the Pacific Sociological Association, and the American Sociological Association. Those who offered specific advice and encouragement include Joe Mills Braddock, Susan Brownell, Michael Burawoy, C. L. Cole, Herman Gray, Keith Harrison, Richard Lapchick, Doug McAdam, Michael Messner, Aldon Morris, David Roediger, Jeffrey Sammons, David Wiggins, and Wayne Wilson. Thanks also to Ed Derse, Mary Drew, Chris Elzey, Tim Gustafson, Ted Hamm, Michael Palm, Pauline Swartz, and old friends at Project South in Atlanta.

The Postgraduate Fellowship Program at the Olympic Studies Center in Lausanne, Switzerland, provided a stimulating and productive environment at a crucial phase in the project. An early version of some of the material in the first half of the book was published as "The Politics of Race and Sport: Resistance and Domination in the 1968 African American Olympic Protest Movement," *Ethnic and Racial Studies* 19, no. 3 (July 1996): 548–566.

My family has been there throughout this entire process: my parents, Robert and Esther; my kids, Emma (who only recently realized her middle name wasn't sports) and Ben; and especially my wife Teresa.

This project first began to take shape at the University of Chicago as a course project and then as a thesis in the interdisciplinary Masters of Arts Program in the Social Sciences, so it seems only fitting that it has come to fruition back at the University of Chicago Press. I have Douglas Mitchell and his wonderful staff to thank for that. Thanks also to Drusilla Moorhouse for all her efforts to make the text tighter and more readable. Finally I want to acknowledge, once again, the two individuals who, in their very different ways, inspired me to appreciate and try to understand the social significance of sport and its complicated relationships to race. One is Larry Hawkins, the educator, administrator, activist, and coach from the South Side of Chicago, whose program introduced me to contemporary realities of race and sport. The other is John MacAloon. Some years ago, Professor MacAloon told me that the best way to become a scholar was to find a model to emulate. As much as possible, I have tried to follow that advice and his example in researching and writing this book.

INTRODUCTION

Our passion for categorization, life neatly fitted into pegs, has led
to an unforeseen, paradoxical distress; confusion, a breakdown of
meaning. These categories which were meant to define and
control the world for us have boomeranged us into chaos; in
which limbo we whirl, clutching the straws of our definitions.

—James Baldwin, *Partisan Review* (1949)

What do they know of sport who only sport know?

—Paraphrased from C. L. R. James, *Beyond a Boundary* (1963)

Chapter 1

Unforgettable Fists

There's somethin' happenin' here,
what it is ain't exactly clear.
. . . .
Young people speakin' their minds
Getting so much resistance from behind.
I think it's time we stop, hey, what's that sound?
Everybody look what's going down.

"For What It's Worth," Steven Stills, for the band Buffalo
Springfield (1966)

It begins, in this version at least, with a race, a simple footrace.
Entering the Games of the nineteenth Olympiad, the men's 200-meter
dash seemed destined to make history—a race, as the old sports cliché
goes, for the ages. Tommie Smith was the favorite according to most
knowledgeable observers at the time. Smith—the Jesse Owens or Carl
Lewis of his day, when track and field was still a major American sport—
held eleven world records both indoors and out, at distances up to 400
meters, and he had once long jumped 25 feet, 11 inches. And for all of
this, the 200 meters was his specialty, the distance at which he reigned
as world champion. Yet Smith was to receive a serious challenge from
John Carlos, his collegiate teammate at San Jose State. Though a relative newcomer to the international scene, Carlos had beaten Smith for
the first time only a month earlier at the U.S. Olympic trials, clocking a
world-record time of 19.7 seconds in the process (a record never officially
recognized because Carlos was wearing "brush spike" shoes, a short-lived
innovation that, though never shown to aid runners unfairly, was ruled
illegal at the time). So clear was the athletic brilliance of these two sprinters that the *Chicago Tribune* proclaimed that regardless of the outcome of
their personal battle, there was "no question that the United States would
be represented by the greatest 200-meter team in its history"—no small assertion considering that the United States had dominated the event since

it was first run in 1900, winning eleven of fourteen times and capturing twenty-nine of the forty-two total awarded medals.[1] Making the contest even more captivating were the personal differences that distinguished the two athletes. Although both came from poor black families and now ran out of coach Bud Winter's "speed city" in San Jose, they were otherwise a study in contrasts. Smith was from California, Carlos from Harlem; Smith was the calm, cool, hardworking, and graceful veteran; Carlos the cocky, brash, hugely talented and yet notoriously unpredictable upstart. It was to be a classic duel. But even in view of all this hype, hyperbole, and intrigue, few could have predicted the kind of history this event would make.

By all accounts, the race itself was glorious (as were so many of the track-and-field performances in Mexico City's high altitude: an astonishing fifteen world records were broken in track and field alone, including Bob Beamon's miraculous 29-foot long jump).[2] Smith and Carlos were assigned side-by-side lanes. Smith, who had taken no practice starts to avoid aggravating a severe hamstring pull he had sustained in a qualifying heat just two hours prior to the final, came out of the blocks gingerly, not knowing for sure whether he would even be able to complete the race, much less compete with Carlos. Next to Smith in lane four, Carlos came away from the start perfectly and rounded the turn holding a full meter and a half lead on Smith and the rest of the field. But Smith, who was using short, quick strides around the turn to keep pressure off his injured inside leg, appeared to be gaining confidence. He closed rapidly on his front-running teammate and then, with 60 meters to go, Smith burst by Carlos on the strength of a powerful and familiar kick—his fabled "Tommie-Jets." From there, Smith was a sight to behold: his long, smooth, classic sprinter's stride carried him gracefully, forcefully—*beautifully*—across the track. Even to see the race on tape today one cannot help but be struck by the sheer aesthetic brilliance that some consider the raison d'etre of high performance sport. Smith's victory, in fact, was almost anticlimactic: he won so decisively that even before he broke the tape he was smiling and waving in a jubilant, euphoric celebration that may, some have claimed, have cost him the greatest 200-meter time ever. Meanwhile on his right, Carlos had to settle for third place. When he turned his head to watch Smith go by, Carlos was surprisingly overtaken by the Australian Peter Norman, who, like Smith, had run the race of his life. The official result showed that Smith had won the race in a new official world-record time of 19.8 seconds, with Norman and Carlos finishing second and third respectively with identical times of 20 seconds flat. "It was a fine race, one that Smith could be proud of," *Sports Illustrated* commented, but not what he would be remembered for. Instead, the magazine correctly predicted, Smith "will be remembered for what happened next"—that is, what happened during the victory ceremony shortly thereafter.[3]

Immediately after the race, according to the standard practice of the time, the runners were taken to their dressing rooms underneath the stadium to await the presentation of their medals. It was there, in dungeon-like confines, that Smith produced the black gloves that would serve as the focal point of the gesture that was to follow. Giving Carlos the left-handed glove and keeping the right one for himself, Smith explained to Carlos what he wanted them to do and what it would stand for. He stressed, above all else, the gravity of what was to happen: "The national anthem is a sacred song to me," he said. "This can't be sloppy. It has to be clean and abrupt."[4] The two Americans also gave a button reading the "Olympic Project for Human Rights" to the Australian Norman who, after having been privy to these deliberations, wanted to show solidarity with their cause. And everything was set for their victory ceremony.

As dictated by established Olympic protocol and practice, the three athletes were led across the stadium infield by the awards presenters, three young Mexican women in embroidered native dress and a group of senior representatives of the appropriate international sports organizations. The Americans mounted the awards podium clad in sweat suits and black stocking feet and carrying white-soled Puma sneakers. Smith wore a black scarf around his neck, Carlos a string of African-style beads. Both men (along with the Australian) displayed their OPHR buttons. Presiding over the ceremony was the president of the International Amateur Athletic Federation, Lord Burghley, the marquess of Exeter. The marquess, the 1924 Olympic 400-meter hurdles champion later made famous as a composite character in the film *Chariots of Fire*, had requested that he present these medals in order to personally honor Smith as the greatest long sprinter who had ever lived. Years later, in fact, Smith would recall that the warmth and peace radiated by this man (whom he mistakenly identified as the Irishman Lord Killanin, the future president of the IOC) helped him to compose himself for what was to come. Along with his gold medal, the IOC official presented Smith a box with an olive tree sapling inside, an ancient emblem of peace, which the sprinter smoothly accepted into his own symbolic space. And then it was time. The "Star-Spangled Banner" began and the stars and stripes of the United States flag were lifted upward to honor the nation of the Olympic champion. In a stark break with convention, however, Smith and Carlos thrust black-gloved fists—Smith his right, Carlos his left—above lowered eyes and bowed heads.

Protocol, custom, and fear demand that everyone—strangers, rivals, and enemies as much as countrymen and teammates—rise and remain silent and respectful for the duration of the anthem. Thus, as Olympic scholar John MacAloon has observed, the entire ritual company, even the stunned Lord Burghley, had no choice but to stand at formal attention, as if nothing unusual were happening, for the full ninety seconds of the American national anthem. And yet, obviously, something extraordinary was happening. In this moment was born one of the most vibrant and poignant images ever generated by that international spectacle of symbolism and myth-making we call the Olympic Games. In its aftermath, Smith gave a brief but powerful explanation of the meaning of these symbols and of his and Carlos's actions. It was an explanation that would be reprinted many times after it first appeared in *The Revolt of the Black Athlete* (1969).

> My raised right hand stood for the power in black America. Carlos's raised left hand stood for the unity of black America. Together they formed an arch of unity and power. The black scarf around my neck stood for black pride. The black socks with no shoes stood for black poverty in racist America. The totality of our effort was the regaining of black dignity.[5]

Smith would not talk publicly about this moment again for more than twenty years. But over the course of those years, the image he had helped to engineer would come, for American audiences and many others around the globe, to define the 1968 Mexico City Olympics and, in many ways, to transcend sport itself.

Making Sense of an Icon

In 1968 the Vietnam War, the assassinations of Martin Luther King Jr. and Robert F. Kennedy, the Democratic national convention in Chicago and riots in many other cities (including the student uprisings in Paris, troops rolling into Czechoslovakia, and both in Mexico itself) produced many vivid images and powerful historical icons. Yet the image of Smith and Carlos's victory-stand demonstration was reported with and has been remembered amid all of them. Within two days, Smith and Carlos's gesture was pictured on the front page (not the sports page, the *front* page) of newspapers across the United States and around the world. And still today, more than a third-century later, references to this image appear—a paragraph here, a sentence or two there, or more often than not just the photograph itself—with a surprising degree of regularity in a wide variety of contexts.

Pictures of Smith and Carlos have been used to illustrate American high school history textbooks (see, for example, Linden, Brink, and Huntington 1986), and posters of the image have provided inspiration and strength for generations of college students. The image of these two athletes has long been an object of reflection for artists, whether as the basis for the "civil rights" creations of Chicago-based Alanzo Parham or as an example of the more overtly political African American aesthetic practiced by Murray DePillars. Smith, Carlos, and their fists were emblazoned next to Malcolm X's picture on the "By Any Means" T-shirts and sweatshirts popularized by several Spike Lee films in the late 1980s, and a few years later Hollywood's Oliver Stone seriously considered making a feature-length motion picture based on Smith and Carlos's story. In 1988 the image of Smith and Carlos was prominently placed in a special *Time* magazine retrospective issue called "1968: The Year That Shaped a Generation," and many of that small cottage industry of books on the 1960s have given it prominent treatment as well.[6]

Home Box Office (HBO) Films eventually did produce the widely publicized *Fists of Freedom* documentary (1999), but this was long after Kenny Moore's landmark feature on the story behind the image supplied the backdrop and promotional vehicle for a two-part *Sports Illustrated* cover story, "The Black Athlete," in the summer of 1991. The twenty-fifth anniversary of the demonstration in 1993 occasioned a nationwide series of retrospective stories and commentaries. Said one writer, "[it was] the most significant athletic image of my sports life . . . I recall the black, gloved fists as if they were raised yesterday."[7]

Smith and Carlos's demonstration subsequently served as a touchstone for public reporting of events ranging from the USOC's "Tonya Harding dilemma" during the 1994 Winter Olympics to George Foreman's unlikely return to professional boxing (and eventual heavyweight championship) and O. J. Simpson's infamous double-murder trial. Since then the picture has appeared on the cover of a special issue of the academic journal *Race and Class*, was featured in a controversial European advertising campaign (juxtaposed next to duck-stepping Nazi soldiers), and was ranked among *TV Guide*'s one hundred most memorable moments in television history (number thirty-eight to be precise).[8] The memory of Smith and Carlos figured in John Berendt's account of African American tastes in hard liquor in *Midnight in the Garden of Good and Evil* (1994, p. 319), and in the new millennium the image served as the focal point of a pivotal scene in the feel-good Hollywood picture *Remember the Titans*. My own surveys and interviews indicate that even those who claim to care nothing for sports and/or know nothing about the image itself—men and women alike—often experience strong emotional reactions to it. Although it is received enthusiastically these days, in more than one library I have come across documents pertaining to Smith and Carlos or their demonstration that have been defaced or purged entirely.

No Olympic anthology, history of sport in the United States, or treatment of the African American athlete seems complete without some acknowledgment of Smith and Carlos's demonstration, and Jim Riordan and Arnd Kruger's recent (1999) volume on the international politics of twentieth-century sport is graced by a picture of the demonstration on its cover. A surprising number of sports biographies and autobiographies devote some sustained attention to the episode. Virtually all 1968 Olympic alumni—white or black, male or female—are eventually coerced or compelled to discuss their views on the episode because, as one 1968 Olympian told me, "their protest *is* the 1968 Olympics for most Americans."[9] But it is probably Smith and Carlos's African American male teammates who understand this best. Speaking in 1991, Jimmy Hines, the 100-meter gold medalist in Mexico City, sighed: "I've done maybe a thousand speaking engagements and after each I've had the question: 'Were you the ones . . . ? The ones who . . . ?' I guess that's forever."[10]

Each of these references, contexts, and anecdotes constitutes a portion of what the sociologist Wendy Griswold (1994) might describe as the social significance embodied in this cultural form. Despite its prominence and power as an object of meaning and collective memory, however, most Americans "know" little more than the image itself. Typically the picture of the two athletes is displayed (or the image rhetorically appropriated) without any critical commentary or explanation, as if its significance were wholly self-sufficient or self-evident, a picture worth literally a thousand words. One striking such example can be found in William O'Neil's (1978) widely read "informal history" of 1960s America. In one of the two photograph galleries that supplement the text is a picture of Smith and Carlos on the victory stand. It is presented under the caption "A Black Power salute at the Olympics, 1968," and yet, incredibly, no further reference to the image can be found in the entire book—not in the chapters involving black power, not in the discussion of the year 1968 itself, not even in the section devoted specifically to the decade's sporting events. Similarly, K. Sue Jewell's more recent book on the role of cultural images in the construction of American public policy, *From Mammy to Miss America and Beyond* (1993), features visual cues to Smith and Carlos on its cover that are not touched upon in any way in the text itself. Even Riordan and Kruger's recent volume on the international politics of sport, which has the image on its cover, contains only two scant references to the demonstration itself (one of which is historically inaccurate).

I received one of my first and most powerful lessons on this point when I began working with high school students from the South Side of Chicago after graduating from college in the late 1980s. I was, at the time, drafting a very early version of the narrative that would eventually become the first part of the present volume and wondered what these students knew about the image that had inspired me. I was especially interested in their understandings because I had seen many of them proudly sporting the Spike Lee sweatshirts that juxtaposed Malcolm X with Smith and Carlos's fists at the time of the release of the film *Do the Right Thing*. But to my surprise, none of these students knew anything at all about the image. They liked it—thought it was "hip" and "straight-up" and all the rest—but could say little more. I remember in particular a conversation I shared with about eight or nine African American junior high school girls—many of whom were athletes (volleyball players), most of whom fancied themselves as having very progressive racial politics, and all of whom planned to attend college. To a person, they found the image very appealing and yet were almost embarrassed to admit having absolutely no sense of where it had come from or what its enactors had intended it to mean. This is not to say they were uninterested in the story—they simply didn't know and hadn't even imagined that such a story existed.[11]

In the preface to *The Sixties: Years of Hope, Days of Rage* (1987), Todd Gitlin observes that in late twentieth century American culture,

> "The Sixties" [have] receded into haze and myth: lingering images of nobility and violence, occasional news clips of Martin Luther King, Jr. and John F. Kennedy, Beatles and Bob Dylan retrospectives, the jumble of images this culture shares instead of a sense of continuous, lived history. "The Sixties": a collage of fragments scooped together as if a whole decade took place in an instant. (p. 3)

What Gitlin says about "the Sixties" must surely apply to the Smith and Carlos demonstration: it is—or at least has become—one of those familiar, spectacular, and utterly peculiar icons that fascinates the American imagination and satisfies its sense of news and history.

As with so much of popular culture, a great many concerns are raised by the superficial, impoverished sense of the past contained and conveyed in such images. To the extent that it is only an "image," a picture without a story, the particular social relations and historical conditions that occasioned Smith and Carlos's demonstration and that help account for its deeper social meaning are effectively trivialized, diluted, or even erased altogether, rendering our memories of their gesture either shamelessly sentimental and meaningless on the one hand, or subject to political manipulation, reckless commercialization, and all manner of wanton co-optation on the other. These patterns of appropriation, subversion, and exploitation are familiar and disturbing enough for those of us who have studied the social life of cultural products in a mass commercial society, but their effect assumes tragic proportions if and when they serve to mystify and perpetuate the social injustices that created them in the first place—as has been the case for so much of African American culture throughout American history.[12] Such considerations make it easy to agree with Gitlin when he argues that the history behind such images needs to be "reclaimed."

A good portion of the work that follows will, as I pointed out in the preface, be devoted to reconstructing this history, to showing how this demonstration is actually best understood as the final product of a failed effort to organize an African American boycott of the Mexico City Games, a protest initiative that itself grew out of the frustration with the slow pace of post–civil rights racial change on the one hand and the emerging frustration of African American athletes with their treatment in the world of sport on the other. But this image has a kind of second life or history as well, one that is both easier to miss and yet just as important to grapple with, involving the social meanings and collective memories that have been invested in and attributed to this image over the years. In recent years—especially around the time of the twenty-fifth anniversary of the demonstration in 1993, but beginning as early as the 1984 Olympic Games—Americans have tended to view Smith and Carlos and the demonstration in generally positive, if not downright celebratory ways. Indeed, in the 1991 *Sports Illustrated* story in which Smith finally provided his account of the demonstration, the former sprinter is described as a "civil rights hero" . . . "cloaked in pride and dignity," a reading extended and further popularized by the 1999 HBO documentary *Fists of Freedom* and in TNT's 2002 treatment in their *Fifteen Minutes of Fame* series. In our comfortable era where Michael Jordan reigns supreme and Muhammad Ali and Martin Luther King have become icons for mainstream, middle-class America, it can be difficult to comprehend the historical specificity of these recollections. But the constructedness of these memories is made manifest when we consider them in contrast to the controversy and outrage Smith and Carlos engendered in mainstream America back in 1968.

It began immediately. Even before they had returned home from Mexico City, American newspapers were overflowing with reports, heated editorials, and emotional letters-to-the-editor criticizing and condemning the protest. The *New York Times* claimed that "a majority condemned [the protest] as disgraceful, insulting and embarrassing,"[13] and the mainstream media clearly did what it could to consolidate such a consensus among the American public. On its main editorial page, the *Chicago Tribune* called the demonstration "an embarrassment visited upon the country," an " act contemptuous of the United States," and "an insult to their countrymen," predicting with unmitigated disgust that these "renegades" would come home to be "greeted as heroes by fellow extremists."[14] *Time* magazine saw it as an "unpleasant controversy [that] dulled the luster of a superlative track and field meet," and *Sports Illustrated* relegated what it called the "Carlos-Smith affair" to four pejorative paragraphs buried on the fifth page of an otherwise verbose twelve-page story. ABC's official thirty-five-minute highlight film of the Games (which emphasized American performances almost exclusively and in fact concluded by playing the national anthem behind images of American flags and Olympic victors in competition and on the victory stand) made absolutely no mention of the events surrounding Smith and Carlos—despite the fact that the network had followed the story closely during its live coverage. One of the harshest indictments against Smith and Carlos was issued by a young staff writer for the *Chicago American* named Brent Musburger. Writing from Mexico City, Musburger began:

> One gets a little tired of having the United States run down by athletes who are enjoying themselves at the expense of their country. Protesting and working constructively against racism in the United States is one thing, but airing one's dirty clothing before the entire world during a fun-and-games tournament was no more than a juvenile gesture by a couple of athletes who should have known better.[15]

Calling their demonstration an "ignoble performance" that "completely overshadowed" a magnificent athletic one, Musburger likened Smith and Carlos to "a pair of dark-skinned storm troopers" and concluded that "they should have avoided the awards ceremony altogether."

Obviously, then, the project of reclaiming the history of Smith and Carlos's demonstration has as much to do with understanding the meanings and memories that have been attributed to the image as it does with grasping the motivations and intentions of its actors in the first place. Given that the image itself did not change at all during this period and that neither Smith nor Carlos said or did anything that could have affected how it was interpreted, the only recourse for explaining this dramatic transformation is the sociological one: to look to the broader sociohistorical context within which its meaning was produced and imputed—putting "text" in "context," to use the language Herman Gray (1995) has given us. [16] The developments that led to the dramatic rebirth and transformation of memories about Smith and Carlos, in fact, constitute the focus of the second part of this book.

But even for those who know the story behind this image and who have some appreciation of the sociohistorical context in which American understandings of it have been constructed, contained, and transformed, the Smith-Carlos demonstration itself remains as enigmatic and puzzling as it has been powerful and persistent. In 1984, to take one notable example, the sports historian Donald Spivey (1984, pp. 249–251) was still puzzling over what he called the "1968 Olympic boycott movement," describing it in one instance as "nothing more than a few symbolic gestures" and yet, in another way, as somehow "more than the sum of its parts." It has been this way ever since Smith and Carlos first clenched their fists and bowed their heads. *New York Times* sportswriter Robert Lipsyte, who had covered the OPHR throughout 1968 and was on location that day in Mexico City, remembers being disappointed, wondering "Is this all there is? . . . [T]wo handsome college students . . . raising their arms and bowing their heads did not seem exactly like wild in the streets." [17] In its 1968 Olympics retrospective *Ebony* magazine registered even more confused, contradictory impressions:

> In a nation where black protest has reached such heights as ghetto riots, school boycotts and impassioned requests for a separate state, the Smith/Carlos demonstration should look like child's play. In a nation where white Vietnam protesters have flaunted Viet Cong flags, burned and torn American flags and burned draft cards, the Smith/Carlos demonstration appeared as solemn as a church service. [18]

How could a reputable African American publication compare the demonstration to the play of children in one sentence and the seriousness of a church service in the next, without further comment? How can it be that one of the most thoughtful and well-positioned sports journalists in the country recalls being "disappointed" by the gesture at the time, only to still be writing about it more than twenty-five years later? Is Spivey's fundamental ambivalence, in the end, the only rational conclusion that can be drawn?

These are not puzzles and paradoxes we should move past too quickly. The fact that Smith and Carlos's victory-stand gesture was such a powerful and contradictory image back in 1968 and remains so today in spite of (or perhaps even because of) the absence of any substantial or "real" history is, I believe, interesting and in need of explanation itself.

In certain ways such questions call to mind the curious and contradictory historiography of Smith and Carlos's contemporaries and sometime collaborators Stokely Carmichael and H. Rap Brown, and the organization with which they were famously associated. Much like the Smith-Carlos demonstration, the Black Panther Party is at once known and unknown, symbolically central to the 1960s and yet historiographically underdeveloped. In a recent and very important rethinking of this uneven historical legacy, Nikhil Pal Singh (1998) suggests that much of the paradox of the Panthers is a function of a general American ambivalence about "black liberatory aspirations" and the persistent problems of race in the United States. This is certainly the case for the Smith and Carlos demonstration and the memories and meanings that surround it: they reflect the ambiguities and tensions embedded in the ongoing African American struggle for social justice.

Singh goes on to argue that the Panther's distinctive local and global "appeal" cannot be understood apart from the realities of translocal and transnational intercultural transfer and exchange. More specifically, he maintains that the Black Panther's multifaceted commitment to counternationalism, anti-imperialism, and decolonization is (and was) profoundly unsettling, if not simply subversive for the usual narratives that perceive America as a unified national community, an ideal awaiting realization. This radical reading has profound parallels and implications for a demonstration that unfolded in the context of one of the most powerful and popular international institutions of the modern world—the Olympic Games. Indeed, the inherently global, international, and cross-cultural character of the Olympic movement ensures that issues of nationalism, internationalism, and racial colonization resonate in and through Smith and Carlos's victory-stand demonstration.

That said, it is far from clear that Smith and Carlos held the decisively radical if not fully revolutionary anticapitalist, transnational vision Singh claims for the Panthers. On the one hand, the dramatic black-gloved, clenched-fist salute at the emotional center of Smith and Carlos's victory-stand display is easily (and typically) described as a "black power salute." This gesture has a long history as a symbol of challenge or revolt in both formal and vernacular gesticulation.[19] Yet, at the same time, it is important to note that Smith (and, though to a lesser extent, even Carlos) pointedly did not describe it in this way. While he mentioned the "power in black America" in the phrase quoted above, Smith instead utilized the less explicitly radical language of "black pride" and "unity," moderate labels that were matched by the dignity and solemnity of bowed heads. If Smith and Carlos's gesture is implicated in the politics of race in the United States, then, its "authors" would seem to have had less do with the radicalism of the Left and more with the challenge of the center. Indeed, I believe that it is largely because of this subtle rhetorical moderation that Smith and Carlos's demonstration was so readily rehabilitated in mainstream American culture in the late 1980s and early 1990s.

But there is something else that is ideologically distinctive about this story as compared to that of Singh's characterization of the Panthers. It has to do with its sport-specific nature, its status as a product of the popular cultural practices of the athletic world. Such attitudes about popular images and popular cultural forms in general are reminiscent of Pierre Bourdieu's famous description of the paradoxical social status of the sociology of sport: "[S]corned by sociologists," he notes, "it is despised by sportspersons." The challenge, then, to overcome the artificial, parochial divisions engendered by the study of all manner of popular culture by seeing what is so memorable and meaningful about images and practices—such as the Smith-Carlos gesture—that are essentially dehistoricized and disembodied.

Here it is instructive to recall that Bourdieu used a parable about black athletes in prestigious American universities in the 1970s to make his point about the problems of studying sport and all manner of popular culture. Despite their seeming prominence and importance, he noted, these student-athletes found themselves in "golden ghettos" of isolation where conservatives were reluctant to talk with them because they were black, while liberals were hesitant to converse with them because they were athletes.[20] If Bourdieu used this example to call attention to the problems of studying sport and popular culture more generally, my intent is to take this case even more literally and a step further to suggest that there is something about race as well that is peculiar and particularly problematic in American society, liberal democratic political ideology, and sport culture itself, something that comes out in Olympic symbology in general and the meanings inherent in the Smith-Carlos demonstration. Here it is imperative to realize that this image has a structure and history that is interesting, important, and all its own—independent of the movement that gave birth to it and separate from the historical context that subsequently enveloped it, yet intimately and inherently linked with the relationships between race and sport at the heart of this study. To fully capture the demonstration in this way, we must shift gears and take a slight detour through the lure of the Olympic Games and the sociologics of Olympic ritual and symbolism. I draw heavily and directly on the work of Olympic scholar John MacAloon, the anthropologist who is not only the foremost American expert on the international Olympic movement but who has produced the most compelling explanation of the power and significance of the Smith-Carlos demonstration to date.

The Sociological Structure and Power of Olympic Ceremony

John MacAloon's pioneering body of work explicating the various performative and symbolic aspects of Olympic sport provides the structural
framework within and against which to begin to understand the sheer
emotional impact of the Smith-Carlos demonstration and its image.[21]
The modern Olympic Games, even though barely one hundred years old,
have grown into what MacAloon calls "a cultural performance of global
proportion" (1984, p. 241). Participants in the Games come from almost
two hundred countries and number in the tens of thousands; live spectators from all over the world number in the millions. Broadcast audiences
are estimated in the billions and generate revenues of comparable scale,
although, as MacAloon points out, what may be even more significant
than these sheer numbers is the fact that—quite unlike the audience for
any other sporting event, and to an extent little programming can match
(at least in the United States)—the demographic composition of Olympic
television audiences closely reproduces actual sociological structure. The
Games are almost universally recognized for their importance in international commerce and politics (among the world's developed nations, in
fact, only the United States lacks a cabinet-level minister of sport), as well
as their cross-cultural sway over individual hopes and dreams. For reasons
large and small, MacAloon seems justified in concluding that "Insofar as
there exists, in the Hegelian-Marxist phrase, a 'world-historical process,'
the Olympics have emerged as its privileged expression and celebration"
(1984, p. 242).

Many factors, of course, contribute to the remarkable social status of
sport in the modern world, but one of the factors unique to the Olympics
is what MacAloon describes as "its encasement of sociological and ideological elements within evocative ritual performances":

> Olympic rituals, like all rites, are sets of evocative symbols or-
> ganized processually in space and time. Olympic rituals take body
> symbolism, join it with symbols of determined social categories and
> meld the whole into expressions of Olympic ideology that the ritu-
> als are designed to render emotionally veridical. (p. 242)

MacAloon attributes much of the global import of the Olympic Games
to the striking and consistent effects generated by the Games' particular
constellation of performance genres, calling them the "closest we have
been able to come to true world rituals" (1988b, p. 286). The central objective of Olympic participation for many national delegations is simply
to march in the Opening and Closing Ceremonies and thus allow their
country to assume its place alongside the nations of the world commu-

nity. This is not surprising, MacAloon points out, when we consider that 40–50 percent of the participating nations have their entire delegation eliminated in the first round of competition, and fewer than 30 percent actually win a medal. (He also asserts that the United Nations' inability to generate ceremonies of comparable force and consistency has been one of its greatest failures as a world organization, which helps account for UNESCO's largely forgotten attempt to take over the Olympic movement in the 1960s and 1970s.) In any case, it is in the context of international spectacle and ritual that we really begin to appreciate the power and prominence of Smith and Carlos's victory-stand demonstration.

Although little noticed by American observers (stemming in large measure from conventions of American media coverage of the ceremonies and the utilitarian, antiritualistic nature of American culture more generally), the rituals and icons of the Olympic Games pay homage to a specific triad of identities: those of the individual, the nation, and the whole of humanity itself. These are displayed in various ways but largely in the Opening and Closing Ceremonies and on the victory stands. In the Opening Ceremonies, national and transnational (i.e., Olympic or broadly "human") symbols are juxtaposed and stressed: this is accomplished, in the first stage of the rite, as athletes and officials "march" into the stadium in national groups marked by distinctive flags, anthems, emblems, and costumes, while the presentation of the Olympic flag, the playing of the Olympic anthem, and the lighting of the flame follow in the second stage. Consistent with the universal humanist ideals that have dominated the International Olympic Movement since its restoration under Pierre de Coubertin over one hundred years ago, the role of national symbols is significantly downplayed in the Closing Ceremonies. Only the anthems of Greece (the birthplace of the Games), the host nation, and the nation that will host the next Games are heard; additionally, the flags and name cards of each country are separated from the athletes and carried into the stadium by anonymous young people from the host country. The athletes then process in a rather unruly, ad hoc band, ordered in no particular fashion that, ever since it emerged in Melbourne in 1956, is said to offer a ritual expression of the bonds of friendship and mutual respect transcending differences of class, ethnicity, ideology, and language the athletes are supposed to have achieved during the festival. It is also thought to express the higher "humankindness" said to be necessary for all moral men and women as well as to display Coubertin's overriding conviction that patriotism and individual achievement are not only compatible with true internationalism but in fact indispensable to it.[22]

While individuals are obviously the actors who compose the Opening and Closing Ceremonies, their identity *as* individuals (the third level of identity expressed in Olympic ritual) is brought to the fore only when the results of the athletic contests themselves are confirmed and consecrated in the victory ceremonies. Here, the athlete's body itself serves as the primary symbolic capital (though the effect is enhanced by the medals, flowers, and an olive branch cut from the grove of Zeus at Archiaia Olympia presented by a high-ranking member of the International Olympic Committee) representing the best and the brightest individual among "us," the highest exemplar of the species known as human being. This victory ceremony in itself is so well known and enacted across nations, continents, and cultures that MacAloon considers it alone "the object of a genuinely global popular culture" (1988b).

Though I have left out many details along the way (most notably, the liminal "rites of passage" that mark and define Olympic ceremony and festival from "ordinary life"), this description captures and conveys what MacAloon calls the "normative exegesis" of Olympic symbology (1984, 1988b) that can be distilled from official Olympic protocol and broadly confirmed by observation and the experience of participants, athletes, officials, and spectators alike. What is significant about all of this, in the context of the Smith and Carlos demonstration and this study as a whole, is what is missing. Olympic symbology provides no formal space for representing various nonnational social categories such as race, religion, region, ethnicity, or gender, the collective identities and social solidarities that for many Olympic participants define most fundamentally who they are, the very essence of their being. It is precisely in the face of this tripartiad ritual structure that Smith and Carlos—whose identity as black Americans constituted their foremost political and existential preoccupations—were confronted with a challenge, that of interjecting their own blackness into a ceremonial system that (not unlike classical, color-blind liberal democratic ideology) quite literally had no place for them.

The Structure—and Power—of Smith and Carlos's Demonstration

Before we go into how Smith and Carlos were able to maneuver within and around—or, to be more precise, directly through—the powerful constraints imposed by this ceremonial system, let us first consider the victory-stand experience of another 1968 Olympic champion, Dick Fosbury, the American who revolutionized the high jump that year with his backward leap—now known as the "Fosbury flop"—over the bar.[23]

Again, this case is the product of John MacAloon's extensive scholarly engagement with the Olympic Games and Olympic ritual in particular. It comes from an interview he conducted with the high jumper in the 1970s. After Fosbury recounted how he felt while jumping ("his sense of absolute risk and absolute control . . . and the certain though unspeakable knowledge that he would prevail"), MacAloon asked Fosbury to describe his victory-ceremony experience. Fosbury's initial responses are what any casual observer would probably expect. He talked about getting "really emotional" and nearly crying, about family and friends who had helped him to get there, and about all of the different emotions that "surged in waves" through his body (1988b, pp. 288–289).

According to MacAloon's careful report of the exchange (which I am forced to condense unmercifully), Fosbury continued, struggling to account for the powerful emotions he had "never experienced before," only to stop and abruptly change the subject moments after he had recalled welcoming some sort of "patriotic feeling." When he returned to the matter a bit later, it was to insist—quite incongruously—that he "didn't need the victory ceremony at all"; that he had not appreciated being put "on a pedestal," had not wanted to be a "role model" or a "hero," and felt like he had been forced to serve as a vessel for something foreign to himself (1988b, p. 289). Fosbury clearly detested being a symbol of any kind. But it became clear moments later that there was something quite specific, quite personal about his distaste for the victory ceremony:

> Being a college student at that time, I was against everything the government was doing as far as Viet Nam and as far as resisting any kind of protest the people were doing legitimately. So I was really against the United States government and so I really felt kind of anti-patriotic. And then I go to the Olympic Games and they play the anthem and I get this overwhelming feeling and it was pretty confusing. I couldn't believe what was happening. I guess it didn't make any sense to me. Maybe I did feel proud to be an American and proud to be from Oregon and proud to be representing my friends and different people from my hometown, but at the same time I didn't respect the government. (1988b, p. 290)

Fosbury's remarks clearly highlight the tensions and contradictions between nationalism, patriotism, and the state, and an individual's sense of self and his (or her) collective commitments contained in the victory-stand ritual. Above all else, Fosbury's account (which, in spite of Mac-Aloon's efforts to the contrary, remains outside the domain of either public or scholarly knowledge about the rite) highlights the compelling and unyielding structure of the victory-stand ritual, as well as the demands and pressures it can put upon individuals whose personal sense of self is not fully satisfied or properly expressed in the classic Olympic triad of individual, national, and global identities.

If Fosbury found himself caught up in these contradictions and confusions, unable to express them then and still pressed to even begin to understand them many years later, it might seem easier for athletes with intense or even overwhelming loyalties to religion, race, region, or politics to downplay the ceremony, laugh it off, or simply avoid it altogether. And, in fact, prior to the 1968 Games one of the protest possibilities entertained by Smith, Carlos, and their colleagues in the OPHR (strongly endorsed by some, as we shall see) was to simply boycott Olympic ceremonies—the victory rite in particular—altogether. Four years later in Munich, in fact, two of Smith and Carlos's friends and teammates, Vincent Matthews and Wayne Collett, enacted the symbolic equivalent, standing casually during the anthem, at one point twirling their medals on their fingers. Obviously Smith and Carlos did nothing of the sort. Quite the contrary, they chose to remain squarely within the confines of the ritual ceremony. But rather than giving themselves fully over to its conventional structure and implied sociological meanings, they tried—by the force of a logic they may not have been able to articulate in any other way—to reshape its symbols and sociologics into a meaningful expression of their own racially inflected sense of self and social solidarity.

Given their social interests and the established symbolic structure and sociological function of Olympic ritual, MacAloon (1988b) argues in what has been one of the only sustained intellectual commentaries on the episode, Smith and Carlos's actions could not have been choreographed and performed more perfectly. Precisely as the flag rose, the anthem began and the words "Oh say can you see / by the dawn's early light / what so proudly we hailed" resonated silently in the hearts and minds of American spectators, these two black athletes bowed their heads and fixed their eyes on the ground, refusing—in stark symbolic opposition—to "see" or "proudly hail" the nation they were supposed to represent. By rejecting the ritual celebration of a national identity they could not unconditionally accept, denying what and when the "script" of the ritual called for them to affirm, they recast the ceremony to function in a way that it was surely not intended, flipping it upside down; denying, surely not honoring, the integrity of their native United States.

Theirs was not simply an expression of negation or opposition, however. Having countermanded the symbols upon which the ritual usually depended, Smith and Carlos had created what MacAloon (1988b, p. 287) describes as a "sudden symbolic void." This void allowed them to draw the spotlight onto themselves and the clothing they wore, the "new" symbols of the ritual: clenched fists for unity and power; "human rights" patches covering their U.S. emblems; black stocking feet for black poverty and the myth of black economic progress through sport; a black scarf for black pride and tribal beads to pay homage to their own African heritage; and, perhaps most simply of all, their own black bodies. Introducing these new, more appropriate symbols at *exactly* the right time, Smith and Carlos co-opted and supercharged the Olympic victory ritual—"hot-wired" it, as MacAloon has put it—to send a solemn and powerful message to Americans and the world that attention and honor should be directed away from mainstream America, deflected even away from their personal selves and redirected instead toward the problems of race in the United States.

Rarely is human expression as focused, elegant, and eloquent as Smith and Carlos's was that day. Whatever else we discover about their politics, personal lives, and ideological commitments, this gesture must be recognized, as John MacAloon has suggested (1988b, p. 288), as an act of inspiration, passion, and originality, of sheer expressive genius—truly, by these standards or any others, a work of art.

Agency and Understanding in the Performance

To speak of this performance as a work of art is, of course, to ascribe considerable critical and creative capacity to Smith and Carlos themselves. It is a degree of agency and intention that has regularly been minimized or denied ever since. For example, for many years highly placed USOC officials whispered that Smith and Carlos were "put up to" the protest by an American newsmagazine in search of a cover story. While this charge (leveled against *Newsweek* and its longtime sports reporter Pete Axthelm) has long since been denied and dismissed, a great deal of prevailing wisdom attributes the demonstration not to Smith and Carlos but to the lead organizer and spokesperson of the Olympic Project for Human Rights, Harry Edwards. To this day, their Olympic sprint coach Stan Wright insists that "Smith and Carlos didn't plan the protest by themselves. I think Harry Edwards exploited [them] and used them for his own movement."[24] Historian Donald Spivey (1984) reports that the black boycott movement was "practically a one-man show," a "virtual one-man crusade," kept alive only by Edwards, who, during the final days before the Games, "could be found working out of the back of his rented van near the Olympic Village" urging prospective spectators not to attend (pp. 245, 248).

Edwards himself has done little to dispel these impressions. As he told a magazine reporter in 1993, "If I am remembered for nothing else, I want to be remembered for 1968. . . . Of all the things on my resume . . . the thing that's most important to me is the thing I have not put on [it]: my role in organizing the Olympic Project for Human Rights in 1967 and 1968."[25] Yet a huge portion of Edwards's substantial resume has been predicated directly on his role in these events. His first major work, *The Revolt of the Black Athlete* (1969), recounts the 1968 demonstration and the protest organization behind it: both the back cover and the foreword describe Edwards as "the architect of the rebellion." Most of his subsequent writings (which are still recognized among the authorial voices of the American sociology of sport), furthermore, seem to be either informed by or directly predicated upon these experiences (cf. Edwards 1979, 1980), and few of his numerous public appearances fail to mention them as one of his major accomplishments (Leonard 1998). Even his legendary tenure battle at the University of California, Berkeley, in the 1970s (which Edwards won only after the state governor intervened on his behalf over and above the objections of his department, the Academic Senate, and the Office of the President) seems to have been impacted decisively by his activism in and around sport.

I don't want to be misunderstood here. Edwards is a central figure in all of the pages that follow. As a young sociology instructor Edwards played a crucial and indispensable role in organizing and sustaining the OPHR, as well as in educating African Americans like Smith and Carlos about the racial injustices they experienced as athletes and in society as a whole. In addition, it is clear that Edwards was central to the discussions of how the athletes would express these discontents, and *The Revolt of the Black Athlete* has been the standard source of information on 1968 Olympic protest activities all the years since. Perhaps most important of all, Edwards led the movement for racial justice in and around sport in the aftermath of the Mexico City Games and helped to transform the academic subdiscipline of sport sociology in the process. But none of this should be confused with Smith and Carlos's victory-stand demonstration. There is no indication in the historical record that Edwards (or anyone else, for that matter) formulated any strategy resembling the one these two athletes put into action on October 16, 1968. The protests suggested by Edwards and his OPHR to politically conscious black athletes (such as wearing black armbands or socks) were vague and halfhearted at best. Unable to settle upon a mutually agreeable gesture prior to the Games, in fact, activist-minded athletes had resolved simply to do their own protest "thing" at the Games (much to Harry Edwards's disappointment, as I will discuss in chapter 5).

And if it is true, as Edwards would later write, that they agreed that the victory-stand ceremonies would be the focal point of the protests, it is also evident that his idea at the time was to boycott the rite entirely. Thus, sitting in the stands that day even fellow teammates and friends such as Vincent Matthews would be "shocked" by "the spontaneity of [Smith and Carlos's] protest." According to Matthews, there had been "little evidence until then that any form of protest might be forthcoming" and "it wasn't until [Smith and Carlos] were under the stadium waiting for the ceremony that they decided what to do" (Matthews with Admur 1974, p. 197).[26]

Many years later, speaking publicly on the topic for the first time since 1968, Smith described the difficult situation he and his teammates faced in Mexico City as they searched for some kind of a gesture to express their frustrations and discontent. "It had to be silent—to solve the language problem—strong, prayful and imposing. It kind of makes me want to cry when I think about it now. I cherish life so much that what I did couldn't be militant, not violent." Smith went on to recall how his sisters cringed at his activism even before the Olympic Games because they didn't want him to embarrass the family by describing how poor they were. But, as he saw it, they were poor and this fact alone was nothing to be ashamed of—which is why still today Smith is convinced they did the right thing: "[W]e had to be heard, forcefully heard, because we represented what others didn't want to believe" (Moore 1991a, p. 72).

Again, MacAloon's structural analysis of the victory-stand ritual should help us understand how—by calling attention to their own black bodies in a space where their blackness was otherwise seen but not seen—Smith and Carlos succeeded in "forcing" those who may not have "wanted to believe" what they had to say about the problems of American race relations at least to be confronted with some representation of them. But there was also more to it than this. In working *through* sport (or, to be more precise, through the ceremonial system of the Olympic Games, one of sport's most cherished and sacred expressive venues), rather than protesting *against* it (as the symbolic logic of a boycott would have had it), Smith and Carlos challenged an institutional-symbolic system that had made great claims about being a positive, progressive force for African Americans to explicitly recognize and represent race, to finally—and formally—live up to its claims. This is not to say that Smith and Carlos consciously planned the demonstration symbolic-detail-by-symbolic-detail, nor to claim that they would have been able to situate it in the comprehensive analytical context MacAloon provides. But it is to insist that Smith and Carlos's performance was founded on—indeed literally embodied—an exceptionally deep and comprehensive *understanding* of the sociological elements of

Olympic ritual and the potential for political expression also made possible by what was simply taken for granted and by what was left out altogether.[27]

Even so, the problem remains that over the years the two athletes—intense rivals then and never really friends—have offered different versions of the story.[28] On the one hand, Smith claims he "knew what [he] would do" a few days before the race and waited to tell Carlos until afterward because the two athletes were, after all, competitors as well as teammates. Carlos, for his part, says he suggested some sort of a gesture immediately prior to the race to Smith, who then agreed to go along. Indeed, in an interview with one of my research assistants on this project, Carlos called Smith's recollections "imaginative," saying he had "let" Smith win the race because his priority was to make a nonviolent demonstration, insisting that one day "we'll know the real truth; if I have to live to wait for that day to come, I will."[29]

But Carlos's claims are both dubious and vague. For one thing, it was Smith who produced the gloves that he and Carlos wore on the victory stand. His wife and the wife of another teammate had bought them a day earlier after watching black teammate and 100-meter champion Jimmy Hines refuse to shake hands with IOC President Avery Brundage, who presided over his gold medal ceremony. No one, as far as I am aware, has ever disputed this. Second, existing video footage makes it clear that Smith took the lead both in stepping onto the podium as well as in initiating the clenched-fist gesture. At least one psychologist, in fact, claimed that the bend in Carlos's arm (clearly discernible in photographs) indicates that he was somewhat less certain of his cause than Smith, whose arm is clearly ramrod straight.[30] More telling, perhaps, is that Smith offered a concentrated and coherent explanation of the protest's symbolism immediately following the ceremony, while Carlos was only able to (re)produce a familiar, if inflammatory, political rhetoric.[31] Moreover, ever since he first spoke out in 1991, Smith's recollections (incorporated above) have proven powerful, consistent, and compelling. It is for all these reasons that I consider Smith the primary architect of the demonstration and why I followed his account of the exchange leading up to the demonstration in the opening pages of this work.

In a certain sense, of course, this attention to the details of attribution may seem to succumb to fundamentally asociological (if not simply trivial) fascinations with individual intention, authenticity, and creative genius that are precisely the opposite of the expressed intent of this narrative. One reason I have spent so much energy on attribution is that any commentary that minimizes Smith's (and Carlos's) role in the demonstration—whether intended to absolve them of responsibility or take credit away from them—simply plays upon and reproduces insidious cultural stereotypes about athletes and African Americans being incapable of creative or intelligent labor. But there is much more to it than simply giving credit where credit is due. For credit, in this case, has a great deal to do with the meaning and significance bound up with this image, the very lessons about race, sport, and culture in the United States that it has to teach and we have to learn.

Following the account originally offered by Harry Edwards in *Revolt,* most commentators in the world of sport scholarship have highlighted the role of the organizing committee Edwards created and directed for the purposes of promoting an Olympic boycott (he called it the Olympic Committee for Human Rights, the OCHR) and its various protest activities in the year leading up to the Games as a way to explain the demonstration and its impacts.[32] More important, they have interpreted this entire constellation of sport-based protest activities—Smith and Carlos's dramatic stand most of all—as dictated by and directed against racism and discrimination in the world of sport itself. While there is truth in such interpretations (Smith and Carlos were certainly part of a movement and an organization that was much larger than them), it is not the whole truth. What such interpretations miss is that Smith and Carlos's demonstration carried racial meaning and significance far beyond the world of sport and its particular racial problems. Even at the level of motive and intent, this vision is misleading and misinformed. As we shall see in the next chapter, when Smith and his colleagues initially put forward the idea of race-based Olympic protest, they were careful *not* to criticize sport on racial grounds. Their hope was to use the Olympic Games to spotlight their concerns about race and racism in the United States broadly conceived.

Whether cause or consequence, these narrow, one-sided interpretations are closely connected with the muddled theorizing that has marked the conventional sociology of sport in the United States ever since. The primary program of this work has been to demonstrate that dominant sociopolitical structures and relationships—especially in the particular social categories of race and gender—tend *not* to be challenged and overcome in the sports world but instead are maintained and reproduced there. To be sure, these critiques initially provided a much-needed deconstruction of the sport-as-positive-social-force discourse that has been dominant to the point of being oppressive in the Western world. Yet, these formulations—grounded, as they tend to be, in conventional functionalist and reductionist theories of cultural domination, mystification, and/or hegemony—have simply exchanged one kind of totalization for another. They have thus failed to grasp the complex ways in which sport (not to mention popular culture more generally) is bound up with the constitution, reproduction, transformation, and, in some cases, contestation of racial order in societies organized according to liberal democratic principles.

Demonstrating this crucial and complicated vision is, of course, one of the primary objectives of this book.[33] It is also what brings us back, once again, to the particular understanding of sport and its problematic relationship to race that Carlos and especially Smith intuitively grasped and literally embodied on the victory stand in Mexico City. What is it, then, that they understood so well? What insight about sport and its significance for race was embodied in their victory-stand demonstration?

The answer to this question is complicated by the fact that it was not at all clear what import, if any, their demonstration was intended to have for concrete, political action. Even the interpretations they offered to the international media served to perpetuate rather than clarify its practical implications. If, for example, they had utilized a gesture many recognized as a "black power salute," then it was also the case that, as I alluded to earlier, Smith had refused to name it as such: the "power in black America" and "an arch of unity and power" was as close as he came, phrases he immediately qualified by referring also to the "regaining of black dignity." Along these same lines, it is hard to reconcile the radical black power nationalism associated with the clenched fist salute with the bowed heads that were also a part of the demonstration, especially when viewed through the lens of Christian iconography as a sign of submission and powerlessness. Thus, the gesture was full of paradox and ambiguity: at once subversive and respectful, silent but resounding, seemingly empty of political content, on the one hand, yet packed with meaning and significance on the other.

In many cases, such opacity would be the mark of confusion, expressive inefficiency, or a more basic indecisiveness. But my reading in this instance is quite the opposite. I believe that this very ambiguity constitutes the final portion of brilliance and meaning contained in their gesture. Standing on the victory stand with clenched fists jutting powerfully over silently bowed heads, Smith and Carlos captured, in a single and singularly powerful gesture, the complicated, controversial, and contradictory constellation of racial experiences, ideologies, and political programs swirling around them, in sport and in society at large and in the relations between sport and society. They made race a problem that could not be dismissed or avoided. And, in capturing, without fully commenting upon, the problematic nature of race both in and outside of sport, Smith and

Carlos opened a unique symbolic space for dialogue and debate about these issues. More than that, given the intrigue and emotion their gesture typically generates, they virtually obligated people—especially sports fans and historians and social scientists like myself—to recognize and make sense of all of this for themselves.

And so it was in the twenty-odd years that followed. Tommie Smith's adamant refusal to speak on public record about the gesture can and should be read, as John MacAloon insisted (unpublished manuscript), as an extension of that same demonstration, a protracted, personal, and highly successful effort to "force" Americans to confront the issues of race, sport, and the relationships between them that meant so much to him.

Ever since Smith's version of the story was made part of the public record by *Sports Illustrated* in 1991, much of the intrigue and controversy surrounding the demonstration seems to have dissipated. I am not convinced that this development has been wholly positive, especially given the straightforward, civil rights frame that now seems to surround the story. Indeed, I daresay it is time for us to return to this remarkable episode, to reexamine the social and cultural structures that endow it with meaning and the historical forces that help us understand how our memories and perceptions of it have shifted and changed over time. The drama of Smith and Carlos's victory-stand gesture deserves and demands nothing less.

PART ONE

The Movement, 1967–1968

He didn't know where he was going, but he knew he had to run, because it was rapidly making little sense and he knew if he was still for a minute to digest everything he would have to give up. . . . He had to run, search, look, fight—but more than anything, not give up.

—Barry Beckham, *Runner Mack* (1972)

Chapter 2

Agents of Challenge

On Thanksgiving Day, November 23, 1967, several hundred young black activists gathered at the Second Baptist Church in Los Angeles for a meeting designated as the Los Angeles Black Youth Conference. "Liberation Is Coming from a Black Thing" was the theme of the conference, one of a series of regional meetings proposed by that summer's first-ever National Black Power Conference to help plot the course for the next phase of the African American struggle for social justice in the United States. Its keynote address was delivered by James Foreman, the director of the International Affairs Commission of the increasingly militant and fractious Student Non-Violent Coordinating Committee (SNCC). But what made this meeting national news then and historical narrative now was the announcement that the approximately two hundred participants in a workshop titled the "Olympic Project for Human Rights"—Tommie Smith and UCLA basketball star Lew Alcindor among them—had "unanimously voted to fully endorse and participate in a boycott of the Olympic Games of 1968."[1]

This was not the first time the idea of an African American Olympic boycott had been conceived by activists, or introduced into the U.S. public culture. Only months before (in July) delegates to the national Black Power Conference had passed a general resolution urging black athletes to refuse to participate in the 1968 Olympics or in professional boxing matches until Muhammad Ali was restored to his former title as heavy-weight boxing champion (stripped by the World Boxing Association after he refused induction into military service for the Vietnam conflict). The basic idea had been around since at least the 1960 Olympics, when a reporter asked eventual gold medal decathlete Rafer Johnson about the possibility of his participating in such a boycott in connection with civil rights protests in the American South.[2]

The man whose name was linked with both variations on the boycott theme was Dick Gregory, the nationally known comedian and political satirist who had become an outspoken social activist during the course of the civil rights movement. Gregory, himself a former scholarship athlete at Southern Illinois University, apparently adapted the athletic boycott concept from antiapartheid plans that were beginning to be widely circulated among African Olympic nations about the same time.[3] In the summer of 1963, some three years after originally floating the idea, Gregory tried to convince black athletes at the Amateur Athletic Union (AAU) national track-and-field championships in St. Louis to boycott the American team that was being assembled to compete against a Russian side in Moscow as part of a prominent and hotly contested U.S.-Soviet dual-meet series. Gregory was convinced that a poor showing by an all-white American contingent overseas would "bust" racial problems in the United States by "embarrassing" the country on a world stage.[4]

In recent years scholars have suggested that international interests and pressures had a critical if not decisive impact on the American civil rights movement and domestic race policy in general.[5] Nikhil Pal Singh (1998) has gone so far as to argue that the enduring appeal of the Black Panther Party cannot be understood outside of an international context and without attention to their radical transnational politics. Gregory didn't necessarily share this revolutionary transnational vision. But his boycott proposal certainly was an effort to leverage Cold War American international interests against domestic racial problems.

Although Gregory's initiative didn't find any immediate support among black athletes, it got a boost the following March when three-time Olympic champion Mal Whitfield (800 meter and 400 meter relays in 1948; 800 meter in 1952) offered what he called "a shocking proposal" in *Ebony* magazine: "I advocate that every Negro athlete eligible to participate in the Olympic Games in Japan next October boycott the games if Negro Americans by that time have not been guaranteed full and equal rights as first class citizens." According to Whitfield, it was time for Negro athletes to "join in the civil rights fight," on the one hand, and, on the other, for "America to live up to its promises of Liberty, Equality and Justice for all or be shown up to the world as a nation where the color of one's skin takes precedence over the quality of one's mind and character." Echoing Gregory, Whitfield maintained that an Olympic boycott would "force" the United States to "live up" to its democratic ideals.[6]

At least two interrelated factors made these claims plausible and potentially potent. The first was the crucial role that black athletes played on U.S. sports teams. The 1967 record books, for instance, indicate that in track and field alone—which was then, even more than now, the crown jewel of Olympic competition—black athletes accounted for more than one-third of the gold medals won by the United States since World War II and 18 percent of all medals total.[7] The second factor underlying the appeal of a boycott as a tool for promoting racial change was the importance of Olympic-style sport for American foreign policy concerns at the height of the Cold War. The Olympics, after all, were not just any athletic contest but an international event of unparalleled scope and prominence. These international festivals of sport functioned as extensions of East-West (communist-democratic) ideological battles between the United States and the Soviet Union, and a black boycott would certainly have compromised American interests in the all-important medal counts vis-à-vis the Soviets.[8]

The American public and its leadership were more aware of this than today is often assumed. Before the 1960 Rome Olympics, for example, a *Newsweek* article titled "Men—Medals —Marxism" openly acknowledged that when the Games began "the United States and Russia will revive their athletic competition" in which each athlete "realizes that he is a pawn in a hot athletic war that is a phase of his country's cold political war." In January of 1963 U.S. Senator (and future Vice President) Hubert Humphrey penned an article for *Parade* magazine called "Why *We* Must Win the Olympics" (italics added) arguing that the Games represented the "relentless struggle between freedom and communism." A year later U.S. Attorney General Robert F. Kennedy insisted that it was a matter of "national interest" that "we regain our Olympic superiority—that we once again give the world visible proof of our inner strength and vitality." Inspired by Kennedy, Humphrey, and others, former Assistant Secretary of Defense Franklin Orth made headlines all over the country in 1964 when he headed up an attempt to reconfigure the institutions of the American amateur athletic establishment to "restore the supremacy of the United States in the Olympic Games."[9]

In addition to competing *against* each other in Olympic sport, these two super-powers were also competing *for* the attentions and affections of other nations around the world as well. Of particular consequence in this regard were the Third World nations of Africa and South America, the Western European democracies, and the Eastern European satellites—

all of whom, for different sets of reasons, found cause to be critical of American democratic ideals (and thus side with Soviet socialist interests) concerning matters of race. In other words, the racial discontents and injustices that an African American Olympic boycott was intended to highlight would be particularly damaging because it was precisely on the score of race that American democracy was most vulnerable before the world and in comparison with Soviet communism.

None of this was lost on Gregory or Whitfield. Writing for *Ebony*'s primarily black audience, Whitfield, who held college degrees in both physical education and urban planning, insisted:

> Even the people of foreign lands know that we are still not free in this country. In Africa, South America and all the nations of Europe, they know that the day-to-day civil rights struggles of the American Negro are but expressions of his earnest desire to break loose from the shackles that keep him from making his place in the sun. They know this, and they watch with discerning eyes to see what the outcome will be.

Gregory's boycott vision appealed even more explicitly to American nationalism. "An American Negro can go to Moscow and run in an integrated track meet on *enemy territory*," he told young black athletes, "but he can't run in an integrated meeting in parts of *his own country*. . . . [I]f Khrushchev came to this country with his Russian track team and demanded that the meet be held in New Orleans he would beat *us* because no Negroes could compete" (my italics). Gregory was so convinced of (if not simply invested in) the power of nationalist interests and ideological preoccupations that he believed black athletes "could have saved it right there. They would have embarrassed this country so bad it would have cleaned house."

But they didn't. Whatever its possibilities, the idea of an Olympic boycott had never taken hold among athletes prior to the fall of 1967. In 1960 Rafer Johnson had simply brushed aside the idea. In 1964 all that materialized was a handful of nonathletic pickets (led by Gregory) at the U.S. Olympic trials and some vague complaints from black Olympians about unsatisfactory social activities, athletic assignments, and housing accommodations in Tokyo—insignificant incidents quickly resolved by Olympic authorities and quietly sidestepped by the American press. And the African American Olympic boycott proposed in the summer of 1967 seemed to have no more chance of coming to fruition in 1968 than in these previous years. Only one athlete—two-time Olympic medalist long jumper Ralph Boston—would even comment on Gregory's Black Power

Conference resolution publicly, only saying, "I don't see that anything would be accomplished. We at least have this much freedom. If we boycott, we are throwing it away."[10]

In Gregory's view, black athletes were "young" and "didn't want to embarrass their country . . . on an international level." The latter point is particularly instructive. There were deep national-cultural taboos, or "unwritten laws" as Bayard Rustin put it (quoted in Marqusee 1999, p. 32), against civil rights activists and African Americans in particular protesting in any way in international arenas or in front of foreign audiences. It was, as Mike Marqusee (1999) has recently suggested, his internationalism as much as his black nationalism and his conversion to Islam that made Muhammad Ali such a despised figure in American culture at the time. Marqusee makes this point by recalling what the NAACP's Walter White—at the request of the State Department—said about internationally renowned entertainer, activist, and former football star Paul Robeson in the 1940s: "Negroes are American. We contend for full and equal rights and we accept full and equal responsibilities. In the event of any conflict that our nation has with any other nation, we will regard ourselves as Americans and meet the responsibilities imposed on all Americans" (Marqusee 1999, p. 32). If anything, African Americans were expected to bend over backward to prove their patriotism in international arenas.

Obviously, by the fall of 1967 something had changed. One way or another, some black athletes were beginning to think differently about the idea of an Olympic boycott. Gregory and Whitfield's proposal was, in other words, beginning to be taken seriously.

The Boycott Idea Finds Life

The first public indication that support for an Olympic boycott among black American athletes might be gathering was revealed on September 3, 1967, at the University Games in Tokyo, when a Japanese reporter asked Tommie Smith about the possibility with regard to the upcoming Mexico City Olympic Games. In response, Smith—a fifth-year senior-to-be at San Jose State—acknowledged that some black athletes might boycott the upcoming Games in order to protest racial injustice in America. Even though little else was known about the exchange—no one seemed to know, for example, what motivated the question, why Smith answered as he did, how many athletes he spoke for, or what the likelihood of such an action might be—American wire services picked up Smith's comments and they were reported across the country.[11]

That such a brief and offhanded comment attracted such national publicity signifies the deep threat posed by a black Olympic boycott. Even more telling was the commentary the story generated. Despite the lack of concrete information contained in the press dispatches, sportswriters across the country responded with remarkable hostility. They accused Smith of being "ungrateful," "childish," and "unpatriotic." Some suggested the American team would be better off without him, and others (against their better judgment) went so far as to speculate that even a complete black boycott would have little or no impact upon the American contingent's ability to produce Olympic medals. Smith himself began to receive hate mail, which would continue throughout the year, filled with insults, vulgarity, obscenity, and threats of violence and retribution.[12]

But the twenty-three-year-old track veteran refused to back down. A couple of weeks later (after he had returned to the States and resumed his classes), Smith, this time along with his San Jose State teammate Lee Evans, reiterated that there was a "good chance" of a boycott happening. Together, Smith and Evans, who were close friends as well as teammates, echoed Gregory and Whitfield's earlier claims, saying that they believed such a boycott would "hurt" the United States a great deal and in doing so contribute to the struggle against racial injustice within the nation's borders.

No matter how much observers wanted to believe otherwise, they were forced to admit that Smith and Evans had a point—at least as far as American Olympic interests were concerned. Not only had black athletes anchored the American track-and-field effort in previous Olympic games, but a 1968 boycott, according to the canonical *Track and Field News*, promised to be "keenly felt" in the featured sprints, relays, and all the jumps except the pole vault.[13] Their projections indicated that black athletes would account for 55 percent of the medals (eighteen of thirty-three) American athletes could reasonably be predicted to win in Mexico City. In the 100-meter dash, for example, where four medals were possible (three in the individual event and one in the team relay) only ten of the top thirty-five sprinters in the country were white—and none of them had run fast enough to rank among the serious Olympic contenders. *T&FN* didn't specify names, but Smith and Evans were undoubtedly two of the black sprinters expected to contribute to the American medal count.

The pair's track credentials were not only impeccable, they were truly incomparable. By 1967 both Smith and Evans were regular members of the American teams assembled for international competition, and between them held at least portions of *eleven* different track world records. Most of those belonged to Smith, who, during the course of the previous season (his fourth and final year of eligibility as a college competitor), had

Fig. 2. Tommie Smith and Lee Evans in world-record-setting 400/440 at San Jose State, May 1967. Photograph courtesy Jeff Kroot.

established new world standards in an unprecedented (and never again equaled) six of a possible eight individual outdoor sprint events. Only the 100-meter/yard distances remained for him to conquer, and his personal best of 9.3 seconds over 100 yards was already world-class. For his part, Evans, three years younger than Smith with two years of collegiate eligibility remaining, was already the top-ranked quarter-miler in the world, having lost only once in the event before he was injured in a European summer meet. (His loss, incidentally, was to Smith in one of his world-record-setting performances. It was the first and last time they faced each other in competition. See fig. 2.) The two were also accomplished relay runners, representing one-half of San Jose State's world-record 800 and 880 relay teams and one-half of the U.S. national team that owned the world record in the 1600 meter and the American record in the mile relay. What is more, Smith and Evans trained with Bud Winter, the most successful American sprint coach of his generation, and a group of sprinters that was among the greatest ever assembled in track-and-field history.

Between San Jose State and the Santa Clara Valley Village Youth Track Club (also based in San Jose), no fewer than *seven* of Winters's protégés—all of them African American—ran 9.4 or faster in the 100-yard dash (a time not one white sprinter in the country had achieved). It was an array of sprint talent so amazing that in the track world San Jose was known simply as "Speed City." (See fig. 3.)

If their athletic prowess was what marked their boycott discussions as worthy of public attention, it was also what would seem to have numbered Smith and Evans among the most unlikely of boycott proponents. For one, like so many of the great sprinters in track-and-field history, Smith and Evans were highly competitive and fiercely individualistic. Their personal running styles, for example, could not have been more different (Smith was known for his flawless technique and his incomparable top speed, Evans mostly for his tenacity and his indefatigable finishing kick), and their personalities were as distinctive as their running styles. "Smith was contained. Evans was funny and bold. Smith was liquid grace. Evans was burly, head-rolling determination," as their Olympic teammate Kenny Moore (1991, p. 64) would recall many years later. More important, their desire to compete in the Olympics was intense. Evans, for example, readily acknowledged having dreamed of participating in the Olympics since he had first started running, and Smith, in a prescient

Fig. 3. The "Speed City" crew, San Jose, 1968. Photograph courtesy Jeff Kroot.

figure of speech, told audiences that he would gladly "give his right to win a gold medal."[14]

In addition to the pride of personal achievement, an Olympic championship also held the promise of widespread public adulation, commercial endorsements, and, for lucky athletes, professional contracts in other sports. These financial incentives, it should be emphasized, were not nearly as large, direct, and predictable as they are for Olympic champions today. Nevertheless, for individuals like Smith and Evans—the children of poor, uneducated laborers in Northern California—they represented immediate entree to a way of life that could otherwise only be dreamed about. These two athletes grew up within thirty miles of each other in the verdant San Joaquin Valley (Evans in Fresno, Smith in the small town of Lemoore), and their backgrounds are remarkably similar; Smith's father, Richard, was a utility man who eventually got a job for the Lemoore Naval Station School; Evans's father, Dayton, was a hod carrier. Both men and their families were recent migrants from the South. Their families were large (Smith was the seventh of twelve children, Evans the fourth of seven) and both of their mothers (Dora and Pearlie Mae) often had to find work for themselves—and often their children—at jobs such as domestic service, lawn mowing, and migrant labor to supplement the family income. Both Smith and Evans knew what it was like to pick cotton and years later could speculate about having bumped into each other as children working the Northern California vineyards.[15]

And then there were the prevailing standards of amateurism and the lack of publicly supported facilities in the United States, which together made it all but impossible for most American Olympians to train at an elite level after college. Also considering the notoriously short prime of a top-flight sprinter, the four-year interval that separated each Olympiad, and their dreams of Olympic glory, the Mexico City Games represented a once-in-a-lifetime opportunity that neither Smith nor Evans seemed inclined to give up for any cause.

Nor, it was widely assumed, should they have to—even (or perhaps especially) if they wanted to contribute to the advancement of their race. This assumption was rooted in both recent historical experience and prevailing cultural logic. In a society where oppressive racial prejudices and discriminatory practices had effectively restricted the mobility of most African Americans, it almost went without saying that a black athlete could make his or her (but usually his) greatest racial contribution simply by minding his own competitive business, playing "by the rules," and letting his athletic presence and accomplishments speak for themselves— and, by extension, for the race. Sport was understood as an institutional

lm where personal, private interests and larger, collective
reinforced each other but found near-perfect synthesis.
ious black athletes didn't have to make a choice between
1al desires and their identity as black Americans; they
:ake and eat it too.

world champion heavyweight boxer of the 1930s and
___, was one of the most widely cited examples. Simply by "allowing his
fists to talk for him," as historian Lawrence Levine (1977, p. 433) puts it,
Louis was "a breaker of stereotypes and a destroyer of norms."[16] He didn't
need to make personal sacrifices or public statements about racial matters; his athletic presence and prominence was statement enough. Four-
time Olympic champion Jesse Owens, who won his medals at Hitler's
1936 Berlin Games, was another case. An even better example may be the
African American who integrated Major League Baseball, Jackie Robinson.
For it was only because of his fully conscious, enlightened understanding
of himself as a representative of the race and leader in the struggle for
African American justice, as Jules Tygiel (1983) describes in his seminal
treatment, that an individual as proud and defiant as Robinson absorbed
the taunts and attacks he received from racist players and fans in his first
years in the league. This pattern was thought to hold not only for nationally known athletes such as Louis and Robinson (or Smith and Evans) but
also for local sports standouts in cities and towns, high schools and colleges across the country. Quite unlike any other set of actors in the civil
rights drama, it was believed that the best contribution athletes could
make toward the cause was simply to make a name for themselves by
leaving the racial ghetto.[17]

As late as the summer of 1967, neither Smith nor Evans exhibited any
indication of deviating from this rags-to-riches, golden-gateway-out-of-
the-ghetto script. In a featured profile in *Sport* magazine that summer,
Smith, for example, was portrayed as a solid citizen, a model of social
mobility and racial integration.[18] The article dealt mainly with his on-
track exploits and accomplishments, but it nevertheless duly reported
that Smith was completing his fourth and final year of ROTC at San Jose
State and emphasized that he studied hard and expected to be commissioned an Army lieutenant upon graduation. He had also been drafted by
the Los Angeles Rams: the team hoped Smith might follow in the footsteps of the great 1964 gold medalist sprinter Bob Hayes, a star wide receiver for the Dallas Cowboys. Smith stated that poverty was "no excuse
for anything" and, according to the report, mentioned his race only "jok-
ingly" to suggest that his lack of recognition in the United States may
have stemmed from the fact that white people think "all Negroes look
alike."

This lighthearted, conciliatory Tommie Smith stands ir trast to the one who would openly speculate about giving pic dreams to participate in a black Olympic boycott jus later. Smith's conversion seemed so stark, so dramatic, s that many of his contemporaries—friends, acquaintances, alike—speculated that the boycott was being foisted upon th by militant and manipulative black leaders, outsiders who had no interest in Smith or involvement in sport. Smith, as we will see shortly, did not pretend to be an isolated, autonomous agent. But he also made it clear that his consideration of an Olympic boycott reflected a deep personal commitment that was carefully thought out and fully self-conscious. "My comments in Japan," Smith noted just a few weeks after first speaking out about the possibility of a boycott, "came as a result of quite a bit of listening and reading and thinking for myself."[19]

Anything but a stereotypical, single-minded "dumb-jock," Smith was an intelligent, articulate, well-traveled young man who was finally beginning to understand the deep and abiding problems of race in the United States, especially insofar as they impacted African Americans. "It began," Smith explained, "when I started walking and thinking 'I am a Negro' . . . I said, 'here's a white man, I'm a Negro. He can walk into this store, why can't I?'" And this transformation was far less impulsive and dramatic than public appearances suggested. According to Smith, it had been in ferment for several years at San Jose State.

> . . . as a senior in high school I looked upon my ability as something no one else had, and looking at this ability alone I neglected to realize that there might be something else to life than just track. It's only been in the last two years that I have begun to see that there are problems, and that I must learn to cope with them.[20]

"It really started last semester," Smith continued a bit later, when "I took a class in black leadership. It started me to thinking: What the hell is going on in the U.S.? I'm a human. What kind of rights do I have? What kind of rights don't I have? Why can't I get these rights?" The answers to these questions, Smith came to conclude, revolved around what he called "racial ostracism" in the United States.

In this context, it seems safe to assume that there was biting irony in the comments about race that *Sport* magazine had taken as Smith's "playful banter" just a few weeks earlier—and that the writer didn't realize this probably did little to alter the track star's sense of his country's racial issues.[21] But Smith wasn't interested in just analyzing or commenting upon America's racial problems. Indeed, after having spent the past couple of years "coping" with them personally, what he was really interested in and creasingly committed to was confronting these problems at their larger, systemic levels. This, obviously, is where the idea of an Olympic boycott came in.

Smith's tentative endorsement of an Olympic boycott was not the first thoughtful, self-conscious, and deliberate contribution by a black athlete in the struggle against racism in the United States. Far from it. I have already mentioned Jackie Robinson's vital and acute self-consciousness of being a representative of his race in integrating Major League Baseball. In 1966, Boston Celtics basketball star Bill Russell had published *Go Up for Glory* in an attempt to place the struggles and sacrifices of professional black athletes "in perspective." And then there is the case of Muhammad Ali, the man whose experience had helped inspire the revival of the Olympic boycott idea. What made Ali, or Cassius Clay as he was still called by most reporters and sportswriters in the mainstream press, one of the most famous and controversial personalities of the period were his very public and very unpopular positions on issues ranging from racism to religion and the Vietnam War.[22] Following in the footsteps of the man they thought of as their "patron saint," Tommie Smith and his friend Lee Evans (who offered a very similar account) were thus part of the first generation of African American athletes who believed that in order to make a genuine contribution to their race and to the struggle against what they called "racial ostracism" they had to do something more—or at least something different—than just excel athletically.

Many in the media and the public concluded that the willingness of athletes like Smith and Evans to support an Olympic boycott must have had something to do with racial discrimination in sport itself. Such charges, as we will see in chapter 4, would soon dominate the discussion. (Just a few weeks earlier at a press conference in New York City the NAACP's renowned Legal Defense and Education Fund had announced a lawsuit charging that Negro athletes appeared less often on television than comparable white athletes and for lower fees.)[23] But Smith and Evans asserted that their boycott considerations were motivated by racism and discrimination outside of sport—not in it. These young, activist-minded black runners insisted they were simply trying to use the cultural prominence and power afforded them as athletes to contribute to the larger movement against racial ostracism. In other words, Smith and Evans tried to portray their use of sport in much the same pragmatic terms that black Americans had come to understand their participation in any social institution or practice during the struggle for civil rights: as a form of structural power or symbolic capital that could be mobilized against racial injustice. As Smith put it a few weeks later: "I recognize that Negroes have had greater opportunities in sports in general and the Olympics in particular than they have had in other fields." However, "I am an athlete, I have stature only in the field of athletics and any action I take can only be effective in [that field]."[24]

The simple and straightforward desire to contribute to the African American struggle, argued Smith and Evans over the course of the fall, explained and justified their consideration of an Olympic boycott. It was also the rationale that Olympic Project for Human Rights organizers (Smith and Evans among them) would draw upon in their Thanksgiving statements to the press announcing the proposal, and in the explanation they would formalize shortly thereafter. "The roots" of the protest, as OPHR spokesperson Harry Edwards would later write, "spring from the same seed that produced the sit-ins, the freedom rides and the rebellions in Watts, Detroit and Newark." Common to these protests, he explained, was a fundamental "dissatisfaction" with the "racist germ" that had "infected" American society and corrupted the ideals of "equality, justice . . . and the attainment of the basic human and civil rights guaranteed by the United States Constitution and the concept of American democracy."[25] "There have been a lot of marches, protests and sit-ins on the situation of Negro ostracism in the U.S.," Smith observed.

> I don't think that this boycott of the Olympics will stop the problem but I think people will see that we will not sit on our haunches and take this sort of stuff. Our goal would not be just to improve conditions for ourselves and our teammates, but to improve things for the entire Negro community. . . . Maybe discrimination won't stop in the next 10 years, but it will represent another important development [in that direction].[26]

"You must regard this suggestion," Smith insisted, "as only another step in [this] series of movements."

Smith's moderate, matter-of-fact tone recalls Arthur Ashe's description of the OPHR and its boycott proposal as "a logical extension of the overall racial climate" (1988, p. 190) and the historian Adolph Grundman's claim that "given the mood of the era . . . it would have been strange indeed if sport had remained unaffected" (1979, p. 79). Such characterizations are appropriate and typical, but ultimately misleading. They are appropriate because the developments connected with the civil rights movement were obviously the catalysts that prompted athletes like Smith and Evans to finally take the idea of an Olympic boycott seriously. And they are typical in the sense that accounts of the OPHR and its boycott quest routinely—indeed almost uniformly—situate it against or within this sociohistorical

backdrop. But this typicality is also where such characterizations can begin to become misleading. Generalizations such as "the overall racial climate" or "the mood of the era" are trotted out so often and recited so
formulaically (and connected with sport protest so logically and unprob-
lematically) that they cease to be meaningful or useful. What is worse,
they can blunt or blur the challenges, complexities, and controversies that
racial activism—in any social arena but especially in sport—necessarily
involved at this point in time and the complicated question of why this
effort emerged when it did. In order to avoid such misunderstandings,
therefore, and really get to the heart of why an African American Olympic
boycott was being taken seriously for the first time in American history,
we must situate these boycott deliberations within a concrete, nuanced
understanding of the challenges African American activists faced in the
immediate post–civil rights period.

The Challenges of Race in the Post–Civil Rights Period

There was, at this time, a real split within the once-solid civil rights coalition. On the one side were those—represented by organizations such as
the NAACP and the Urban League—who believed that the civil rights
movement had done its work and that the new imperative for African
Americans was to move *from* the extra-institutional politics of protest *to*
the more usual institutional politics of the electoral-legislative system and
social processes of civil society (including, of course, the free market). To
the extent that additional protest or activism was deemed necessary at all,
in this view, it was only to ensure that the civil rights of African Americans
remained intact (that is, to prevent backsliding) or to extend the rights
and guarantees of full and equal citizenship to spheres of society that
still lagged behind. On the other side were those—including members of
organizations ranging from the Southern Christian Leadership Council
to the Student Non-Violent Coordinating Committee and the Congress
on Racial Equality to the Black Panther Party—who were convinced that
it was not enough to leave African American freedom and equality to the
workings of institutional politics, civil society, and human history itself.
In this view, additional social action and activism was necessary for true
racial justice to be achieved in American society.[27]

Underlying this split were two different conceptions of racial justice
and perhaps the more fundamental question of whether race remained a
problem at all in view of the accomplishments of the civil rights movement. Having already accomplished the formal goals of individual freedom from discrimination as well as legal and political equality of oppor-

tunity (symbolized and embodied most dramatically in the Civil Rights and Voting Rights Acts of 1964 and 1965), it seemed to many Americans, black as well as white, that the problem of racial injustice was finally being dealt with, that at long last African Americans had finally won the right to participate fully and equally as American citizens. It would be only a matter of time before the workings of the market and civil society fully integrated and assimilated blacks into the American mainstream. This is what might be called a "procedural" notion of racial justice (Bellah et al. 1985, p. 335). What made the racial order just was simply that the laws, rules, and norms of society had been equalized, made fair. If additional racial protest and activism was necessary, it was not to revolutionize the social order but simply to extend civil rights into spheres where they had not been applied before.

Yet large portions of the African American community were also coming to realize that these procedural reforms mattered very little in their daily lives. They discovered deeper and more persistent structural causes to their fundamentally unequal condition: institutional racism, economic shifts, deep cultural stereotypes, and so on. In other words, in spite of all the victories of the civil rights movement, African Americans still found themselves in a world of hegemonic racial stereotypes and socioeconomic structures of inequality that appeared to have little possibility of abating. And, unlike voting rights abuses, overt segregation, or outright physical violence, they were not forms of racism and inequality that could be easily overcome. Indeed, African Americans were beginning to suspect that procedural fairness and individual freedom would not be enough to overcome the injustices embedded deep in culture and institutional practices. If true racial justice was to be achieved, in this view, Americans would have to move beyond the liberal, procedural understandings of social justice and think about these problems in more structural, collectivist, even sociological terms. As Martin Luther King Jr. put it in 1966:

> So far, we have had the Constitution backing most of the demands for change and this has made our work easier. . . . Now we are approaching areas where the voice of the Constitution is not clear. We have left the realm of constitutional rights and we are entering the area of human rights . . . [whose objectives] will be a lot more difficult and require much more discipline, understanding, organization, and sacrifice. (King 1986, p. 131)

The tensions inherent within American understandings of liberal democracy and the civil rights coalition itself had been sensed early on by the fieldworkers of the Congress for Racial Equality (CORE) and especially the Student Non-Violent Coordinating Committee (SNCC). For example, immediately following A. Phillip Randolph's 1963 March on Washington, the moment of King's famous "I Have a Dream" speech, many of these student activists had become convinced that the nation was finally beginning to confront the anachronisms of Jim Crow social life and that black Americans would eventually win their full and unrestricted citizenship. Confidently expecting the passage of legislative measures prohibiting discrimination and segregation, they decided instead to direct their energies away from protesting against "the system" and toward working within it. Projects such as the Mississippi Freedom Summer, designed to organize the otherwise poor and powerless black majority against their own poverty and discrimination at the ballot box, became the focus. But their best efforts at institutional-electoral politics did not produce the results they had expected. Even after the passage of the federal Voting Rights and Civil Rights Acts (laws that were supposed to have equalized the racial playing field), large portions of the black community—in the rural South but increasingly in other portions of the country as well—found little difference in their daily lives. These activists began to realize that racism, discrimination, and inequality were far more deeply entrenched than any of them had realized.

Nowhere were these barriers more formidable (and did the discontents they engendered erupt more unexpectedly) than in the urban North. There, the successes of the Southern struggle had accelerated the hope and aspirations of ghetto blacks but had done nothing to improve the conditions of their daily lives, nor their prospects for the future. These developments have been neatly summarized by social historian Harvard Sitkoff:

> The panoply of court decisions, congressional acts and executive orders failed to affect the subordinate status of blacks in the North. None of the marches, pickets, rallies or other forms of peaceful protest abolished filthy dope-ridden streets or inferior segregated schools. No lawful strategy of social change dented the hostility of police departments or the discrimination of labor unions. All the tactics that had worked in the South miscarried against greedy slumlords and their intransigent political allies. Steadily the gap widened between what blacks desired and what they obtained, between what they expected and what they attained. (1981, p. 208)

If racial justice were to be achieved, in this view, it would require both new forms of activism and new understandings of racial justice itself. The idea of an Olympic boycott spoke directly to both these concerns.

That the boycott idea itself had been revived at the first-ever national Black Power Conference is only the most obvious testament to the more radical, post–civil rights racial politics of the prospective boycotters. Their use of the phrase "human rights" also signaled the shift. Just two years earlier, in his autobiographical *Go Up for Glory,* basketball star Bill Russell had written a remarkable chapter with just this title. Russell followed Malcolm X in arguing that "Civil rights today has become too tranquil, too filled with compromise."[28] Evans was even more explicit: "I think Negroes are realizing that the white man doesn't go by his own rules, such as civil rights." So, too, was Smith. Referring to the limitations of the usual American political process, he said, "We're not going to wait for the white man to think of something else to do with us—as in politics which is currently working against us."

Smith's reference to the importance of a college course he had taken on "black leadership" for his emerging racial consciousness is another, subtler indication of the more radical ideals and commitments that informed the boycott proposal. The failure of black leadership was the explicit subject matter of Harold Cruse's seminal 1967 black nationalist text *The Crisis of the Negro Intellectual.* One suspects that Cruse's work—which took black elites to task for failing not only to establish and sustain a more collectivist consciousness among black Americans but also to use various cultural and popular cultural forms to reach out to the black masses— may have been influential for these activist-athletes in ways that cannot be reliably demonstrated from available evidence. Neither was it incidental that their chief adviser, teacher, and strategist at San Jose State, Harry Edwards, was himself an instructor and Ph.D. candidate in sociology. Almost everything the potential boycotters had to say about the problems of race in the United States—from their critique of the racial order to the collectivist, structuralist solutions they hinted at—was grounded in a sociological perspective that was fundamentally foreign to American thinking about civil rights and social justice. As Evans himself recalled many years later: "A lot of militancy was rising in the black community. We stopped referring to ourselves as colored or Negro. You were black or you were not black. An Afro haircut was a statement of black nationalism. Nineteen sixty-seven was the first year I was proud of my skin being black."[29]

The point here is not that Smith and Evans were more radical than an earlier generation of self-conscious African American athletes. In fact, Smith and Evans vehemently resisted anyone who attempted to label them as "militants," "radicals," or "revolutionaries" and quite deliberately avoided associating themselves explicitly with "black power" politics. Furthermore, they regularly tried to characterize their racial critiques and boycott considerations as an extension of earlier instances of racial activism both inside and outside of sport. The point, instead, is that the broader social context within which their athletic participation was rendered racially meaningful had changed dramatically. Only in the context of the deep ideological and political challenges facing post–civil rights, African American activism can we understand why these young African Americans athletes even began to consider the boycott of an institution that they, like almost all other Americans, considered one of the few that had afforded them a relatively full, fair, and free opportunity to participate in American society.

Where previous generations of progressive black athletes had once contented, constrained, and controlled themselves in the knowledge that they were in the vanguard of progress for their people simply by virtue of their presence and performance in elite, integrated sports, this younger generation of aspiring activist-athletes was finding it increasingly difficult to make this argument sound convincing, either to themselves or to racially progressive others. However slowly and unevenly it had come about, black athletes were beginning to be accepted as part of the American sporting establishment. By the late 1960s, to take one important example, even the most recalcitrant, segregationist Southern colleges and universities were recruiting and admitting black students to compete on their athletic squads (Doyle 1994). As significant an advance as it was to see black athletes prominently represented in integrated settings all across the country—and it was a truly historic development, one that constituted very real social progress in both concrete and symbolic terms—the presence of these athletes was quickly becoming so widespread and widely accepted that it could no longer be said to represent dramatic progress or change. Both in sport and symbolically in society, black athletes had become part of the status quo, the expected, the taken for granted. What had once constituted genuine social progress had become commonplace social process. While this general shift represents a certain kind of success, simply being a successful black athlete could no longer be considered a form of activism in the late 1960s.

Furthermore, the post–civil rights phase of the movement required action directed against deep structural constraints and toward the accomplishment of concrete, collective progress. In this respect the old athlete-as-silent-symbol model not only seemed limited but suddenly appeared as part of the ideological problem that was being struggled against. It was, after all, precisely an individualist vision of racial justice that activists in the post–civil rights phase of the movement were trying to call into question. Individual success was no longer a great contribution in an era where the problems of race were now clearly structural and collective. As a contribution to the movement, individual athletic participation and success was being rendered almost obsolete.

Remember that the proposed Olympic boycott was *not*—at least as it was understood by Smith and Evans or approved by the OPHR workshop assembly—a criticism of, much less an attack upon, the Olympic Games or even sport in general for being racist or discriminatory. Rather, these young, activist-minded black athletes were trying to use their involvement in sport to contribute to the movement beyond civil rights.[30] These athletes seem to have hoped that justifying the boycott in this fashion might help individuals in the sporting world see their way to accepting, if not supporting, the more ambitious agenda of the post–civil rights phase of the struggle for racial justice.

A San Jose State Education

No matter how deeply committed an individual may be to a cause that requires tremendous personal sacrifice, such sacrifices rarely are carried out, much less conceived, in isolation—that is, in the absence of a face-to-face community of equally committed and like-minded colleagues and supporters. This is why the personal history and immediate social context of any actor or set of actors—their "habitus" and "field," to appropriate Bourdieu's formal social-theoretical terms (cf. Bourdieu and Wacquant 1992)—are always such crucial historical concerns. In the case of Smith and Evans the education and experience they received at San Jose State—an education, once again, made possible by their athletic prowess—both predisposed them to take the idea of an Olympic boycott seriously and then reinforced and radicalized these early boycott speculations.

We have already seen several indications of how important Smith and Evans's education at SJS was in terms of helping them to develop a deeper, more structural understanding of the history and circumstance of racism in the United States. It was no accident, for example, that Evans attributed a good deal of his own personal development to the reading he had done, or that Smith claimed that a course on black leadership had finally opened up his eyes to prospective solutions to the problem. Indeed, when they were first asked what inspired their "activist roles" a few weeks after their boycott ruminations became public, Smith and Evans gave identical, one-word answers: "thinking."[31]

San Jose State also brought them into intimate and uncomfortable contact with white culture, power, and privilege, and racism itself. The inability to find suitable housing close to campus was perhaps the most immediate and direct experience they faced. But the contradictions in their treatment as athletes and as black students were surely an important part of this as well. Evans gave the example of how San Jose State's white professors interacted with them. "They only talk to us because we're athletes," he said. "They don't talk to the next Negro who passes by." Smith added that his white instructors never wanted to discuss his performances on exams or anything about his personal life; they only wanted to talk about his races and his world records. Evans took this to mean: "They know us as the fastest nigger(s) on campus. . . . They don't say nigger but that's what they mean."[32] These words would become a refrain for prospective boycotters.

At San Jose State Smith and Evans also learned what was involved in trying to instigate change in racist policies and practices through hands-on, strategic experience. An Olympic boycott was not their only answer to their concerns about racial discrimination and ostracism in the United States. In fact, Smith and Evans were also part of a newly formed group of black students at San Jose State called the United Black Students for Action. During the first week of classes that fall the UBSA (whose membership included 59 of the roughly 75 black students among the student body of some 23,000) organized a series of rallies, pickets, and protests targeted, on the one hand, against institutional racism and discrimination among fraternities and sororities and intended, on the other, to achieve fairness in housing, more representative admissions policies, and reform in the athletic department.

The UBSA protest was perhaps the most important aspect of their education and experience at San Jose State as far as an Olympic boycott was concerned. By all accounts, the protest was the brainchild of a young sociology instructor named Harry Edwards.[33] Born and raised in the ghettos of East St. Louis, Edwards had attended San Jose State as an undergraduate on an athletic scholarship. After completing his master's degree in sociology at Cornell University, Edwards returned to his alma mater to teach and continue working toward his Ph.D. But the new instructor was disappointed to find that very little had changed at SJS during his years away from the campus. Rebuffed after his initial inquiries into the situation, Edwards grew frustrated with what he perceived as the administration's insensitivity to these concerns. To force the issue, Edwards, together with Kenneth Noel, who was working on his master's degree in sociology at San Jose State (he, too, had been a scholarship athlete as an undergraduate there), concocted the back-to-school protest.

The kickoff event took place on the first Monday of the fall term. During a rally attended by hundreds of protesters and onlookers, the UBSA presented a formal list of grievances to San Jose State president Robert D. Clark. In order to allow students "to register their complaints and to let other people respond if they wished to," Clark called for hearings to begin on campus that afternoon. The chief administrator assigned two of his vice presidents to sit on a panel that included both UBSA representatives (Harry Edwards among them) and spokespersons from the groups under attack.

These developments were, in many ways, typical of the numerous campus confrontations that unfolded in those years (such confrontations, of course, were also focusing increasingly on the Vietnam War). However, the San Jose State protest came to national attention when its leaders announced that the first home football game of the year, scheduled to be played against the University of Texas, El Paso, would be targeted for protest. More specifically, UBSA leaders promised that the SJS football field would be covered with as many as one thousand demonstrators if their demands weren't met.[34] (Conveniently for protesters, UTEP had failed to graduate a single one of the starting five basketball players that had led them to an NCAA championship in 1965, when the school was still known as Texas Western.)

It is difficult to capture the intense scrutiny and genuine fear provoked by the mere mention of a football-based protest. Tensions mounted and pressures soared both on and off campus, and rumors that the exclusively white sorority and fraternity houses might also be attacked and burned down resulted in the precautionary evacuation of Greek Row. Local businesses and community members worried that any disruptions could spill off campus and replay the urban riot scenes that had so unsettled the nation as a whole. Eventually, President Clark, with the national media looking on, canceled the game over and above the vehement objections of California governor Ronald Reagan. Governor Reagan (himself a former athlete and sportscaster who played the role of Notre Dame's legendary football coach Knute Rockne during his Hollywood days) had insisted that the game be played, offering to call in the California National Guard "to preserve order" and avoid what he called "the appeasement of lawbreakers."[35]

These UBSA experiences were foundational in a number of respects for Smith and Evans and their boycott idea. Not only were Smith and Evans among the group's advisory leaders, but current or former student-athletes composed the vast majority of the membership. What is more, one of the UBSA's most forceful complaints was that the 2 percent of the college admissions known as "special admissions" (a precursor to affirmative action) were almost all based solely upon athletic ability.[36] Though this aspect of the UBSA action was typically downplayed or trivialized by the national reporters who covered the story, sport itself was one of the most important and concrete arenas of contention at San Jose State. The cancellation of the college's first football game was a particularly important learning experience for aspiring sport-based activists.

One year later Edwards would depict the football boycott as a central feature of UBSA calculations. "Our strategy was basically a simple one," he recalled. "[W]e decided to use something . . . central to the [social and economic] concerns of the entire local community structure—athletics"—as "a power lever" that would "force" the community, student body, and administration into a "pressure situation."[37] But while Edwards's conclusions reveal how he and his colleagues *came to understand* the possibilities of athletic boycotts and strikes, the available archival evidence suggests that this threat to disrupt the football game was not a major part of the UBSA's original plans, nor was it subject to their direct control.[38] What seems to have happened instead is that, once mentioned, the football game protest emerged suddenly and virtually unexpectedly as a flash point of contention. This, in turn, alerted Edwards and his colleagues to what they would come to understand as "the power to be gained from exploiting the white man's economic and almost religious involvement with athletics."[39] In other words, the football protest was part of an emerging awareness of the utility of using sport as a tool for confronting the problems of race that persisted in the United States.

That Smith and Evans's commitment to an Olympic boycott was reinforced and radicalized by their experience at San Jose State is not mere speculation. Just a few weeks later, Smith would explicitly confirm as much: "[The UBSA football protest] has forced me to read and think about the problems of this day and age—even more than 6 months ago."[40] All this was unfolding when Smith and Evans were first beginning to speak publicly on the possibility of a black Olympic boycott. It is no accident that Smith initially addressed the possibility of an Olympic boycott just as fall classes were beginning to get underway. Or that he and Evans jointly reaffirmed the possibility of such a boycott during the same press conference in which the UBSA announced that it had agreed to proposals by the SJS administration to put an end to discrimination in fraternities and sororities, housing, and athletics. This was also the moment Tommie Smith chose to use the powerful and provocative words we saw above to explain why he was contemplating an Olympic boycott: "It is very discouraging to compete with white athletes. On the track you're Tommie Smith, the fastest man in the world, but off it you are just another nigger."[41]

At the center of almost all of this, of course, was Harry Edwards, the young sociology instructor who taught the classes on race relations and black leadership to which Smith and Evans referred. Edwards was far more than just a classroom teacher for Smith and Evans. Energized by his encounters with black radicalism the previous summer, Edwards, along with Noel, Smith, and Evans, would spend the better part of the fall refining the boycott idea and organizing the workshop around it. Although only twenty-four years old, Edwards was well suited for such a leadership role. He was intelligent, intense, well-spoken, and critically inclined, and, at 6'8" and 240 pounds, he had a commanding, charismatic presence. During the course of the 1967–68 school year, Edwards's class on race relations grew in attendance from sixty to six hundred students. As their teacher, Edwards also had daily personal contact with Smith, Evans, and their teammates, giving them the conceptual tools by which to make sense of the racial order around them and their role as athletes in it. Many years later Smith would recall Edwards's influence on their thinking and activism: "Harry challenged you. He used whatever he could to stop you in your tracks and get you to listen—black jargon, profanity, jokes, threats, or a Ph.D. soliloquy on history."[42]

The Olympic Committee for Human Rights

For the first time since the idea had been suggested in 1960, then, a group of African American athletes and activists was perfectly positioned to appreciate and mobilize around the idea of a black Olympic boycott. It was out of this group that the Olympic Project for Human Rights would emerge. However, a tremendous amount of organizing occurred between the time that Smith and Evans affirmed their personal commitments to an Olympic boycott and the November workshop in Los Angeles where a formal boycott resolution was collectively passed. This is where Harry Edwards emerged as a major player in the Olympic boycott movement.

In *The Revolt of the Black Athlete* (1969), his account of the OPHR, Edwards describes a private meeting he had with Smith early in the fall of 1967. In it, he says, they reflected upon their recent experiences with activism and sports and discussed what, if anything, they should do next.[43] Out of this conversation came a decision to assess the attitudes of others regarding "a revolt . . . over the problems facing black athletes and the black community in general." What they discovered, according to Edwards, was that "a number of black athletes (in addition to Smith and Evans, Edwards names sprinter John Carlos, Otis Burrell, Lew Alcindor, and his UCLA teammates Mike Warren and Lucius Allen) had given a great deal of serious thought to the idea of boycotting the 1968 Olympic Games."[44]

Alcindor's is an interesting and illustrative case. The celebrated seven-foot center had left his native New York City to come to the University of California, Los Angeles, because he expected that Southern California would offer an open, color-blind social environment. "I wasn't happy about leaving my parents and my old neighborhood," Alcindor recalled a few years later, "but I had to face the fact that there was prejudice in New York and there was a semi-permanent riot situation in the Harlem that I once loved."[45] But he found that racism and racial prejudice existed in Los Angeles as well, if in subtler, more insidious forms. Indeed, in the second installment of a two-part series in *Sports Illustrated,* Alcindor put it starkly: "UCLA Was a Mistake." Distraught by the realization, the basketball star turned to his studies and to books like *The Autobiography of Malcolm X:*

> I got more and more lonely and more and more hurt by all the prejudice and finally I made a decision: . . . I pushed to the back of my mind all the normalcies of college life and dug down deep into my black studies and my religious studies. I withdrew to find myself. I made no attempt to integrate. I was consumed and obsessed by my interest in the black man, in Black Power, black pride, black courage. That, for me, would suffice.

Alcindor's was thus another case in which a star athlete's university experience brought him in contact with the depth of American racism. At the same time it also gave him a way to begin to make better sense of the problem. "I was full of serious ideas. I could see the whole transition of the black man and his history. And I developed my first interest in Islam." In addition, Alcindor, who would soon change his name to Kareem Abdul-Jabaar, notes, "[I] learned about the third force in the world and the rising tide of black nationalism. I read LeRoi Jones' poems and plays. My head was filled with things, spinning with new ideas." According to Alcindor, these new ideas and views of the world came not only from classes but from conversations with his black teammates and friends, his "like-thinking brothers." The idea of an Olympic boycott provided for Alcindor, and others like him, a way to translate these deeply personal ideas and ideals into politically consequential action.[46]

Satisfied that the boycott had some chance of finding support among thoughtful, politically inclined black athletes like Alcindor, Edwards and Smith proceeded in earnest with their collaboration. In order to "plan and map a strategy," as Edwards tells it, a meeting was convened at his home in Northern California on October 7. Those in attendance—in addition to Noel, Smith, and himself, Edwards mentions George Washington Ware, a fieldworker for SNCC; Jimmy Garrett, an experienced organizer and chairman of the Black Student Union at San Francisco State College; and Bob Hoover, an activist and counselor at San Mateo Junior College—produced the idea for a workshop "to spell out formally the direction that the Olympic boycott . . . would take," as well as a committee—the Olympic Committee for Human Rights (the OCHR)—to organize it.[47]

While this organizing obviously entailed the regular dirty work of pulling together any conference, including phone calls to get commitments from prospective participants as well as countless administrative tasks, only limited information about the actual work of the organizing committee is available. And as with so much of the entire boycott effort, most of it comes directly from Edwards. He claims the OCHR was a three-man committee (composed of Edwards as chairman, Kenneth Noel as "chief organizer," and most likely either Smith or Evans)[48] assisted by a cadre of "student volunteers" at San Jose State who performed clerical work and tried to "locate and get information to" as many black athletes as possible. This was also the group responsible for the procedures that strictly limited media access to the workshop. As Edwards explained later, they had learned from previous black activism that "the less information about Afro-American intentions and plans released to . . . the mass media, the better off black people were" and therefore decided "to make the press dependent upon our reports and interpretations of what went on in the workshop rather than permitting them to observe the activities of the workshop at first hand and thus possibly influencing the proceedings by the very fact of their presence."[49]

This behind-the-scenes planning, of course, had not yet become a matter of public knowledge. All that most Americans knew came through and centered around Lee Evans and especially Tommie Smith. Interestingly, Smith and Evans coyly insisted time and again that they were not actively encouraging other athletes to boycott and were not even sure that a boycott would transpire. They would only say that should there be a boycott, they would take part in it. "There is a chance it will happen, but it just depends," Evans said. He believed that upward of three-quarters of world-class African American athletes would be willing to forsake their "opportunity to compete; they'd hate to but then you've got to do something," but the long sprinter also realized that athletes in other parts of the country did not understand the urgency or complexity of the problems of race in a way that would incline them toward making the personal sacrifices necessary to pull off a boycott. "[I]f you go to the south or southwest,"

Evans explained, "these are the guys who are catching the most hell in the streets and they just don't understand the need for a boycott."

> The schools in the south simply aren't the same as in the west. So, these guys aren't aware of what's happening. The schools don't get them to thinking and the guys don't read about the problems. They don't think about their jobs and what their parents were doing. They're just thinking about themselves and what the Olympics would mean.[50]

And even to the extent they were aware of the larger issues, Smith added, fear and intimidation discouraged many athletes in all parts of the country from participating. Because of these obstacles, the two San Jose sprinters claimed they themselves were waiting until the Los Angeles workshop to make a decision on boycotting.

If they were not "actively" trying to "organize" a boycott, Smith and Evans were certainly prominent and provocative voices on its behalf. "The Olympics are something that I have dreamed of participating in ever since I first learned to run," Evans told people. "If the door . . . to freedom for black people . . . can be opened by my not participating, then I will not participate." Smith took his earlier theme of self-sacrifice even further: "I would give my right arm to participate and win a gold medal, but . . . I am quite willing not only to give up my participation in the Games but my life as well if necessary to open a door by which the oppression and injustices suffered by black people in the U.S. might be alleviated."[51] In fact, the first public indication that a formal meeting would take place seems to have come when Smith raised the "delicate subject" in a November 5 speech to a service club in his hometown of Lemoore, California. At that time, Smith claimed that even though he personally was against such a boycott and was desperate for his chance to win Olympic gold, he would honor the decision reached by a meeting of Negro athletes scheduled for Thanksgiving Day at UCLA.[52]

Obviously, the specific details of the meeting had not yet been finalized. Not only did Smith say the meeting would take place at UCLA (which it did not), he also claimed that Wilt Chamberlain, Bill Russell, and Jim Brown would be among the attendees. They were not; in fact, reporters quickly realized that both Chamberlain and Russell, who played professional basketball for the Philadelphia 76ers and Boston Celtics respectively, had home games scheduled for that date. And this was not the only snafu the OCHR experienced. By Edwards's own subsequent admission, they were "only partly successful" in even contacting athletes, much less enticing them to come to Los Angeles to take part in the meeting.[53] In addition to these organizational stumbling blocks, many more fundamental questions and confusions lingered around the objectives, ideals, and discontents that motivated the boycott idea.

Many critics wanted to know, for example, why members of the OCHR would single out the Olympics—an institution widely believed to be relatively free of discrimination or bias—for boycott while continuing to compete for a school they deemed guilty of actual discrimination. Part of the reason for this was simply pragmatic. They were, after all, still college students whose very education and future livelihoods had been made possible by and still depended upon athletic scholarships. "Athletic scholarships," as Smith remarked, "mean our lives to us." But the real factor, they insisted, was that sport was only a tool, not a target. Evans addressed this point by reiterating that societal racism—or "racial ostracism" as Smith had called it—was the real target of their protest.

> The school is just part of this country. So I think we should hit at the top. . . . [An Olympic boycott] is where you can hit them the hardest. This is one of the major areas where the U.S. gets its international sports propaganda. The Olympics are a big thing and the press help to create this. So, if the people want us Negroes to help promote U.S. sports propaganda, they can help us too.[54]

But even those who were genuinely sympathetic to the OPHR cause were uncertain, confused, or simply unconvinced as to what could be accomplished by an Olympic boycott. At a very basic level, potential supporters wanted to know what Smith and Evans actually wanted, what they hoped to accomplish, and what it would take for them to drop their boycott consideration. Given their silence on this matter, the question quickly became whether boycott proponents were really trying to "force" social change by leveraging American Olympic performances against domestic racist practices (as was implicit in Gregory's original proposal), or whether they simply meant to "call attention to" racial injustice and inequality using the boycott (or its threat). Even though Smith and Evans were adamant about their intention to honor a boycott if it came down to that, they also refused to offer definitive statements when asked whether they were trying to accomplish "concrete objectives" or simply trying to make a "symbolic statement."

I do not mean to imply that Smith and Evans and their OCHR colleagues were confused on these issues. Even though it was composed mostly of college students, the organizing committee was actually quite sensitive to many of these issues, had considered them in some detail and then chosen, as an organizing strategy, to avoid discussing them specifically so as not to alienate potential supporters anyway. Instead, Smith and Evans and their collaborators focused on the three things that they were most convinced of and committed to: first, that, despite all of the advances of the civil rights era, racism was still a problem in the United States; second, that it required concerted public attention and deliberate measures; and third, that an Olympic boycott represented one powerful and provocative forum for raising these issues in an increasingly difficult era for racial activists. And this much is certain: whatever other ambiguities and tensions may have been embedded in the idea of an Olympic boycott, these convictions proved sufficient to bring some two hundred activists and athletes to Los Angeles on Thanksgiving Day for an Olympic Project for Human Rights workshop.

The Thanksgiving Day Workshop

Because no white reporters had been permitted in the building, and those black reporters allowed in were prohibited from taking direct quotes, interviewing participants, or taking pictures, little more was—or is—known about the Los Angeles workshop than what I reported at the start of this chapter. The only full account that remains is the one provided by Harry Edwards himself in *Revolt*.[55] According to Edwards, he personally opened the workshop with a short talk on the factors that led to the proposal of the boycott. After that, several black athletes (including Smith, Evans, Alcindor, and Burrell) offered up their own comments and viewpoints. It was apparently the seven-foot tall Alcindor who set the tone of the meeting:

> I'm the big basketball star, the weekend hero, everybody's All-American. Well, last summer I was almost killed by a racist cop shooting at a black cat in Harlem. He was shooting on the street— where masses of black people were standing around or just taking a walk. But he didn't care. After all we were just niggers. I found out last summer that we don't catch hell because we aren't basketball stars or because we don't have money. We catch hell because we are black. Somewhere each of us have got to make a stand against this kind of thing. This is how I take my stand—using what I have. And I take my stand here.[56]

Alcindor's remarks, in Edwards's account (which has since been widely quoted), drew a five-minute ovation from the assembly.

According to a reporter on the scene for *Sports Illustrated,* arguments for and against the boycott proposal were then heard for almost two hours, with most of the arguments against the boycott (or for some form of compromise action) being raised by the older attendees. (Edwards singled out Dan Towler, a professional football player from the Los Angeles Rams, claiming that Towler's critical comments were met with "a chorus of boos" and were inevitably "shouted down.") Before a formal vote could be taken, however, the meeting was disrupted by a violent episode outside the meeting hall. The clash seems to have pitted black power leader Ron Karengas and his "US" group against various members of the American Communist Party. Although the exact cause of the disturbance or its connection to the workshop is difficult to establish, the chaos that ensued forced workshop participants to express their support for an Olympic boycott via a rather hurried, disorderly mass acclamation. While not quite the "unanimous vote" reported to the press, this voice vote provided the organizing committee with the "endorsement that it sought." "The first step in the mobilization," as Harry Edwards would write little over a year later, "was complete."[57]

Edwards wasted little time in taking the next step. In a prepared statement released to the press immediately following the workshop, the young sociology instructor described the proposed Olympic boycott as a "significant stand."

> I know of no other group of people who can make our feelings known. I hope the country can see what these black athletes have done. This is the last chance to avoid racial catastrophe in this country. This is our way of pointing out that the United States has no right to set itself up as a leader of the free world. It is a simple fact that America has to be exposed for what it is. America is just as guilty as South Africa ever was.

The goal of the boycott, Edwards concluded in dramatic fashion, was to "put the question before the United Nations," to "take it out of the sphere of civil rights and bring it into the sphere of human rights."[58]

It was a heady moment, but the unity achieved behind closed doors didn't last long. Prominent workshop participants began backing away from the resolution they had supposedly voted to uphold almost immediately. In an interview with the *Los Angeles Times,* for example, Lew Alcindor refused to "unequivocally" confirm either that a boycott would occur or that he would not compete for the U.S. basketball team. "I can't comment on what Mr. Edwards said," Alcindor said. "All I can say is that everybody agreed it would be a good idea to boycott. That does not speak for any one person. Everything was done anonymously. Actually, there is no boycott as of now. There can be no boycott until it's time for anybody to boycott."[59] According to the article, Alcindor's comments were significant for two reasons: first, because he claimed that the boycott resolution did not bind him personally, and second, because of the discrepancies between Edwards's and Alcindor's versions of what happened in the meeting.

Alcindor's UCLA teammate Mike Warren denied that he had even attended the workshop and was quoted as saying that his preference was for "something more constructive than a boycott" anyway.[60] A few days later, yet another prominent boycott proponent, Otis Burrell, withdrew his support because he felt that the "lack of unity and organization of this proposal" would have rendered a boycott a "useless sacrifice" (a sacrifice underscored by the fact that Burrell claimed already to have been denied a Christmas job because of his attendance at the workshop).[61] Even Tommie Smith himself denied the "official" OPHR press release just two hours after it came out, telling a San Jose *Mercury-News* reporter: "Harry has taken it upon himself to make a statement. He was not authorized to do so. No, I won't verify it. I'm giving no statement."[62]

The man in question had departed Southern California immediately after the Olympic boycott workshop to attend the National Conference of Student Body Governments in San Francisco where he was to supposed to deliver an address on "Student Government Responsibility and the Crisis in Race Relations On American College Campuses" the next day. Edwards's invitation to speak at this conference was based upon his recent activism at San Jose State (whose student government was the host school for the meeting), but reporters were waiting at the Sheraton Place Hotel to find out more about the Olympic boycott announcement of the previous day. After giving his scheduled talk, the sociology instructor read and distributed copies of what he called a "rough statement on the results of the Olympic boycott workshop" to the nearly one hundred reporters present. The statement read, in part:

> RESOLUTION DRAFTED AT BLACK YOUTH CONFERENCE, LOS ANGELES, NOV. 23, 1967 OLYMPIC BOYCOTT, HARRY EDWARDS, CHAIRMAN
>
> Whereas: The United States has failed to use its power—governmental or economic—to effectively alleviate the problems of 22 million black people in this country,
>
> Whereas the United States has openly and flagrantly carried out and endorsed acts which have operated—by plan—to the detriment of black people in this country,
>
> Whereas the United States has engaged in acts which constitute a direct affront and humiliation to the basic humanity of black people in this society,

Whereas the United States has hypocritically put itself up as the leader of the Free World while right here in this country we have 22 million black people catching more hell than anyone in any communist country ever dreamed of,

Whereas the United States government has acted in complicity with other racist elements of this society to strip black athletes of their prestige and athletic status based upon racist whim,

Resolved: Black men and women athletes at the Black Youth Conference held in Los Angeles on the 23rd of November, 1967, have unanimously voted to fully endorse and participate in a boycott of the Olympic Games in 1968.

What is more, Edwards insisted that workshop conferees had, in two separate resolutions, also "unanimously voted to boycott" any sporting events connected with the New York Athletic Club or involving participants from South Africa or Southern Rhodesia.[63]

In the absence of additional historical evidence, it is difficult to judge the accuracy of Edwards's account and interpretation of the proceedings in Los Angeles. But at least three points are certain. One is that the conspiratorial, apocalyptic vision that animated Edwards's fiery rhetoric was calculated to stir up controversy in the public sphere. A second is that this was not a public stance with which most of the athletes who had participated in the workshop were comfortable. And thirdly and most important, the boycott push was on, the movement, for better or for worse, had begun. All they could do now—or at least for the moment—was sit back and see how their proposal would be received.

Chapter 3

Of Civil Rights, Culture Fights, and Abstract Ideals

The day after the OPHR released its declaration in favor of a black American Olympic boycott, major newspapers across the country gave the announcement prominent coverage, with at least one (the *Chicago Tribune*) making it a front-page story. Most of these accounts simply described the boycott announcement and named several of the athletes reported to have participated in the workshop. In addition to Tommie Smith, Lew Alcindor, and Lee Evans, UCLA's Mike Warren and UNLV trackman Otis Burrell were among those named. Many also reported Harry Edwards's comments—at this point he was quoted as an "unnamed black spokesman"[1]—on the importance of black athletes in the United States and their intention to use the boycott to demonstrate to the world the pervasive racism of American society.

But while the national media was clearly poised to substantiate and elaborate the story, additional details proved difficult to come by. Reporters had only the Edwards press statement at their disposal and that came to them indirectly, through a black Los Angeles sports reporter. A handful of reports recalled that Tommie Smith had expressed similar sentiments several weeks earlier, but except to say that the conference organizers promised more details sometime the next day, there was little else to report about this late-breaking Thanksgiving Day story.[2]

All of this, recall, was by the design of Edwards and the organizing committee. Over the course of the year to come, Edwards's ability to understand and manipulate media conventions would become one of the primary resources of the entire boycott effort. Unfortunately, these initial forays into what we might now call spin control were less than a complete success. For one thing, reporters (who covered the story on site but were not allowed to observe the proceedings) had only the names of those who had been in attendance to report—something the athletes had explicitly wanted to avoid. Even worse, the lack of other information meant that as much attention was paid to the events that unfolded outside the church as to the meeting that was held inside it.

The *Los Angeles Times,* to take one important example, devoted an entire story to the commotion. According to the *Times* account, Ron Karenga, a recognizable militant activist often at odds with other "black power" leaders, and his followers had clashed with a band of some fifty members of a Marxist-Leninist branch of the American Communist Party. In the melee that ensued, the *Times* reported, several shots were fired and two of the communists sustained undisclosed injuries.[3] The *San Francisco Chronicle* reported that Karenga and his supporters (who appeared "with shaved heads and wearing orange and yellow shirts with a picture of Karenga on the front") "chased eight other Negroes and a white man (later identified as Michael Lasky, a self-described local Communist Party official) and pummeled the latter before he was rescued by police." This account, compiled from the Associated Press and United Press International wire services, reported that no one was seriously wounded.

The precise cause of the disturbance remained cloudy. The *Chronicle* says that the fight broke out after the group with Lasky shouted, "Down with bourgeois Negroes!" The *Times,* however, simply notes that Karenga and his troupe had been serving as a "security guard" for the conference. (*Sports Illustrated*'s story on the workshop, written by a young African American reporter named Johnathan Rodgers, made no mention of the incident at all.) Whatever actually happened outside the OPHR workshop and however it was associated with the boycott proposal, the media's use of the incident to frame the boycott story signals how the Olympic Project for Human Rights would be perceived by the mainstream American press and public.

A Storm of Controversy and Confusion

In lieu of more concrete and immediate information from workshop organizers, sportswriters and reporters set about trying to determine the actual likelihood of a boycott for themselves. What they discovered seemed to suggest that it was little more than an idle threat. Not only were the most prominent athletes associated with the boycott proposal backing away from the resolution they had supposedly voted to uphold, but fewer than half of workshop participants (no more than fifty or sixty, according to most accounts) had actually been athletes, and of those only a handful possessed the world-class skills that marked them as potential Olympic qualifiers. Only two other prospective Olympians (sprinters Bill Gaines of San Jose State and East Texas State's John Carlos) subsequently declared their support of the boycott, while many others—including track-and-field standouts Ralph Boston, Charlie Greene, Jimmy Hines, Art Walker, and University of Houston basketball star Elvin Hayes—were adamant about their opposition to it.[4] Perhaps even more telling, prominent black athletes reportedly sympathetic to the boycott declined to speak directly on its behalf—instead choosing to speak out only against its critics. Outspoken NBA star Bill Russell, for example, criticized Owens and Boston for opposing the boycott and said that a boycott would not harm their race's struggle for equality, but he would not go so far as to call himself a supporter. "A man should do what he feels is right," Russell said. "If anything, it might help call attention to the problem."[5] At this point, the controversial boxer many American journalists insisted on calling "Cassius Clay" was the sole African American athletic star to voice public support for the proposal.[6]

Many black athletes were sympathetic to the racial discontents that motivated the proposal and were even willing to take some action against them, but they remained unconvinced that an Olympic boycott was the best way to do so. Some, simply unwilling to give up something they had worked their whole lives for, were determined to try to compete in the Olympics Games no matter what. Others, perhaps a majority, had more fundamental concerns. High jumper Ed Caruthers was one. "Athletics have been mighty good to the Negro. Our participating in the Olympics has given the young Negro kids something to look up to. It is a prideful thing to be able to participate in the Games."[7] Sprinter Charlie Greene considered a boycott un-American: "It all comes down to a matter if you're an American or you're not. I'm an American and I'm going to run." Similarly, Elvin Hayes insisted, "It is not a one-color country, it is an all-person country."[8] Sprinter Clarence Ray elaborated:

> I feel the U.S. should be represented by the best athletes regardless of race, creed, color or religion. I think the boycott will exploit the fact that there is a racial problem in the U.S. but on the other hand we are not alone in racial differences as other countries have the same problem. I couldn't say that the boycott will solve our

racial problem here in the U.S., but I can say that if we are not represented by the best athletes this will hurt America. Attempts must be made to solve these problems, but a house divided by itself cannot stand alone; . . . We must always keep our personal affairs to ourselves for solving America's problems is a problem for Americans alone. By division, we show disunity and America's image will be destroyed. I am an American first, last and always.

Ralph Boston, who had been involved in political discussions the previous summer, was also against a boycott but for a much different reason: "I don't feel that the Games should be used as a political crutch," Boston said. "I don't feel that politics should enter into the Olympics at all."[9]

For all these reasons, black athletes and sports figures lined up (or were lined up) against the proposed boycott. According to the *Chicago Tribune,* "Negro athletes throughout the nation yesterday generally expressed their opposition to the announcement from Los Angeles"—a claim based on a "survey" of black athletes from all levels of sport: Olympic, collegiate, and professional.[10] A story that came out of San Francisco on the UPI wire had Bob Hayes (1964 100-meter gold medalist and professional football player for the Dallas Cowboys), Rafer Johnson, and Jesse Owens along with Boston—probably the four most well-known black track athletes in the country—all on record as opposing the threatened boycott.[11] Johnson, the former decathlon gold medalist who had been party to boycott discussions almost a decade earlier in 1960, called instead for the establishment of a "Committee for the Perpetuation of Friendship through Sport" based upon the twin notions that the Olympics were a competition strictly between individuals and that sports were the great racial equalizer.

USOC director Art Lentz said that his organization "resents being used as an attention-getter no matter how worthwhile the cause may be," while the U.S. track-and-field team's head coach, Payton Jordan of Stanford University, suggested, "There must be some coercion to have an individual who has worked so long and hard [to qualify for the Olympics] change his mind in the middle of the stream."[12] In many communities local sports personalities were sounded out for their views as well. In Chicago, for example, alderman Ralph Metcalfe claimed that there had been a proposal to boycott the year he was an Olympian. "There was talk of boycotting Hitler and his doctrine of Nordic supremacy," said Metcalfe, "but we thought we would make a contribution. There were more Negroes on that team than any previous United States Olympic team. We won and it stuck a pin in the balloon of Hitler's doctrine."[13]

Jesse Owens, of course, was the most famous and celebrated athlete of those 1936 Berlin Games. As legend had it, his gold medals in an unprecedented four events (the 100- and 200-meter dashes, the 100-meter relay, and the long jump—this won with the help of German rival Luz Long, who suggested the American move his takeoff mark back six inches in order to avoid fouling out of the competition) had so upset Hitler that the führer refused to shake Owens's hand in congratulations. Though Hitler's "snub" has since been revealed as Owens's personal myth-making, the story was upheld in 1967 as evidence against the proposed boycott, and Owens himself emerged as one of its most outspoken and widely quoted critics.[14] In Owens's view, the boycott was nothing but "political aggrandizement," which he condemned on the grounds that "there is no place in the athletic world for politics." Instead, Owens claimed, "The Olympics help bridge the gap of misunderstanding of people in this country," thus promoting the "way of American life."[15] In a follow-up statement published under the title "Olympics a Bastion of Non-Discrimination," the legendary figure added that athletic scholarships help youngsters to attend the colleges of their choice.[16]

Owens was surpassed as the most strident, obsessive, and omnipresent public critic of the boycott only by Avery Brundage, the Chicago businessman who was president of the International Olympic Committee. Speaking from his vacation home in Southern California the day after it was announced, Brundage characterized the boycott resolution as "foolish" and "opposed to the basic philosophy of the Olympic movement." According to Brundage,

> The Olympics is the one enterprise that has protected the rights of all people. The basic philosophy of the movement is no discrimination of any kind—racial, political, religious or anything else. It is the one great enterprise that has been fundamentally against all forms of discrimination. When starters mark the line, all are equal.[17]

Brundage promised to use his influence to urge the athletes who had endorsed the resolution to reconsider. In the event they decided to follow through on their threat, however, he predicted that their spots would be "eagerly taken by others" and would make little difference in the showing of the United States in Mexico City. According to Brundage, "These misguided young men are being badly misadvised" and would "only be depriving themselves of an opportunity that comes only once in a lifetime." His conclusion was at once patronizing and menacing: "If these boys are serious, they're making a very bad mistake. If they're not serious and they're using the Olympic Games for publicity purposes, we don't like it."[18]

Just a few weeks later, in its December edition, the *Track and Field News* reported that of the twenty-seven black contenders for Olympic track berths either quoted in the press or polled by the editors themselves, only nine said they would even consider a boycott, and not one said they would unequivocally support one. At this time, the newsletter quite correctly surmised, the boycott was "strictly a proposal, with few takers"; it was, in short, little more than a hypothetical idea.[19]

However, despite the lack of tangible support for the idea—track and field was, after all, the sport where the boycott had originated—the mainstream media continued to treat the Olympic boycott proposal *as if* it were a realistic protest possibility. In fact, the proposal triggered what an astonished *Track and Field News* would quite accurately call "perhaps the greatest explosion of interest and controversy in the history of track and field." Sportswriters and reporters continued to devote extensive coverage to the story for much of the following week. Alternately fascinated and horrified by the proposal, those in the public press were, in a very real sense, obsessed with it. More than this, in tones ranging from disbelieving and skeptical to critical and openly hostile, they took it upon themselves to formulate detailed criticisms and condemnations of the boycott idea.

In a commentary run on its main editorial page, the *Chicago Tribune* recounted the boycott vote and quoted Harry Edwards as saying "that the Negro oppression in this country is 'as bad as that of South Africa,' and that the United States should be 'exposed' before the United Nations for having 'exploited' Negro athletes." "This chatter," as the *Tribune* called it, "is as silly as it is intemperate. Athletics is one field in which discrimination hardly exists." The newspaper based its assessment on the fact that sports teams at every level of competition in football, baseball, and basketball "have Negro athletes who are stars and whose exploits are applauded." And as for exploitation, the paper dismissed the claim simply by suggesting that the salary checks of professional black athletes "would tell a different story." The final paragraph of the editorial appealed to "the Olympic ideal" of "a more generous humanity" as a proven way to improve race relations, but concluded in disgust that "the Negro athletes and those who arouse them think it better to boycott their own country and humanity."[20] A month later on Christmas Day, the paper would include the Olympic boycott story in an article titled "Stories We Could've Done Without in '67."

One of the strongest and most vitriolic variations on this theme was delivered by A. S. "Doc" Young, a longtime sportswriter for the *Chicago Defender:*

> If Tommie Smith . . . believes "I'm nothing but a nigger" when he isn't performing on the track, then he is "nothing but a nigger."

When one considers that millions of American Negroes have with-stood the worst of Southern bigotry without ever being reduced to the acceptance of that state, what is Tommie Smith crying so much about? I have nothing but contempt for people who complain be-cause we don't have enough heroes but who spend their time trying to destroy the showcases for which heroes are produced and dis-played. The charge that "America is as racist as South Africa" is the most extravagant lie in our times.

Saying that "Dick Gregory and his 'crowd'" were wrong to have men-tioned the idea in the first place, Young claimed, "There actually is no way of telling just how important Negro athletic heroes have been to the cause of racial equality in this country. Whenever a bigot cheers for an integrated team in this country, he loses a bit . . . of his bigotry." If these "Instant Leaders want some causes," Young declared, they would do well to devote themselves to the "elimination of riots . . . school dropouts, youthful crime, grime in the ghettos—for starters."[21]

As this fierce resistance would suggest, the mere idea of a black Olympic boycott was truly a startling challenge, far more threatening in 1968 than it may appear from our perspective a third of a century later. But what was the nature of its threat? Why was a protest proposal that seemed to have little or no grassroots, rank-and-file support taken so seriously? What was at stake in this controversy? Answering these questions requires something of an interlude from this basic historical narrative but will establish the complicated constellation of cultural ideals about race, sport, social justice, and civil rights that prefigured, animated, and constrained black athletic protest and the counterstruggles against it.

Making Sense of the Threat

For mainstream, middle-class white Americans not deeply or directly in-volved with sport, the threat of an African American Olympic boycott was probably just one more example of the stark divisions, cataclysmic struggles, and chaotic changes of the period. With Vietnam and class war-fare, with feminism and black power, with students in the streets and pop culture icons and practices suddenly the stuff of politics and public policy, this period was a watershed, a parting of the waters. In 1968, as Stuart Hall and his colleagues (1978) described Great Britain, "the whole fulcrum of society turn[ed] and the country enter[ed], not a temporary and passing rupture, but a prolonged and continuous state of semi-siege. . . . The po-litical polarization which it precipitated fractured society into two camps:

authority and its 'enemies.'" Volumes have been written about this period, much of it focusing on the year 1968. I won't attempt a recounting here except to point out that one of the things that seems to have made all the transformations and struggles that were part of 1968 so threatening and disconcerting for those who felt under attack were the strange, peculiar forms these struggles assumed. On the one hand, they were composed of new groups of challengers—women, students, environmentalists, and most of all minorities—with unfamiliar grievances and objectives, and some of whom seemed to have no fundamental concrete grievances or objectives at all. Connected with this, these actors expressed themselves in forms and forums that had never seen protest or politics before. No one, it seemed, perhaps not even the actors and activists themselves, fully understood the meanings and causes or the consequences and implications of the social dramas being played out. "This spectacle," as Hall and his colleagues called it, "mesmerized the right, the center and the apolitical, precisely because it refused to assume the recognized forms of classical class conflict and the politics associated with it."[22]

With its connections to black power activism and anti-Vietnam protest, its ambiguous and uncertain aims, and its location in the middle of that playful and heretofore "apolitical" realm of sport, the African American Olympic boycott proposal, then, was for many simply one more instance of the incomprehensible spectacle of social chaos and upheaval, another example of a world gone—or going—mad. Disentangling the connections among and between each of these various issues and forces can be both difficult and dangerous. However, in this case at least, it is obvious that the racial politics of the prospective boycotters were at the center of the boycott controversy. In a country already wracked by the fragmentation of the civil rights coalition, urban violence, militant "black power" protest, and white backlash, there was simply little public sympathy or political support for those dramatizing the problems of race in any form, much less on a stage for all the world to see. And few groups felt more strange about this than white sportswriters.

That black protest in the United States had simply gone "too far" was the theme of *Los Angeles Times* sportswriter Charles Maher's first column addressing the resolution that had been passed in his city on Thanksgiving Day. According to Maher,

> American Negroes struggled for years to reach the mainstream of American sports. And they finally made it. But now some of them— a few of them—are swimming furiously away from the mainstream. Their determination to withdraw is a product of frustration. They

have decided, or have been led to believe, that their people will never achieve social and economic equality in American society. Rather than fight a hopeless situation, they have elected to get out. The trouble is that no course of action could be more hopeless than the one these Negro athletes propose to follow.

For Maher, the Olympic boycott was symbolic of certain segments of the black population that had given up on the democratic process. It was not a development he condoned. "[W]ithdrawal is not the Negro's answer," the Los Angeles columnist concluded. "In this country, sports have given the Negro an effective means of communicating with the white majority, of demonstrating that he can fit in. Destroying this line of communication hardly seems calculated to serve the Negro's cause."[23]

This depiction of the boycott as outside the boundaries of acceptable social protest was further developed a few weeks later in a column written by John Chamberlain (copyrighted and distributed by the King Features Syndicate) titled "Boycott of Olympics Is a Boycott of Reality."[24] Chamberlain described the proposed boycott of the Games as "the most recent outbreak of 'Black Power' apartheid virulence in the United States" in his very first sentence. For Chamberlain, "The 'Black Power' advocates seem to be more and more committed to turning the United States into an 'apartheid' nation, which is the very thing they profess to hate about South Africa." The trouble with their point of view, he went on, is "that it implies a perfectionist standard that no country in the world has ever reached. The perfectionist who cannot see that historical evolution is a rugged process commits a crime against a lot of his live-and-let-live brothers who want to see slow improvement in their own daily lives." Chamberlain then used Jackie Robinson's integration of the major leagues to justify the claim that "what happens in athletics in America is always a precursor of what happens in society as a whole," and to support his larger conviction that "Whatever the 'Black Power' extremists say, the Negro is slowly winning his fight against discrimination in the U.S."[25] Chamberlain concluded:

> The Negro athletes who elect to go to Mexico City in 1968 will not be representing an abstraction; they will be representing a people who hold all shades of opinion about "race." Don't [those] who constitute a prime example of integration in America have their right to be represented at Mexico City by the best athletes we can assemble regardless of race? . . . This is a question that track star Tommie Smith might ponder.

Chamberlain's blanket characterization of boycott supporters as "black power extremists" was, of course, not entirely accurate. We have already seen considerably more ambiguity and indecision among them on matters of racial politics than Chamberlain was aware of—or, perhaps, could allow. Recall that Smith (among others) clearly repudiated the anti-American, black power militancy Chamberlain associated with him, and went out of his way to distance himself from Harry Edwards's inflammatory public comments. Nevertheless, Chamberlain was correct in identifying boycott proponents as part of the coalition of black activists who believed that civil rights had not gone far enough.

Not only was this one of the points that brought boycott advocates together in the first place, but what support the initiative found in the days immediately following its announcement came from spokespersons and leaders of organizations who shared this basic conviction. One of those was Charles Hamilton, professor of political science at Roosevelt University in Chicago and coauthor (with SNCC's Stokely Carmichael) of the influential and still widely read *Black Power* (1968). "The boycott is very necessary," Hamilton argued. "It gives us another way of confronting the system of racism in this country. . . . What Black Power people are saying is that those of us who have 'made it,' star athletes or whatever, have a responsibility to bring our people along with us."[26] Another was Lincoln Lynch, a national CORE spokesman, who suggested that the boycott "should be extended to all black athletes who take part in every phase of athletics in the United States." Even more, Lincoln promised that CORE would support the continuation of an all-sport boycott "until we see some real evidence that the power structure is prepared to deal with black people on the basis of equality."[27] And finally there was Martin Luther King Jr.

Andrew Young, King's top assistant and the newly appointed executive director of the SCLC, spoke on behalf of the Nobel Prize–winning civil rights leader in strong support of the boycott effort. Young situated King's support in the context of the SCLC's fledgling "Poor People's Campaign" (the initiative King was working toward when he was assassinated in Memphis just a few months later). "Dr. King applauds this new sensitivity among Negro athletes and public figures and he feels that this should be encouraged," Young reported. "Dr. King told me this represents a new spirit of concern on the part of successful Negroes for those who remain impoverished. Negro athletes may be treated with adulation during their Olympic careers, but many will face later the same slights experienced by other Negroes." According to Young, King understood it was a lot to ask a Negro athlete to give up the possibility of an Olympic gold medal but nevertheless felt that "the cause of the Negro may demand it."[28]

Once again, in the context of the polarized racial politics of the era, such assertions alone were probably enough to have provoked an antagonistic, critical response from many, if not most, Americans. They represented, in the mainstream American imagination, that place where African American activism crossed the line from being legitimate, civil rights protest to extremist black power radicalism. Even King, it should be recalled, had fallen out of favor with most Americans because of his evolving structural critique of American society and his continued involvement in contentious, extralegal protests and organizations. In many ways this was one of the lessons of the UBSA protests that Edwards, Evans, Smith, and Noel had been involved with at San Jose State just two months earlier.

After four successive days of hearings, demonstrations, and negotiations following the UBSA's disruption of the football home opener, SJS president Robert Clark's administration placed all twenty-seven fraternities and sororities on probation, ordered the athletic department to provide equal treatment for all athletes (especially as far as recruiting practices were concerned), and appointed a special ombudsman to look into other racial problems such as discriminatory local landlords. The SJS administration also promised financial backing for a black students program to tutor and recruit minority group high school students for college.[29] It was, by most local accounts, a quick, amicable, and just settlement. Edwards proclaimed it "an historic occasion," displaying "the possibility of men sitting down as men to meet deeply rooted problems." "If it can be done at SJS," Edwards proclaimed, "I cannot see why it cannot be done in Detroit, New York and Newark." Pictures of the initial Monday UBSA rally show a poster that compares SJS with the Universities of Alabama, Georgia, and Mississippi. Another banner asked: "If it can't be done at SJS, then Where?"[30]

The suggestion that the SJS experience might be a model for colleges and universities across the country infuriated California governor Ronald Reagan. He publicly reprimanded Clark and demanded the termination of Harry Edwards's teaching contract.[31] "I disapprove greatly of what Edwards is trying to accomplish," the future president proclaimed. "Young athletes are going to be victimized by such an action. Edwards is contributing nothing toward harmony between the races."[32] Edwards, in return, suggested that Reagan was the one who needed to be relieved of his duties, calling him "a petrified pig, unfit to govern."[33] But Reagan was far from alone. He had the strong support of California state superintendent of public instruction Max Rafferty,[34] and many Republican legislators were clearly on his side. One California Republican state senator described the UBSA threats as "a poker game bluff" and worried that the cancellation of the football game could set "a dangerous precedent." It was one small example of the beginning of the white electoral backlash that would help elect President Nixon less than a year later.

In sum, then, although UBSA student leaders and an overwhelming portion of the university community considered the settlement of these disputes satisfactory, even laudable—an example of reasonable, nonviolent demonstration tactics and of appropriate give-and-take on the part of the black students and college administrators—prominent state officials branded the protesters as radical, unlawful extremists and characterized the settlement as weak-kneed appeasement. In other words, despite the apparent "solution" to the protest, the university found itself—mainly in the symbolic figurehead of its president (who resigned less than two years later)—under siege from the conservative forces of the state government.[35] Given that formal procedural freedom and equality had been guaranteed, in this view, any activities or protests motivated by the belief that racial justice had not yet been achieved—that civil rights had not yet gone far enough—were almost by definition illegitimate and unnecessary, or, in the language of the era, militant, radical, and extremist. The young activist-athletes realized this quite clearly. "As soon as you become aware of what is happening to your people," Lee Evans explained, "you're considered militant. The UBSA is considered a militant group because we got things done on the campus."[36] Reagan and his many supporters would certainly have concurred with Evans's analysis, although just as certainly they would have rejected his conclusion that the San Jose campus was now a better place and a model for schools nationwide to emulate.

Sport as Special

As clear as the polarized racial politics implicated in the boycott initiative seemed to be, what is surprising—and this is a crucial point—is that Maher and Chamberlain found themselves among a very small minority of critics who focused explicitly on the racial dimensions of the prospective boycott. Many different arguments against the boycott were given, not all of which were mutually consistent. Some said that sport participation was an inherently positive and progressive racial force already, or that the Olympics were supposed to be a humanitarian gathering of individuals, a place for overcoming—not calling attention to—social differences and distinctions. Others argued that a boycott was un-American or that such a protest was political and thus had no place in the world of sport. Still others suggested that the boycott was being foisted upon naïve young athletes by opportunistic, nonathletic others, outside agitators of a sort. But the argument that the racial views behind a boycott transgressed the boundaries of acceptable, civil rights—oriented activism was almost never among those offered up by critics. If and when matters of race were invoked by boycott critics, it was only briefly—usually to preface their reprehension of the boycott with some general declaration of support for racial equality, integration, or "civil rights," occasionally to argue that things were actually getting better for African Americans, or simply to assert that however troubled the racial situation in the United States, it was still much better than in a country like South Africa. Otherwise, racial issues were almost absent from the discourse—either unspeakable or unthinkable, perhaps somehow taboo. Clearly, this was not the usual, post—civil rights politics of race; something else was going on.

That "something" had to do with the social realm that was the platform for this activism. The unifying theme running throughout the otherwise diverse and disorderly cacophony of arguments aligned against an Olympic boycott was that it was wrong simply because sport itself was an inappropriate venue for any kind of racial activism. Nationally syndicated sports columnist Red Smith, for example, charged Edwards with "setting his sights on the wrong target."[37] Art Rosenbaum of the *San Francisco Chronicle* claimed Edwards "and his crowd" were "boycotting the wrong store,"[38] and *Life* magazine ran an editorial arguing that a "Negro Olympics Boycott Is Off Target."

The *Life* case is particularly important and revealing because the periodical had a well-established reputation for being open to black radicalism (a reputation that probably contributed to its own demise four years later), and in discussing the boycott proposal the magazine's editors went out of their way to point out that African Americans had often made good use of "the boycott weapon" and even defended "Black Power" as a diffuse rallying cry that "appeals to Negro pride." Nevertheless, *Life*'s editorialists felt compelled to draw a line when it came to the question of an *Olympic* boycott. "In their long and unfinished struggle for equal rights," they wrote, "Negroes have often made good use of the boycott weapon especially against discrimination in jobs, restaurants, etc. where the target was clear and vulnerable." But "what," they asked rhetorically, "can they accomplish by boycotting the Olympics, which have been notably free of racial discrimination?"[39]

Thus, racial issues were missing from most boycott critiques because sport was seen as somehow unique, a special case that didn't require or allow their consideration. Even in an era when no aspect of American culture seemed beyond question, when virtually nothing was sacrosanct, boycott critics were united around this sentiment. So deeply ingrained was this belief in the sanctity of sport that many critics assumed—directly in contrast to the way boycott proponents formulated and presented their proposal—that the boycott was aimed at the Games themselves, that it was an attack on sport.

Part of what made sport so special, in the eyes of boycott critics, had to do with the widely held belief that it was, in the words of Red Smith, "gloriously free of discrimination." The next chapter shows this to be a dubious proposition at best. But at this particular historical moment, this claim went basically unchallenged. Recall that even Smith and Evans had essentially conceded the point in the weeks leading up to the Los Angeles workshop. Many critics would go even further to argue that sport was a positive, progressive force for American race relations. For them this set up a broader and more basic claim: that the sanctity and integrity of athletic competition could not be compromised or disrupted by the presence of activist-athletes, whether they were protesting race conditions or anything else.

In a certain sense, this view of sport as a social realm that had to be protected and preserved from all outside influences and social forces was a version of the old argument in the worlds of art and literature that "high culture" has to be kept separate from "politics," that such spheres are either outside of or above such complexities and complications. But in the sporting context, this argument sometimes assumed a different, somewhat "lower" guise: that sport shouldn't be taken so seriously to begin with, that it was nothing more than a diversion, a form of entertainment and release from the complexities of everyday life. In either variation, this sport-as-separate-sphere argument was based on the belief that athletic competition had to be the first and most important priority. Anything that interrupted, disrupted, or violated its integrity in any way—as an Olympic boycott obviously would do—had to be opposed and expunged. Critics who took this line believed that as long as sport itself wasn't racist or discriminatory, there was no reason for the sporting world to expose itself to the controversy and upheaval of dealing with this contentious social issue.

If boycott critics were concerned simply with preserving the purity and integrity of the pure play realm of sport—that is, with maintaining the boundaries between sport and everything that wasn't sport—this might suffice as an explanation for the peculiar absence of racial issues in the arguments offered against the proposed boycott. We could simply conclude that those in the sports world were committed to preserving and protecting the integrity of athletic competition for its own sake and above all else. This would not be a particularly inspiring position, but it would be fairly straightforward and consistent. However, as is almost inevitably the case for sport idealists, what made sport special in the eyes of boycott critics was actually even more complicated and ambitious than this separatist formulation would allow. For at the same time critics wanted to preserve and protect sport from the corrupting influence of a racial boycott, most also refused to let go of their claim that sport was a leader in the struggle for African American advancement and racial harmony and justice in general. Critics like Avery Brundage and Jesse Owens almost never made one point without the other. "Doc" Young, the black sportswriter who had taken Smith so sternly to task for supporting a boycott, had written a whole book on the subject, proclaiming sport as "the door-breaker [for] Americans of color [in all] walks of life" and the "proof to the world that democracy can work."[40] The *Chicago Tribune* sounded the call frequently and forcefully. "Few if any aspects of American life demonstrate fair racial practices more thoroly [*sic*] than sports, or had demonstrated it longer. Pillars of church and university might like to be able to say that they have led the way, but they have to admit that sports did."[41]

Although considerably more complicated and uncertain than inflated sportswriting hyperbole would allow, there is no question that sport had been in the vanguard of racial progress in the United States in the first sixty years of the twentieth century.[42] The prominence and prowess of African American athletes presented a strong rebuttal against insidious assumptions of racial inferiority; provided African Americans with much-needed heroes, role models, and leaders; and presented both communities and the nation with examples of the possibilities and benefits of racial integration. Even Harry Edwards would have admitted as much. But this was not really the bone of contention between boycott proponents and critics. Most sports idealists went well beyond the experience of recent history to claim that a boycott wasn't necessary because African American athletic participation was linked to racial progress inherently and inevitably. So commonsensical, so natural, so inevitable did the relationship between sport participation and African American advancement seem that most Americans were simply shocked to hear that anyone—much less a group of athletes themselves—would make the claim that sport needed to be used in a more deliberate, calculated fashion if it were to be a positive force in the movement against racism and for racial justice. It ran counter to everything they knew and assumed about sport when it came to matters of race. Sport was simply and unquestionably a positive and progressive racial force. Elevated to the level of ideology by the 1960s, this was an article of faith not only held by sports idealists but also accepted by those who knew or cared very little about sport.

As far as idealistic boycott critics were concerned, then, sport was thus doubly inappropriate for race-based activism: it was off-limits to non-sport intrusions, and it was an institution that produced positive and progressive racial results. As long as it remained unquestioned, this two-dimensional idealization of sport served the sports commentators and elites very well. It enabled the sporting world to take credit for all positive racial results achieved in and through sport, while allowing that world to disavow the need to engage any controversial racial issues.

It would be a mistake, however, to conclude that the specter of racial politics was not involved at all in the judgments pronounced against the Olympic boycott. There are at least two reasons for this. One is that Smith and Evans had pointedly and deliberately avoided criticizing sport while promoting the boycott proposal. Indeed, they explicitly tried to frame the boycott as consistent with sport's long legacy of commitment to African American advancement in the United States. Thus the idea of an Olympic boycott *could* have been understood as a logical, reasonable extension of the belief that sport was a positive force for African Americans and race relations (rather than antisport protest) if a more specific racial politics were not somehow involved. Indeed, it was likely with this hope in mind that Smith and Evans had refused to discuss discriminatory racial policies and practices in the world of sport that they were obviously well aware of and deeply troubled by. Closely connected with this is the curious fact that those in the sporting establishment who led the way in criticizing this activism were often the very same officials, reporters, and athletes who had celebrated sport for its contributions to the advancement of the black race for so many years before. No matter what these critics did (or did not) say, then, something about the racial politics they associated with Edwards, Evans, and Smith was deeply and directly connected with their objections to them and their boycott proposal.

These implicit tensions and contradictions would lead Harry Edwards and his OCHR collaborators to accuse their critics of being racists, anti-Semites, and "Uncle Toms" hiding behind one form or another of sports idealism. Although the connections between sports idealism and a more conservative racial politics were not coincidental, I would not go so far. On the one hand, it is simply impossible to accept (much less prove) that so many athletes, coaches, sportswriters, and leaders had changed their racial views so dramatically or were so fundamentally racist to begin with, or that painting them with this brush helps us to understand what was really going on here. On the other hand, no matter how simplistic, mythologized, or duplicitous this rhetoric about the sanctity of sport may seem (and I do mean to suggest it was deeply problematic), boycott critiques formulated along these lines were far too passionate and publicly convincing for us not to take them at face value. Indeed, a good deal of the power and effectiveness of these critiques derived directly from the fact that they involved so little subtlety, nuance, or refinement. Instead, I argue that if there were some sort of connivance between sport idealism and racial conservatism here, it was a much deeper, more diffuse collusion of the interests and ideals embedded in the idealized discourse surrounding sport itself. What is crucial to understand, therefore, is the logic by which this romanticized sport discourse worked to obscure, erase, or mystify the racial issues problematized in and presented through the boycott proposal—how, in other words, the idealism or idealization of sport recognized, endorsed, and celebrated certain forms of racial progress while labeling others as "protest" and therefore inappropriate uses of sport.

At the core of the explanation are the remarkable affinities between the sacralization of sport and dominant American conceptions of liberal democracy, racial progress, and color-blind, meritocratic social justice. And nowhere were these connections made more clear than in the ideas and attitudes of Avery Brundage, the self-made American businessman who presided over the International Olympic Committee.

The Conflated Ideals of Sport Culture, Civil Rights, and Color-Blind Justice

Brundage's opposition to the proposed Olympic boycott stemmed from his conviction that the Olympic movement was a "20th century religion, a religion with universal appeal which incorporates all the basic values of other religions, a modern, exciting, virile, dynamic religion."

Brundage's embrace of this religious analogy and its implied conception of the sacred provided a near perfect rhetorical device for synthesizing the dual, seemingly contradictory senses in which sport was perceived by its supporters to be special. The religious imagery of the sacred allowed Brundage to insist, on the one hand, on the institutional autonomy of sport from the rest of social life (distinguishing the sacred from the profane, as it were). On the other hand, the idea of the sacred as purity distinct from corruption and threat also gave Brundage a way to make the broader and more fundamental claim that sport was a purely positive, progressive social force in modern society. This notion was core to the official aims of the Olympic movement, as outlined in *The Olympic Charter*. They included "promoting the development of those physical and moral qualities which are the basis of sport"; "educating young peo-

Fig. 4. IOC President Avery Brundage, circa 1968. Courtesy of University of Illinois, Department of Special Collections.

ple through sport in a spirit of better understanding, and of friendship, thereby helping to build a better and more peaceful world"; and "creating international good will" by "spreading Olympic principles."[43]

Many Americans today would probably dismiss this kind of talk as mere rhetorical excess from an old, out-of-touch aristocrat. Indeed, in view of Brundage's infamous dictum that "the Games must go on" even in the aftermath of the tragic assassinations of Israeli athletes at the Berlin Olympics in 1972, sports historian John Hoberman (1984) argues just this: that these concepts are empty and substantively meaningless, designed primarily to bring as many peoples and nations into the Olympic movement as possible without regard for practical consequences or moral implications. It is a stance Hoberman dismisses as "amoral universalism." But as with the racial idealization of sport, I think it is important to take this rhetoric a bit more seriously, if only to try to make sense of the peculiar cultural "logic" constituted in and through such ideals, the values and worldviews it appeared to validate and confirm. Not only is this cultural logic important on its own terms, it is clearly relevant to (if not determinate of) attitudes toward the sanctity of sport culture as they concerned matters of race.

At the core of the conviction that sport promotes and ensures salutary social results is the theory of culture, sport, and social order bequeathed by the founder of the Olympic restoration, Pierre de Coubertin, to the modern Olympic movement (MacAloon 1981): namely, that mutual respect flows from mutual knowledge and understanding, both of which flow from social interaction. All social goods, in short, are thought to emerge naturally and inevitably out of human connection, interaction, and even competition. This idea was—and is—grounded, in both conception and practice, in a thoroughly Durkheimian theoretical logic: that "social density" is thought to lead automatically to "moral order" (usually expressed in abstractions such as peace, friendship, or harmony) through the processes of communication and understanding cultivated in and through social interaction. This is what John MacAloon, redeploying a famous phrase from the anthropologist Lévy-Bruhl, calls Olympic sport's "participation mystique."[44]

The key to this ideology is a belief in the order-generating property of social interaction itself, something uniquely ensured in athletic participation, according to its adherents. Brundage was fond of quoting a passage from John Galsworthy to make this point:

> Sport, which still keeps the flag of idealism flying, is perhaps the most saving grace in the world at the moment, with its *spirit of rules* kept and regard for the adversary, whether the fight is going on for or against. When if ever, the *spirit of sport*, which is the *spirit of fair play*, reigns over international affairs, the cat force which rules there now, will slink away and human life emerge for the first time from the jungle.[45]

Sport thus provided a space and a structure for interaction, and it did so in a way that was absolute and certain, applied equally to all individuals regardless of race, class, creed, or any other social characteristic.

What is most important about the sports world's participation mystique, in my view, is its parallels with liberal democratic political ideologies, especially in their American conception and application. Although these two sets of discursive practice were (and are) much more complicated and complex than I can fully elaborate here, they held several fundamental tenets in common. At the most foundational levels, these two constellations of ideals and values shared beliefs in the sanctity of free and fair play within the established, abstracted rules of conduct, on the one hand, and the freely acting individual as the fount and source or building block for all human creativity and social order on the other. In this dominant view, individuals are believed to be judged and rewarded not because of any sociological characteristics such as skin color but solely on the basis of their personal merit, worth, and hard work, their exercise of freedom under the absolute equality of the law. Furthermore, it was assumed that an appropriate balance between rights, freedoms, and the law would, through the competitive workings of the free market and civil society, be the fount and source of all social progress, the greatest possible good, and, most crucial to our concerns here, ethnic harmony and racial justice. Sport not only exemplified these political-ideological commitments, it embodied them.

These overlapping and mutually sustaining ideological parallels or "homologies" encourage the common conception in American culture of sport as a metaphor for social life, a linguistic trope (along with play and game) that the literary historian Michael Oriard (1991) has explored in detail. For many Americans, sportspeople or not, as many of Oriard's examples reveal, sport is even more: a literal model, the ideal or moral standard to which social orders should aspire and by which just social life is constituted and maintained. Martin Luther King Jr.'s well-known fascination with St. Paul's use of the footrace as a metaphor for social justice is just one example of how deep the connections between the culture of Western sport and individual meritocratic understandings of social justice "ran"—and run—in American culture. The claim that a fair society, like a fair race, required all individuals to be afforded equal opportunity was one that King and many other African American leaders employed many times and quite successfully to legitimate the civil rights struggle as morally just and right. For those who thought like this, participation in sport was naturally about racial justice and civil rights. To put it even more starkly: sport *was* just and right, the concrete, institutional embodiment of the ideals of justice promised in liberal democratic ideology, the essence of social justice.

Of course, despite their timeless and universal appearances, the ideals expressed in this synthesis were (and are) very, very particular. I can only mention here the "masculine" character of the discourse itself—

the idealistic, rule-oriented conception of social justice that the Harvard psychologist Carol Gilligan (1982) has argued that men prefer over the more concrete, caring-and-concern orientation prioritized by women. More to the immediate point, this particular combination of abstract ideals yielded a standard of racial justice and appropriate civil rights activism that was thoroughly individualist—color-blind we might call it— and therefore had no place for the kind of structuralist racial critique (much less collectivist solution) implied by potential boycotters. This was neither incidental nor necessarily inconsistent. Quite the contrary, the only role for race in this abstract, universalist moral system was as a social phenomenon to be set aside, transcended, or overcome. As long as individuals were not discriminated against on the basis of race (or other social characteristics such as religion, class, or gender, for that matter), sport had lived up to the vision of justice that was promised. No one could want or expect any more.

The fact that sport culture and liberal democratic ideology were so closely and unquestionably intertwined made it impossible for outsiders to the racial injustice and discontent that persisted even after the accomplishments of the civil rights era to even begin to understand the protesters' collectivist grievances and concerns. To the extent that civil rights had been grounded in this fundamentally individualistic, competitive, and contractual understanding of social order and process, the achievement of civil rights in and through sport was seen and celebrated as a natural, inevitable, and wholly desirable outcome. But, because of the homologies between sport culture and liberal democratic ideology (and the sociostructural relationships these metaphorical relations both reflected and reinforced), calls for racial change absolutely had to fit within this moral frame. Otherwise, they would be recognized as based in power relations and not moral consensus—that is, as political. As soon as black activists started to step out of or go beyond this commonsensical, unquestioned set of moral commitments, they suddenly lost their legitimacy and acceptability. To put it somewhat differently, they were construed as "political" and thus unacceptable, calculated racial protest rather than natural social process, an attempt to force their will and their own group interests on those of the majority.

Ironically, then, the same juxtaposition of liberal democratic and sport ideals that had for so long constituted sport as an arena of racial mobility and integration eventually made it impossible for the sporting establishment to accommodate (much less recognize) the claims of prospective boycotters. In other words, the ideals of sport culture and American liberal democracy were confronting the new realities and deeper ambiguities of civil rights as a social movement and a set of moral principles, and the deeper nature and logic of racial injustice in American life.[46] Here we see why the boycott proposal not only engendered opposition but why the opposition was so intensive despite the fact that an actual boycott seemed so unlikely. It threatened to undermine, indeed directly disrupted, the assumed homologies among sport participation, racial progress, and social justice. It revealed cracks, fissures, limitations, and inconsistencies in this otherwise seamless web of sports idealism, color-blind social justice, and liberal democracy itself.

Much of this was actually foreshadowed in the moment when the idea of a black Olympic boycott was reintroduced to the press and public in 1967 by Dick Gregory at the national Black Power Conference in Newark. The coverage by the *New York Times* is illustrative. In both its commentary and its reporting, the *Times* was extremely critical of the conference proceedings, and of the entire tone of the discussions and black power itself. A large part of this was because of what it called "the strength of the black separatist sentiments" that emerged from the meeting. (One *Times* editorial on the matter was instructively titled "Black Racism.") Even more telling, however, is that the editors used the Olympic boycott resolution itself to convey just how "extreme" the tone of the conference was. The *Times,* in fact, titled its front-page story on the conference "Boycott of Sports by Negroes Asked" and printed this lead: "Resolutions calling for Negro boycotts—including boycotts by athletes of international Olympic competition and professional boxing—were shouted through today at the concluding session of the first National Conference on Black Power."[47] If post—civil rights racial activism was considered extreme, activism in sport was clearly the apex of such extremism.

If the idealization of sport rendered many observers unable to make any other sense of an Olympic boycott, it reduced others to almost outright irrationality. Once again, Avery Brundage strikes a revealing pose. His commitment to the "religion of Olympism" was so completely consistent and single-minded that it often made Brundage oblivious to the social realities of human life, the sources of solidarity and collective identity that mediated between (or were in tension with) individuals and their larger national and cosmopolitan concerns. A notorious example was Brundage's obdurate, oft-repeated conviction that "95 percent of all Olympic medals are won by 'poor boys.'" Brundage's position was utterly indefensible from an empirical point of view. Sport sociologists had repeatedly shown that "poor boys" were quite underrepresented at the Olympic Games. Yet Brundage ridiculed such findings and in one case went so far as to blame sociologists for not doing their scholarly work adequately, accusing them of contaminating youth "by their laxity in enforcing regulations."[48] In one circular to the members of the IOC, in fact, Brundage wrote that he had "never known or even heard of one single athlete who was too poor to participate in the Olympic Games." (Brundage also had to be aware of privilege: one of his highest ranking colleagues on the Executive Committee, the Lord David Burghley, the Marquess of Exeter, was himself an Olympic gold medalist.)

And so it was with the racial conditions that prompted the black American Olympic boycott initiative, as far as Brundage was concerned: as long as they did not prevent or discriminate against individual black Americans from competing in the Olympics, he believed these problems of race either did not exist or were of no meaningful consequence. Brundage was so convinced of the sanctity of sport and its connections with racial justice and civil rights that he was unable or unwilling to recognize any claims to the contrary. To take some of the examples his biographer Allen Guttmann provides, Brundage refused to "inquire into the social factors that determined [black] dominance in sports like boxing or their absence in fencing or tennis," nor was he "especially sensitive to discrimination outside of sports." Furthermore, Brundage "seems not to have asked himself about the injustice done to a black athlete who competed on the field as a member of a racially integrated team and was then turned away from the hotel where his teammates sat down to their victory banquet." If none of this necessarily proves that Brundage was "a racist" (as Guttmann claims), at the very least it demonstrates how the idealization of sport worked to support certain kinds of racial politics while dismissing others.[49] All the rest was, for Brundage, relegated to the unsavory category of "the political"—and therefore had no place in the sacred, pure-play realm of international Olympic style sport.

Desperate Times, Desperate Measures

Situated in the context of these cultural structures (or strictures), what may be most surprising about this entire episode is not that the boycott idea was so widely criticized and condemned, but rather that it found any support at all among African American athletes. To a certain extent, the fact that it did is a powerful reminder of the difficult, almost impossible situation of African American activism in the late 1960s and the passion and deep commitment of these athletes to contribute to that struggle. No one really knew what an Olympic boycott would or could accomplish (much less if they could pull one off) but they felt they had to "do" something. Recall that Smith himself, when confronted with the question of what he expected a boycott to accomplish, harbored no false illusions that a boycott would eliminate racial problems; he simply insisted that it was important to demonstrate that his people would not just "sit on their haunches and take this sort of stuff." "With politics working against us," Smith and his circle of friends and supporters had simply concluded, "we're not going to wait for the white man to think of something else to do against us."[50] Only in this context of searching for new and more forceful means of activism did African Americans even begin to consider protest in a cultural realm they had long considered one of the most fair and racially progressive in American society.

Those few figures in the sports world who offered public support of the boycott resolution tended to justify their stance on just such grounds. Jackie Robinson, the man who had integrated Major League Baseball a generation earlier, was one of those:

> I know very well this is not going to work. However, I have to admire these youngsters. I feel we've got to use whatever means, except violence, we can to get our rights in this country. When, for 300 years, Negroes have been denied equal opportunity, some attention must be focused on it.[51]

Although two weeks late and characteristically fatalistic, Robinson's support is revealing. Robinson was no radical. Indeed, he was a rare black Republican who had supported Richard Nixon's run for the presidency in 1960 and by this time was working as a special assistant on community affairs for New York's Republican governor Nelson Rockefeller. However, when it came to issues of racial injustice, the former baseball great was in the middle of a long if ultimately unsuccessful attempt to stake out a progressive Republican approach to race relations in his nationally syndicated newspaper column. As other options were exhausted, Robinson found himself, somewhat uncomfortably and uncertainly, gravitating toward sport-based possibilities.[52]

In addition, there was the unsettling sense, just beginning to be recognized by politically inclined athletes, that the problem they were facing was not just that sport participation was no longer a positive, progressive force (as it had been in earlier generations) but that there were ways in which it was actually impeding racial progress. In the previous chapter I discussed how participation in sport was becoming a less meaningful contribution to the African American struggle because it had become so commonplace, so much a part of the racial status quo. But things were even more complicated and pressing for genuinely progressive, activist-minded athletes. The large numbers of successful black athletes in elite, integrated sport settings in the late 1960s seemed to be making it easier for white Americans (many of whom had their only meaningful contact with blacks through sport) to simply assume that the country's racial problems had been solved, that full freedom, equality, and justice had been achieved, making it no longer necessary or even justifiable for African Americans to push for (or liberals to try to legislate or deliberately engineer) further racial reforms. "Look how well Negroes are doing in sport," the implicit symbolic logic went. "If they can make it there, they can certainly make it elsewhere with the proper effort, initiative, and dedication." In other words, the unparalleled success of African American athletes gave white, mainstream Americans a way to rationalize their treatment of African Americans in other social realms; in social scientific parlance, it served to legitimate the existing racial order. Here, the profile *Sport* magazine had produced on Tommie Smith the previous summer comes immediately to mind, in which the sprinter was portrayed as contented and satisfied and upwardly mobile, willing to laugh off the problems of race in the United States.

Such portrayals grated on the athletes, who were well aware of the racial interests that these stories were serving. World-class high jumper Gene Johnson, one of Smith and Evans's earliest supporters, described it as a "credibility gap" between "the treatment accorded our Negro stars and the black masses in general."

> I would like to pose this as a question: what would be the fate of a Ralph Boston were he not a 27-foot broad jumper? Or of a Charlie Greene if he were not a 9.2 sprinter? They would be "faceless" black men caught in the same system of racial discrimination as many other black citizens.

"The United States exalts its Olympic star athletes as representatives of a democratic and free society," the high jumper observed, "when millions of Negro and other minority citizens are excluded from decent housing and meaningful employment."[53]

For socially conscious, politically progressive African American athletes like Johnson, Smith, and Evans, it was not as simple as choosing whether or not to support the OPHR: they were forced to consider whether they would inadvertently harm the civil rights movement by allowing themselves and their performances to justify the racial status quo. An OPHR organizing pamphlet being assembled at the time put the issue bluntly: "We must no longer allow this country to use black individuals of whatever level to rationalize its treatment of the black masses. We must no longer allow America to use a few 'Negroes' to point out to the world how much progress she has made in solving her racial problems when the oppression of Afro-Americans in this country is greater than it ever was."[54] Malcolm X's famous line was never more apropos: athletes felt as if they were either part of the solution or part of the problem; there was no middle ground. Thus it was that Gene Johnson decided to support the boycott proposal. "I am proud," the high jumper concluded, "to see that those proposing the boycott have enough social awareness to realize that this struggle of the man in Fillmore, Watts and Harlem is their struggle also. The efforts of Negroes in athletics have benefited only the athlete involved. The Civil Rights Movement or struggle requires the aid and contributions of all black men regardless of station in life. Negro athletes should not be exempt, nor should they divorce themselves from this struggle. The fact that a great sacrifice is involved such as foregoing an opportunity to participate in the Olympics points to the urgency."[55]

Given all this, along with their previous protest experiences at San Jose State, Smith and his OPHR collaborators must have expected—and may even have wanted—to provoke a strong, critical reaction from mainstream American audiences. Harry Edwards certainly did. In announcing the boycott resolution to the press, Edwards was intent on exacerbating rather than softening the threat of the proposed boycott. "Is it not time," he asked rhetorically, "for black people to stand up as men and women and refuse to be utilized as performing animals for a little extra dog food?"

That Edwards was prepared to take this hard line, to radicalize, to move away from the politics of consensus and coalition building in favor of the politics of boundary drawing, consciousness raising, and confrontation came out in the defiant, aggressive posture he assumed in the previously cited *International Tribune* profile that appeared in mid-December.

> We must reassert the basic masculinity of black people and force the white man to stop taking their services for granted in a country where we can't take simple things like personal safety for granted, where we can't drive across the country and expect to be served food or treated with humanity.

Talking to—or, perhaps, through—acclaimed sports journalist Robert Lipsyte, Edwards continued: "I think the time is gone when the black man is going to run and jump when the white man says so, and then come back home and run and jump some more to keep from being lynched." It is time for "the auction block to come down. Black masculinity is no longer for sale." Edwards here was no longer just appealing to sport's (and American democracy's) better impulses and ideals, assuming that racial progress would happen in due time. Rather, he was insisting that African Americans had to continue to push for racial change for themselves. Echoing Malcolm X, the twenty-four-year-old sociology instructor insisted: "We have to use whatever means are available to wake up the country."

Edwards's thoroughly gendered language, his direct appeal to manhood and masculinity (and Malcolm X), obviously mirrors the hyper-masculinity exhibited by many African American male activists during the period, especially those associated with the "black power" wing of the movement (for descriptions, see S. Evans 1979; Davis 1997). Stokely Carmichael's infamous declaration that the proper place of women in the movement was "prone" may be the most recognizable and revealing such illustration of this sentiment, but one that is just as graphic and more directly connected to the concerns of this project can be found in Elridge Cleaver's period classic *Soul on Ice* (1968). The book—which proclaimed the boxing ring as the "ultimate form of masculinity in America" and anointed the controversial Muhammad Ali as "the real Mr. America"— actually begins with an impassioned explanation and defense of the sexual attacks on white women—Cleaver calls them "insurrectionary acts" (p. 13)—that landed the future activist in jail for the better part of his early adult life.

Dating back at least to Michele Wallace's provocative *Black Macho and the Myth of the Superwoman* (1978), much has been written about the complicated relationships between race and gender in African American activism.[56] On the one hand, these works also call our attention to the ways in which this masculine orientation led to the marginalization and exclusion of women as well as of feminist ideas more generally. This in mind, I would be remiss if I didn't point out that Edwards and his colleagues failed to reach out to African American women athletes (whose Olympic medals counted every bit as much as their own in the all-important national rankings) in their attempt to create a boycott and then, as we will see in the next chapter, rather deliberately snubbed female athletes when they tried to involve themselves in the movement later in the year. On the other hand, the best of these works have also helped us to understand how the obsession with masculinity among African American male activists was largely a response to racist and colonial systems that, as Franz Fanon famously described in *Black Skin, White Masks* (1986, especially pp. 112–115), otherwise feminized and emasculated black men.

The historian Robin D. G. Kelley has discussed the relationship between African American activism and masculinity in terms of the historic problems workers, especially black workers, have faced in terms of jettisoning the "mask of deference" that is conventionally such an important part of a worker's identity. Because their work (and thus their resistance) was more public and potentially productive of violence, black men, as Kelley (1996) has put it, "had to contend with gender conventions that regarded defense and retreat from conflict as less-than-manly." As a result the "racial politics of manhood has centered not only on 'standing up' to racism and other indignities but the failure or inability to do so has frequently been described in terms of feminizing black men" (p. 24; see also 1992). It should be no surprise, then, Kelley argues, that black and white workers often found common ground on the terrain of gender— their identity as men being crucial to their ability to stand up for their rights and freedoms as workers. In this context, I suggest, following Ben Carrington (1998), that sport—precisely because of its masculine character and its traditional domination by men—provided an activist like Harry Edwards an especially potent mantle of manhood to leverage against the racial status quo. It was a compelling challenge for any self-respecting, African American male. This emphasis on masculinity had the additional and final virtue of making it difficult for the male-dominated sporting establishment to dismiss the boycott proposal without at least acknowledging the specific problems associated with race in the United States—this, because of the way the appeal to manhood cut against sport's otherwise hegemonic and taken-for-granted association with masculinity itself.[57]

A great many of the possibilities and problems of the gendered dimensions of Edwards's public defense of the proposed boycott came to a head, literally and symbolically, in the person of Muhammad Ali, as has been discussed by the sports historian Jeffrey Sammons (1995). Focusing on Ali's "blatant displays of black cultural styles in body and mouth," especially his "wolfing" or "trash talking," his self-promotional poetry, and his trademark Ali Shuffle, Sammons calls attention to the way in which Ali inverted the traditional masculine culture of boxing by "harping on his good looks," calling himself "pretty" rather than "handsome," and playing up his emotions, often to the point of hysterics. Sammons calls this Ali's "dandification" of boxing. All this, according to Sammons, challenges "the pattern set by the humble, unassuming, no-frills demeanor and style of Joe Louis. If Louis stood for quiet dignity then Ali represented loud arrogance. If Louis was blue-collar then Ali was somewhere between zoot suit and dinner jacket" (p. 161). This explains what it meant for Elridge Cleaver to proclaim Ali the "real Mr. America" and why Ali was reviled by so many in the sporting establishment and outside it. Here it is worth recalling how, when Ali had his heavyweight championship taken away by the World Boxing Association on the grounds (later overturned by the U.S. Supreme Court) that he could not be a conscientious objector to the Vietnam conflict, African American leaders such as Louie

Lomax and Floyd McKissick described Ali's treatment in graphically gendered terms as symbolic of the nation's intent "to castrate any black man who stands up for truth."[58] That Dick Gregory's original boycott proposition was tied to a demand that Ali's championship be reinstated takes on a deeper meaning in the context of the cultural construction of black masculinity here as well.

In any case, it wouldn't be long before Edwards's personal appearance, his mode of public self-presentation, would match his hard, masculine talk and radical racial ideas. In the photograph that accompanied the *New York Times* profile, Edwards wears black-rimmed glasses, a short, neatly trimmed Afro and goatee, and a dark coat and tie—the look we now associate with Malcolm X and the Nation of Islam. It was distinctive, of course, but well within the basic parameters of mainstream African American fashion and decorum. Just a few months later, however, Edwards would be dressing the part of the militant, black power radical. His Afro would grow much longer, and he would soon take to wearing black sunglasses and a black beret along with African dashiki shirts and beads. The activist sociologist would, in short, soon fit historian Allen Matusow's description of H. Rap Brown perfectly: "Lean, cool, menacing, peering impassively at the world from behind his dark glasses, he was white America's dreaded image of the New Ghetto man" (Matusow 1984, p. 365).

It would be easy enough, in a society built around values of consensus and cooperation, to criticize Edwards and the OPHR for their more radical racial ideologies and political posturing or, alternatively, to simply dismiss these symbolic gestures in a popular cultural realm. But this, I think, would be to miss their true significance. One of the truisms of struggling for social change is that marginalized, disempowered peoples and movements are often forced to resort to unusual and unconventional means of contesting the power and authority of the established social order. They must come up with what Doug McAdam (1983) calls "tactical innovations." Part of this involves pushing the "radical flank" (Haines 1988) of the movement, pursuing more radical demands that in turn make those of the center seem more reasonable and attainable. But ideas and symbols and style itself are crucial as well. Indeed, in the late 1960s, progressive black activists were pushing not only for additional resources and institutional changes but also for fresh and more radical ways of thinking about the goals of the movement, about standards of racial justice and harmony, and about the identity and culture of African Americans themselves. These kinds of ideological transformations and innovations were often expressed best through the idiom of style, what I would call, following Dick Hebdige (1979; see also Kelley 1992 and Van Deburg 1992), the "cultural politics of style."

In the realm of sport studies, the cultural politics of style at least with respect to race has been associated largely with Richard Majors's writings on the "cool pose" (Majors 1998) he says is assumed by so many African American male athletes. Useful as they have been, Majors's formulations have the unfortunate tendency to minimize the political import of black athletic style, because they render such cultural forms as an escape from the harsh realities of racial subordination. In contrast, following the lead of Jeffrey Sammons's previously cited treatment of Muhammad Ali and others,[59] I call attention here to the broader and truly consequential meaning and symbolic import of these rhetorical and theatrical presentations. In an era where the forces of capital and power were learning to insulate themselves against traditional, materialist forms of social protest (cf. Harvey 1990), such symbolic gestures and radical rhetoric were quickly becoming models of social contestation and struggle, ways of locating one's self and one's community in the social terrain and of thus disrupting, at both the level of substance and style, aspects of social order that were otherwise taken for granted and normalized. The boycott proposal involved tactics of both style and substance, and Edwards's rhetoric and theatrical affect would prove to be incredibly effective on both fronts.[60]

Such symbolic politics were conceived and contrived precisely as a means to keep the media and mainstream public engaged with (or enraged about) matters of race in the post–civil rights era. More than this, the boycott proposal, based as it was on the understanding that participation in sport was not automatically and inevitably progressive, also provided a direct challenge to dominant individualist American understandings of political legitimacy and racial justice otherwise embedded in the racial discourse surrounding sport. Closely connected with this, the act of calling attention to their own blackness and their own political dislocation also helped to build a distinctive African American identity and style, a collective consciousness that was both an end in itself and a crucial step in the post–civil rights struggle. As Edwards, when asked about the aim of the boycott movement a couple of months later, would put it, "It's simple: Black dignity. I will use any tool, political or otherwise, to bring about unity within the black race."[61] And it is no accident that sport would quickly emerge as one of the most important sites for the creation and presentation of a distinctive African American identity and aesthetic (cf. Van Deburg 1997; George 1992): post–civil rights substance and style were intimately linked in the context of activism in the heretofore apolitical realm of sport. Viewed in this way, the boycott became not only a moral challenge to mainstream America but also a way to raise the political consciousness of African Americans and a strategy by which to call into question the very legitimacy of dominant, liberal meritocratic visions of racial progress and social justice.

But if all this is true, then it is important to ask why so many of these young activist-athletes shied away from the boycott proposal almost as soon as it was publicly announced by Harry Edwards. Several things were probably involved here—and they all foreshadow both the general challenges of using sport for post–civil rights racial activism and the concrete organizing obstacles Edwards and his associates would face in the months to come.

One of the reasons so many of these young activist-athletes were having second thoughts about the resolution they had supposedly voted to uphold was that this was their first foray into any kind of public activism. The misgivings generated by these new experiences were pushed to the breaking point when pitted against the hostile reaction the proposal engendered and the almost complete lack of support it found among other African American athletes. Another factor is that many of them seem to have been quite uncomfortable with Harry Edwards and the leadership role he had assumed. I am thinking here not only of Edwards's militant rhetoric and his aggressive public posturing but also of his description of the Los Angeles workshop itself—his account of what had been discussed, how it had been discussed, and what had been decided at the workshop in Los Angeles. Edwards's version of the story simply did not square with the experience, recollections and impressions of many other participants.

Even more fundamentally, most OPHR activist-athletes may never have intended to give up liberal democratic ideals or consensus-based, coalition politics in the first place. We have already seen the extremes to which Evans and Smith went in trying to avoid being painted as radicals or extremists. Clearly there were deep and abiding tensions among boycott supporters themselves on the ultimate objectives of an Olympic boycott and the ideals of racial justice it was to serve. The caveat about "violence" Jackie Robinson had included in his statement supporting the boycott initiative is revealing in this regard. While Robinson was adamant about the need for additional racial activism, he also worried that "the [Olympic boycott] leadership may not be right. I don't go for the kind of things we saw on the streets; I don't go for violence."[62] For Robinson, who was surely referring to racial ideology as much as he was to specific protest activities, the Olympic boycott as promoted by Edwards and the OPHR was a bit too radical and militant.

More moderate racial political views and ideals also helps to explain why Mal Whitfield, one of the original boycott proponents back in 1964, reversed his position on a boycott when informed of the OPHR proposal in 1967. Speaking from Kampala, Uganda, Whitfield stated: "It would be wrong to boycott the Olympics which have given the Negro athletes so much international attention. Members of the so-called boycott movement have not been able to give any solid reason for such a move.... Negro athletes compete on equal terms with white athletes when the US Olympic team is chosen. The Black Youth Conference with its unfounded statements is trying to damage the image of my country, causing misunderstanding abroad." Whitfield, who was by this time working as a cultural envoy (or an "ambassador of sport" as some journalists put it) for the U.S. Information Service, had always been a clear supporter of individualistic notions of civil rights and, therefore, seems to have been satisfied that civil rights protest and activism had fulfilled their objectives.[63] It appears that for Robinson and Whitfield, who almost certainly represented the sentiments of many others in the athletic world, the idea of an Olympic boycott was a good one only so long as it was about guaranteeing civil rights and extending them to all aspects of American social life. In other words, it was simply a powerful institutional forum from which to make this kind of a statement and nothing more.

Of course my analysis in this chapter suggests that even this vision had far more radical implications than its advocates were willing or able to realize. Although it may not have been intended as an attack upon sport or color-blind, individual-meritocratic visions of racial justice, the Olympic boycott proposal was nevertheless an implicit challenge against the unquestioned symbiotic relationships between sport culture and racial progress that had previously defined public conceptions of both sport and race. Sport was viewed as not only special but essentially sacred, above question, comment, or critique. And the ideology of sport as a positive racial force, recall, emphasized *participation*. An Olympic boycott, in contrast, implied that sport participation was not enough, that sport was a tool that had to be "used" (or not used, as a boycott implied) if it was to continue to contribute to the advancement of the race. Thus, the mere idea of an African American Olympic boycott (whatever its particular political objectives) marked a significant, even revolutionary shift in the terms by which the relationship between sport participation and racial progress was understood.

Few boycott supporters grasped the full depth and consequence of these cultural assumptions before the boycott proposal was made public, however. Even the most radical and fully committed among them tried to avoid criticizing sport in any way. They seem to have been taken aback by the fact that they and their boycott ideal were attacked so vociferously, and that their platform was perceived as being antisport. This, more

than any other factor, may explain why many of the initial boycott supporters suddenly felt the need to reassess their participation. Even those
who genuinely sympathized with the grievances and goals of the prospective boycotters (such as the editors of the *Track and Field News,* who one
month earlier had provided Smith and Evans an unprecedented opportunity to explain their position) found themselves cautioning against a
boycott mainly on the grounds that the idealization of sport was simply too deeply ingrained in the American imagination to allow effective
protest.

These obstacles could well have been the end of the boycott initiative.
But Harry Edwards refused to give into them: "If there is a religion in
this country," Edwards told Robert Lipsyte of the *New York Times,* "it is
athletics. On Saturdays from 1:00 to 6:00 you know where you can find a
substantial portion of the country?: in the stadium or in front of the television set. We want to get to those people, to affect them, to wake them
up to what's happening in this country." Always the strategist, Edwards
tried to turn this apt religious metaphor to his organizing advantage by
taking on the conflation of sport participation and racial progress directly.
Edwards would ask athletes: "Who is to say that any area is too sacred to
be used as an avenue to relieve the suffering [of black Americans]? . . .
Black athletes . . . must brush aside the 'holy' cries that sports should be
a sacred arena, 'off limits' to political issues. The life and death struggle
[of all black Americans] . . . enables Black athletes to recognize the simple
truth that there are no 'sacred arenas.' In whatever arena—cultural, religious, civic, economic, education, political—an assault against the Old
System must be waged and won."[64]

Edwards's was a radical cultural analysis requiring confrontational politics that would seem to have left little room for compromise or ambivalence. But at least it was a response, and one that not only kept the boycott possibility alive but that also offered the germ of a whole new way
of thinking about sport and its relation to race—and to social life more
generally. Would this new, realist vision of sport answer the reservations
of prospective activist-athletes, however, and help Edwards transform the
Los Angeles resolution into a full-fledged boycott?

Chapter 4

Movement Mobilizing

Whether because of or in spite of the furor provoked by their November boycott proposal, the Olympic Committee for Human Rights emerged from its maiden foray into the national spotlight determined to push for a black Olympic boycott. Harry Edwards and his colleagues were convinced, as they wrote in their organizational pamphlet, that an Olympic boycott represented "the commonality of interest between black athletes and the masses of black people" and "presented one of the few alternatives to violence for the effective expression of the plight of black people." In particular, they believed an Olympic boycott would make race "an issue that the U.S. would have to face before the world"; "re-establish . . . the fact that no Afro-American really 'makes it' in [American] society"; and, finally, "afford the proven men of black society an opportunity to share in the preservation of this society and of the black race."[1] Then there was also the basic conviction that they could "no longer allow" mainstream America to "*use*" (their emphasis) black athletes to "*rationalize* [my emphasis] its treatment of the black masses." In a nationally syndicated *New York Times* profile carried across the *International Tribune* wire in mid-December, Edwards was steadfast. "We're not just talking about the 1968 Olympics," he said, "we're talking about the survival of society." Rhetorically, he asked: "What value is it to a black man to win a medal if he returns to be relegated to the hell of Harlem?

And what does society gain by some Negro winning a medal while other Negroes back home are burning down the country?"[2]

But no matter how powerful and provocative the idea of an African American Olympic boycott may have appeared to its supporters (or detractors, for that matter), it was little more than just that: an idea. And, mob scenes or utopian daydreams aside, a good idea does not a boycott—much less a movement—make. With few active supporters and a host of outright opponents, OPHR organizers obviously had a tremendous amount of work to do if they were to turn the idea of an African American Olympic boycott into some kind of movement reality.

We have already seen that the organizing committee's initial impulse seems to have been to essentially sidestep this task and instead to simply use the threat of an Olympic boycott as a platform from which to promote their broad and otherwise unpopular critique of American race relations. Smith himself adopted this line after a track meet early in the indoor season in Los Angeles. In the city where he had first publicly affirmed his support for an Olympic boycott, the crowd had greeted Smith with "scattered boos," which quickly turned into "deafening cheers" when Smith lost an indoor quarter mile for the first time in his life. *Sports Illustrated*'s Pete Axthlem called it "the first raw emotional reaction to what he was doing" that the track star encountered. Of it, Smith said: "I think I expected it to happen and in some ways maybe I'm kind of glad."

> I think I would have been disappointed if I had gotten no reaction from people like these. If they felt upset enough to boo me I guess I must have had a pretty strong effect on their consciences. . . . Incidents like the one tonight only make me more convinced that I'm doing the right thing. I realize now that a lot of people are hoping I'll lose races so that they can stop paying attention to what I have to say. But I won't let them bother me. I'll go on and try to win and stand up for what I believe in.

If they couldn't change people's minds, the OPHR activist-athletes believed they could at least use their status as athletes and future Olympians to force mainstream Americans to acknowledge the issues they cared about—even if it meant being vilified in the process.[3]

Such accomplishments should not be taken lightly. It was not easy to keep the media and mainstream public attentive to matters of race in the post–civil rights era. As I suggested above, in an era where social leaders were becoming well versed in dealing with traditional forms of civil rights activism, strong statements and radical posturing in ostensibly apolitical, popular cultural realms were now emerging as the most effective means of social contestation and struggle, the best way to engage the American audience and authorites (Hall 1981; Singh 1998; Hall et al. 1979). Nevertheless, this hard-line, symbolic politics of race faced one very obvious and very serious limitation: the boycott itself had almost no support among the athletes themselves. Given the almost overwhelming media attention the boycott threat generated upon its initial proposal, this might be easy to overlook. But in order for this radical posturing to continue to generate public comment, condemnation, and controversy, the boycott had to be perceived as possible, a threat that could be actualized. A boycott didn't have to be seen as morally legitimate by mainstream America, but unless more athletes soon came around to supporting the boycott proposal (or, at the very least, reserving judgment on it), its threat would soon be revealed as an empty one.

New Directions

For help, Edwards and the organizing committee turned to nationally syndicated columnist, best-selling author-historian, and veteran civil rights activist Louie Lomax. Together, Edwards and Lomax (who were already acquaintances)[4] devised a new plan for OCHR organizing. It included "bring[ing] as many recognized leaders as possible into the movement" and avoiding those associated with organizations such as the Urban League and the NAACP, which they regarded as too "Negro oriented." At the heart of their scheme was a set of "intermediate" or "secondary goals" designed to shift the focus (at least temporarily) away from an Olympic boycott. Flanked by Martin Luther King Jr. and Floyd McKissick (director of CORE), Edwards and Lomax unveiled these goals on December 14 at a press conference in New York City's Americana Hotel in the form of six separate "demands."

1. Restoration of Muhammad Ali's title and right to box in this country.

2. Removal of the anti-Semitic and anti-black personality Avery Brundage from his post as Chairman of the International Olympic Committee.

3. Curtailment of participation of all-white teams and individuals from the Union of South Africa and Southern Rhodesia in all United States and Olympic Athletic events.

4. The addition of at least two black coaches to the men's track

and field coaching staff appointed to coach the 1968 United States Olympic team (of whom Stan Wright is deemed unacceptable).

5. The appointment of at least two black people to policy making positions on the United States Olympic Committee.

6. The complete desegregation of the bigot-dominated and racist New York Athletic Club.[5]

Despite the fact that five of the six planks of this plan had already been bandied about publicly in the days following the L.A. workshop (only the call for Brundage's removal from office—which the IOC leader claimed was based on "a monstrous lie"[6]—was really "new"), the press conference was widely and fully reported in the national media. For the second time in less than a month, in other words, the Olympic Project for Human Rights had found a national audience.

Much of this publicity can be attributed to Martin Luther King's appearance. Speaking not only for himself but also "as the president of the Southern Christian Leadership Conference," King announced "absolute support" for the OPHR. "This is a protest and a struggle against racism and injustice and that is what we are working to eliminate in our organization and in our total struggle," he insisted. The famed civil rights leader also furnished the sound bite that many in the media used to define the press conference: "[N]o one looking at these six demands can ignore the truth of them."

In fielding a series of questions from the press, King literally dominated the press conference and its coverage. King commended the "outstanding athletes [some of whom, he noted, were white] who have the courage and the . . . determination to make it clear that they will not participate in the 1968 Olympics in Mexico City unless something is done about these terrible problems, these terrible evils and injustices." Having been assured by Edwards that there was "great support among the athletes," King held up their commitment as an example of successful Negroes' obligation to help those who remained impoverished or excluded. "Freedom always demands sacrifice and . . . they have the courage to say 'We're going to be men and the United States of America have deprived us of our manhood, of our dignity and our native worth, and consequently we're going to stand up and make the sacrifices . . ." King concluded that these athletes would not be "losing ground"; rather, "whenever one takes a stand for justice, he is gaining ground in the process."[7]

From our perspective early in the twenty-first century—when the civil rights leader's life and work have been deified and in effect depoliticized— it would be easy to mistake King's endorsement as an indication that support for the OPHR and its boycott initiative was beginning to build either among athletes or in the public realm (or both). Nothing, however, could be further from the reality of King's public place in the late 1960s. Because of his opposition to the Vietnam conflict and his planned nationwide, multiethnic "Poor People's Campaign," King, at this point in his life, had alienated many of his earlier supporters (liberal whites, the federal government, and more moderate and conservative blacks, in particular). And yet, driven chiefly by his deep commitment to consensus and his hopes for a grand progressive synthesis, King remained reluctant to align himself too closely with the more militant branches of the movement (not to mention the fact that he was viewed suspiciously by them). In a time when there was little room for moderation or compromise on matters of race in the United States, the nation's most famous civil rights leader was becoming (if he had not already become) an increasingly marginal, ineffectual figure. Even his own Southern Christian Leadership Council was wracked by internal dissention and confusion.[8] It is in the context of his own precarious and ultimately untenable position that King's description of and support for the OPHR as one of the few remaining avenues for nonviolent protest must be understood.

If King's endorsement of the OPHR was a sign of the narrow, almost nonexistent tightrope traditional civil rights activists were trying to walk, the situation was even more precarious for the activist-athletes of the OPHR. For not only were they confronting the general societal opposition to further racial change, but, as we saw last chapter, they also had to overcome the charge of having interjected racial politics into the sacred realm of the sports world. And it is with this in mind that we must carefully consider the tactical maneuvering involved in the announcement of these six new goals.

On the face of it, this plan appears as a straightforward attempt to shift the focus of the OPHR away from an Olympic boycott toward the more moderate and concrete goal of bringing about institutional change within the sporting establishment. In a booklet outlining the revised aims and foundations of the Olympic Project for Human Rights, Edwards and Noel suggest as much. They follow King's lead in arguing that the "justice" of this new direction was "incontestable." They say that it was too much to expect that "the whole racial situation in this country . . . be cleared up by the onset of the 1968 Olympics." Instead, the OPHR leaders relented and—in what would seem to be a dramatic change of heart and strategy—allowed that "a sufficient indication of good faith to forestall the proposed boycott" would be for "society and the sports world" to "rectif[y] the situations" specified in the New York press conference."[9]

While there is no reason to question the sincerity of this pledge, it is nevertheless highly doubtful, in my view, that Edwards, Noel, and their advisers really expected to have to carry it out. After all, no agency or institution in the country had the power or authority to implement the reforms they were calling for. Moreover, the OPHR threat of an Olympic boycott provided virtually no leverage against targeted organizations such as the World Boxing Association, the New York State Boxing Commission, the New York Athletic Club, or the International Olympic Committee—all of which, not incidentally, expressed surprise, confusion, or anger at being named in the demands. These "demands" are better understood as part of a larger and ingenious organizing strategy conceived with an Olympic boycott still in view.

On the one hand, these demands—which clearly abandoned Smith and Evans's studied refusal to speak critically about sport's own racial practices—were an obvious rejoinder to the claim that sport was an inappropriate realm for racial activism, that a boycott would interject racial politics into the heretofore politically pure and racially progressive realm of sport. Edwards told Robert Lipsyte, the white *New York Times* sportswriter whose piece was published by the international wires in December, that they would "no longer allow the Sports World to pat itself on the back as a citadel of racial justice when the racial injustices of the sports industry are infamously legendary." What is more, in pointing out the racial injustices of an institution believed to be a model of racial progress Edwards hoped to call attention to the depth and persistence of racial problems in the country. "We want to get to those people [who watch sports]," the athlete-turned sociologist told Lipstye, "to affect them, to wake them up to what's happening in this country, because otherwise they won't care. . . . It seems as though the only way we can reach [these people] is by showing them that all is not well in the locker room. Then maybe they'll see beyond the locker room."[10] Perhaps more important, Edwards and his organizing associates appealed to athletes themselves in a similar fashion, pointing out not only that they faced racism and discrimination outside of sport but also in sport in terms of confronting quotas, contract disparities, opportunities in management and coaching.

All of this was what we have come to recognize as a classic organizing technique: using small, symbolic projects to orient otherwise reluctant or ambivalent participants (and audiences) toward increasingly ambitious forms of resistance. Nowhere is it more obvious that an Olympic boycott remained the OCHR's focal point and ultimate goal than in the press conference itself. The wire services quoted McKissick as saying that a boycott would remind people that "an athlete is only on the field two or more hours after which he becomes a black man again subject to the same discrimination other black men must live with." Echoing this theme, Lomax characterized "[Cassius] Clay's loss" of the heavyweight title as "a total castration of the black people in this country." Then, after reminding the audience that 22 of the 126 medals won by Americans at the Tokyo Games four years earlier had gone to Negroes, he claimed that a "long list" (though he refused to disclose the names) of Negro athletes had already agreed to go along with the boycott, which would "cripple" the U.S. Olympic effort.[11] A look back at King's comments reveal that he too was preoccupied with the idea of the Olympic boycott.

I do not mean to criticize the OCHR for introducing these six demands for institutional reforms within the world of sport. Nor do I mean to diminish their fascination with the idea of an Olympic boycott. Both had their purposes and were clearly linked with a political consciousness and commitment beginning to emerge among African American athletes. But deep ideological and practical issues divided and distinguished these proposed institutional reforms from an Olympic boycott. (Perhaps most obvious in this regard was that the racial discontents that made these six demands "just" and "incontestable"—with which even the mainstream media seemed to agree; remarkably little criticism was directed against them—were much different than those which inspired an Olympic boycott.) More than this, such differences would have to be overcome, and doing so would be a major and rather improbable mobilizing achievement. We can be fairly certain that Edwards and the others, with the guidance and support of protest veterans like Lomax and King, had some understanding of what they were up to (and up against) here. But we don't know exactly how many others shared this understanding, or whether these young athletic activists had come up with an organizing strategy that would allow them to overcome these challenges. For better or worse, this tension—between the traditional civil rights agenda that promised to excite and involve both athletes and other supporters and the structuralist, collectivist critique that the boycott was initially and ultimately intended to address—would animate and dictate the course of the movement in the weeks and months that followed. It played out clearly in the next and most successful direct action with which the OPHR was involved.

Boycott in New York

The first real test the newly focused Olympic Committee for Human Rights chose for itself and for its new organizing strategy was its proposed boycott of the New York Athletic Club's annual indoor track meet. The NYAC meet, which rivaled the Milrose Games at the time as the most prestigious event of the American indoor circuit, had long been a favorite of the black athletes and drew crowds of spectators. It was the athletic club that sponsored it, however, that made the meet an extremely attractive target for the OPHR and race-based protest in general.

Described by one sportswriter as "intransigent and obtuse," the NYAC was a genuine "old boy's club." The club counted few Jews and no Negroes among its membership, and during the course of the track-and-field season bestowed official sponsorship and funding upon only white athletes. Such discriminatory policies and practices were neither isolated nor unusual as far as contemporary elite American sporting clubs were concerned. According to a survey of twenty major American cities conducted by *Sports Illustrated* one month after the meet, only one nationally ranking athletic club (in Washington, D.C.) had any African American members (and most had only "token numbers" of Jews).[12] As black athletes and many others saw it, such policies and practices were especially insulting and hypocritical given how important a role black athletes had played over the years of the club's showcase track-and-field event. Vince Matthews, an emerging long sprinter who had run at several previous NYAC meets, explained:

> [O]n the one hand, it was telling blacks that they weren't welcome inside their building on Fifty-Seventh Street because of their color and justifying this policy on the premise that it's a private club entitled to invite whomever it pleases. Yet the AC turns around and tries to recruit or invite these same black athletes to a New York AC track meet. Now the policy is reversed: the blacks are good enough, as athletes, to compete in the club's meet and help sell tickets so that the club can continue to support only white amateur athletes on the circuit.[13]

As Matthews—and many of his fellow competitors—saw it, the way the NYAC dealt with black athletes was characteristic of the double standards and hypocrisy that defined so many black-white relationships in the society at large. This broader symbolism was particularly appealing to Edwards and his colleagues. Their aim, as Edwards later wrote, was "not to force the club to integrate . . . but rather to regain some of the dignity that black athletes had compromised over several decades by participating for a club that would not allow a black person to shower in its facilities."[14]

If the New York Athletic Club's sponsorship made the meet a vulnerable target for protest, the fact that it was sure to attract a large national audience made it an especially desirable one. Not only did the meet have a long and prestigious tradition in the media capital of the country, but the 1968 edition marked the hundredth anniversary of the club's first indoor meet and was to be the first track-and-field meet at New York City's brand-new Madison Square Garden. In celebration, meet director Ray Lumpp and his staff planned a huge, festive competition. With all the media attention this hubbub seemed guaranteed to provide, the meet provided a perfect forum for the OPHR to meet its dual agendas of focusing national attention on discriminatory racial practices within the world of sport and beginning to generate support for an American Olympic boycott.[15]

The mobilization proceeded quickly. By the end of January strong support for the protest was falling into place. Athletes had met at the Milrose Games and then again at a Boston meet (both took place in mid-January) in order to discuss plans for the NYAC boycott. A number of prominent athletes, including Smith, Evans, Carlos, Bill Gaines, Martin McGurdy, Kirk Clayton, and Otis Paul Drayton announced their support. Drayton, a two-time Olympic medalist from Villanova, explained: "I don't want to join the NYAC. I'm not telling them to change their policy. I just don't see why I should support it."[16] Other athletes, according to *Sports Illustrated,* "came up with a variety of excuses not to attend" in order to "avoid rupturing team loyalties or offend[ing] old friends."[17] USC's two-sport star and future Heisman Trophy recipient O.J. Simpson, for example, claimed he "couldn't fit it into [his] training schedule," though he told some reporters, "I wouldn't run that weekend if my mother was holding the meet."[18]

On January 30, a coalition of four East Coast colleges (Manhattan College, Villanova, Maryland State, and Morgan State) issued public assurances that they would not require individual athletes to participate in the meet. The Manhattan College Faculty Committee on Athletics, for example, stated:

> While Manhattan does not ban participation by its athletes in the meet, it recognizes the right not to complete for any member of the team who believes that he cannot in good conscience take part in a track meet sponsored by the New York Athletic Club.[19]

The Manhattan faculty also added the disclaimer that if athletes from their school eventually did participate in the meet, it should not be taken as an endorsement of the NYAC or its policies. Shortly thereafter, coaches from New York University, St. John's, and Rutgers said their teams would attend the meet but that individual athletes would not be required to compete. At the same time, all public and Catholic high schools from the

New York area—whose participation was another traditionally venerated aspect of the meet—announced that they would not attend. Several days later, two of the foreign squads that had been expected to add international luster to the field—West Germany and the Soviet Union—declined their invitations to attend as well. Finally, and just a few days prior to the meet, the U.S. Service Academies (the single largest supplier of athletes to the U.S. Olympic team at the time) also released their athletes from the obligation to take part in the event.

Meet director Lumpp continued to insist that "Negro athletes too numerous to mention" were entered, but his words were beginning to lose their credibility. ABC Television, which planned to show the event on its popular *Wide World of Sports* program, reconsidered. Only after a great deal of internal debate, according to coordinating producer Jim Spence, did they decide to go ahead with their plans to broadcast the event, but not without receiving assurances that "some Negroes" would compete. They also took "extraordinary precautions" to protect their equipment, arranging backup programming and informing the NYAC that, should developments warrant it, the network was prepared to cover the event "like a news story."[20]

The official NYAC response throughout was to avoid public comment, but several reports indicated that there was some split within the membership.[21] Privately, one member said that he was not against a change in membership policy but just did not want to be "clubbed into it," while another suggested dropping the meet altogether to simply avoid the "public controversy."[22] "Public opposition" would probably have been a more appropriate choice of phrase. In marked contrast to how the Olympic boycott was received, public sentiment was clearly and decisively against the Athletic Club and in support of the boycott. Major, mainstream New York human rights agencies such as the NAACP and the American Jewish Council gave their support to the boycott and even promised to help organize a picket outside the Garden on the night of the meet. (In fact, as far as I can determine, the Urban League was the only major civil rights organization that explicitly declined to support the protest effort.) The City of New York's Commission on Human Rights announced its intentions to investigate the NYAC for its use of city-owned Randall's Island for sporting events.[23] White journalists took up the cause with a vengeance as well. Alumni of Notre Dame University were also encouraged to "get into the act" by Bob Woodward, religion editor of *Newsweek* and a Notre Dame graduate. Woodward implored his fellow graduates to resign from the club unless its membership policies were fully disclosed and explained. "The New York Athletic Club has a reputation for being a

Catholic club—more particularly an Irish Catholic hangout. This brings it very close to Notre Dame," Woodward explained in justifying such unprecedented, concerted measures.[24] Tellingly, when longtime syndicated *New York Times* sportswriter Arthur Daley wrote a column supporting the NYAC (or, at least, opposing a boycott of its meet), the only argument he was able to muster on its behalf was that if discrimination existed, it was nevertheless within the legal rights of a private club. Even so, Daley maintained that he was only playing "devil's advocate."[25]

Edwards, Noel, and their supporters did what they could to organize the New York boycott from their base in San Jose. Edwards says they established telephone contacts with a number of New York—based organizations and individuals, among them Omar Ahmad (cochair of the 1967 Black Power Conference), H. Rap Brown (newly elected chair of SNCC), and Jay Cooper (chair of the Columbia University Black American Law Students Association). These leaders and their organizations served as contact staff for the boycott and assumed the primary responsibility for bringing people to the picket on the day of the meet. A black AAU official named Marshall Brown served as Edward's East Coast connection and personally called many of the athletes and schools that were scheduled to be represented in the field. Edwards and his staff of students mailed out letters and pamphlets to colleges, high schools, and top individual athletes in the West and Midwest, and encouraged athletes to gather at meets leading up to the event to discuss the boycott. They also sent telegrams to the Russian Embassy in Washington asking for Soviet recognition of the boycott.[26]

Edwards himself eventually made the trip across the country. The day before the meet, he and his associates held a press conference in the office of Jessie Gray, the leader of a recent rent strike against city slumlords. After detailing the anticipated extent of the boycott, the group (which included H. Rap Brown, Ahmad, and Ray Ennis of CORE as well as a number of other boycott organizers and supporters) issued a press release claiming that the "intransigence of the NYAC" was merely "indicative of the present demeanor of White America toward taking real steps to deal with racism in this society." We aren't up against "just racist *individuals*," the statement continued, but a much larger "racist *conspiracy* involving many of the would-be great institutions of the society." In the realm of athletics, the statement went on, these institutions included the AAU (which had not only refused to unsanction the meet but was also said to be contributing funds to bring in foreign competitors to restock the depleted NYAC field) and the administrators of Madison Square Garden as well as the NYAC itself. In order to "rectify this situation," Edwards and his supporters promised to picket the meet, "white-list" any universities or colleges that participated in it, and initiate legal action against the NYAC.[27] At some point during the conference, H. Rap Brown, in his characteristic style, insinuated that the Garden itself might even be "blown up" if the meet went off as scheduled.[28]

Brown never showed up the next evening but almost everything else went the protesters' way. Although NYAC promoters reported that a near-capacity 15,972 tickets were purchased, several reports estimated the crowd at less than half of this total, and one magazine photograph shows twenty or thirty bewildered tuxedo-clad NYAC officials standing at track level looking up at virtually empty seats.[29] Many of the meet's traditional schools and clubs stayed home (the high school division was canceled entirely), and numerous black and white athletes belatedly joined the boycott—including Olympic champion long jumper Ralph Boston. Boston's withdrawal was, in the view of many reporters, "perhaps the most significant aspect" of the boycott. This was because Boston, who was African American, had been an outspoken critic of the OPHR and its proposed Olympic boycott, going so far as to engage Smith in an extended debate on the matter that ran just days before as a feature in *Sport* magazine. As the *San Jose Mercury News* saw it, "Boston still may

Fig. 5. Harry Edwards press conference, early 1968. © Bettmann/CORBIS.

oppose [an Olympic boycott] when it's time to leave for Mexico City, but his withdrawal from the NYAC meet now leaves his plans definitely in doubt."[30]

Of those athletes who did participate in the meet, very few were black (nine, according to the *Times* and many other sources, though this is a matter of some uncertainty) and the performances of the competitors were poor.[31] Perhaps most important, all was dutifully reported in the national press, which meant that many athletes not directly involved in the boycott as well as a large spectator audience were nevertheless directly affected by it.

Much of this, of course, was anticlimactic. That drama that did transpire, it seems, occurred outside the Garden, where Edwards and the other organizers had promised to assemble a picket line. Even though Brown did not appear, the large numbers of police officers that typically accompanied his public appearances in those days did, and, for some portion of the night, they actually outnumbered the pickets assembled.[32] Kenneth Noel provided what *Newsweek*'s sports editor Pete Axthelm described as "the first dramatic moment of the evening" when, standing in front of a bus carrying athletes from Holy Cross and Providence, he held up a sign that read: "RATHER THAN RUN AND JUMP FOR MEDALS, WE ARE STANDING UP FOR HUMANITY. WON'T YOU JOIN US?" As the cheering crowd gathered around, the bus was forced to turn around and find another entrance at which to deposit its passengers. The chant heard throughout the evening was "Muhammad Ali is our champ," though most of the demonstrating seems to have been saved for the photographers and cameramen.[33] Several times over the course of the evening young marchers advocated taking the Garden by storm, but each time Edwards, speaking through an electric megaphone, convinced them otherwise. According to Axthelm (the prominent white reporter who was making the Olympic boycott story part of his regular beat), Edwards would say something that "sounded properly militant to the kids" but that concluded something along the lines of: " 'why get our heads busted to get in with a bunch of honkies? We're here to keep the blacks out, not to go in and join the damn whites.' "

Just as significant as these displays of public bravado were the face-to-face conversations and confrontations that took place just outside the athletes' entrance. In one that Axthelm observed, Noel asked Larry Livers, one of the handful of blacks scheduled to compete, "Brother, why would you want to go in there?" Livers, a hurdler from Oakland, hesitated and then explained: "I wanted the plane trip to New York to see my family. And I wasn't really notified about the situation here." Charlie Mays, a quarter-miler from a New York club team that supported the boycott, told him, "Larry, you can't let the rest of us down by going in there." Noel nodded silently and waited. Gradually, Livers's expression began to lighten, until finally he turned away from the door.[34] This was just one of the many decisions and developments that made the NYAC boycott an almost unqualified success.

A Tale of Two (or Maybe Three) Boycotts

With all of this success came many questions. Why had such a large number of people—athletes and spectators, liberals and conservatives, black and whites alike—ultimately supported this boycott? What did their actions indicate; what did they symbolize? More specifically, what did all this mean for the future of an Olympic boycott?

Not surprisingly, Harry Edwards and his organizing committee were among the first to answer these questions, and (also not surprisingly) their answers reflected very nicely on their own contributions to the protest and its implications for their larger Olympic initiative. The OPHR organizers argued that the NYAC boycott was their idea, that they had helped organize it, and that they had attracted the national publicity that multiplied its impact far beyond the boundaries of New York City and the world of sport. What is more, they claimed their success indicated growing support for an African American Olympic boycott. It demonstrated, in Edwards's words, that "black dignity was no longer for sale at any price." The OPHR, Edwards proclaimed, had "passed" another "serious challenge" in its quest to bring off a full-scale Olympic boycott.[35]

These factors were enough to persuade the widely respected and well-positioned Pete Axthelm. In the pages of *Sports Illustrated,* he wrote:

> When Tommie Smith and Lee Evans joined Edwards in proposing an Olympic boycott last November, their chances of pulling it off appeared remote. In the three months that followed their cause seemed, if anything, to become even more hopeless. Last weekend this trend was dramatically reversed. . . . A widespread Olympic boycott may be still more than a distant possibility, but it is certainly possible—and it appears far more likely now than it ever did before.[36]

Axthelm, as we have seen, had more sympathy for the Olympic Project for Human Rights than most reporters, especially white ones. Nevertheless, both the press and the public found it difficult to disagree with his assessment of growing momentum for an African American Olympic boycott.

And it was not just because the two boycotts seemed to have so much in common; unrest, discontent, and protest were pervasive in and around the sports world. None of these various incidents and issues had a more direct relationship to and bearing upon the OPHR boycott than the controversy surrounding South African Olympic participation.[37]

The nation had been excluded from the 1964 Tokyo Games and the Olympic movement for its apartheid policies in sport, but in May 1967 the IOC, under Avery Brundage's leadership, began sending signals that it planned to reopen the matter. The newly independent African nations led the international campaign against readmission, but a broad, bipartisan group of Americans chaired by Jackie Robinson and calling itself the "American Committee on Africa" issued a letter to Douglas F. Roby, American IOC representative and president of the USOC, asking him and his organization to commit themselves to keeping South Africa out of the Games.[38] For the better part of the next year, there was little more than occasional public rumor and innuendo on the topic in the American press. But then on February 17, running just above the story of the New York Athletic Club meet boycott, a banner headline in the *New York Times* announced that the International Olympic Committee had decided to readmit the apartheid nation back into the Olympic fold and allow it to field a team in Mexico City.

The IOC claimed (based on what would be called a "highly questionable" investigating commission [Guttmann 1984]) that a great deal of progress had been made toward alleviating the racial apartheid that had prompted the nation's expulsion from the Olympic movement and the 1964 Olympiad. This was an assertion flatly denied by almost every African nation in the Olympic movement. Just twenty-four hours after the IOC decision was announced, six different African nations unequivocally announced their intention to boycott the Mexico City Games if South Africa were allowed to compete. The protest literally snowballed as day after day another African nation announced its intention to withdraw. Then, on February 25, the thirty-five-member nation Organization of African Unity announced that a full-scale boycott would be imposed if South Africa's invitation was not revoked. The American delegation, for its part, sent out a letter on April 10 saying "it is essential for American representatives, particularly those involved in the Civil Rights struggle and concerned athletes, to speak with a clear voice on such a crucial issue."[39] This was just the kind of action the OPHR had probably been hoping for, and Edwards took full advantage of the opportunity. "Where are all the people who say the Olympics should be above racism?" he asked rhetorically. "Who can say the Olympics shouldn't be targeted now? The

[International Olympic] Committee has shown the black man just what it thinks of him. I think things will really begin to heat up."[40]

This presented an extremely awkward situation for American sportswriters and commentators, especially those who held sport up to the ideals discussed in the previous chapter. On the one hand, many of them supported the IOC's decision on the grounds that it protected against the politicization of sport and were outraged about the threatened boycott by African nations. The *Los Angeles Times* and *New York Times,* in fact, took a lead in staking out these positions with editorials published on March 1 and March 2, respectively. (Brundage, it is worth noting, had the Los Angeles and New York editorials included as part of a virtually unprecedented five-page circular distributed to all IOC members, National Olympic Committees (NOCs), and International Sports Federations (IFs) in March of 1968.)[41] On the other hand, these editorialists also had little sympathy for South African apartheid policies and felt extremely uncomfortable confronting the kinds of charges these policy shifts allowed Edwards to make. Indeed, it proved impossible for them to keep these two issues separate. For example, in its February 28 issue, under the heading "In Principle," *Sports Illustrated* drew a careful distinction between the South African—inspired boycott and that of the OPHR. "It is understandable, in the current emotional context, that black American athletes, angry over the International Olympic Committee's decision to allow *apartheid* South Africa to compete at Mexico City, should seriously consider boycotting the Games. But insofar as the U.S. itself is concerned, such a boycott is illogical" (their italics). Two weeks later the magazine weighed in with a second editorial underscoring the same point, this time headed "Politics vs. Principles."[42]

None of this was intentional on the part of the IOC. Quite the contrary, the IOC maintained a studied indifference to the American racial situation and the OPHR boycott proposal, which it considered a strictly local, intranational issue. Only isolated and ambiguous references to the "American situation" show up in the expansive IOC archives of the period—for example, a vague reference in a letter from Compte de Beaumont to Brundage dated December 14, 1967, and allusions in exchanges dominated by other issues between Brundage and Roby in December and January. Remarkably, there is not a single mention of or reference to the proposed American boycott in the fifty-plus letters from NOCs in IOC files pertaining to the proposed readmission of the South African delegation. In fact, the only real, concrete evidence available that IOC was aware of the American situation (and it certainly was) comes in the April *Olympic Newsletter,* which quoted Smith and Ralph Boston in its regular feature on Olympic issues in the international media under the heading "South Africa and the Boycott of Negroes."[43] And were it not for the fact that the IOC president was an American and had been singled out for attack by the OPHR, it may not have been an issue at all.[44]

But no matter how the American mainstream media tried to distinguish and define these two boycotts, the IOC decision, certainly without meaning to do so, threatened to transform the proposed OPHR Olympic boycott from an unlikely, symbolic threat into an actual protest possibility by giving credence to OPHR claims that the world of sport was, after all, tinged by racism and discrimination. Indeed, Edwards's conclusion was what many Americans feared most: "This new issue will force the black man to fight. They've virtually said 'the hell with us.' Now we'll have to reply: Let Whitey run his own Olympics."[45]

The only real qualification on the OPHR claim that the results of the NYAC boycott indicated that an African American Olympic boycott was gaining momentum was that the success of the former could be traced, at least partially, to the tactics of intimidation and coercion Edwards's organizing committee had employed. According to *Sports Illustrated,* for example, Edwards "openly threatened [black athletes who planned to participate] with retaliation by "people back in their home towns" and "injected a spontaneous protest with an unnecessary atmosphere of violence." And a report in *Newsweek* noted that both Jim Hines and Jon Thomas avoided the meet but chose not to endorse the boycott because of bodily threats they had personally received. Also, an anonymous caller had warned Airman 2/c James Dennis at his home in Houston: "Don't compete. If you do, the committee won't be responsible."[46] Edwards would later dismiss these charges as unfounded (*Revolt,* p. 68), but there is plenty of evidence that he and his fellows were not above using intimidation, name-calling, and threats of violence against spectators, athletes, and coaches.

I have already noted that H. Rap Brown raised the possibility that the Garden might be blown up by demonstrators. Inside the meet, there were several reports of unidentified, surly black men with clipboards on the edge of the Garden track taking down names of competitors. Edwards himself would later boast of "informing" the Russian ambassador that the organizing committee "could not guarantee" the safety of Russian athletes who attempted to cross the NYAC picket line.[47] Neither should the potential explosiveness and danger surrounding the boycott and intensified by the Edwards-led OPHR crowd be underestimated. Five black athletes who made the trip from the University of Texas, El Paso, were forced to register at their hotel under assumed names, and OPHR chief organizer Kenneth Noel had to work all night to restrain protesters outside the Garden. Even so, one black competitor had his glasses broken as he tried to enter the arena, and several more appear to have been detained long enough to miss their events. By the end of the evening, Edwards himself was concerned enough to encourage people to disperse to Harlem rather than continuing to congregate around the arena.[48]

These are, I think, disturbing practices for an organization that claimed to be working in service of human rights, and I shall return to them later in this chapter in order to highlight the problems of OPHR organizing tactics. At the same time, however, I think it is also very easy to overstate their contribution to the New York protest. Contrary to mainstream media interpretations and criticisms, the boycott was effective not *because of* these tactics but *in spite of* them. I say this because the success of the NYAC boycott was ultimately the result of conditions, concerns, and commitments much broader and more diffuse than those the media could comprehend, or those attempting to organize an Olympic boycott—Edwards's OCHR—could completely control or take credit for.

One unmistakable indication that the NYAC boycott was distinct from than the OCHR's Olympic boycott scheme in important ways was (or should have been) that while the former carried widespread legitimacy and support among athletes and in the community as a whole, the latter did not. In fact, many athletes who supported the NYAC boycott took pains to separate their participation from Edwards and his Olympic boycott proposal. For example, even before he decided not to participate in the New York meet, Ralph Boston had insisted that a Negro boycott of NYAC events was much different from a boycott of the Olympics.[49] Some white athletes (such as Richmond Flowers) who were sympathetic to the NYAC boycott decided to compete simply because they did not want to be identified with Edwards, H. Rap Brown, and the Olympic boycott. Moreover, there was no indication that the Olympic boycott had gained or was gaining support among black athletes, activists, or agencies. Shortly before the NYAC boycott, an *Ebony* magazine poll indicated that only 1 percent of black athletes nationwide supported the Olympic boycott (71 percent were against it, with 28 percent undecided).[50] Even its organizers had difficulty asserting otherwise. While he frequently claimed to have boycott commitments from a number of prospective Olympians on the West Coast, for example, Edwards would never reveal what that number actually was, nor would he furnish any specific names. Indeed, Edwards himself had downplayed the connections between the two boycotts in the weeks leading up to the NYAC meet. "We're not focusing on the Olympics right now," he said. "We have our hands full trying to coordinate this one. You can't eat the entire pie in one bite or you'll get sick."[51]

There is no way, as I see it, that the NYAC protest could have functioned as effectively as it did had it been simply a subplot of the larger Olympic boycott effort—even if it had been directly connected to the African antiapartheid boycott. Not only had a critical mass of black and white athletes participated in the boycott without regard for OCHR involvement, but the boycott in New York seems to have enjoyed both widespread public support as well as help from well-established local civil rights agencies such as the NAACP and the American Jewish Council. While this support was undoubtedly essential to the success of the athletic club boycott, its significance goes far beyond the formal organizational assistance these agencies and individuals may have provided. It calls attention to a broad, diffuse set of racial inequities, discontents, and unrest in the world of sport itself that was concurrent with the OCHR push to build an Olympic boycott but not reducible to it. A more detailed examination of these grievances will not only help us better understand the relationship between the OPHR and the NYAC boycotts but also will lay bare the fundamental tensions and outright contradictions that defined race-based athletic activism in the late 1960s.

Of Resistance and Revolt

If there is one development that was more important than any other for the OPHR's Olympic boycott proposal, it was the emergence of a generation of racially disgruntled and politically conscious African American athletes. After several previous years of growing frustration, race-based activism and unrest in and around sport "reached a crescendo," as David Wiggins (1997) has put it, in 1968. "Although never approaching the degree of activism evidenced among some members of their community," Wiggins writes, "and not always prepared for the rigor or consequences of racial protest, black athletes in unprecedented numbers became participants in the civil rights struggle . . . denounc[ing] everything from the lack of black executives in professional sport to racial exploitation in college athletics" (p. 105).

The bulk of this resistance and revolt was centered in college and university campuses. According to Wiggins, who has devoted a number of scholarly papers to these developments (see also 1991, 1993, 1994), at least thirty-seven such uprisings took place on predominantly white colleges and universities throughout 1968. The disruptions resulted "from black athletes' complaints about everything from unfair dress codes to inadequate treatment of injuries by prejudiced athletic trainers" (Wiggins 1988, p. 305). Black athletes at the University of Washington accused football coach Jim Owens of various forms of discrimination and threatened to boycott all athletic events until a black coach or administrator was hired on a full-time basis. Nine track-and-field stars (including future gold medalist long jumper Bob Beamon) at the University of Texas at El Paso were kicked off the team by coach Wayne Vandenburge after they refused to compete in a meet with BYU in protest for the Mormon Church's treatment of blacks (see also Olsen 1968). (Every edition of the *Track and Field News* that spring contained at least a couple of snippets regarding incidents of protest or discontent among top-flight black trackmen.) In July, twenty-three of the twenty-five black athletes at Iowa State announced their withdrawal from school effective August 1 because the athletic council rejected some of their eight demands—including one that called for the hiring of Negro coaches in all sports. Even black football players at Michigan State—whose coach Duffy Daugherty had carefully and consciously tried to craft a reputation for dealing fairly with black athletes—brought demands for black cheerleaders, assistant coaches, counselors, and trainers to athletic director Biggie Munn and organized a one-day strike at spring football practice to protest subtler grievances.[52]

Professional athletics were not unaffected either. Black athletes from the St. Louis Cardinals and Cleveland Browns football teams organized protests or demonstrations to call attention to what they deemed to be racist and discriminatory practices in their respective organizations, in some cases openly naming offending coaches and white teammates. On March 3 during the first boxing program held at the new Madison Square Garden—a fight between Joe Frazier and Buster Matrio for the heavyweight championship, the very title that had been stripped from Muhammad Ali the previous summer—several "black militant groups" picketed the arena, displaying signs reading "KO [knockout] racism, KO the draft."[53] While less public in baseball, racial tensions were always just below the surface on Major League teams such as the St. Louis Cardinals or even the New York Yankees (Halberstam 1994; Briley 1989).

So numerous and explosive were such incidents that *Sports Illustrated* began dispatching several "key correspondents" across the country to interview athletes, coaches, educators, and prominent members of the black community about them. What they found—and would report in July in an unprecedented five-part series "The Black Athlete: A Shameful Story" that publisher Garry Valk would describe as "the most socially significant" the magazine had ever printed—was that "Almost to a man, Negro athletes were dissatisfied, disgruntled and disillusioned." Professional athletes were saying they were "underpaid, shunted into certain stereotyped positions and treated like subhumans," while collegiate performers claimed they were "dehumanized, exploited and discarded." At both levels some athletes went so far as to say "they were happier back in the ghetto."[54] Thus it was at the beginning of 1968 that these heretofore occasional and relatively spontaneous disruptions began to coalesce into what might properly be considered a movement—one that seemed certain to connect and energize with the OCHR's attempt to organize an Olympic boycott.

While it was only beginning to be recognized by the sporting community at the time, this bare-bones sketch of black athletic "revolt" is today familiar enough to sport scholars and historians.[55] Still a good deal of work remains to be done in terms of explaining the causes and consequences of these developments, especially in establishing how this emerging discontent related to an Olympic boycott. And it is not enough to simply assert as one historian has that "given the mood of the era . . . it would have been strange indeed if sport had remained unaffected" by the general militancy of the late 1960s, and leave it at that.[56] Such general glosses merely beg the more complicated questions of why such a movement had not emerged *sooner* and *how* it finally and concretely came to be.

It was Harry Edwards himself who, at the height of his activism, christened the movement with its famous title.[57] Edwards, the sociologist-in-training, was concerned to situate black athletic protest in a broader social and historical context. In the book that named the movement, Edwards would argue that protest among black athletes stemmed from a heightened social consciousness:

> The revolt of the black athlete arises . . . from his new awareness of his responsibilities in an increasingly desperate, violent and unstable America. He is for the first time reacting in a human and masculine fashion to the disparities between the heady, artificial world of newspaper clippings, photographers and screaming spectators and the real world of degradation, humiliation and horror that confronts the overwhelming majority of Afro-Americans. (Edwards 1969, pp. xvii–xviii)

Tommie Smith, Lee Evans, Lew Alcindor, and others who worked in concert with Edwards were obviously motivated primarily by their emerging awareness of and desire to contest the myriad of deep, structural injustices that confronted African Americans in the post–civil rights period.

But such a broad, progressive social consciousness really only explains the involvement of the most enlightened individuals. High-minded, altruistic ideas alone have a limited impact upon collective action—such as an Olympic boycott—that requires tremendous individual sacrifice or personal risk. Whatever the limitations of the rational choice theories of collective action inspired by Mancur Olson (1965), they are certainly correct to emphasize that immediate, personal costs and/or benefits are usually the fundamental determinants of the success or failure of collective activity, especially in a society (the United States) and a cultural arena (sport) that both place such a high premium on individuality and competitive self-interest.

Here context and external expectations must be taken into consideration. The successes of the civil rights movement had put tremendous social pressure on black athletes, as representatives of the African American community, to commit themselves to doing something publicly on behalf of their race—and, for reasons touched upon in previous chapters, mere participation in sport was no longer enough. As a black school administrator put it then:

> There is a growing demand that the athlete take part in the affairs of the Negro community, that he use his prestige, the position he's acquired, to make himself a force in the improvement of the position of all Negroes. Negroes are apt to show hostility to a Negro athlete who doesn't take full advantage of his opportunities.[58]

This was particularly true on college campuses, where many of the most fervent advocates for ongoing action against the dominant racial order resided.

In contrast to Edwards's early emphasis on a heightened social consciousness, David Wiggins (1988) has explained the African American athletic activism and unrest of the period with respect to this external, community-based pressure African American student-athletes felt to become more active in campus politics and the larger racial struggle. In his view, these protests had less to do with either abstract racial ideals or radical racial politics than they did with black athletes trying to find a way to answer the call to be involved in the larger struggle against racism in activities that were as uncontroversial as possible and that did not conflict with their identities and commitments as athletes.

In all the cases Wiggins surveys, protests were directed at white coaches, who, he claims, were easy and visible targets "used as scapegoats" by black athletes. Moreover, black athletes were strongly encouraged and supported by black student organizations as well as activist-oriented community leaders, black faculty, and even established African American political organizations such as the NAACP. Perhaps most notably, these activist coalitions targeted not the athletic departments but the university administrations at the highest possible levels. On the other hand,

Wiggins points out, black athletes paid little or no attention to the claims of discrimination or mistreatment lodged by white athletes against the athletic establishment, even when those claims were remarkably similar to their own. And he also notes that such protest activities were "almost nonexistent" at historically black colleges in the period, despite the fact that coaches such as Grambling's Eddie Robinson or Florida A&M's Jake Gaither laid down and strictly enforced the same kinds of rules and regulations black athletes labeled as racist and discriminatory at predominantly white institutions. "By alleging discrimination," Wiggins concludes, "black athletes could at once express empathy with or become actively involved in the black protest movement and convince themselves that they had not violated their proper role as athletes" (p. 329).

Wiggins is certainly correct that these protests were an important and even calculated part of a much broader and largely symbolic attack on antiblack racism in the post–civil rights United States. And he is also right to suggest that African American athletes often had to be convinced, against their initial inclinations, by more politically progressive members of the black community to take part in race-based protests. But he is on dangerous ground, I think, to the extent that he downplays or dismisses the claims of racial discrimination and injustice also involved in these protests. For to do so leaves no recourse but to see these revolts merely as symbolic appropriations of sport; that is, that allegations of discrimination in sport were simply issued for political purpose with no real basis in fact. Moreover, it suggests that these athletes were little more than conservative pawns looking for the easy way out in an otherwise high-stakes political game. And at schools such as San Jose State, Wyoming, and the University of Texas, El Paso, black athletes were clearly leaders more than followers when it came to racial activism on campus.

In this context, it is worth mentioning that Wiggins is not actually clear on whether the charges of racism and discrimination issued against white coaches were based in fact. "Alleged" discrimination is as far as he will go. But crucial to the public legitimacy of these charges and their impact on self-interested, sports-focused athletes was the fact that more than a few coaches were blatantly racist figures in otherwise extremely liberal institutions. Recall that the SEC, for example, had only agreed to integrate its sports teams two years earlier. The vast majority of its coaches were the products of a thoroughly segregated and discriminatory racial mindset and regime. So while these athletes may have been cajoled into actions that had much broader symbolic visibility and consequences, these actions were nevertheless directed against practices and policies that were in fact racially discriminatory. As for most westerners, it was their own, most personal experiences—in this case, with *racism in the world of sport*—that was the catalyst to protest for most black athletes.

The experience of Calvin Murphy, one of the country's most outstanding sophomore basketball players (and a future professional standout), is illustrative:

> I was coming out of the streets into another world. I got angry when I saw people starring at me. First I thought it was because there was a Negro on campus. Then I began to think they were saying, "There's Calvin Murphy, the basketball player." That sounds much better. [59]

But even if it sounded better, it did nothing to alleviate how completely out of place Murphy, like many other black students and athletes, felt on a predominantly white college campus. "I just don't feel lost," he explained, "I felt like I wanted to get lost [*sic*]. With the few other brothers on campus I was fine. But when I had to walk alone among *those people,* I felt like . . . ugh . . ." (ellipses in original). The difficulties he and his white classmates and teammates experienced were often matters of simple understanding. "You know a lot of times we'd be kidding in the dorms and I'd find guys couldn't understand my humor. I would talk my jive talk and they wouldn't understand." The consequences of these differences for Murphy, the black man living in a white man's world, were much more severe for Murphy than his white acquaintances. In words reminiscent of what W. E. B. Du Bois called the "double consciousness" of the American Negro, Murphy realized: "I had to act differently than I do at home. I am two people. I like the one at home better." [60]

It is not incidental, I think, that the strongest sentiments for the movement involved black athletes on predominantly white college and university campuses, for it was precisely there—on campus—that the contradictions among their roles as athletes, students, and African Americans were most obvious and troubling. Many of these problems were outlined by Harry Edwards himself in scholarly work produced in the 1970s.

Financially, some African American athletes were enticed to enroll in schools on the promises of scholarships that did not exist or grant-in-aid loans that had been disguised as full and clear scholarships. Academically, some were brought to collegiate programs they clearly were not prepared for; others were herded into "Mickey Mouse" classes and provided with questionable "tutoring" to keep their grade point averages up and their athletic eligibility intact. They were also encouraged to take a minimum number of course hours so they could concentrate on their athletic careers. Unfortunately, few black athletes graduated in four years, after which time their athletic eligibility and scholarships ran out (and tutoring ended), thus making it difficult if not impossible for them to fulfill requirements for graduation. Socially, almost all of them experienced difficulty in finding off-campus housing, and many were excluded from white fraternities and sororities. In addition, they found few other black students to socialize with and few extracurricular activities that were open or interesting to them.

Racism and discrimination against black student-athletes in and around sport was evident as well. More than a few white coaches and athletic administrators were at best paternalistic toward their black athletes and at worst openly racist. There was a marked absence of black coaches (or trainers, administrators, and cheerleaders for that matter). Players encountered unofficial practices of "stacking," where all black players were assigned to the same position or event in order to limit black visibility to the fans, or discovered that certain positions (such as the football quarterback, the baseball pitcher, or the basketball point guard) were informally set aside for whites. Black athletes were usually expected to perform at higher standards than their white teammates and were often castigated for making mistakes or suffering injuries, and white spectators were often not shy about expressing antiblack opinions and sentiments at sporting events, especially in the only-recently desegregated South.

Most of these contradictions and injustices were the product of a system that treated black athletes not as human beings (much less as students) but instead as workers, whose real purpose for being on campus was simply to win games. As Edwards himself would quite correctly surmise in the later work from which some of these details are drawn:

> [T]he Black athlete in the predominantly white school was and is, first and foremost and sometimes only, an athletic commodity. He is constantly reminded of this fact, sometimes subtly and informally, at other times harshly and overtly but at all times unequivocally.[61]

And if their treatment as athletes was not enough to arouse discontent, the future that awaited them after their days in sport were over was even more disheartening. This, too, would become a familiar theme for Edwards.

> . . . once their athletic abilities are impaired by age or injury, only the ghetto beckons and they are doomed once again to that faceless, hopeless, ignominious existence they had supposedly forever left behind them. At the end of their athletic career, black athletes do not become congressmen . . . [nor do they] cash in on the

> thousands of dollars to be had from endorsements. . . . And all his clippings, records and photographs will not qualify him for a good job. . . . These are only the most obvious of the inequities faced by the black athlete. Others are less obvious but no less humiliating and they have no less a devastating effect on the black athlete's psyche. Like other blacks, black athletes find housing, recreational facilities, clubs and off-season jobs closed to them.[62]

These were not just theoretical possibilities. By 1968, at least one generation of black athletes lived as testament to the limited opportunities that awaited African Americans after their sports careers were over.[63]

None of these racist and exploitative conditions, experiences, and sentiments of frustration were necessarily new. In a paper tracing the historical experience of black athletes in predominantly white colleges and universities, Wiggins (1991) argues that the conditions that produced these frustrations had been around for almost as many years as black athletes had been allowed to participate in white sporting events. In fact, Wiggins shows that the first wave of black collegiate student-athletes in the 1930s and 1940s articulated many of these same problems of academic neglect and social isolation as well as of racial insensitivity and prejudice, though usually in much less vehement fashion than that expressed by black athletes in the 1960s (see, especially, pp. 169–171).[64] As Benjamin Bluitt, an African American forty-four-year-old Chicago high school basketball coach and former star athlete explained: "We pouted a little, but that was all. I think there was some feeling that Negroes had to prove they could 'take it.' But the kids today don't feel they have to go through the same stuff. We took it for them."[65] Black athletes like Murphy were not only beginning to express these discontents as they never had been before; many were ready to act on behalf of them.

The crux of this new impulse toward action among African American athletes goes back once again to the historical context of the civil rights movement itself. In addition to putting external pressure on African American athletes, the movement also made them far less willing to put up with prejudice or discrimination of any sort, especially in the world of sport, which held itself up as a model for race relations. In this era of rapid social change, many of the abuses and injustices black athletes had been willing to tolerate in the name of racial progress only a few years earlier—such as refusing to acknowledge racial taunts from opposing fans and players, turning a deaf ear to racist teammates and coaches, or competing in track meets sponsored by otherwise discriminatory clubs—were beginning to feel like the very discrimination and exploitation everyone else was now challenging. The civil rights movement, in short, had caught up with the world of sport, and in many ways appeared to have passed it by. In a version of Alexis de Tocqueville's famous thesis about rising expectations (that revolutions are most likely to happen *not* when things are bad but instead when they are getting better), black athletes finally had reason to expect and demand truly fair and equal treatment. At the very least, these athletes were simply trying to bring civil rights into the locker rooms and onto the fields and floors of the American sporting scene.

If a mobilization among black athletes was in the works, then, it wasn't so much a movement being organized by the OCHR or any other group as it was a movement emerging out of a general and very diverse accumulation of structural inequities and shared grievances. In protests against old-line, overt forms of racism and discrimination—such as those that marked the New York Athletic Club—these emergent forces gelled nicely together with the broader ideas and ideals at the core of the Olympic boycott proposal. Not only did the boycott against the NYAC target more traditional forms of racism, but it could also serve, as far as those with more radical racial politics saw it, as a public symbol of the need for further racial transformations in American society. By demanding that their own civil rights be respected and enforced in the world of sport, in other words, black athletes could serve both their individual interests and those of the larger collective at the same time.

Yet these two dimensions of athletic resistance were not necessarily congruent. The newfound political consciousness or "militancy" of most black athletes in fact did not result from broad interests in the African American community taken as a whole; rather, the resistance of most black athletes was more about their rights and freedoms as individuals— the very ideals many, more progressive black activists (like those in the OPHR) were trying to move beyond. As an extensive story in *Look* magazine would put it later in the summer:

> Most black athletes are not ready to send stadiums up in flames. Nor are they ready, in large numbers . . . to refuse induction into the armed services. . . . Most, like their white counterparts, are frankly ambitious and practical. [In contrast to Harry Edwards] the typical black athlete . . . wants to win within the system. He knows the system is flawed but he knows too that he has made big strides. [66]

Thus, the resistance of most black athletes, as put on display in the NYAC boycott, were both larger and smaller than the OPHR's Olympic boycott initiative. It spurred far more athletes into action and helped to sustain and legitimate the fledgling and otherwise floundering movement to use athletic protest in service of racial change. But it was ultimately driven and limited by a vision of civil rights well within the bounds of traditional individualist visions of freedom, property, and rights—and, as such, had little possibility of being radicalized in service of the structuralist-collectivist critique prospective boycotters had initially hoped to promote. Edwards and his colleagues were, in short, encountering and participating in a "movement" thoroughly and fundamentally divided on ideals, strategies, and goals.

Organizing Strategies and Tactics

I do not mean to suggest that Edwards and his OCHR colleagues did not understand the structural tensions that constituted the black athletic resistance movement of which they were a part. I have little doubt that they did. But what I do think deserves further consideration is whether the OCHR had an appropriate understanding of how best to be involved with and contribute to this broad, multifaceted movement. This is another issue altogether, especially in view of their veritably all-consuming goal of bringing off an Olympic boycott. Even given that they were trying to transpose the energy and commitment generated by the more moderate elements of the movement onto an Olympic boycott and its more radical racial critique, it is far from clear that Edwards and his colleagues understood how grassroots movement building could accomplish this difficult transference. Most of their energies, as we have seen, were directed toward the media and the mass public and to certain organizational elites. Clearly this emphasis was effective in terms of consolidating a progressive black collective consciousness and delivering this message to a much larger, mostly white mainstream public. But it was not directed toward building the kind of participatory support necessary to nurture and sustain mass-based protests and boycotts.

One of the most important and underappreciated components of grassroots movement building (and one that would be crucial to the success or failure of an Olympic boycott) is the face-to-face, person-to-person, small group communication and exchange in which otherwise reluctant, uninterested, or hostile individuals come to be convinced and committed to collective action. In the case of the NYAC protest, most of this nitty-gritty work seems to have been left to discussions among the athletes themselves. Edwards and his colleagues mainly mobilized local elites and the faceless masses.

I have already mentioned the meetings and conversations athletes held at meets preceding the NYAC event. Vince Matthews, an up-and-coming 400-meter runner who eventually qualified for the fourth spot on the 1600-meter American Olympic relay team, received nothing more than a bland OCHR form letter in December that suggested plans for the NYAC boycott and the following summer. Only after discussions among themselves did Matthews and his teammates at little John C. Smith College (most of whom received no information at all from the OCHR) decide to skip the NYAC meet.[67] Matthews, in fact, recalls that communication between the West Coast–based OPHR and athletes at East Coast and Midwestern schools was "one of the problems of the entire black boycott movement."

> I'm certain that all of us agreed with the general philosophies that Harry Edwards was talking about—the exploitation of the black athlete by a racist white society. But many of us had to settle for secondhand accounts of what actually was happening . . . what was expected of us, who was supporting the movement, how far it had spread, what resistance, if any, it was encountering.[68]

Although he credits the NYAC boycott with beginning to establish contacts between East and West Coast runners (no small task at a time when there was little communication between athletes on either coast, and a good deal of competitive jealousy separating them as well), Matthews did not align himself with Edwards and the OPHR until sometime the next summer. This was simply because until that time he knew little about the prospective boycotters' plans.

Matthews's recollections are corroborated and extended by the Olympic scholar John MacAloon, who at that time was a competitive middle-distance runner at Catholic University in Washington, D.C. According to MacAloon (who is white), he and his teammates (some of whom were black) received no direct information or contact from anyone connected with the boycott effort and, as a consequence, eventually decided to participate in the meet. The decision had been left up to them by their coach. Since they were a fairly good team with rising hopes and the NYAC was a big meet, they decided to go. It was not that they were completely "out of the loop"—according to MacAloon, they had heard enough to know about a possible boycott via his teammates' "black network," but this still was not enough to change their decision. It was a choice, MacAloon says, they came to regret.[69]

Other athletes and audiences took pains to separate their support for sport-based protests like the NYAC boycott from an endorsement of Harry Edwards and his OCHR. According to Dave Morgan, a former Marine who emerged as a leader of the demonstrations at the University of Texas, El Paso:

> ... they ridicule me and say that I'm somebody's misguided child, that Harry Edwards was behind all this. Well, let me tell you something: Harry Edwards was behind *nothing*. He came to this campus and tried to stir the Negroes up. But he didn't have the slightest effect on us. Now you hear all over the campus that Harry Edwards wrote the statement we handed out about our position. You want to know who wrote that statement? I wrote it! *Dave Morgan wrote it.* Harry Edwards has not and will not sway my position in any way whatsoever . . . and neither is anybody else involved in this thing.[70]

In a more recent historical study of an incident at the University of California, David Wiggins notes he could not locate a single, independent confirmation of OCHR involvement at Berkeley in spite of Edwards's public assertions of support and assistance there.[71]

The OCHR's relation to the South African Olympic boycott bid is perhaps even more instructive on this point. Many accounts, including Edwards's own (1969), suggest that the OCHR played an influential role in helping to bring about the proposed international boycott that would eventually result in the re-affirmation of South Africa's expulsion several months later. For example, Spivey's (1984) otherwise balanced narrative says, "The 1968 Olympic boycott movement [referring to the efforts of Smith, Evans, and Edwards] stands as the cornerstone in the awakening of black America, Africa and much of the so-called third world to the power and utility of international athletic competition as a political forum." Other texts have even gone so far as to suggest that the African nations simply adapted the boycott idea laid out by Edwards and Smith in Los Angeles. The truth is clearly the other way around. The South African Olympic controversy and boycott movement had been in motion long before Edwards and the OPHR came onto the scene. Indeed, as I suggested in the Chapter 2, the idea of an African American Olympic boycott seems actually to have drawn its inspiration from the South African boycotts proposed by African sports activists beginning in the late 1950s which, unlike the OCHR initiative, were truly an international issue and power struggle. Indeed, the inclusion of South Africa (and Southern Rhodesia for that matter) to the OCHR agenda seems to have been merely an afterthought or last-minute addition. According to antiapartheid sports activist and analyst Richard Lapchick (1975, pp. 101–102), a few days before the initial American proposal was issued in November, Dennis Brutus, the leader of an integrated group of South Africans who called themselves the

South African Non-Racial Olympic Committee (SANCROC) cabled a fellow South African at UCLA, Dan Kunene, and asked him to approach Edwards about including the South African expulsion among their demands. In essence, then, the issue of South African readmission was an international issue which both predated the OCHR and in which the OCHR was merely a rather insignificant, indirect participant.

To the extent Edwards and his colleagues helped to convince individual athletes not to take part in the NYAC meet, the tactics of coercion and intimidation they employed were not necessarily in the best interests of the larger movement and more progressive consciousness they were trying to build. For example, after seeing his black teammate ("not a guy who scares easily about anything") get so frightened that he was literally shaking after he finished their relay race, MacAloon and his teammates became "very, very angry, really pissed off" and yet "politically confused":

> I stood for everything all the protesters stood for but the fact that there were these black power guys there prepared to take my teammate's name and punish him for making the decision he made— and that we contributed to—made me, well, ambivalent. And I suppose I, maybe out of some guilt for being there at all, I reacted with anger. At one point several of us even kind of pushed up against one of the guys, as if to suggest a certain kind of counterthreat. I don't know if they noticed or not, but I think a lot of people felt the way we did: that this went too far, this notion of punishing individuals. I mean, after all, this was about civil rights. That's a kind of testimony as to how confused everybody was—even activists—about the relationship between black power and threats of violence, and the kinds of civil rights actions we were used to.[72]

MacAloon's recollections raise serious moral questions about the OCHR (not to mention black activism more broadly in 1968): Did they really stand for basic, individual human rights? And if so, how willing were they to set aside these ideals in order to achieve their more immediate political goals? Was there any room for compromise in the rigid masculinist posture they were assuming?

As is so often the case, these ethical dilemmas were closely connected with the practical problems of building support for a protest action that did not enjoy immediate grassroots legitimacy. Consider the behind-the-scenes tactics Edwards and his colleagues were employing in their attempt to build support among African American athletes—specifically, their efforts to pressure black athletes into supporting the boycott by forcing them to choose their racial identity over the competing interests and ideals of sport participation, individual glory, patriotism or antipolitical sports idealism. It was one thing for black athletes to posit such priorities for themselves—as Lee Evans had done back in responding to a letter from a black track coach named Stan Wright who had advised him to consider himself an American first and a Negro second. "We are black men first and athletes second," Evans, adopting a revealing, masculine language, had told the media in explaining his support for the proposed boycott.[73] But to insist that athletes *had* to accept these priorities or else be exposed as race-traitors was an altogether different approach.

First, it relied upon a high degree of racial consciousness and commitment and a rather sophisticated analysis of the structural problems faced by African Americans in this country, and one with which even some educated and enlightened activists did not necessarily agree. Indeed, this forced black athletes to unwillingly choose between ideals, interests, and identities. This comes through clearly in the remarkable rebuttal Ralph Boston had offered up against the boycott proposal in *Sport* magazine just prior to the NYAC boycott:

> I am a Negro and I want to make it very clear that I am proud I am a Negro and I would not want to be anything else. I do not believe Negroes have had equal rights or have enjoyed equal status in this country and I believe that it is good and right that we fight for our people . . . but there are different ways of fighting and one man's way is not necessarily the right way, nor does it have to be my way. . . . . I believe it is my duty as a Negro and as an athlete and as an American citizen to speak up for what I believe but I do not believe I should be called names or shunned for it.[74]

Second, such tactics easily (and often very quickly) deteriorated into personal threats, intimidation, and name-calling. Such interactions did very little for building the kind of deep and abiding legitimacy necessary for bringing about something as controversial as an Olympic boycott. If anything, they were probably counterproductive because they alienated many otherwise ambivalent or uncommitted athletes. Directly to this point, we will see in the next chapter that some athletes came around to supporting the OPHR belatedly because they had to overcome the image of Edwards and the Olympic boycott proposal they had gotten from the media and their participation in events like the NYAC boycott.

This brings me back to the deeply gendered, indeed thoroughly masculine style Harry Edwards and the OCHR had borrowed from erstwhile black radicals like Elridge Cleaver and H. Rap Brown. I discussed some of the historical context and cultural significance of this gendered style in the previous chapter. Here, I focus on its costs and consequences. Conspicuous by their absence in all the OPHR posturing and planning were black women athletes. Given the history of gendered language and style, it should come as no surprise that Edwards and his colleagues neglected to reach out to these women. Worse, in a few short months Edwards and his colleagues would actually rebuff African American women who had qualified for the American Olympic squad when they approached the men with the idea of participating in the OPHR initiative. For reasons that are almost certainly connected with the sexist, homophobic, and hypermasculine traits of many black-power-style activists, OPHR leaders declined their offer.

Wyomia Tyus recalled many years later: "It appalled me that the men simply took us for granted. They assumed we had no minds of our own and that we'd do whatever we were told."[75] It is a truth, according to writer Kenny Moore, that Tommie Smith still struggles with. "They should have been involved," he says. "It just wasn't done, but it was not meant to be denigrating. So many things were happening, and there was so little time. It was an inadvertent oversight."[76] Moore's article suggests it was probably much more than that.

This is not to suggest that African American women had no influence in the OPHR initiative (or, for that matter, the broader black power push). Indeed, one of the more interesting and unappreciated subtexts of the entire saga is how deeply influenced Evans, Carlos, and especially Tommie Smith were by their wives. Pete Axthelm's July write-up in *Newsweek* makes a point, in fact, of quoting Smith's "intense and intelligent" wife, Denise, on racial issues, noting that she too was a former world-class track star. Later in the same story Axthelm also mentions how Denise Smith accused meet officials at the Los Angeles trials of deliberately assigning her husband an unfavorable lane on the far outside of the track in one of his races.[77] Moreover, recall that it was Denise who actually purchased the infamous black leather gloves in Mexico City that Tommie Smith and John Carlos would wear on the victory stand. Nevertheless, it is true that the most prominent, public aspects of OPHR activism—which Edwards had described back in December as an attempt to reestablish the masculinity of the race itself—were considered the realm of men.

But more important than whether women were involved were the masculine ethos and action orientation at the roots of the OPHR's mission and organizing strategy. This obviously recalls the graphic masculine imagery that many of the male leaders used in introducing the idea of the boycott or in talking about the injustices done to African American athletes like Muhammad Ali. As Edwards had put it: "It was important to reassert the basic masculinity of black men and force the controlling white forces in the United States to stop taking the black man's services for granted." Besides excluding women, this masculine mindset and activist orientation left no room for compromise or the creation of a more sophisticated consciousness of the complex relationship among athletes, athletics, and race—and the alternative protest possibilities therein.[78]

In this context it is worth recalling Edwards's public critique of sport as a "sacred arena" (Edwards 1969, pp. 190–192). "Who is to say that any arena is too sacred to be used as an avenue to relieve suffering," Edwards had written. Instead he insisted that black athletes had to "brush aside" such "holy cries" and realize that they were talking about a "life and death struggle" where "the simple truth is that there are no sacred arenas." Edwards went on to say that "any black person who allows himself to be used . . . is not only a chump . . . but a traitor to his race." On the other hand, he promised that black athletes who went along with the boycott would become "heroes of humanity," "emblazoned in the minds of mankind forever." What makes this rhetoric and way of thinking particularly interesting is that in rejecting the sanctity of sport (or self-interest or American patriotism, for that matter), Edwards ironically employs his own rhetoric of the sacred, wherein the "black liberation" struggle must be accepted and celebrated above all else. It is an audacious and aggressive move, one that in my view actually buys into the abstract, universalizing, rights-based style of thought at the heart of liberal democratic social theory. Indeed, Edwards is not rejecting Western social thought and activist style so much as he is trying to turn them to his advantage by insisting that racial rights must be more fully realized and operationalized therein.

Pressing On

The OCHR and its boycott initiative were not without their organizing accomplishments in the weeks and months following the NYAC boycott. Perhaps most important and easiest to overlook was Edwards's ability to keep the Olympic Project for Human Rights in the news. As stories about disgruntled African American athletes began to appear in newspapers and magazines across the country, they almost inevitably mentioned Edwards, the OPHR, and the boycott initiative. Edwards himself became something of a household name—commenting on these disturbances and traveling to campuses around the country to participate in the proceedings. And Edwards never failed to bring these appearances back around to the Olympic boycott proposal. In March he penned a commentary for the *Saturday Evening Post Magazine* titled "Why Negroes Should Boycott Whitey's

Olympics,"[79] and just two months after that the *New York Times Magazine* published a major biographical profile on him. Edwards, who by now had fully assumed the part of the revolutionary black activist, makes masterful use of radical political style in interviews reported in this piece. When asked what changes America had to undertake, Edwards launched into a lengthy diatribe:

> For openers, the federal government, the honkies, the pigs in blue must go down South and take those crackers out of bed, the crackers who blew up those four little girls in that Birmingham church, those crackers who murdered Medgar Evers and killed the civil rights workers—they must pull them out of bed and kill them with dull axes. Slowly. At high noon. With everybody watching on television.

Elsewhere he calls LBJ "Lynchin' Baines Johnson," describes Jesse Owens and Willie Mays as "traitors," and reserves sainthood for Malcolm X. "Talking with Edwards," according to the story's author Arnold Hano, "is amusing when it is not chilling. Sometimes it is both."[80]

There were more concrete organizing achievements as well. One that received only minimal attention at the time, but which would eventually have major implications for all parties involved, was John Carlos's decision to transfer to San Jose State for the spring semester of 1968. Carlos, who was not only one of the few athletes in the nation who had been outspoken in his support of the OPHR but was also an emerging world-class sprinter, arrived at San Jose State via East Texas State. He came to San Jose for a variety of political, personal, and competitive reasons. Unlike Smith or Evans or others of the Speed City contingent, Carlos came from the East Coast, New York City. He was a product of Harlem's P.S. 90, Frederick Douglass Junior High, and Manhattan Vocational and Technical High School. He left New York City after graduating from high school in 1966 hoping to find in Austin a comfortable life for his new wife Kim and the child they were expecting. But he found there a completely different set of racial conditions than those of the northeastern urban environment he was accustomed to. "A [black] man couldn't get a beer in Austin, in the Texas state capital," he recalled years later, "and football coaches called a black receiver who dropped the ball 'Nigger' or 'Nigra' or 'boy.'" He said that when he was interviewed by a reporter from the school paper and described the racism he had observed on campus, the athletic department called a meeting of black athletes and told them: "You don't like it here, you can leave." Eventually Carlos did, going back home to New York City around the time of the OPHR's press conference in December of 1967.

There he apparently met King, Andrew Young, and Harry Edwards, who together helped him enroll at San Jose State, supported by student loans instead athletic grant-in-aids.

It wasn't just their politics that lured Carlos to California. He was also drawn by the challenge of competing with and against sprinters like Smith and Evans. Indeed, many years later Carlos claimed he actually went to San Jose hoping to avoid controversy, having told Smith, Edwards, and Evans that they should not expect him to support any of their militant stands. If he had intended to avoid political controversy, he was certainly not shy about inviting athletic contest. "Hoarse, abrasive, hugely talented, a fountain of jive, . . . a master of the gunfighter braggadocio of sprinters," was the way one author recently recalled Carlos's air and attitude at the time. "I'll save you niggers a piece of the tape," he would tell the competition while settling into the starting blocks. "He made it a rule to ignore the rules, giving the impression that his manhood was somehow sullied by the need to train" (Moore 1991a, p. 66). A "kaleidoscope" was the term that San Jose sprint coach Bud Winter used to describe Carlos in 1969. "He always seems to be changing but deep down I don't think he ever changes at all. He's unpredictable, but he's always unpredictable. He's moody and often mean. He's the strangest person I've ever known, the toughest I've ever tried to coach, the most frustrating I've ever tried to reach."[81] Of course, the edginess that made Carlos tough to train also made him well-suited to the political style and strategies that Edwards was building the boycott initiative around.

Another organizing success came when some twenty of the top amateur basketball players in the country—including three members of the defending national championship UCLA basketball team, Lew Alcindor, Mike Warren, and Lucius Allen; and standouts such as Louisville's Wesley Unseld, Dayton's Don May, Larry Miller of North Carolina, and Elvin Hayes of Houston—declined invitations to try out for the 1968 American Olympic squad.[82] Many excuses were given. Unseld claimed he was "tired," May that he was "exhausted," and Miller that he was injured. Hayes had signed a contract with the San Diego Rockets of the fledgling American Basketball Association, thus making him ineligible for Olympic competition. Then there was the poor timing of the tryouts and the Games themselves. The trials were to commence immediately after the collegiate season right in the middle of the academic year, meaning that many players were in fact tired and would be forced to miss classes; then, the Games themselves were to be held in October and would mean more missed classes, in many cases requiring student-athletes to take the entire semester off. Nevertheless, most observers also recognized that many of the defections had something to do with the proposed Olympic boycott.

The case of the UCLA players is particularly revealing. In a statement explaining the selection procedure, NCAA executive director Walter Byers noted that Alcindor, Warren, and Allen had been "contacted concerning their availability" but that "UCLA replied that none of the three was interested in the Olympic trials and none would accept the invitations."[83] According to Byers, they gave no reason for their disinterest. But if these players supplied no formal statement as to why they were not interested in trying out for the team, that was not because they didn't have one—or even that basketball officials themselves didn't know what it was. Their sympathy and support for Edwards and his OPHR boycott had been clearly reported in the media back in November.

The problems these players faced comes out in an interview Lew Alcindor gave a few months later.[84] Early in the interview, Alcindor said that his decision not to try out for the team was "misquoted and misunderstood," as much a product of his desire to stay in school and graduate on time the next June as it was of the racial situation in the United States. Alcindor then described the New York City "Operation Sports Rescue" program he was planning to spend his summer working with instead. ("We've got to convince black youngsters and Puerto Rican youngsters to stay in school. Otherwise, they will not be properly equipped for the world of tomorrow." Sport, according to Alcindor, was one way to help break the "pattern of the ghetto.") Even so, later in the interview he went on to say: "[E]ven after South Africa was barred, many black athletes decided to make some sort of protest against the way black Americans are treated. My decision not to go to the Olympics is my way of getting the message across."

> Other people have asked me: "Don't you owe an obligation to your country to compete in the Olympics?" Yes, I owe an obligation to my country, but my country also owes an obligation to me as a black man, an obligation that has not been fulfilled for 400 years. There has to be a lot of equalizing before I can start talking about the obligations I owe this country. For too long I have been a second-class citizen . . . I am talking collectively about me as a black man. I'm not a sociologist or a politician but it would seem to me that America should put first things first. My people need to eat, they need clothes, they need to own their own homes. I think we have to rectify that situation before we can talk about what the future is going to be like.

In 1970 Alcindor also placed his Olympic decision in the context of misperceptions about African Americans in sport. "When Jackie Robinson broke in, it was good enough for him to get base hits because white people thought he wasn't good enough to do it. But it isn't enough anymore. Black intellectuals don't want black athletes for leaders. They feel there have been enough black symbols in sports and jazz. I know that. I'm figuring it out."[85]

Perhaps the most significant development as far as the boycott initiative was concerned was a tragedy that had little to do with sport: Martin Luther King Jr.'s assassination in early April. If the South African readmission provided compelling evidence of OPHR claims of persistent racism within the world of sport in general and the Olympic establishment in particular, witnessing King's death and the public's reaction to it pushed more than a few previously unconvinced African American athletes in the direction of more radical racial politics.

The newly arrived John Carlos was one of those. Carlos, who had transferred to San Jose State after speaking with King in New York in December, had placed all his hope for an Olympic boycott in the slain civil rights leader. Indeed, he claims to have spoken with him again in New York City in March: "I felt he'd find support for athletes who boycotted. He was the only guy who would and could. Edwards was not in any position to do that then."[86] Another athlete deeply affected by King's assassination was Ralph Boston. Early in the year, recall, Boston had steadfastly opposed an Olympic boycott. In the wake of the King assassination, however, the two-time Olympic long jumper began to reassess his position. In a candid interview with *Sports Illustrated,* Boston expressed his thoughts and emotions: "For the first time since the talks about the boycott began," Boston began, "I feel that I really have a valid reason to boycott." He went on to explain how he came to this realization:

> I sat and thought about it and I see that if I go to Mexico City and represent the United States I would be representing people like the one that killed Dr. King. And there are more people like that going around. I feel that I shouldn't represent people like that. On the other hand, I feel if I don't go and someone else wins the medal and it goes to another country, I haven't accomplished anything either. It is disturbing when a guy cannot even talk to people and he is shot for that. It makes you think that Stokely Carmichael and Rap Brown are right. All my life I felt that violence wasn't the way to deal with the problem. How do you keep feeling this way when things like that keep coming? How?[87]

Whether supportive of a boycott or not, few black athletes were unaffected by King's death and the public reaction to it. Much of the anger and resentment of these young men came out on the track. On the day of a meet, for example, University of Tennessee track star Larry James learned that King's death touched off a standing ovation in the student center in Knoxville. He carried that knowledge with him across campus where he was supposed to represent the university at an intercollegiate track meet. As he jogged to the stadium, James recalls, "A VW passed and I heard, 'run, nigger, run!' I immediately started to walk. And I began to internalize things." And then channel it. James went on to win the 440 in the third-fastest time ever of 45.2 and three weeks later completed a running-start 440-relay leg at the Penn Relays in 43.9. As one writer closely connected with many of these athletes and events has put it, "Every black athlete of that generation had experiences like [James's]. They transformed fear, loss, and rage into performance." Many years later, Tommie Smith himself would concur and suggest: "It was in us, the will to prove our worth."[88]

Such comments and experiences are, I think, expressly significant in that they reveal a link between racial politics and athletic performance. What Smith's observation calls attention to is that the only thing these athletes had that was uniquely powerful and political—that allowed their controversial claims a place in the public eye—were their bodies and performances. Their politics, in other words, were expressed in what they did, how they did it, and what they were able to say because of their having done it. Their performances were their politics. Indeed, it seems likely that during this period the seeds of an alternative to boycotting may have begun to emerge in the deep, intuitive recesses of Smith's political consciousness. And it didn't hurt that seeing sport in these terms (rather than in terms of a boycott) also gave more moderate black athletes a way to express their racial conscience and commitment without that expression necessarily becoming an endorsement of more radical, separatist political ideals.

What Next?

All these were significant developments, of course. But they were also limited and their connections with the OPHR Olympic boycott initiative were less direct and obvious than Edwards and his group probably would have preferred, and this is basically where things stood as the spring wore on toward the crucial June qualifying trials for the American Olympic track-and-field team. It was not an ideal situation either for grassroots mobilizing or for drawing media attention to their cause, especially given that the American track-and-field season was in full swing and the Olympic trials were on the horizon. And there was one old issue, quite outside of OPHR purview of control, that finally appeared to be resolved.

For months the IOC, under the direction of President Avery Brundage, had tried to maintain its original decision to readmit South Africa. But on April 20, with thirty-nine nations having affirmed their intention to boycott and a host more threatening to do so (including the USSR and, by extension, the satellite nations of Eastern Europe), the executive board of the IOC finally (if reluctantly) consented to poll its members regarding the withdrawal of the invitation to South Africa. The results of the ballot were not surprising: an overwhelming majority of member nations voted to reinstate the exclusion of the apartheid nation. When the vote was finally, formally recognized and the ban against South African participation in the Games reinstated, the move was viewed by many in the black community as an unqualified triumph for race relations, a "victory" as Jackie Robinson, one of the leaders in the struggle, called it in his syndicated column.[89] Ironically, however, it meant something quite different for the OCHR and its attempt to build an African American Olympic boycott. This "victory" robbed the OCHR of its broadest and most compelling reason to boycott the Games—namely, that the international Olympic establishment was not committed to racial progress or even above racism itself.

The *New York Times* called the reversal "a help" to the U.S. Olympic team. Even more significantly, the paper reported that both Tommie Smith and Lee Evans were now having "second thoughts" about an Olympic boycott as a result. The story, whose headline implied they had already called off the proposed boycott, quoted Payton Jordan, the head U.S. track coach as saying that he was "personally pleased to see this problem resolved."[90] Jordan and the *Times* were obviously projecting their own hopes and desires here. A careful reading of their comments reveals that Smith and Evans may have been reevaluating their boycott proposal but had done nothing to rule it out. Nevertheless, these developments created a whole host of new questions, doubts, and ambiguities among the athletes themselves. At a meet in San Diego on June 1, Vincent Matthews asked fellow 400-meter runner and OPHR activist Lee Evans what boycott advocates planned to do next. Evans told Matthews that the movement was "big and probably going to get bigger." At the same time, as Matthews recalls, he was also "somewhat vague about exactly what direction the Olympic Project for Human Rights was taking." As Matthews came to understand it, the group was "mostly concerned about gathering as much support as possible for whatever position the group adopted." Evans summed up the OPHR view of things to Matthews in this way: "Nobody knows where it's going, but we've got to stick together."[91]

Chapter 5

Power Plays:
Trials, Triumphs, and Polarization

On the eve of what at one time was to have been the official U.S. Olympic track-and field trials late in June, somewhere between
twenty-five and forty black athletes gathered in the competitors' quarters
at California Polytechnic University in Pomona for a closed-door meeting on the status of the Olympic Project for Human Rights and its proposed boycott of the Mexico City Games. When the International Olympic Committee bowed to international pressure and finally reinstated its
ban on South African Olympic participation, the OPHR was robbed of
its most compelling argument; the boycott movement seemed to have
been stalled or, in the words of one well-placed observer, "on the wane."[1]
This June meeting, therefore, was held to review these developments and,
finally, settle on a concrete plan of action. As Lee Evans had told Vince
Matthews earlier in the month, " 'Nobody knows where it's heading, but
we've got to stick together.' "[2] Harry Edwards, by now the clear and undisputed leader of the initiative, had more than "sticking together" on his
mind, however. He was committed to doing all he could to bring off the
boycott he and his colleagues had proposed the previous fall. In what
was described as "his most impassioned rhetoric," Edwards reminded the
athletes that South Africa had never been a major target of the OPHR
boycott. "The point," he told them, "has always been to dramatize racial
injustice right here at home."[3]

Returning to the themes he had sounded time and again in the preceding year, Edwards explained, "We're not just talking about the 1968 Olympics. We're talking about the survival of society." As far as he was concerned, there was no value to an Olympic gold medal for a black man if, when he returned, he was relegated to "the hell of Harlem." An Olympic boycott would help "reassert the basic masculinity of black men" and "force the controlling white forces in the United States to stop taking the black man's services for granted." Four-hundred-meter specialist Vincent Matthews recalls that Edwards made "a very powerful pitch" with which "many athletes . . . agreed."[4] It should not be surprising that so many athletes agreed with Edwards: since the April assassination of Martin Luther King Jr., many of them had been politicized to an extent they never before could have imagined. They had already held meetings, demonstrations, and, we can imagine, many informal conversations at the various meets (events such as the annual AAU Track and Field Championships, West Coast Relays, and the California Relays) that made up the outdoor track-and-field season and served as tune-ups for the official U.S. qualifying trials in this Olympic year.

At one of these meets (Edwards says it was the AAU event held several weeks earlier that year in Sacramento) it was decided that if two-thirds of the black athletes agreed before the June trials were held, then the boycott would be "on." Edwards and the OCHR had clearly been doing their homework. A number of those who had been uncommitted or stood in stark opposition to the OPHR only a few months earlier were now wearing its buttons on their sweat suits. According to Charlie Greene, who had once spoken strongly against the movement: "I was misled by newspaper reports that made Harry Edwards sound like some kind of a fanatic. Now I've talked to him personally and I'm impressed."[5] Likewise, Ralph Boston—who claimed he had been led to believe Edwards had "two heads"—now said, "I've met him and he's only got one head and it's a very good one."[6] But if some kind of general agreement had emerged that *something* should be done, it had also become clear that there was no consensus as to what that would be—except that an Olympic boycott did not appear to be a viable protest strategy. As two athletes wearing the OPHR buttons had explained to concerned officials: "They're just buttons. They show some sympathy for an idea. They definitely don't mean a boycott."[7] No matter how forcefully he preached, Edwards could not reverse this sentiment. Among the twenty-six athletes present and virtually assured of making the team, only twelve favored a boycott while thirteen were against it (one athlete abstained).[8] The OPHR power play, in other words, had seemingly come up short.

But the operative word here is seemingly. For despite the backroom collapse of the boycott, the Olympic Project for Human Rights was far from over. This chapter shows how Harry Edwards, Tommie Smith, and their OPHR associates kept the Olympic protest initiative alive, and the different kinds of games they played and symbolic resources they utilized in order to do it. The Cal Poly meetings revealed that the OPHR had two things in its favor. First, if these prospective Olympians could not agree to a boycott, they nevertheless shared a strong sentiment for dramatizing the plight of African Americans in some fashion. In fact, there was a lengthy discussion about other forms their protest might take. Some of the alternatives suggested included wearing black armbands, shoes, or socks, or competing in plain black uniforms, removing the U.S. insignia from their uniforms, refusing to mount awards platforms, or marching as a separate group in the Parade of Nations during the Opening Ceremonies.[9] While none of these suggestions received approval from the group as a whole or were even necessarily feasible, a few stalwarts nonetheless pledged that in lieu of an all-out boycott they would, at the upcoming trials, refuse to mount the victory stands, accept awards, or join the ceremonial athlete's march that traditionally concluded the event.

These discussions and decisions were just precursors to the cat-and-mouse power games—involving Edwards, black Olympians, the USOC, the IOC, the media, and to a certain extent the U.S. government—that were to come. But the second and probably more important thing that came out of the OPHR meeting was what didn't come out of it. No one, in the weeks that followed, publicly revealed the content and outcome of these closed-door sessions. More specifically, no one confirmed whether the boycott proposal had been definitively accepted or rejected. What this meant, of course, was that the *threat* of a boycott was still alive, that the OPHR still had what it believed to be its most powerful protest weapon. The fact that we know now that the threat was strictly a matter of perception is precisely why this chapter reveals the political power and possibility and ultimately explosiveness of politics in a popular cultural arena such as sport.

Counterresistance and the Boycott Collapse

Several years later Vince Matthews would write that the collapse of the boycott was a case of too little, too late. "It was not that some athletes cared less about the plight of blacks," he insisted; rather, this was only the "first taste of what the Olympic Project for Human Rights was really all about" for many, and they had not been exposed to it long enough or directly enough to share the intensity Lee Evans or Tommie Smith possessed after spending the year around Edwards at San Jose State.[10] Personally, Matthews said, "I felt a certain allegiance with the boycott movement, but it was difficult for me to be as intense as Harry Edwards hoped every black athlete would be. I was only twenty years old, I wasn't a man of the world and most of my relationships with whites had come from the subtle racism of the North." In addition, the implications of large-scale demonstrations and threats of reprisals scared many athletes, especially those who had fairly certain job offers or secure teaching positions. Others did not want to risk losing lucrative endorsement deals, which themselves were still covert, due to prevailing regulations regarding "amateurism."[11] None were idle possibilities in an era where simply having one's name printed in an article associated with the OPHR—whether supporting the boycott or not—had clear political implications. Many explanations offered over the years have focused on the personal interest each athlete had in competing. As Lee Evans put it: "Imagine the eagles we had there. And we were going to run. But what else could we agree to do? . . . People were scattered, thinking of the careers they were going to, some to football, some to the military." Years later his former teammate Larry James argued that even baser motives should be taken into account. "It boiled down to cash, between the goal—doing good for all mankind—and the gold: the individual's self-interest. There was, shall we say, counseling back and forth to sort out the two."[12]

Though less often mentioned than these various personal and internal pressures, the widespread mobilization against the boycott—the counterresistance and counterproposals it generated or provoked—may have been an even more decisive factor. Probably the most famous and noteworthy was the nationally reported March 29 press conference at which the vice president and civil rights champion Hubert Humphrey urged Negroes (as the headlines put it) to "compete" and "forward the cause" in the name of "Olympic harmony."[13]

Humphrey's remarks came at the conclusion of the first official meeting of the newly enlarged President's Council on Physical Fitness and Sports, of which the vice president had just assumed the chairmanship. While this long-awaited reorganizational meeting was not actually occasioned by the threat of a black Olympic boycott, this matter occupied a good deal of the discussion during the session and most of the press conference that followed it. In a letter to the NCAA (which included a complete transcript of the press conference), in fact, V. I. Nicholson, Humphrey's director of information for the PCPFS, notes that "the formal recommendations adopted by the Council are concerned primarily with the proposed Olympic boycott and matters closely related to that boycott."[14]

The significance of Humphrey's interest and involvement goes beyond his formal political office. Though he had only recently assumed the chairmanship of the President's Council, the vice president had a long history of interest and involvement in issues of athletics, international sport, and especially the Olympic Games. As a prominent liberal senator in the 1960s, Humphrey had championed the Olympics, much as he had championed civil rights, on the grounds that they "contribute to understanding and harmony among the races." But, like most Americans, Humphrey's notions of "understanding" and "racial harmony" were, in the context of international athletics, essentially American code words for Cold War interests. His distinctly American nationalist understanding of the Games was revealed most obviously when American Olympic teams began to falter in the national medal counts in the middle of the decade. In 1966 Humphrey (serving now as vice president) said: "What the Soviets are doing is a challenge to us, just like Sputnik was a challenge. We are going to be humiliated as a great nation unless we buckle down to the task of giving our young people a chance to compete." Humphrey concluded these remarks by insisting that the United States had to prove conclusively that a free society produces better athletes than a socialist one.[15] And in 1968, as the chairman of the President's Council on Physical Fitness and a soon-to-be candidate for the presidency, Humphrey's concern was acute. During his campaign for the White House, in fact, Humphrey actively sought the support of athletes, black and white. A picture in *Revolt,* for example, shows him standing with four black and two white professional football players.

Torn between the equality concerns of black athletes, their rights as individual citizens, and the foreign policy interests inherent in the Olympic Games, Humphrey's comments on the proposed 1968 boycott read as a classic example of political doublespeak. Although he admitted that he had not consulted with any of the black athletes and had no immediate plans to do so, Humphrey insisted that a boycott of the Olympic Games was "not in their best interest." Instead, the vice president suggested that winning their medals and then speaking out was the surest way for black athletes to fight for their rights in front of the world. "I can't think of any better way to forward the cause of equal opportunity in America," he explained, "than having the [Olympic] champions speak up." Ignoring the example of Muhammad Ali, Humphrey declared, "When he is a champion, it is hard to say he is wrong because he has already been a winner and more likely the other guy has been a talker."

> Surely the spirit of the Olympic Games cannot thrive on a hypocrisy that fails to acknowledge that even the highest individual achievement does not save a black athlete from the indignities and

injustices visited upon him as a man. Surely the spirit of the Olympic Games requires us, as white participants, to explore all the means at our disposal to further the cause of brotherhood and the claims to equality of our black colleagues.[16]

In order to counter any such hypocrisy, Humphrey had agreed the previous day that there was a need for more Negro coaches on the Olympic team and that blacks deserved "wider opportunities" in sports as well.[17] He also noted: "I believe that these matters are matters of individual choice. I haven't had to experience some of the things these men have. I just want them to know how proud we are of their abilities. And not only proud of their abilities, but I want to see those abilities fully recognized in every area of life." In the end, however, Humphrey's implication was clear: whatever it took, he wanted to ensure that black athletes would compete in the 1968 Mexico City Olympic Games.

In spite of Humphrey's sermonizing, no tangible actions directly relevant to the athletes seem to have come out of these meetings. At the very least, the vice president's level of interest and concern suggests just how seriously the nation took the idea of an African American Olympic boycott and the kind of public pressure working against it.

A response to the boycott threat that was more directly targeted to African American athletes themselves came from former professional football star, actor, and black activist Jim Brown. Almost exactly a month before Humphrey convened his session, Brown told some eight hundred people at a Claremont (California) Men's College conference on urban unrest that "black militancy" was not the solution to the Negro's problems in the United States.[18] According to Brown, "Negroes" were being forced to choose between two extremes: either taking a militant route or being a "puppy" for the establishment. "The issue today is not race," Brown countered. "The issue is between the rich and the poor, the haves and the have nots." He called for more job opportunities, the uplifting of neighborhoods and the elimination of discrimination. "Nobody can dispute these things," Brown claimed. He also asserted that an organization he had recently founded, "The Negro Industrial and Economic Union," was "one of the few groups left that is a link between white America and the black ghetto." The NIUC, or Black Economic Union as it later came to be known, had been set up (with a grant of over one million dollars from the Ford Foundation) to promote black entrepreneurship through a network of African American athletes and MBAs—which may also explain why some newspapers put Brown's proclamation against black militancy on the front page of their sports sections (despite the fact that Brown, once named as an OPHR supporter, apparently did not discuss a potential Olympic boycott or athletic protest more generally at the Claremont conference). In a tactic that soon-to-be-elected President Richard Nixon would assume as his own, the market—not militancy—became Brown's preferred sphere for dealing with the problems of African Americans.[19]

Directly connected with the backlash against the OPHR's Olympic boycott proposal, Harry Edwards's favorite nemesis Jesse Owens found his sagging endorsement and public speaking career rejuvenated. That spring (after being delayed for the better part of three years), producer and director Bud Greenspan finally found a network and corporate sponsor for a documentary on the 1936 Olympics titled "Jesse Owens Returns to Berlin," which played to rave reviews across a then-unprecedented 180 television stations nationwide. The title was inspired by Owens's own return to Berlin Stadium in 1951, and Owens himself narrated the documentary (which was distributed by Sports Network, Inc. and sponsored by the General Electric Company). According to a *New York Times* review, "Mr. Greenspan's film was uncommonly well done, capturing the full essence of a remarkable occurrence in international sports. And, if he so chooses, Mr. Owens should have no trouble in obtaining further jobs as a TV narrator. He is very good." The review did not fail to mention why the documentary had suddenly found a network, sponsor, and audience: "The documentary inevitably was made more timely by the controversy over Negro participation in this summer's Olympic Games in Mexico City," though it also noted that even though "Mr. Owens had disapproved of any boycott . . . last night's film . . . was not revised or amended to include such developments."[20]

The most deliberate and concerted attempts to discourage or disable an Olympic boycott, however, had come from those agencies most directly responsible for fielding an American Olympic team: namely, the United States Olympic Committee (USOC), the Amateur Athletic Union (AAU), the National Collegiate Athletic Association (NCAA), and the old American Track and Field Association. In the absence of accessible papers and cooperative officials, it is impossible to document the full range of specific tactics and reprisals these organizations plotted and carried out against the OPHR and the boycott supporters. These are not, after all, the kinds of records that usually endure, and even today few surviving coaches and officials feel comfortable enough to talk about them on the record. There were certainly no direct references to these concerns in official athletic publications, hindered as they were by their strict refusal to address such "political" issues. But if we look closely, reading between the lines and paying attention to what was not said, we can begin to see the outlines of a deliberate counteroffensive against the boycott.

Previous chapters have already revealed the extremes to which the NCAA and national basketball officials went in their (unsuccessful) attempts to guarantee full participation in the basketball trials in April. They also showed how quickly various officials, aided by the national print media, jumped to spin the expulsion of South Africa as the final nail in the coffin of the boycott initiative. But these were only the tip of the counterresistance iceberg. To take the official magazine of the AAU, *Amateur Athlete,* as an example, there are references, all subtly derogatory, to the possibility of an Olympic protest of some sort scattered throughout the fall, winter, and spring issues of 1967–8. The most direct references to the OPHR boycott initiative can be found in an unusual May profile celebrating Jesse Owens's athletic and racial accomplishments while emphasizing his dim views of the OPHR's proposed racial protests.

Another indication of the extreme measures taken by relevant American track-and-field agencies can be seen in an announcement they issued late in the spring:

> The winners of the 18 events have been promised a spot on the 1968 United States Olympic team by edict of the Olympic track and field committee, provided they shall have demonstrated fitness and competitive excellence (in September) to the satisfaction of the Olympic track and field committee.[21]

The statement goes on to say that because USOC officials had "dedicated themselves" to organizing the best possible team for Mexico City, they would reserve training for South Lake Tahoe. And according to the policy, "All final decisions by the committee is [sic] reserved until the Selection Trials." What is important and revealing about this announcement is that always before and ever since, the U.S. track-and-field trials have been tantalizing, do-or-die, sudden-death affairs in which only the three top performers on the appointed day qualify for the American Olympic team. What occasioned this strange and entirely unprecedented shift in 1968 has remained (at least officially) a matter of considerable controversy and debate. The official USOC justification was that the higher altitude at Lake Tahoe would more closely approximate the environment athletes would face in the high altitude of Mexico City (which had in fact provoked a great deal of controversy and concern among coaches, doctors, and officials worldwide). It was probably also an attempt to accommodate an unusual number of ailing American stars such as famed Kansas miler Jim Ryun.[22] Many, however, saw the moves as part of a concerted attempt to quiet and dispel potential boycotters. The final results of the Los Angeles meet, after all, would mean squads comprising only African Americans in seven of eighteen events—leaving the USOC (which either did not know about the apparent collapse of the boycott or was simply unwilling to take any chances whatsoever) at the mercy of a subsequent pullout.

A letter written to IOC President Avery Brundage by USOC President (and American IOC member) Douglas Roby later in the summer confirms this suspicion. Roby assures Brundage that the USOC was taking other steps behind the scenes as well. He tells Brundage, for example, of the hiring of Stan Wright, an African American, as an assistant track coach, and describes how all athletes competing in trials were required to sign a pledge that they would "not take part in any boycott or demonstrations." Roby is most optimistic about the creation of what he describes as a "Board of Consultants." This group, which included former athletes Rafer Johnson, Hayes Jones, Nell Jackson, Bob Mathias, and John Sayre, with none other than Jesse Owens serving as its chair, would provide consultation and mentoring to American Olympians and a liaison between the USOC and its frustrated and disgruntled athletes. For his part, Brundage informed Roby he had instructed Mexican organizing officials to take steps to deal with the prospect of demonstrations in connection with the victory ceremonies.[23] Noteworthy in all of this, Olympic officials were still being forced to react to the actions and statements of Edwards and his associates.

A Strategy of Chaos

Even though any possibility of an all-out, rank-and-file black Olympic walkout had effectively evaporated at the pre-trials Cal Poly meeting, few people outside the OPHR circle were aware of this outcome. And even those who were in the know were, for one reason or another, reluctant to publicize it too openly or definitively. Sportswriters such as Pete Axthelm and his associate Johnathan Edwards may have hesitated so as to allow the OPHR as much continued media attention as possible. For those on quite the opposite side of the political spectrum (such as the sportswriter John Underwood or authorities within the various athletic agencies), it may have been because of a fundamental uncertainty about the accuracy of their information. In other words, they probably knew about the vote (Edwards certainly suggests that there were some suspected moles among those black athletes at the meeting) but were not sure whether it could be trusted.

In any case, this was just the opening Edwards, Smith, and their boycott threat needed. Always the movement strategist and media manipulator, Edwards hid the collapse of the boycott from the public at the Los Angeles meet and focused only on the positive. "Now that so many brothers have awakened," he proclaimed, "there's nothing we can't accomplish."[24] Smith echoed the refrain: "It's unbelievable how much momentum we picked up in a few days."[25] A few days before the qualifying meet began, on June 31, Edwards announced that the OPHR had shifted its strategy somewhat and might not announce its intentions for or against the boycott until even after the teams had reached Mexico City in October. He also hinted that other forms of protest might be employed at the Games, although he declined to specify what those might entail.[26]

And there was plenty of radical posturing to back this rhetoric. Wearing his now-familiar dark sunglasses and a black tam, Edwards, for example, attended the Los Angeles Olympic Trials with outspoken Boston Celtic player-coach Bill Russell. Together the controversial pair sat with a host of black followers in what they called "the poor people's section" of three-dollar general admission seats, attracting a good deal of attention from both the spectators and the media.[27] But this was the time for the athletes to be in the spotlight—Tommie Smith most all. Later that month, Smith would wear his trademark wrap-around black sunglasses as the poster child for *Newsweek*'s cover story, "The Angry Black Athlete." Smith, who had been suffering from a minor muscle pull, was acutely aware of all the attention that was focused on him and what he represented. "A lot of people would love to see me lose. But I'll win. I'm really psyched up—I've never been so conscious of running for my people."[28]

Never had Smith been so correct in so many ways. In the 200-meter trials, he burst to one of the fastest starts of his life (for a sprinter, Smith was notoriously slow out of the blocks) and held off a tenacious Jimmy Hines with ease. After jogging to a stop, he stood still for a moment, hands on hips. Then, defiantly, he pushed his sunglasses up on his forehead, looked up into the crowd, and, in a foreshadowing of what would come later, raised a fist in triumph. As its lead, the *Newsweek* article recounted how moments later a Los Angeles radio reporter thrust a microphone in his face and began, "Tommie, you ran with real power out there," at which point Smith interrupted him: "Call it *black* power," he corrected, and abruptly ended the interview.[29] These were powerful images and provocations.

It seems safe to assume that Smith was one of those athletes who had pledged to enact some form of protest during the trials. However, neither he nor anyone else ever had the chance to carry through on their promises. The United States Olympic Committee abruptly canceled its traditional parade of athletes and victory ceremonies and scheduled additional training and tryouts for Lake Tahoe in September. But none of these measures could keep Smith, Edwards, and the boycott threat out of the media spotlight. The outstanding athletic performances of African American athletes who dominated the Los Angeles meet afforded them and their discontents in general a tremendous degree of media attention. And with this success, news of the broad black athletic unrest and protest that I detailed in the previous chapter finally began to reach a wide public audience.

The African American athletic unrest was, for example, a front-page feature in the *Wall Street Journal* (June 19), spotlighted in numerous national magazines including *Newsweek* and *Look*, and the focus of an extraordinary cover story and five-part series in the nation's foremost sports periodical *Sports Illustrated* titled "The Black Athlete."[30] As the table of contents page summarized the *Newsweek* account (written by Pete Axthelm): "The black college athlete is an angry young man. No longer willing to buy the argument that sport has been 'good' to the Negro, he is striking out at the white sports establishment and as the Olympic Games draw close, such militants as champion sprinter Tommie Smith of San Jose are planning how . . . to make their protest felt. . . . [There is] a growing mood of militancy—a movement powered by everyone from basketball stars to some of the nation's leading track men."[31] And if this athletic discontent was not exactly the black power revolt often characterized by Edwards, the attention it attracted nevertheless allowed Edwards and his OPHR colleagues to give voice to their controversial post–civil rights racial politics.

Much of this was accomplished simply by keeping the threat of an Olympic boycott itself alive. Single-mindedly and often single-handedly, Edwards simply refused to let the boycott idea die. As the month progressed, he raised more specific, often ludicrous possibilities. On one occasion, for example, Edwards suggested that Tommie Smith might run a 52-second 200-meter dash in the Olympic finals (Smith was said to be capable of a sub-20-second time). Writing for the *Times* of London, Neil Allen envisioned African American athletes wearing all-black outfits, concealing the U.S. insignias on their uniforms, or completely refusing to participate in victory ceremonies. All this was, of course, strictly theoretical. Nevertheless, Allen concluded that such "dramatic steps" were "very possible," indeed "an almost logical next step."[32]

None of it was an "easy sell." Evidence was beginning to emerge (quite accurate, as we now know) that the actual boycott had fallen apart. Several athletes admitted as much to various authorities and members of the media. Edwards himself would deny reports that the boycott was off but then offer conditions (such as nationwide attention to black murders and providing black criminal offenders with speedier trials) under which he claimed he would consider withdrawing the boycott proposal.[33] Even more telling is that the very sympathetic article compiled and written by *Newsweek* sports editor Pete Axthelm and his staff made it pretty clear that a boycott would not happen. Although Axthelm himself avoided saying so explicitly, a careful retrospective reading of the piece reveals that he clearly implied it in several places, quoted several athletes who suggested the boycott had collapsed, and printed nothing that would absolutely refute it. The magazine's table of contents page even reported that "such militants as champion sprinter Tommie Smith of San Jose are planning how—probably short of an actual boycott—to make their protest felt."[34] Then, late in July, Lee Evans, one of the boycott's original and most avid supporters, made a statement to the effect that the boycott was off.[35] Edwards, remarkably, remained undaunted and informed the press that such confused and contradictory statements were in fact part of a deliberate "strategy of chaos." As he put it, "There is only one thing more confusing than a rumor and that's a million rumors."[36] Indeed, a few days later, appearing on British television shortly after winning the 200 in a London track meet, Tommie Smith claimed he would back any Olympic boycott:

> The problem has been brought into the open. We are making progress. The black athlete may launch the boycott next week. It may come in a month's time or just before a particular Olympic race. But when it starts, I am sure a lot of people will be involved.[37]

Echoing themes he had sounded for many months, Smith insisted that he was not the leader of this movement but rather "just another athlete . . . behind the move."

This "strategy of chaos" proved to be amazingly effective. Even though they refused (or avoided) spelling out any specifics, and many in the media were beginning to suspect that the OPHR lacked the necessary backing to make such an effort effective, the idea of a boycott continued to captivate the American press. Somehow Edwards was able to keep the possibility of a boycott alive and the issues (and himself) in front of the microphones and cameras, and in the papers. The *Chicago Tribune,* for example, issued yet another general editorial against the proposed boycott and ran numerous stories on it throughout the month of July.[38] Arthur Daley of the *New York Times* drafted his own critical commentary titled "Edwards Casts a Black Cloud Over the Olympics" that was syndicated nationally and widely reprinted.[39] Most of this coverage was marked by a fearful and foreboding tone, and, if anything, the rhetoric grew more heated and confrontational as the OPHR stubbornly refused to relinquish its boycott threat.

Lew Alcindor's stormy guest appearance on NBC's *Today* show suggests the attitudes and emotions surrounding black athletes and their threat of an Olympic boycott. On Friday, July 20, one of the show's hosts, Joe Garagiola (himself a former big league baseball player), asked Alcindor why he did not try out for the U.S. Olympic team. This overtly hostile question provoked the following exchange:

> ALCINDOR: "Yeah, I live here, but it's not really my country."
> GARAGIOLA: "Well, then, there's only one solution: maybe you should move."
> ALCINDOR: "Well, you see that would be fine with me, you know, it all depends on where are we going to move."[40]

The exchange was interrupted by a preplanned station break. When the program returned to the air, the discussion was resumed briefly—but not long enough for Alcindor to clarify what he may have meant by his comments. This incident created quite a stir in Alcindor's hometown of New York and, one would expect, many other parts of the country as well. "What I was trying to get across," Alcindor explained on Sunday afternoon to a reporter from his home in Hollis, Queens, "was that until things are in an equitable basis this is not my country." As Alcindor put it, "We have been a racist nation with first-class citizens and my decision not to go to the Olympics is my way of getting the message across." But he also tried to make it clear that boycotting the Olympic Games was not the only thing he was doing to tackle problems of racial inequity. In fact, the basketball star had agreed to appear on the show in the first place in order to promote the inner-city Operation Sports Rescue Program he was organizing for that summer in New York City.[41] Of course, they never got around to talking about that. "I expected that I would be asked about the Olympics. I guess I knew," Alcindor admitted, but "I don't really know what Garagiola meant . . . Where did he expect me to go to—Africa? A lot of people get discredited by occurrences like this."

While episodes like this one demonstrate that the continued publicity surrounding an Olympic boycott generated more than its fair share of backlash (as Edwards for one had certainly learned to expect), all this coverage also inspired some new supporters as well. For example, just after qualifying for the Olympics, an all-white group of rowers from Harvard— including Scott Steketee, Curtis Canning (captain), J. Cleve Livingston,

David D. Higgins, and Paul Hoffman (coxswain)—released the following statement:

> We—as individuals—have been concerned with the place of the black man in American society and his struggle for equal rights. As members of the United States Olympic team each of us has come to feel a moral commitment to support our black teammates in their efforts to dramatize the influences and injustices that permeate our society. . . .
>
> It is not our intention or desire to embarrass our country or to use athletics for ulterior purposes. But we feel strongly that the racial crisis is a total cultural crisis. The position of the black athlete cannot be, and is not in fact, separated from his position as a black man or woman in America. America can only acquire greater dignity and greater hope by facing its most grievous problem openly and before the world. Surely the spirit of the Olympic Games cannot thrive on a hypocrisy that fails to acknowledge that even the highest individual achievement does not save a black athlete from the indignities and injustices visited upon him as a man. Surely the spirit of the Olympic Games requires us, as white participants, to explore all the means at our disposal to further the cause of brotherhood and the claims to equality of our black colleagues.[42]

This statement—written and released immediately following their qualification to the U.S. Olympic team but announced by Robert Lipsyte in a column in the *New York Times* a week later (on August 1)—seems to have taken shape as their involvement with the American Olympic movement began to intensify. They had been intrigued by the proposed Olympic boycott, then communicated with Evans earlier in the year and met Edwards at the qualifying event in California. But they also claimed that the report released by the well-known Kerner Commission also convinced them it was time to speak out. As Scott Steketee told Lipsyte:

> It's certainly regrettable we have to take this stand, but everything about the plight of the black man in this country is regrettable. And in a sense, our stand is an expression of brotherhood with our black teammates and that's my idea of the spirit of the Olympics, at least the original plan of the Olympics.

While they did not know exactly what form the black athlete's demonstration would take or what (if any) role the rowers might play in such a demonstration, Steketee noted that they decided to help "make contact with other white athletes selected for Olympic teams and create a group that would help whites understand the goals of the black protesters." He also emphasized the legitimacy of their support for the black athletes: "We've invested all our efforts in athletics for so long and we've worked so hard, that I think we've earned the right to use our main area of interest to express our main concerns."

The Harvard rowers set off a flurry of activity behind the scenes among American amateur athletic officials. The acting executive director of the USOC, Everett Barnes (acting on the behest of President Roby), sent out letters to various rowing officials and coaches asking for "suggestions" on "handling this problem." The USOC Rowing Committee headed up the response. Their initial inclination, according to internal records, was to try to force them to sign a "cease and desist statement" or else risk being dropped from the U.S. Olympic contingent. Eventually, however, they settled on asking the crew to sign a statement that read in part: "I . . . hereby agree that if I had planned to take part in Mexico in any demonstration of support for any disadvantaged people in the United States, that I hereby immediately give up such plans and activities."[43] While seven of the eight crew members signed the statement, this would not be the end of their involvement in racially based Olympic protest activities. Never one to miss an opportunity, Edwards himself commented, "It was beautiful to see some white cats willing to admit they've got a problem and looking to take some action to educate their own."[44]

But smoke and mirrors can only captivate and provoke for so long, and Edwards knew that he could not continue the charade of an Olympic boycott without losing his credibility as an organizer and media informant. A formal announcement had to be made. As his audience, Edwards chose what was certainly a friendly crowd at the 1968 National Conference on Black Power held in Philadelphia the last week of August. In a special to the *New York Times* drawn from Edwards's statement to the convention, journalist C. Gerald Fraser confirmed what the press and public was beginning to suspect: "The proposed boycott of the 1968 Olympic Games by United States Negro athletes is off."[45]

Edwards, who was unable to deliver the message personally because of an automobile accident, began by citing the "accomplishments" of "this phase of the athletic movement." Among those Edwards detailed were the exposure of white nationalism and racism in the sports industry; the exposure of the Olympic Games as a white nationalistic, racist political tool of exploiting oppressive governments; the opening of international avenues of communication and cooperation, especially between African nations and black Afro-Americans; the banning of South Africa and Southern Rhodesia from the 1968 Olympics; and the education of black people as to the degree of racism in the United States. He summed it up by saying, "We have gotten world-wide recognition of the plight of black people without a single drop of black blood being spilled."

Asserting that "the majority of athletes *will* participate in the Olympics," the charismatic sociologist claimed that there was "consensus on protest at the Games" and promised that "many will engage in some form of protest." In particular, he maintained that Negro Olympians would *not* participate in "victory stand ceremonies or victory marches; some athletes have decided to boycott the Games and lesser forms of protest will be carried out by others." Edwards also indicated that all had agreed to wear black armbands and "demonstrate their support of the black power movement in some manner during the course of the Olympic Games" and that the protesters would include a "sizable contingent of white athletes." Finally, along with an entire agenda of athletically based protests to be carried out in the next year, Edwards resolved that an awards banquet to honor the athletes who made a "tremendous contribution to the black liberation struggle" should be held. (Tommie Smith, Lew Alcindor, Mike Warren, and Lucius Allen, all members of the UCLA basketball team, and Nevada track star Otis Burrell were among those Edwards named.)

According to Edwards's account in *Revolt,* the final official act of the OCHR was to hold a news conference "to clear up any additional questions the press might have."[46] Semantically, it may have been true that the boycott movement "officially came to an end" here (though the OCHR itself seems to have been little more than Edwards's ghost organization anyway); but the Olympic protest movement was far from over.[47] Black athletes themselves met in Denver, where the USOC was handling outfitting and processing en route to Mexico City. It was there that they planned to make another attempt to settle on what they might do to express their discontents collectively. As Matthews recalls Evans putting it: "We can't go down there without deciding something. We've put this off for too long as it is."[48] A sense of urgency was also introduced into the meeting, as Lee Evans recalled later, when they learned that Brundage had said something to the effect that "black athletes were lucky to be allowed on the team at all." Indeed, according to Evans's recollections many years later, this was a decisive moment: "If he hadn't come out like that, I don't think anything would have happened."[49] Even so, the athletes were once again unable to settle on any form of collective action. According to Matthews, all the various protest possibilities were "hashed over" once more in a meeting that lasted several hours, but, as with previous gatherings, "each time a suggestion was brought up, it was promptly shot down." In the end, the athletes were left with Ralph Boston's suggestion that "it should be left up to the individual." No one seemed particularly pleased with this plan, but under the circumstances it was all they could agree upon.[50]

Writing in *Revolt* the following year, Edwards would put his own twist on what had happened and why:

> It was decided that each athlete would determine and carry out his own "thing," preferably focusing around the victory stand ceremonies. In this way, potential repercussions from a so-called "Black Power" conspiracy could be avoided and, also, each athlete would be free to determine his own course of protest. The results of this new strategy, devised for the most part by the athletes themselves, were no less than revolutionary in impact.[51]

If Edwards correctly surmised that the consequences would be "no less than revolutionary," it is also quite clear from all the accounts available that there was no way he or anyone else would have been able to predict what actually transpired in Mexico City. And this was in large part, as I suggested in the previous chapter, because Edwards and the OPHR had been so completely committed to the idea of an Olympic boycott that they had spent very little time thinking about alternative options; thus, they had very little understanding of (or hope for) what they might achieve in its absence.

It is remarkable how little theorized the strategy of a boycott seems to have been. While there was a great deal of talk about sport protest and the overarching problems of race, there was actually very little consideration of the underlying purpose and specific rationale for choosing an Olympic boycott over other forms of activism. Basically, it seems as if Edwards and his colleagues simply assumed that because it had stirred up such a controversy, an Olympic boycott must be the most powerful means to use sport in service of racial struggle. This was, once again, because of the importance of nationalism and the assumption that winning the Games was essential to the Cold War foreign policy goals Americans associated with international sport. But Edwards seemingly had very little vision of the powerful political potential inherent *in* sport itself, due to its close semantic connections with liberal democratic theory and practice. That is, sporting events as focused gatherings provide a forum or opportunity to do other kinds of politics. This is the tension between the boycott as a mode of structural power to force change (as Edwards uses it here) and as a way to focus cultural attention on social issues such as race.

It was only in mid- to late June that Edwards began to portray the boycott as part of a much larger effort to "dramatize" racial problems in and through sport. Based upon an interview with Edwards, *Los Angeles Times* sports columnist Charles Maher explains: "As I understand it, the boycott is part of a broad movement designed to dramatize the predicament of the Black man in America. I think I can appreciate that predicament but, after reading dozens of stories on the subject, I still can't see how Harry's caper is going to do much for the man in the ghetto. . . . The trouble with Harry's boycott, it seems to me, is that it doesn't apply enough muscle to people who might be in a position to help the Black man." Maher quotes Edwards on "saving the country" and comments, "I don't understand it, but if Harry can really save the country and all it costs us is an Olympic victory, I'm for it."[52] In an article published just one week earlier, Edwards had been able to give no real response to a *Wall Street Journal* interviewer who asked him specifically how an Olympic boycott would push forward the movement for black liberation. "If nobody plays, everybody is equal," was all he said.[53] Much of this ultimately fell on Smith, who had more consistently portrayed the boycott as an attempt to "dramatize" issues of sport and race, rather than an attempt to "force" social change.

Races and Race in Mexico City

As with every Olympic Games, the Games of the XIX Olympiad were invested with deep symbolic significance. In terms of the official Olympic and governmental authorities, this revolved around the fact that Mexico was the first "third world" nation to host an Olympic Games, having won the right despite concerns that it might be dangerous for athletes to compete in its high altitude conditions. For Mexican authorities the Games were also a conscious attempt to promote the country's revolutionary-progressive heritage. Avery Brundage promoted the official IOC and Mexican government line in portraying the Olympic movement as making a contribution to "the most stable and fastest growing country in Latin America." But these conventional claims were haunted by deep social and political unrest in Mexico itself, as Harry Edwards alluded to throughout the OPHR organizing efforts. It all came to a fever pitch on October 2, just days before the scheduled start of the Games.

Though even today the details remain shrouded in uncertainty and controversy, hundreds of students were killed or injured when police and soldiers opened fire onto a crowded public plaza. Student demonstrators contended that the government had no place spending $150 million on a sports spectacle while millions of Mexican citizens still lived in poverty. Indeed, students had been insisting for months that they would deliberately disrupt the Games. They were also demanding the firing of top police officials, dissolution of the city's notorious riot squad, and abolition of various national antisubversion laws.[54]

Smith and Evans and their teammates entered Mexico against this backdrop, and it certainly had some impact on them. They had, after all, been well aware of the Mexican student protests in the months leading up to the Games, because these struggles were often connected with the fight against South African apartheid as well as the Soviet squelching of the recent Czech uprising in Prague.

It was a political context that weighed heavily upon American authorities as well. Although they tried to downplay their significance, Olympic officials were aware of the potential connection between these issues and the threatened African American racial demonstrations. One of the more sympathetic (and forthcoming) officials explained: "Like in our own country, you can't move too fast on these things." In fact, the USOC made a point of having the U.S. ambassador speak to American Olympians upon their arrival to Mexico City about the privilege of being "ambassadors of good will" and competing for their country.[55] The event was replete with a flag-raising ceremony and the singing of the national anthem. Assisting official sports leaders in this effort to insulate American athletes against the influence of other international controversies was the American media. Indeed, it was generally they who took the lead in formulating a counterresponse to shield the American athletic organization against such attacks. The story about the ambassador's reception, for example, received wide circulation via the UPI wire; it made sure to mention that "every one of the black members of the team" participated in the event—including John Carlos, who reportedly "sang as loud as anyone." The story went on to quote head track coach Payton Jordan, who insisted: "We have a fine rapport on our team, maybe the best any team has ever had." He was backed up by his African American assistant Stan Wright, the man President Roby considered so important to USOC counterboycott measures: "I don't expect [a demonstration] and the least said about one the better." The New York Times, for its part, profiled a number of "non-militant" black athletes in sports such as boxing, wrestling, and basketball. One of those featured a twenty-six-year-old wrestler named Bobby Douglas, who was quoted as saying he viewed his participation in the Games as an attempt to "dispel the boycott idea" and "prove Harry Edwards wrong." "I can do more by competing than by sitting on the sidelines and yelling black power," he said.[56]

The sprints began on October 15, the second day of the track-and-field competition, with the first of the sprint finals being the 100-meter dash. In what he later called "the greatest race of my life [and] the greatest thing that will ever happen to me," Jimmy Hines won the race in a world-record time of 9.95, literally running away from Jamaica's Lennox Miller and his African American teammate Charlie Greene. The two Americans stood poised in respectful attention throughout the victory ceremony, giving no public indication of any protest or dissatisfaction. Greene, who would go on to a twenty-year career in the military, recalls, "I thirsted for glory and I wanted the USA to be better than every other country. I loved that." But Hines, who had always made it clear that he would not participate in any kind of a boycott, was not so sanguine. In fact, he had "let it be known" that he would refuse to shake hands with Brundage when and if the IOC president went ahead with the medal presentation as scheduled.[57] (Brundage would not officiate at any further victory ceremonies, but he was far from out of the story.)

The same day as Hines's triumph, a number of other African American athletes—Tommie Smith and John Carlos among them—wore black socks and black berets in their preliminary heats. Carlos sported a button reading "Olympic Project for Human Rights." Earlier in the week several black athletes had talked of joint actions to protest the "atrocious" conditions of hotel rooms assigned their wives; a rumor of a massive black sit-down strike turned out to be little more than a handful of sprinters resting near the track—and the room problem was quickly resolved by the authorities. All such expressions of discontent were conveniently overlooked by coaches and officials and downplayed by the media. A reliably well-positioned Pete Axthelm believed that "the long-awaited black protests have produced far more rumor than trouble. The American blacks apparently will settle for some mild gesture like wearing Afro-style Dashikis over their U.S. sweat suits on award stands." [58] Assistant coach Stan Wright was quoted as saying, "I was not informed of any demonstration. As far as I know, they wore high stockings because it was cold, but they may have intended it to be a demonstration. If they did, it is their business. We are here to win medals."[59] However small and personal and palpable such gestures may have been, they were only a precursor of what was to come from Tommie Smith and John Carlos. But first they had to win.

In analyzing the symbolic composition of their famous demonstration in the first chapter, I described the spectacular 200-meter race that qualified them to stand on the victory rostrum. What I did not discuss at that point was how lucky both Smith and Carlos were to have competed in the race at all. In his preliminary heat just two hours earlier, Smith had suffered a painful muscle pull that easily could have hobbled him during the race or kept him out of the finals altogether. Smith himself was not convinced that the leg would hold until he had completed the turn and the straightaway. This much is well known by sports historians, but Carlos had his own troubles. Even though he had easily won his heat, replays revealed that Carlos had clearly stepped out of his lane, an infraction that could have resulted in an automatic disqualification if officials had caught the error.[60] It is, perhaps, with such uncertainties about athletic competition in mind that we can more fully appreciate the drama that unfolded as Smith and Carlos stepped onto the victory stand after having finished first and third respectively in the fastest 200-meter dash ever recorded at the time.

If the demonstration evokes a certain calm, controlled, dignified defiance for most Americans today (and many others around the world), the reactions it provoked in 1968 couldn't be more different. Almost as soon as Smith and Carlos stepped off the victory podium, the president of the International Olympic Committee, the American Avery Brundage, and his henchmen were looking for heads to roll. ABC's crack reporter Howard Cosell tried to track down Smith, the gold medalist, to "explain himself" to the huge American television audience, to give voice and concrete meaning, as it were, to the otherwise ambiguous message he had used his body to convey. But neither Smith nor Carlos were anywhere to be found. After having been escorted off the podium, across the infield, and over the track by an unidentified Olympic official (at which time Smith—walking straight and tall and staring straight ahead—offered another clenched fist salute),[61] the two athletes had disappeared.

Working on a tip from his ABC colleague Hayes Jones (himself a former Olympic gold medalist) Cosell discovered that Smith and his wife were at the Diplomat Hotel, where he visited them early the next morning. However, he found the 200-meter champion hesitant to do an interview because of all the criticism he had already received: "You'd think I committed murder. All I did was what I've been doing all along, call the attention of the world to the way the blacks are treated in America. There's nothing new about this."[62] Somehow, Cosell convinced Smith that it would be a good idea to come to the ABC studio in the Central Control Tower for an interview. It was there and then that Smith verified, in the solemn, simple words that would remain his only substantial public comment on the demonstration for over twenty years, the symbolic significance of their performance.

In his self-titled book, Howard Cosell recalls that the interview generated so much excitement at the ABC studios "it was as if the Games had come to a halt"; in fact, in an Olympics that would be a breakthrough for television coverage the story proved to be ABC's biggest of the Games.[63] This was not simply happenstance. Even before the Games, executive

Olympic producer Roone Arledge had guessed something might happen on the racial front, and, in order that no newsman would "beat" them to the story, had put Cosell—the white reporter who could talk to blacks—to work on the angle for several weeks. (Arledge himself had broken a network blacklist to use Cosell for precisely this reason. Among other things, Cosell piqued many Americans by calling his boxing broadcast partner Muhammad Ali by his chosen name at the 1968 Games. By 1972 one national poll revealed that Cosell was both America's most respected and most hated sportscaster.) When the demonstration finally went down, Cosell had hustled immediately to the stadium infield, but since ABC had no official rights to interview the champions (much less a place to do it at the stadium), he was unable to catch Smith. Only with good fortune and some cajoling—in which Smith's wife Denise wavered first but then advised Smith to trust Cosell—was the interview arranged. Afterward, according to Cosell, Smith and his wife (and later John Carlos) thanked him for giving them a "fair treatment."[64]

The story for Carlos is much different. Carlos's statements—especially those most widely reported in the media—tended to be much harsher and more inflammatory. To take one widely quoted example, Carlos explained:

> We feel that white people think we're just animals to do a job. We saw white people in the stands putting thumbs down at us. We want them to know we're not roaches, ants or rats. If we do the job well we get a pat on the back or some peanuts. And someone says "good boy." I've heard "boy, boy, boy" all through the Olympics. I'd like to tell white people in America and all over the world that if they don't care for the things black people do then they shouldn't sit in the stands and watch them perform.[65]

Carlos would have much more to say in the next few days. While walking down the *Avenida Revolucion* with a reporter, he, too, would offer a somber accounting: "We wanted all the black people in the world—the little grocer, the man with the shoe repair store—to know that when that medal hangs on my chest or Tommie's, it hangs on his also."[66] But these dimensions of Carlos's personality, perspective, and experience were not widely reported. In a finely honed, time-honored media motif, Smith and Carlos's different temperaments were played up by the press. As much as possible (given the heated criticisms and condemnations their actions provoked), Smith was portrayed as the controlled, measured, rational one. He clearly and thoughtfully articulated the purpose and meaning behind their symbolic acts, trying not to associate himself with one political faction or another. Not long after the Games, in fact, Jesse Owens himself described Smith as a "good boy" who had gotten some "bad advice." Carlos, on the other hand, was portrayed as intensely emotional, radical, and militant. He was represented as the black power character, the ghetto black, the "bad nigger." His quotes, which tended to be much stronger and more provocative, were more widely reported and reacted upon. More than one journalist recounted a loud, profane argument between Carlos and another American, an argument that was prevented from being a fistfight only when a Canadian reporter named Dick Beddos interceded—at which point Carlos apparently told him to "get to the back of the bus, whitey."[67]

A photograph of Smith and Carlos on their return to San Jose on October 21 captures the extent to which both men assumed these roles as well. Smith is dressed in a blazer over a turtleneck top and single string of African beads. Next to Smith, Carlos is dressed casually in baseball cap and T-shirt, with a large gold chain and medallion around his neck; he is nonchalantly picking his nails. At the airport Smith and Carlos were deluged by reporters but "reluctant to talk with local newsmen." Smith, who handled the comments, offered one-word answers or "no comment." The next day in front of an SJS rally of some fifteen hundred people on the college campus Carlos told the crowd, "We'd do it again tomorrow" (Smith, interestingly, was not quoted directly).[68] Indeed, it was Carlos who appeared at post-Olympic press conferences with Harry Edwards, H. Rap Brown, and Stokely Carmichael threatening suit against the USOC.[69] It wasn't until almost a year later that Carlos was offering a more consistently circumspect explanation: "It wasn't an easy thing to do. We could have been shot. But we felt we had to do something. We held up our fists to proclaim ours as a victory on behalf of black men everywhere. We lowered our heads not out of disrespect for our country, but to pray for the cause of black people."[70]

Avery Brundage was little interested in what Smith and Carlos had to say one way or the other. He was convinced that their actions had been "an insult to their Mexican hosts and a disgrace to the United States," requiring immediate and decisive measures. He also wanted Paul Hoffman punished for providing the two with the OPHR buttons they used in their demonstration. The October 16 entry from Brundage's official Olympic journal (which itself was to serve as the basis for the IOC's official statement on the matter) reveals the deeper and more familiar source of his objections:

> One of the basic principles of the Olympic Games is that politics play no part whatsoever in them. This principle has always been accepted with enthusiasm by all, including of course the competitors. Yesterday U.S. athletes in a victory ceremony deliberately violated

> this universally accepted principle by using the occasion to adver-
> tise their domestic political views. The U.S.A. Olympic Committee
> carries the responsibility for its competitors. The executive board of
> the IOC saw Mr. Roby the president of the U.S. national Olympic
> committee early this morning. He stated that he has immediately
> called a meeting of his committee and will report.[71]

After a series of lengthy meetings the next day (four to ten hours, depending upon whose account you follow),[72] the USOC responded with a
formal apology to "the International Olympic Committee, the Mexican
organizing committee and the people of Mexico" for Smith and Carlos's
"discourteous" and "immature" behavior, saying it violated the "basic
standards of sportsmanship and good manners highly regarded in the
United States." Warning of "penalties" for further "black power acts," the
USOC declared that no formal action against Smith and Carlos would be
taken because their act was "an isolated incident."[73]

This relatively light censure, however, triggered its own storm of controversy and political maneuvering. Brundage (with little IOC consultation) had already threatened to cancel all victory ceremonies if there was
no stronger guarantee against any repetition or even approximation of
such actions by others. Now, the IOC's Executive Committee formally
chastised USOC president Douglas Roby for not being able to "control"
"his" athletes and threatened him with the expulsion of the entire American contingent. While the latter was almost certainly political posturing,
it captures the absolute outrage of the Executive Committee and was used
by the USOC to justify the action it was forced to take later that evening.
Another round of meetings followed. This one included athletic consultants John Sayre and Billy Mills, who claimed that "decisive action" was
needed to calm the "explosive atmosphere."[74] Embarrassed and outposi-
tioned USOC officials composed an updated statement (released early on
the morning of October 18) that announced the suspension of the two
men from the American team and ordered them "to remove themselves
from the Olympic village." (Contrary to lingering popular beliefs, Smith
and Carlos did not have their Olympic medals stripped.) With their suspension, Smith and Carlos had their Olympic identity cards invalidated
and were hounded from the Olympic Village and eventually Mexico itself. As a result of IOC pressure, even Peter Norman, the Australian silver
medalist who had simply pinned an "Olympic Project for Human Rights"
button on his uniform, was sternly reprimanded by his own national
committee.[75]

Whether or not these sanctions were dictated by Olympic regulation and necessary to ensure proper ritual conduct for future Games, their impact at another level was unmistakable. Until their suspension two days after the fact, Smith and Carlos's demonstration had been little more than a page-two sports story even in the most Olympic-obsessed American papers. In the wake of these disciplinary actions, however, their gesture was marked as an object of intensive public attention and found its way into high-profile newspaper, magazine, and television reports both nationally and worldwide. In other words, in trying to suppress Smith and Carlos's demonstration (not to mention prevent a repeat performance), the various Olympic authorities actually delivered it—in colorful, spectacular fashion—to an audience far larger and more diverse than the protesters themselves could have imagined in their wildest dreams.

This irony did not go unnoticed by American commentators. Many of them blamed the entire controversy on Olympic officials for overreacting to what they now claimed (trying to minimize the impact) had been a relatively insignificant, even benign demonstration. According to syndicated sports columnist Red Smith, for example, "By throwing a fit over the incident, suspending the young men and ordering them out of Mexico, the badgers multiplied the impact of the protest a hundred fold." Or, as *Time* put it: "The IOC bullheadedly proceeded to make a bad scene worse."[76] And if anything is certain here, it "got worse" before it got better. Even after Smith and Carlos had gone home, an unidentified sportswriter for the international publication *The News* could report that "the echoes of their . . . gestures on the Olympics medal platform have not diminished. In fact, they seem to have become amplified around the world, and here around the Olympic village and the various press centers."[77]

As with all audiences, however, this one would "read" and respond to the act in many different ways. That much had already been made manifest in the reactions of the international audience that witnessed the original demonstration unfold. In spite of Brundage and the IOC's claims that the demonstration had been taken as an affront against Mexico, the predominantly Mexican crowd did not register much of a reaction at all, indicating, we can infer, some combination of amazement, indifference, or bewilderment about both the gesture and any commotion that surrounded it.[78] And there were certainly some Mexicans who immediately recognized Smith and Carlos as allies.[79] In any case, the Mexican press seemed more confused at the fury the gesture occasioned rather than offended by it. Given the international spectators' general lack of knowledge regarding Smith and Carlos, their sympathies and intentions, this is probably not surprising.

As events unfolded and additional information became available, however, more elaborate (if contradictory) interpretations and definitive reactions proliferated. Many—perhaps the majority—came to recognize the fist itself as a reference to the militant "black power" wing of the civil rights movement or some larger, transnational pan-African movement. Others focused on broader symbolic details and saw the demonstration as a general indication of defiance against the powerlessness of blacks in American society or its government more specifically, a gesture of support for black America, the so-called athletic revolution, or human rights most broadly. In any case, according to the dispatches of journalists from a variety of countries worldwide, "Reports from various countries indicate a lot of people were shook up by the two men's display," while at the Games themselves "anybody [could] start an argument at the drop of a name."[80] For example, while there were Europeans who, not unlike Norman, admired Smith and Carlos for vague egalitarian reasons, most others thought it a " 'racialist' assertion of black power over whites . . . [or] even an uncomfortable reminder of the fascist salute."[81] On the other hand, other European commentators were surprised by the intensity of the opposition to the protest. As the official magazine of the British Olympic Association commented: "If this was to be the full measure of Black Power protest on the victory rostrum, then it was a well conceived plan involving the most effective of gestures without, it seemed, giving direct offense to anyone."[82] Perhaps even more significantly, reporters from the United States had little trouble locating both black African observers who pronounced themselves either uninterested or unimpressed with the gesture and Soviet officials who rather enjoyed pointing out how many track-and-field gold medals won by the United States had been won by *black* Americans.

But for those who knew Smith and Carlos and what they had been up to in the months leading up to the Games—mostly Americans, we can assume—there was little room for passivity or indifference. "The Incident," as Arthur Daley of the *New York Times* called it, proved "divisive" and "precipitated reactions that were violent but mixed."[83] Charlie Greene, the bronze medalist in the 100 and a member of the victorious 4×100 relay team, remembers, "There was a gasp . . . I don't remember booing, but a gasp in the section where I was sitting with a bunch of Americans. All of a sudden around me the atmosphere changed. There were negative comments, racial comments about what they were doing. The atmosphere became explosive." Carlos himself recalls, "Those singing the anthem started screaming it out."[84]

One of the first to issue a statement of support for Smith and Carlos in the States was Robert Clark, the president of their alma mater

San Jose State. According to Clark, who knew the athletes personally, "all Americans"—not just those in San Jose—"should be proud of . . . the achievements of Tommie Smith and John Carlos in the Olympic Games." And what Clark meant by their "achievements" was not just their triumph in the 200-meter dash but also the very gesture that resulted in their expulsion. As the academic leader saw it, their act sent a message about the conditions of blacks in the United States that "should be of real concern to all Americans." And while he regretted that Smith and Carlos felt they had to use the Olympic Games to express themselves, Clark emphasized that Smith's explanation of the demonstration's symbolism was "calm and rational" and "his sincerity unquestioned," in contrast to the "ambiguous moralistic posture" of the American Olympic committee. In any case, Clark (who had been subjected to Governor Ronald Reagan's criticisms for his handling of athletic protest organizers earlier in the year) tried to focus attention on the treatment of black athletes and minorities more generally in the United States that prompted such drastic measures. "I hope," Clark concluded, "their gesture will be interpreted properly," and that "[t]hey do not return home in disgrace but as the honorable young men they are, dedicated to the cause of justice for the Black people in our society."[85]

But the embattled Clarke was hoping against hope. In a country already wracked by the fragmentation of the civil rights coalition, urban violence, militant protest, and white backlash—in the context, that is, of the polarized racial politics of the post–civil rights period—there was little sympathy for any persons calling for additional racial change, much less those who did so on the supercharged international stage of the Olympic Games.

As I described in the first chapter, Smith and Carlos were seen by most Americans—even those in the ostensibly neutral and objective American media—as radicals or renegades, villains or traitors, and described in emotionally charged language usually reserved for the most violent and threatening figures Americans could possibly imagine: terrorists, communists, even Nazi storm troopers.

The virulence of the condemnations of Smith and Carlos was matched only by the unrestrained praises directed toward another black American gold medalist, nineteen-year-old heavyweight boxer George Foreman, who had waved a small American flag around the ring following his championship bout. *Sports Illustrated,* for example, concluded its Olympic report by describing the Foreman story as "a fitting tribute to a surprising U.S. Olympic team" and an example of how "a lot of people found a lot of wonderful ways of overcoming [the problems of the Mexican

Olympics]."[86] This was not coincidental. Even before capturing the gold, Foreman had been unsympathetic to Smith and Carlos's cause, saying, "That's for college kids. They live in another world."[87] When he won his championship bout with a technical knockout of Soviet Inoas Chepallis, Foreman went a great deal further by parading around the ring waving a small American flag and, according to at least one source, calling out "United States power!"[88] Foreman's actions were widely interpreted and paradoxically celebrated as both a statement against Smith and Carlos and a spontaneous display of patriotism. Even Brundage himself made a special point to appear with Foreman and the American "Negro" boxers who had invited him in order, as Brundage's diary puts it, "to erase the bad impression left by Track and Field athletes."[89]

"In the Olympic Games," as one American periodical put it, "race normally suggests a contest, but this year it became an issue."[90] And indeed, if there is one point that is clear about the image of Smith and Carlos on the victory stand, it is that the image was a polarizing one, a lightning rod or litmus test, a radical symbol that individuals and groups could use to situate themselves in various communities and contexts.

The Workings of Power

While power struggles over how to deal with Smith and Carlos went on in the media spotlight, other significant and telling battles were being waged behind the scenes in the athletes' quarters. The USOC sent in none other than Jesse Owens—the black American who had supposedly disproved Hitler and his Aryan theories of racial superiority by winning an unprecedented four gold medals thirty-two years earlier in Berlin—to brief a group of about twenty-five supposedly "radical," mostly black American athletes. Owens's real mission, of course, was to ensure that such episodes were not repeated. According to one of the athletes present, he tried to get them to agree on some form of "humanitarian" protest—minus the black gloves. Unfortunately, these athletes were in little mood to hear a lecture from Owens—a man most of them had long since dismissed as a rather pathetic "Uncle Tom"—on what Smith and Carlos had done wrong or how they should behave as a result. When white hammer-thrower Hal Connolly suggested that Smith and Carlos's victory-stand gesture was no more political than the United States's own long-standing refusal to dip the American flag to the Olympic banner during the Opening and Closing Ceremonies, Owens apparently became enraged and asked that he be allowed to speak to his "black brothers" alone. Lee Evans and Vincent Matthews, however, insisted that Connolly had a point, as well as a right to be there. The meeting broke up shortly thereafter, leaving only anger and frustration in its wake.[91]

This was only the beginning of the fallout. Even as Smith and Carlos were being excused from the Olympic Village and sent home to the States, USOC officials confronted and reputedly threatened many of the athletes suspected of being sympathetic to them. Several helped to circulate a rumor that the IAAF (the international governing body for track and field) was preparing to ban anyone from future competition who violated its regulations and traditions regarding amateurism. Its overtones were obvious: that Smith and Carlos had taken money from Puma, whose shoes they had incorporated into their demonstration. (The fact that many, if not a majority, of high-profile Olympic athletes had similar deals was conveniently overlooked by Olympic authorities.) The night before the eight-oar final, coxswain Paul Hoffman of the Harvard crew that had issued the statement of support for the OPHR earlier in the summer was ordered to appear before a meeting of the highest ranking USOC officials. There he was accused of conspiring to violate the Olympic spirit, ostensibly because he had given Smith an OPHR button earlier in the week. Though Hoffman (employing his best "prep school manner") was absolved of the charges, the committee nevertheless threatened to send him home unless he pledged that even if he did not win a medal, neither he nor his crew would demonstrate in any way. On related fronts, two athletes on leave from the army received calls from their commanding officers, while others heard from ROTC units, athletic departments, or employers advising (or threatening) them to not engage in further actions.[92] No one, however, felt this pressure more intensely than 400-meter man Lee Evans.

Evans was torn between running his race the next day or withdrawing in order to protest the treatment Smith and Carlos were receiving. Smith's classmate and close friend and one of the OPHR's earliest and most ardent supporters, Evans was said to have mirrored Smith and Carlos's salute from his own seat in the coliseum during their ceremony. Only after Smith advised him (and all of his teammates) to compete did Evans decide to run at all; then, moments before the final, Evans got locked up in a nasty face-to-face confrontation with the USOC president himself, Douglas Roby. (According to eyewitnesses, the exchange nearly came to blows before the two were separated. Roby himself would tell later of being yelled at for referring to Evans and his teammates as "boys.")[93] Somehow Evans overcame—or perhaps channeled—all of this and turned in another of the remarkable high-altitude performances of Mexico City, leading Larry Farmer and Ron Freeman to an African American sweep of the event in a time that would stand for over twenty years as the world record. All of which merely set up another moment of truth: What, if anything, would Evans and his teammates do? Would there be a repeat performance? Would they, could they, do something even more theatrical, more demonstrative?

Rumors, expectations, warnings, and threats circulated wildly in the moments leading up to their ceremony. With tensions at fever pitch, the trio—led by Evans—approached the podium wearing black tams and just prior to the formal start of the ceremony waved fists (ungloved) close to their heads. But then, at that crucial moment when the anthem started to play, the flags rose, and the eyes of the world came to focus upon them, Evans and his teammates blinked, as it were. They removed their hats and stood frozen in solemn attention.

Standing on the podium after the whole thing was over, Evans and his fellow Americans would again display clenched fists, but these lacked Smith and Carlos's impact, not only because they took place at the conclusion of the ceremony but also because they were accompanied by smiles and waves to the crowd (see fig. 6). Even so, as Larry James remembers it, the first twenty questions they faced in the interview room involved "demonstrating": "Are you holding back?" the reporters wanted to know. "Have you done enough?"[94] The real question on everyone's minds was whether Evans and his teammates were simply waiting to take their final stand until after the 4 × 400 meter relay (which they were understandably expected to win). Their answers to all these questions and suggestions were evasive or sarcastic—for example, when asked why they had worn hats, Evans simply replied, "it was raining and we didn't want to get wet"—and thus did nothing to change the conciliatory impression their actions had conveyed.

Other gestures that made reference to Smith and Carlos would follow as well. Evans, Farmer, and Freeman, this time along with teammate Vincent Matthews, would repeat a similar scenario after winning the 4 × 400 meter relay. Wyomia Tyus, Barbara Ferrell, and the black women of the 400-meter relay team (the same women who had been rebuffed by Edwards and his organization earlier in the year) would dedicate their gold medals to their teammates, and both the Cuban men's and women's 400-meter relay teams presented their silver medals to African American political leaders in honor of the two suspended sprinters. It is interesting to note that Ferrell recalls her initial impression of the demonstrations as being negative, this changed, she said, only after Smith and Carlos explained to their teammates "where they were coming from." After that, "it became a solid thing."[95] One wonders if the USOC and IOC overreaction didn't also contribute to Ferrell's change of heart. Even erstwhile moderate African American athletes like Bob Beamon and Ralph Boston

Fig. 6. Lee Evans and teammates at the 400 meter medal
ceremony. © Bettmann/CORBIS.

were so incensed that they donned knee-high black socks while they received their medals for the long jump (Beamon's gold for his miraculous
twenty-nine-foot long jump that was the defining athletic moment of the
Olympiad). But these were all anticlimactic. Evans and his teammates, by
doing what they had done on the victory stand—or, more precisely, by
not doing what they might have done—had allowed the social solidarities
and hierarchies Smith and Carlos had so successfully challenged to stand
now unquestioned. All of which is confirmed by the fact that Everett

Barnes, the acting director of the USOC, could say, "Everything worked out fine. Lee Evans accepted his medal in fine style."[96]

Even as they walked back through the tunnel and in the press interview, Evans's teammate Vincent Matthews would recall, it was obvious that "people" (it is not clear whether he is referring to their supporters or detractors) "expected even more from us."[97] Edwards, among others, would criticize Evans unmercifully in the months and years that followed, saying Evans had "disappointed his people" and even accusing him of having "sold out" for the chance to sign a professional football contract. According to Edwards, Evans had tried "to stand up and be counted on both sides of the fence at once . . . [in] a struggle with no middle ground."[98] It may be, in an immediate sense, that Evans did sacrifice sociopolitical solidarity with Smith, Carlos, and their racial cause for personal interests of some sort or another. Several years later his teammate Vincent Matthews would write:

> In retrospect, it was clear that all of us harbored some type of fear over possible reprisals. We knew we wanted to do something significant on the victory stand, but it was like we had allowed ourselves to become brainwashed. . . . We were all young and felt that we might be jeopardizing our future careers in the sport . . . [99]

Evans himself publicly acknowledged as much upon his return to the States, telling one reporter, "I wish I'd done what Tommie and John did. I wish I could have been more militant."[100]

Tempered by my sociological inclinations, however, I see something besides personal or moral failure in this episode. What I prefer to focus on instead is how solidly the forces of power must have been stacked against any further demonstration by the time Evans and his teammates finally mounted the victory platform. Evans, after all, was a committed and dedicated supporter of Edwards and the OPHR initiative in the year leading up to the Games. His statements to the press were as forceful as any Carlos or anyone except perhaps Smith uttered. In recent years, in fact, Smith has even claimed that it was Evans who convinced him to get involved with the OPHR in the first place.[101] And the fact that Evans and his teammates were searching for some way to express their outrage and sympathy for Smith and Carlos is undeniable. Matthews, for example, recalls how Evans suggested that prior to the awards ceremony for their relay they walk out with their left fists under their warm-up jackets just to plant the seeds of doubt and fear in the minds of the authorities.[102] Such juvenile gestures ultimately failed miserably, of course, but not only, I think, for a lack of will.

By the time Evans and his teammates had run their races and mounted the victory podium, the stakes were higher, much higher than they had been for Smith and Carlos, whose demonstration was so unexpected that the forces of power—the various Olympic organizations, government officials, commercial interests and the like—had absolutely no opportunity to line up against them. As Smith would put it: "Lee ran after I ran, so he was on the spot."[103] Here, I am not just referring to the threat of Olympic expulsion or the promise of a professional athletic contract, both of which were certain to follow, contingent upon their actions. In addition, Evans and his teammates had to consider permanent banishment from the world of sport (heretofore the only world they had ever known) or blacklisting that would have changed their lives forever, whether they stayed in sports or not. And then there were the vague but ominous threats of violence and even death against them and their families. For a black man in the 1960s, living in the shadow of Martin Luther King Jr., Malcolm X, and many, many others, these possibilities were probably more real and more compelling than any of us can imagine today.

I believe that if there was no middle ground in the struggle over national and racial identities in the Olympics (as Edwards quite correctly saw it), neither was there much ground at all left on the side of the struggle where Smith and Carlos now stood. Matthews described what he and Evans and the others now faced:

> We had seen what had happened to Tommie and John and it wasn't the fact that they had been thrown out of the Olympic village that hit home as much as the absence of any meaningful support for their cause. No one understood what Tommie and John did or why they did it, and no one wanted to understand. It was as if they couldn't wait to get rid of them.[104]

It is difficult to imagine what a public affirmation of solidarity might have consisted of, or what it could have accomplished. Smith and Carlos had already charted those waters and captured those headlines. And even if such a demonstration could have been conceived, it clearly would have come at a far greater and more certain price than the one Smith and Carlos eventually paid for their actions. To put it another way, I think that the demands and pressures placed upon Evans were more irreconcilable than any expectations Smith and Carlos may have faced prior to their protest. For him to have done anything that even smacked of confrontation would probably not only have failed, but would have meant certain symbolic, if not literal, martyrdom.

Evans was under tremendous pressures from all sides, and it showed.

His physical confrontation with USOC president Douglas Roby just before the 400-meter final was only the most public example. Evans admitted having been too shaken to eat during these days and found himself actually crying several times. He recalled senselessly beating his fists against elevator walls on the very day he would try to realize his lifelong dream of winning Olympic gold. If the metaphor of an emotional roller-coaster was ever appropriate, it would certainly apply to what Evans went through in these twenty-four hours. A photograph in a French magazine captured it perfectly: Evans is standing on the victory stand above his two teammates after having just mounted the victory podium for the first time. On what should have been one of the triumphant moments of his life, the new Olympic champion is staring off into space, biting his lips, a hand on one hip and the other clutching his Olympic awards. What teammate Larry James recalled feeling prior to the ceremony might well have held for Evans as well:

> By then I could do without the ceremony. They could even keep the medal. It was the year and a half of getting ready for this that was important. The long siege of a season, the training at Tahoe, the air, the guys, the war stories. All that floods back. That's what I lived for. The victory ceremony? That seemed as if it were for someone else. [105]

It was, to reappropriate an old sports line, the thrill of victory and the agony of activism. In this respect, it may be Evans and his experience (more than Smith and Carlos and theirs) that really helps us understand both how high the stakes of Olympic protest actually were and who, ultimately, held the better hand in this power play.

PART TWO

The Aftermath, 1968 to 1978 and Beyond

Men fight and lose the battle, and the thing they fought for comes about in spite of their defeat, and when it comes, it turns out not to be what they meant, and other men have to fight for what they meant under another name.

—William Morris, *A Dream of John Ball* (1886)

Chapter 6

Only Just Begun

Thus the fireworks were finished. Tommie Smith and John Carlos had taken their stand. The forces of power and public opinion had lined up against them. The results would appear to have been decisive: little support materialized and no meaningful change was produced. Save for a few observations about the impact of these events on the subsequent personal lives of these two African American athletes and the requisite hand-wringing about the "politics" of sport revealed therein, the story would seem to be over. Certainly this is how it is often told (if it is told at all). However, such a version, such an abrupt and disappointing ending to the story, is as inaccurate as it is unsatisfying.

For one thing, the image of Smith and Carlos on the Olympic victory stand did not, would not, simply disappear. Burned into people's memories and the public consciousness, it would be referenced, remembered, ruminated upon, and intensely argued about in numerous communities and contexts for years to come. Indeed, the struggle over its meaning and significance was far from over; the image was quickly becoming a contested terrain all its own. The second problem with ending this narrative in 1968 with Smith and Carlos's expulsion from Mexico City is that the movement of which they were part didn't end then or there. Quite the contrary: ideas, ideals, interests, and identities these two athletes represented and quite literally embodied on the victory stand continued to vex the American establishment, athletic and otherwise, for the better part of the subsequent decade. And it is precisely as this struggle is played out that the true outcomes, accomplishments, and ultimate limitations of the revolt of black athletes are revealed. If the fireworks had dissipated, in other words, the struggle over race and sport in the United States had only just begun.

The Image as Contested Terrain

When Tommie Smith returned to San Jose to register for his final semester of college and ROTC classes, he was advised to turn in his uniform and keep his mouth shut. Then Jim Brown, who had loaned Smith money against the football contract he had planned to sign with the Los Angeles Rams, informed the Olympic champion the team was no longer interested in him. In their view, Smith had showed himself to be "too eager"; to add insult to injury, Brown demanded his money back as well. To support himself and his family, Smith spent several aimless years trying to become a professional football player on the Cincinnati Bengals "taxi squad."[1] For a while there was talk of John Carlos and his OPHR lawyers suing the United States Olympic Committee or even the U.S. government, but this never materialized and Carlos, who had collegiate eligibility remaining, rededicated himself to his track-and-field career. He quickly solidified his rank as one of the top sprinters in the world; almost just as quickly (in less than a year after Mexico City) he would reject black militancy and become a "goodwill representative" for the Seafarers International Union School of Seamanship under the supervision of Pappy Gault, the Olympic boxing coach who had encouraged George Foreman to wave the American flag in Mexico City. "I'll still be right along with the black movement," he would say vaguely, "but I'll be more discrete in my actions, . . . changing my tactics." That was as far as his new coach would let him go.[2]

Even more telling, perhaps, is the extent to which the lives of other African American Olympians, Smith and Carlos's teammates, were affected. The 1968 American Olympic team was the only one not invited to the White House after the Games (although a few individual athletes, including George Foreman and Bill Toomey, did make appearances).[3] Some individuals, such as 100-meter champion Jimmy Hines lost endorsement deals and sponsorship contracts (or had such offers slashed dramatically) simply because they were associated—rightly or wrongly— with the demonstration in Mexico City. Hines estimates that Smith and Carlos's protest cost him at least two million dollars. Others, like 400-meter man Larry James, simply lost their bearings. "You got tagged in

'68 and you had to explain who you were and what you'd done without dishonoring the others . . . The whole leadership thing wanted for me [and] I started to question everything."[4]

Still, none of this was enough for Avery Brundage, the man who as IOC president had been so instrumental in bringing the full weight of the Olympic establishment down on Smith and Carlos. When the Mexican organizing committee released its official documentary of the Olympiad featuring the two African American athletes, Brundage, his biographer reports, immediately registered vehement objections against the film. "That nasty demonstration against the United States flag by Negroes," he fulminated, "had nothing to do with sport. . . . [It] has no more place in the record of the games than the gunfire" that had occurred during the student riots in the days leading up to the Games. Brundage was determined to, as he put it, "erase" the image of their medal ceremony from the Olympic record and public memory altogether.[5] When his objections were not upheld, the IOC president went so far as to try to amend his organization's bylaws to allow the Executive Committee itself (*his* committee) to veto the film. Brundage did not win this battle. But he did succeed in eliminating pictures of the protest from the USOC's official report on the Games, and in his own extensive personal film collection kept only ABC's film, which made no reference to Smith and Carlos's demonstration.[6] Moreover, throughout the final four years of his tenure as IOC president, Brundage continued to push the IOC and USOC to enact new rules and regulations guarding against the repetition of any such demonstrations, and guaranteeing the harsh and immediate censure of any athletes who failed to comply. Even so, Brundage could never put the incident behind him. Writing in an unpublished autobiography several years before his death, Brundage would complain: "Warped mentalities and cracked personalities seem to be everywhere and impossible to eliminate."[7]

If these memories proved "impossible to eliminate," it was because there were those—much as the *Chicago Tribune* had correctly if unhappily predicted during the Games—who honored Smith and Carlos and celebrated their demonstration as adamantly as people like Brundage despised them. When Carlos returned from Mexico City, for example, he was presented, before an overflow crowd at Howard University, with a medallion that pictured Malcolm X. He called it his "gold medal."[8] Writing just a few months later, Harry Edwards took pains to show that "back home" Smith and Carlos had been treated as "heroes to black Americans" citing receptions accorded them by African countries at the United Nations and by black Americans in Washington, D.C.; tributes paid by black leaders such as H. Rap Brown, Stokely Carmichael, Adam Clayton Powell, and Elijah

Muhammad; and letters and telegrams sent by whites and blacks from all around the world.[9] Pictures of Lee Evans and his 400-meter relay team in the black berets giving their own clenched-fist salutes appeared on radical postcards and in Black Panther newspapers, and black students took to reenacting Smith and Carlos's clenched-fist salute in athletic contexts and arenas across the country.[10] College campuses were an especially popular forum for celebrating Smith and Carlos's gesture. In a piece for the University of California, Davis, *Daily Aggie* and later distributed to other California newspapers, a young black student named Robert Stanley Oden called it "one of the most beautiful and gallant scenes ever staged by anyone in the Olympics." "Their efforts might not have made things physically easier for Afro-Americans," Oden claimed, "but it certainly gave Black people a mental uplift to see Black Power at work in Mexico City."[11] Wally Jones and Tim Washington's *Black Champions Challenge American Sports* (1972) lamented that the USOC had singled Smith and Carlos out simply "for saying what Black people had been thinking for centuries." Nevertheless, the book came to a defiant conclusion: "Black people all over the country were proud. No more would they sit back and hope hopes would give them what was theirs. It would be taken, if need be, by any means necessary."[12]

The extent of these differences is revealed in a public opinion poll on issues of politics and race conducted by the sports scholar and activist Richard Lapchick early in his career in 1973. In one of the items in this survey Lapchick asked blacks and whites from six different cities across the country if they felt the gestures made by black U.S. athletes in the 1968 Games were "justifiable." He found that 57 percent of the African Americans surveyed thought Smith and Carlos were in fact justified in their victory-stand demonstration (8 percent undecided) while only 32 percent of whites felt the same (again 8 percent undecided).[13] On this point, a pivotal scene in the Hollywood blockbuster *Remember the Titans* provides an apt historical illustration: in it, white and black teammates on a newly integrated high school football team come to blows over a dispute involving a poster of Smith and Carlos on the victory stand.[14]

As with all public opinion research, these figures must be interpreted carefully and cautiously. The racial cleavages stand out clearly, of course. But the fact that almost one-third of African Americans did not approve of the demonstration, while almost one-third of whites did, suggest that factors other than race—or in combination with race—may have been part of the equation. This caution is further reinforced by the fact that several of the black sports histories of the period were, in notable contrast to the Jones and Washington volume, decidedly ambivalent about the

Smith-Carlos demonstration. Jack Orr (1969), for example, called it "the most bizarre moment" of the Games; others simply avoided discussing it altogether. In this case (as with so many others in American culture), it is easy to overstate racial unity and consensus.

And it wasn't just black people who were mobilized and inspired by memories of the demonstration. Posters of the two athletes poised on the victory stand appeared within weeks, as John MacAloon recalls in an unpublished manuscript, in "head-shops, radical churches and student-movement headquarters" around the country. A book called *Protest! Student Activism in America* (Foster and Long 1970) discusses Harry Edwards and black Olympic activism in two separate places. Reflecting on life in the student New Left in the 1960s, former student activists Peter Collier and David Horowitz (1989, p. 290) recall that "Tommie Smith and John Carlos were heroes for giving the clenched-fist salute on the victory stand." During the course of my research, I have come across scores of people—from all different races and many different countries[15]—who recall such memories vividly. Other researchers and writers tell similar stories. Kenny Moore, the author of the important 1991 *Sports Illustrated* profile of Tommie Smith, for example, told me that his own English literature professor kept a poster of Smith and Carlos hanging on the back of his office door in the 1970s. This scholar told Moore that "their strength, their power, and their restraint" inspired everything he did and helped him summon up his own resolve when "the going got tough."[16]

Given how popular the image of Smith and Carlos on the victory stand came to be in the 1990s, it is important to reiterate that positive views of Smith and Carlos were clearly outside the bounds of dominant, mainstream American culture in the immediate post-1968 period. Those who celebrated the demonstration in the late sixties and early seventies usually did so as a way to capture and convey their own alienation, their frustration with mainstream, white middle-class society. That is, the gesture had meaning and significance far beyond the world of sport. It was precisely in this sense that the image served as an object of ideological contention, conflict, and contestation, a symbolic lightning rod by which one could establish one's radical credentials or against which one could ruminate against the supposed excesses of the Left. Indeed, by the end of the decade the Smith-Carlos picture appeared most often as it did in William O'Neil's (1978) widely read history of the American sixties: without commentary, simply as a visual representation of the cleavages, conflicts, and turmoil of recent social history in the United States.

All of this speaks volumes about both the confusing and contested culture of race in immediate post–civil rights era as well as the powerful yet paradoxical role that popular cultural images and practices such as sport played therein. If, however, the image of Smith and Carlos on the victory stand transcended the world of sport in many ways, it also remained an image of the sports world first and foremost. And no other community was as deeply and directly impacted by and preoccupied with the Smith-Carlos demonstration.

For most sports people, the image was a painful reminder of or rude awakening to social forces they believed would better remain outside the world of sport—not just with respect to race but also to issues and interests concerning such things as amateurism, authority, representation, eligibility, and so on. This is what was generally lumped together under the category of "politics"—not just in the United States, but most of the Western world as well. Here, it is interesting to note the Western European perception of Smith and Carlos's demonstration. While Europeans generally claimed themselves to be "sympathetic" to Smith and Carlos's cause (which is to say that they were critical of American race relations), most of them believed that Smith and Carlos had gone too far on the victory stand. At the heart of their critique was the fact that Europeans observers insisted on seeing the demonstration strictly as a "black power" protest. While Americans across the political spectrum used this same label, it had much more differentiated and diffuse meanings and implications in the United States. For Americans, this "black power" label could refer to either a political position or an essentialist racist ideology (or both) and have either a positive or negative connotation; for the sports-minded European, however, it was almost always negative and essentialist. That is, European audiences were largely insensitive to the nuances and subtleties of Smith's statements on race in the United States, not to mention his refusal to describe the gesture itself as a "black power salute." Ironically they were far more comfortable with Carlos and his more radical, inflammatory account. This interpretation led more than a few to draw an unfortunate analogy between Smith and Carlos's victory-stand salute and the duck-stepping Nazis saluting the führer during the 1936 Berlin Games.[17]

If the dominant view of the sporting public was that whatever the Smith-Carlos image was believed to represent it was better kept outside of the athletic arena, there were others in the athletic community—especially young athletes, aspiring athletes, and sports fans with an emerging awareness of broad social issues if not yet a fully developed political consciousness—for whom the image represented just the opposite, something much more complicated and demanding. In the words of Richard Lapchick, "The memory of Smith and Carlos on the victory stand would not go away. It became the Olympic picture. Everything had changed."[18]

New York Times sportswriter William Rhoden recalls that the "militance" of the gesture "allowed me to expand the definition of myself as an athlete." No longer did he have to keep his identities as "student" and "athlete" separate and distinct. "Smith and Carlos made me understand that athletes were not removed from the fray; in fact, their visibility and contact with the public allowed a certain opportunity to speak loudly." More than this, Rhoden concludes, they provided an opportunity to "go on the attack"[19]—all of which brings us, not incidentally, to the second, more concrete and, in many ways, much more significant reason to continue the story of black athletic protest.

The "Revolt," Continued

In his first public statement officially acknowledging the collapse of the OPHR boycott initiative back in August 1968, Harry Edwards had predicted that the aborted effort would be only the beginning of a much larger offensive against racism and exploitation in American sports. He told the delegates to the National Black Power Conference in Philadelphia that there were "many things yet to be done." Saying it was imperative that the struggle for black liberation "push forward," Edwards promised to focus activist-minded athletes on the institutional terrain of sport itself. Among the actions he envisioned, Edwards included "a total movement against Negro and white racist athletic departments at the collegiate level"; "a total move against professional athletes"; "a general endorsement of an athletic boycott against all Mormon dominated schools"; "immediate preparations . . . for the 1972 Olympic Games"; and, finally, the formation of a "Federation of Black Amateur Athletes" to protect them against "the ravages of exploitation."[20]

Edwards made all this sound so logical and inevitable that it is easy to overlook the rather significant strategic shift that had taken place. The idea of boycotting the 1968 Olympic Games had originated out of the notion of using sport to protest general societal racism; now, Edwards was charging sport itself with being racist and discriminatory. In other words, the focus had shifted from calling attention to racism *through* sport to protesting against racism *in* sport.

The groundwork for this subtle but not insignificant shift had actually begun to take shape in the process of trying to build both public and grassroots support for an Olympic boycott. In this process, discussed extensively in chapter 4, Edwards and his colleagues were forced to concede that attacking lingering racism and discrimination in the world of sport itself was the only way to get athletes to even take seriously the idea of an

African American boycott. In many ways, it was better than the boycott threat, because it mobilized a broader constituency and found a good deal more public support. In any case, focusing on racism in sport certainly received a much better reception in 1968—from athletes, the media, and the public at large—than that accorded the idea of a boycott.

Two years later, writing in the preface to the paperback edition of *Revolt,* Edwards was able to tell his readers that "[t]he struggle for justice in the realm of athletics has intensified" (1970, p. xviii). Edwards, playing the media and public as always, almost certainly overstated the case. It was (and indeed, still is) hard to imagine a period when racial unrest and African American discontent in athletics was more intensive and widespread than the Olympic year of 1968. But in making such an audacious claim Edwards was also sending the message—contradicting the hopes and expectations of the sporting establishment—that the African American athletic resistance was far from over.

Edwards cited a number of protests, incidents, and other developments that lent credence to his claim. One was a continuing series of protests directed against the "anti-black policies of the Mormon Church," focusing especially on the flagship Brigham Young University. Another was Curt Flood's suit against the "reserve clause" (or, on behalf of the right to free agency) in Major League Baseball—which, according to Edwards, was an example of an emerging move by black athletes against the exploitative "master-slave" relationships of American professional sports. On the "international scene" Edwards noted that South Africa's apartheid policies were coming under "increasing attack" now that the Olympic ban had been upheld and extended to sports such as golf, rugby, and tennis. (This, especially with South African authorities twice denying a visa to Arthur Ashe, the black U.S. Open Tennis Champion slated to represent the American team in Davis Cup competition.)[21] Also, according to Edwards, a growing number of sports reporters were aiding in the struggle through "sympathetic writings or their outright statements of support." Some, Edwards intimated, had even voluntarily provided invaluable information to "individuals and groups in the forefront of the revolt." Edwards also reported that the black athlete's federation he envisioned with the initial publication of *Revolt* was "well on its way to becoming a reality." As he put it: "Potential officers have been contacted, a number of prominent athletes have been approached to serve as possible charter members of the federation and existing organizations have been contacted about the possibility of taking on the work of contract negotiations, business counseling and so on" (1969, p. 114).

If he had been more theoretically attuned to what I called in chapter 4 the "politics of oppositional style," Edwards might also have talked about the distinctive aesthetic African American male athletes were cultivating both on and off the fields of play. Consider, for example, the touchdown dances in the end zone by someone like Elmo Wright or a bit later Billy "White Shoes" Johnson; or how star players such as Lew Alcindor or Bobby Moore took Islamic names (Kareem Abdul-Jabaar and Amad Rashad respectively); or, perhaps more memorably, of "natural" hairstyles and big bushy Afros sported by black athletes male and female, and of the near complete and utter transformation of basketball into "the Black man's game" as later captured in the work of cultural critic Nelson George (1992). Following the lead of Muhammad Ali, as Jeffrey Sammons (1995) has analyzed, black athletes—especially males—were finding ways to express themselves on "American patriotism, integrationism, athletic codes of behavior and obligatory black humility" (p. 162), all without saying a word.

Likewise, if he had been more interested in grassroots, participatory sport—in school sports, youth development initiatives, and community-based recreation and fitness programs—Edwards would have been able to speak of other, quieter but no less significant revolutions as well. Urban recreation programs (like Lew Alcindor's Operation Sports Rescue or the NCAA's newly created National Youth Sports Program), which actively promoted and put into practice the notion that sports participation could be used for the purposes of outreach and intervention to disadvantaged minority youths, were springing up all over the country. Not only were such programs positioned to transform the conception and delivery of sport to underserved populations, but many of those associated with these programs began making demands that colleges and universities take better care of the African American athletes they recruited, and even to give something back to the neighborhoods, high schools, and communities from which they came.[22]

Edwards touches on this latter point in his study of university life among African American students published just one year after *Revolt* under the title *Black Students* (1970). Indeed, it is in ongoing and even intensifying protests against "athletic exploitation and injustice" at colleges and universities all around the country that Edwards found his most compelling evidence that the revolt would "not soon die." I discussed some of the earliest of the episodes—such as the one involving Bob Beamon and his teammates at the University of Texas, El Paso—previously in chapter 4. There, I argued that these protests were driven by the twin engines of African American athletes wanting to contribute to the post–civil rights struggle for racial justice in the United States and their more basic frustrations with the blatant forms of racism and discrimination that lingered in the world of sport. Indeed, I suggested that the beauty of these protests, in contrast to that of the proposed Olympic boycott, was how they accomplished both goals at once. But in this context, I want to emphasize a different point: the broad scope and deeper systemic significance of this persistent protest and unrest.

In what to my knowledge is the only substantive analysis on the topic, the sports historian David K. Wiggins (1988, 1997) concentrates on the confrontations involving the basketball team at the University of California, Berkeley, in 1968, the Syracuse University football squad the following fall, and the football team at Oregon State in the off-season after that. And in framing these case studies, he also mentions a number of other such episodes. In January 1969, for example, five black football players at Princeton University charged their coaches, Dick Coleman and Walter "Pet" McCarthy, with "racist tendencies in coaching." The players' chief complaint was that they were passed over for starting positions (especially in the so-called skilled positions in the backfield) despite performing well. The following season, in October, the University of Wyoming's football coach Lloyd Eaton kicked about a dozen black players off the team for asking if they could enact some type of protest in their upcoming game against Brigham Young. About a month after that, coach John Pont of Indiana dismissed a number of black players from the football team when they boycotted practice two days in a row on the grounds that Pont had created an atmosphere that was "mentally depressing and morally discouraging to blacks." That winter black athletes charged the University of Pittsburgh's athletic department with racial discrimination. Several black basketball players at Buffalo State quit the team under similar accusations, touching off what Wiggins describes as "a violent disturbance" on campus. Then in 1972 the one and only black baseball player at Oregon State University took his coach Gene Tanselli to court, a move that led to Tanselli's eventual dismissal.

It is difficult to say just how many such episodes actually took place. In *Revolt* (p. 88), Edwards says that 37 occurred in 1968 alone; in a later work he suggests that as many as 180 incidents unfolded during the following academic year (Edwards 1973b, p. 151). Wiggins endorses the estimate Edwards gave for 1968 but simply states that black athletic resistance on college campuses continued on "different kinds of campuses in various locations across the country" over a four-year period (1997, p. 124). For the quantitatively minded, Wiggins's gloss may not be particularly satisfying; nonetheless, it is sufficient. For what is at issue, as Wiggins correctly surmises, is not the actual number and/or frequency of such incidents but rather their intensity, their collectivity, and the consequences and reverberations. Wiggins summarizes:

> The disturbances became so intense on some campuses that black athletes lost their scholarships, black and white athletes became bitter antagonists, coaches either quit or were fired, athletic directors had their power usurped, newly created organizations were established on campus expressly to look into the problems of racial discrimination and national organizations such as the NAACP were called in to settle campus disputes. (p. 124)

In fact, racial protests in sport convinced many coaches, athletic directors, and college presidents that nothing less than the "future of college athletics was at stake." (Wiggins, in fact, uses this phrase—which came from a statement made by a prominent athletic director implicated in one of the cases he focused on—as the title of his study.) "We are facing the greatest crisis in sports history," Oklahoma State and U.S. Olympic basketball coach Hank "Mo" Iba told *Sports Illustrated* in the summer of 1969. "In the next eight months we could see sports virtually destroyed. Nobody seems to realize how critical this situation is."[23]

"It's Not Just Race"

Wiggins focuses almost entirely on the racial dimensions of these confrontations and in the following chapter, for some obvious reasons and a few others I will expound upon shortly, I will as well. However, it is important to first underscore what made such incidents so fundamentally threatening to those on the front lines of the amateur athletic establishment: namely, that most of them were about much more than racial discrimination and mistreatment, and that white athletes were increasingly and more directly involved.

For some athletes, the issues were strictly sports-based—concerns about training techniques, coaching philosophies, eligibility standards, and the like. For others, grievances had more to do with life outside of sport—especially the extent to which coaches and programs could institute curfews, set class attendance policies, or regulate leisure activities. Strange and unlikely as it may sound today, many of these conflicts were focused on such small and seemingly insignificant issues such as hair length, facial hair, and personal hygiene.[24] For still others, the issues were couched in more conventional political terms: for example, whether athletes were required to participate in the patriotic displays that often accompanied sporting events—or, conversely, whether they should be allowed to participate in activist-oriented political demonstrations and protests outside of their respective fields of play.

At stake for athletes on one level was the way they were treated, what might be called "the conditions of their labor."[25] What was also and more broadly at stake was the relationship between sports and the rest of social life—that is, what role sport should play in society and what this implied for the very definition of what it meant to be an athlete. Either way, such activism and unrest presented a direct challenge to the integrity, institutional authority, and social purpose of the sports world as traditionally understood—its standards of discipline, its understanding of and way of dealing with athletes, its sense of its own place in the broader social world. In this respect athletes were very much a part of young Americans' radical rethinking of societal norms and practices at this time. According to UCLA football coach Tommy Prothero, "It's no longer the autocratic society it was when I played where a Bob Neyland or Wallace Wade (two famously successful disciplinarian coaches) would just say, 'you'll do it because I say so.' Now you have to explain yourself. The logic behind it. The philosophy."[26] F. Melvin Cratsley, a basketball coach who lost his job at Pittsburgh's newly formed Point Park College after getting caught up in one of these disturbances, put it like this to a sympathetic reporter:

> I was fired because I was too disciplined. . . . I wanted my players to wear blazers, get haircuts, wear a tie and take a bath once in a while, be on time. They didn't want to do these things. I object to players telling me they want to wear beards, long hair and all the rest because the next thing they want to do is run the team. More important than the beard, is what it represents: rebellion.

"It probably originated as a black problem," Cratsley speculated, "but today it's not just race. It's all types of kids."[27]

In the summer of 1969, just one year after its monumental series on the black athlete, *Sports Illustrated* commissioned John Underwood (the writer responsible for its antidemonstration story on the Olympics the previous year) for a three-part series called "The Desperate Coach." Focusing on those who bore the brunt of the unrest, the series is one of the few public documents at the time that acknowledged and captured what was going on inside the athletic establishment. Coaches, as John Underwood memorably described, were left "bewildered, angry and disillusioned, no longer certain of their mission or, in some cases, their relevance."[28] Again, the fact that these incidents increasingly involved and even featured white student-athletes seems to have shaken coaches as much as anything. For example, Washington football coach Jim Owens told Underwood he felt haunted by two white students he had. They came to campus, "good boys—intelligent, first-rate athletes," he said. "Now you see them and they're all the cliches: long dirty hair, slovenly, anti-war, anti-Establishment. It's frightening. One fellow played for me [just last year]. He went so fast." Many coaches, according to Underwood, had similar stories. Oregon State's Dee Andros's version involved the son of an Air Force colonel. When he entered the program, this athlete was "big and strong and just first-class in every way," Andros recalled, "the best linebacker we ever had on the freshman team." But then something changed. "[I]n the spring, at the time of the boycott, he marched into my office and told me he wasn't coming out. I couldn't believe it. It made me sick to see what I was seeing. He was wearing sandals. No socks. His hair was down to his shoulders. He had a long beard. It was hell for me. The kid just turned my stomach."[29] That summer the NCAA Annual Coaches Convention gave resounding approval to motions to "bring about greater discussion of problems in athletics, whether of an athletic nature or not" (Edwards 1970, p. xxii).

It wasn't long before the discontented athletes found a name for themselves or, more precisely, for their movement: "the athletic revolution." It was a label that, not incidentally, both connected it to and distinguished it from black athletic resistance.[30]

Miguel De Capriles, one of the USOC officials who had been intimately involved in the dealings with Smith and Carlos and the IOC in Mexico City, had an accurate and acute sense of the threat posed by such a movement: "This, to my mind, is a very serious problem which is not limited to the Olympics; it runs right throughout our whole athletics-competitive scheme."[31] Although he didn't elaborate and none of his colleagues picked up the discussion, De Capriles was making an important point, one that many establishment figures understood intuitively even if they lacked the words or resolve to talk about explicitly. It wasn't just the established world of sport that coaches saw as being under attack by disgruntled young athletes; it was the whole, very traditional value system and vision of society that sport had conventionally been associated with. This is what the coaches John Underwood interviewed in the summer of 1969 took to calling, in private places and hushed tones, "the Problem." Cratsley, the fired Point Park coach I quoted above, was one of the few willing to talk about it on the record.

> Athletics are the last stronghold of discipline on the campus. It
> may be that they are in a life-or-death struggle on their own. I read
> somewhere—I clipped it out—that the aim of the New Left is to

replace the athlete with the hippie as the idol of the kids. I don't know if it can be done, but it seems society is intent on destroying Horatio Alger Jr. The oddball is getting control. The good guy is out-numbered. America seems interested only in glorifying the loser.

Legendary Alabama football coach Bear Bryant expanded from Cratsley into an entire critique of the recent changes in American culture. "Kids simply aren't as hungry as they used to be. Paying the price doesn't mean as much because everything comes easy. Folks get more on relief today than my papa did working. You see it on the campus. No matter how poor they are, they all have cars."[32] It wouldn't be long before these views were given much more public expression.

In a speech the USOC reprinted in its monthly newsletter, Amateur Athletic Union president Jesse Pardue told his audience that "important values in amateur sport" were "in danger." His use of the term values had the same impact and implication then as it has had in recent years among conservatives in American social and political culture. For Pardue believed that much of the problem was outside of sport, the result of the cultural changes and dramatic social cleavages of the 1960s. In deeply earnest tones, he spoke of the "erosion and destruction of our civiliza-tion," and in particular of its overemphasis on "entertainment, the lowest form of human appeal." At the heart of the problem, this leader of the American amateur athletic establishment argued, were college students finding "fault with their elders on issues such as the Vietnam War, race relations and their own education." Pardue spoke of the need to "restore high ethical standards to competitive amateur sports and to strengthen sportsmanship as a vital factor in human relations and understanding." He believed collegiate athletics were being attacked because they "depend upon the same principles of understanding and sportsmanship" and "re-spect for tradition and institutional pride . . . and order and discipline" that are part of the "hated establishment."[33]

I have already described how white athletes like Hal Connolly, Ed Burke, and the Harvard rowers stood both publicly and privately in sup-port of their African American teammates and friends at various times throughout the tumultuous year of 1968. These white athletes and count-less others like them seem to have been initially motivated by the desire to show sympathy for and solidarity with their black teammates. But they also began to realize that other issues and ideals were at stake in these en-counters, grand principles and concrete problems that implicated them deeply and directly. This is precisely how it played out for Paul Hoffman and his Harvard teammates on the American Olympic rowing team.

Recall that under pressure from USOC president Douglas Roby (himself under pressure from IOC president Avery Brundage), the team had been asked by U.S. Rowing officials to sign a statement vowing that they would not participate in "any demonstration of support for any disadvantaged people in the United States" prior to the Games.[34] Hoffman and his teammates had essentially complied with this request. But the way in which they crafted their compliance, the reaction their response engendered, and the events that subsequently unfolded tell a much deeper, more complicated, and more consequential story.

The Harvard crew responded to the USOC and U.S. Rowing Federation with a remarkable three-page letter explaining their desire to understand the problems of black Americans, both inside and outside of sport, and to communicate them back to white America. "Our basic premise," the rowers explained, "is that the Olympic Games should provide an opportunity for all athletes to get to know and understand each other better, whatever their backgrounds." Given that "a large number of black athletes are very disturbed," we have tried "to acquaint ourselves with their position" and as a result "feel we have at least a partial understanding of why the blacks feel as they do." The young rowers went on to say that they were now in "excellent position" to facilitate "discussion and exchange between teams [and] across sport boundaries" in Mexico City—which would, in turn, "stimulate and encourage a general interest in bridging the serious gaps of understanding that exist within the Olympic Team and within American society." All of this, the crew members insisted, was fundamentally "in accord with [the] spirit of the Olympics."

> We are sure that you are in basic agreement with us that the promotion of understanding among men is a fundamental part of the spirit of the Olympic Games. We sincerely hope that you will avoid taking stands that might unnecessarily alienate or antagonize members of the Team, thus cutting off the possibilities of communication. We hope instead that you will seek to encourage understanding within the Team, within the United States, and throughout the world.[35]

It is hard to imagine that these Ivy Leaguers were surprised that their attempt to establish common ground with the U.S. Rowing Federation and national Olympic Committee on the issue of racial unrest would prove futile. But they do not seem to have expected the intensity of the opposition they inflamed among Olympic authorities; nor, perhaps more significantly, did they anticipate the treatment that erstwhile leader Hoffman would receive in Mexico City. (Recall again that merely for having given

Smith and Carlos the Olympic Project for Human Rights buttons they used in the demonstration, Hoffman himself was almost kicked off of the team and out of Mexico.) And this seems to have affected profoundly the Harvard rowers and their understanding of the Olympic Games and sport in general.

Just two years later Hoffman's Olympic teammate and Harvard classmate John Cleve Livingston wrote an eighty-page honors thesis on the topic of politics, human rights, and the Olympics. In it, Livingston touched upon issues of free speech and due process, civil liberties, and the meaning of patriotism in the context of Olympic sport. Many of Livingston's criticisms reflected his belief that sport had failed to take full advantage of its opportunities for social betterment. But he was also concerned above all else with the political implications of sport, the meanings attached and attributed to Olympic athletes and the athlete's ability to respond to or resist dominant conceptions and perceptions. "Every athlete owes a certain obligation to his country," Livingston wrote in one passage, "but that obligation is not to represent his country in the best possible light but to represent it as he sees fit. This is the only type of representation which is in harmony with the Olympic ideal. To assume any other attitude toward your country is to portray it as something it is not."[36]

What we see here is that the "human rights" orientation of the OPHR was more than a symbol or slogan for white athletes like the Harvard rowers; it was, in fact, becoming a matter of common cause. Indeed, the early focus for many of the white athletes—especially for those who came out of the antiwar movement and the New Left—was on basic human rights issues: the right to be politically active; the right to refuse traditional stereotypes about athletes (whether it was that they were supposed to be Nixon-loving, hippie-stomping conservatives or simply uninterested, apolitical dumb jocks); the right to train and compete in events and using techniques they saw fit; the right to participate in the organization and administration of their sport; the right to earn a living; and finally, even the simple, seemingly innocuous right of wearing their hair any way they wanted.

Other white athletes took this human rights orientation in another direction. This group began to channel their feelings of alienation, exploitation, and powerlessness into a far-ranging critique of the American amateur athletic establishment, focusing especially on the leaders and elite organizations that sat at the head of the institutional hierarchy. Already simmering years earlier (much like African American unrest), this response began to take shape in the weeks and months immediately following the conclusion of the 1968 Olympic Games.

One of the first and most prominent public announcements came in a remarkable interview with Hal and Olga Connolly, the first couple of Olympic track and field, published by *Sport* magazine early in 1969.[37] The Connollys, described as "sort of unofficial spokesmen for amateur athletes, men and women, in this country," focused their attack on the organization most directly responsible for American track and field, the Amateur Athletic Union (AAU). They charged AAU officials with being "part-timers, businesspeople, wealthy men with no real background in athletics and no real understanding of the social or financial or competitive problems faced by athletes" and insisted that that "the AAU will have to give athletes more of a say in governing themselves." Athletes, Hal Connolly explained, "are demanding a say. And they will get it. And with it will come many reforms." Connolly claimed that one of the first of those would be the "outright abolition of the concept of amateurism as we know it." In his view, with appearance fees, payments from corporate promoters, padded expense accounts, and generous speaking engagements, there was no such thing as an amateur athlete in Olympic sport anyway. "There ain't no such animal," he insisted, derisively speaking instead of "shamateurism" where "everyone was on the take." The problem, in Connolly's view, was not the money itself; after all, athletes had to make a living, and training required huge amounts of time, energy, and funding. Rather, he said, "Everyone gets to make an honest living except the athlete."

The Connollys were not lonely, isolated voices on these matters. Quite the contrary, as Olga Connolly correctly pointed out, athletes around the United States and throughout the Olympic world in a variety of sports were beginning to stand up for their rights and demand institutional reforms to accommodate them. Within months, in fact, athletes in both the amateur and professional ranks would begin to organize themselves into unions, new organizers and spokespersons would emerge (Bay Area—based firebrand Jack Scott most prominent among them), and new points of contestation and struggle would take center stage—including, most notably, women organizing on behalf of gender equity in sport. In other words, this was a social movement very much on par with the revolt of the black athlete itself.

If they hadn't been aware of it already, news of this gathering storm came to the USOC executive board officially, in the form of a statement written by athletes from the 1968 Olympic team in the immediate aftermath of the Games.

> We, the undersigned athletes, are concerned about and committed to the Olympic ideal; have suffered because of the lack of communications between the United States Olympic Committee

and the athletes themselves; therefore, we demand that athletes who have competed in Mexico or in the last two Olympics be well-represented on the United States Olympic Committee in each sport, for the purpose of providing fresh, new and creative ideas.[38]

The statement was delivered to the board by John Sayre, a member of the special team of consultants the USOC had appointed prior to Mexico City in its ill-fated attempt to deal with the complaints and potential demonstrations by African American athletes. (This was the group headed by Jesse Owens; he was unable to make this particular meeting.) As part of his appearance, Sayre gave a detailed informal presentation as well.

Sayre, a former competitive rower and well-respected journalist (he was the sports editor of the Southern California—based *Pace* magazine and had penned a widely circulated preview to the Mexico City Games in 1966), prefaced his remarks by telling the executive board that his group had made one key discovery at the Games:

> It's a very different breed of athlete who represents their countries in the Olympics today . . . completely different from the athletics teams of just eight years ago. They have far greater interest, a far greater concern for what's happening in the world [and] in their country, and they have a far greater interest in participating in what's going on.

It was a point Sayre came back to repeatedly throughout the meeting, emphasizing that the 1968 squad was "the most mature and intelligent team we've ever had" and asserting, "you don't have the 'dumb athlete' of a few years ago . . . [t]hey come from the best universities in the country." Many of these athletes, he pointed out, were married and many were "professional men"—military officers, corporate managers, doctors, teachers, lawyers, engineers, and the like. Most important, according to Sayre, was that this "new breed" wanted to be involved in the Olympic movement as more than just competitors. "They don't want to run it, but they want to have a say and have a chance to participate" in running the contests they competed in. So strong were these impulses that Sayre concluded his formal remarks by saying: "I believe it has gotten to the point, now, where if they don't get a chance of participating, there will be considerably more trouble in 1972 than we had this year."[39]

Some American officials, such as the AAU representative Jay-Ehret Mahoney, tried to characterize the problems Sayre was describing as a mere matter of communication—or the lack thereof—between the USOC and its athletes.[40] Others viewed it simply as the product of a "generation gap." Sayre, however, insisted it was something more. He claimed that athletes wanted to know not only what was happening but why it was happening and, more important, he said they wanted to be participants in the system, part of the decision-making process itself. They wanted, in short, to "be treated as responsible men and women."[41]

Pressed to justify his analysis and ominous forecast, Sayre told the board that the true nature of the changes were revealed not by "the obvious incidents" that took place in Mexico City but by those that didn't. He went on to tell of an individual, whom he described only as "one of the most illustrious athletes the United States has," who had put plans in place to withdraw from the Games because he was "so disgusted with what he felt had happened to the Olympics" and "disgusted with the attitude of the officials" in particular. This athlete went so far as to compose an elaborate letter of resignation from the U.S. team and schedule a press conference for the day before the Opening Ceremonies, just three days before his own competition was to begin, in order to announce his decision. The only reason this individual didn't follow through with his plan, according to Sayre, was because of an emotionally draining, three-hour conversation with his coach, whom this athlete respected greatly. (Sayre calls this coach "one of the great men in the American Olympic movement" and says his genius in this situation was that he didn't try to talk this athlete out of this decision so much as try to understand the interests and ideas that precipitated it and help his athlete consider the implications of [and alternatives to] addressing them in this fashion.) When the board asked for assurances that this individual was not an "isolated" or "unusual" case, Sayre deferred, saying only that this athlete was "not a troublemaker" and reiterating that he was "one of the best-behaved and most concerned, most intelligent young athletes in America."[42]

In retrospect, it is obvious that Sayre was referring to Don Schollander, who, four years earlier in Tokyo (when he was eighteen), had become the first swimmer in history to win four gold medals in an Olympic Games. Schollander would publish an account of his ill-fated personal protest in a book called *Deep Water* (1971) written with Duke Savage, portions of which were widely reprinted in 1972 under the title "The Olympics That Almost Weren't." (Sayre himself signaled as much when later in the meeting he identified Schollander, a Yale graduate, as an athlete who "feels very deeply about the Olympics" and would make an excellent representative to the USOC.)[43]

Schollander's motivations were broad and multifaceted (if not altogether refined), and as such revealing of the unrest that would soon coalesce into a movement. The concern this former Olympic champion put at the top of his list was the intrusion of "politics" into an event he believed was designed to create "international amity and goodwill, thus leading to a happier and more peaceful world." "Before the Games even began," he wrote later, "the whole vocabulary of world dissension had attached itself to the one event designed to foster international goodwill: Revolution . . . repression . . . racism . . . communism . . . imperialism" (1971). Schollander was also well aware of and deeply distressed by the frustrations of black athletes, and the problems associated with drug testing, sex testing, and "payoffs to supposedly amateur athletes." And then there was the enormous pressure to win. As soon as he stepped off the plane in Mexico City, Schollander says he was asked if he would match his medal count of the previous games, even though he was only entered in two events this time around. For a guy who had hoped to savor his Olympic moment in Mexico in a way that had not been possible in Tokyo, this was almost more than he could handle. It convinced Schollander that the Olympic ideal was either "corrupted" or "antiquated." Although he never quite decided which, Schollander was not willing to simply sit idly by. "Something," he insisted in the speech he never delivered, "had to be done to change the direction of the Olympic movement."

On the need for change Schollander struck a chord. It would not be long before he found himself in common cause not just with Hal Connolly, Paul Hoffman, and Cleve Livingston but with hundreds and thousands of disgruntled athletes, black and white, all across the country in a wide variety of sports, at all levels. And Sayre saw it coming. With his colleagues on the USOC's board of consultants, Sayre had already put together a proposal that would have created ten new, at-large voting seats for athletes on the USOC's board of directors.[44] Near the end of his exchange with the USOC, Sayre reiterated his conviction that something had to be done. "If athletes aren't given some kind of responsible voice," he said—pausing, almost as if for dramatic effect, until he was prompted by USOC president Roby's anxious "yes, yes . . ."—"there will be serious trouble."[45]

The "Other" Athletic Revolt

Even more than the resistance of black athletes, the movement that came to be called the athletic revolution was a broad and diffuse constellation of groups, interests, ideals, and objectives stretching across sports, across social groups, and across the different levels of sport in the United States. It was a movement concerned, in one way or another, with the rights, experiences, and opportunities of all athletes, involving the conditions of their participation as well as the broader symbolic meanings and values associated with their athletic performances and sport in general.

Criticisms of the sort detailed above—of the administrative structure of sport and the relative powerlessness of athletes therein—emerged in dozens of sports and turned into demands for "athletes' rights" in amateur athletics and free agency in professional sports. At both levels, unionization became a watchword and a rallying cry. Issues regarding sources of support, rates of compensation, contractual obligations, and eligibility rules were at the core of such organizations, but new concerns such as steroid use, training techniques, and career length also began to take shape. Issues of access and equality were taken up by traditionally underserved populations as well by those in the sport community who saw the need to develop a broader, more democratic and community-based orientation to sport. Women, soon to be empowered and emboldened by the passage of Title IX, were especially activated during this period, advocating not only for equal opportunity but also for altogether new institutions and understandings of sporting practice.

Calls for entirely new models and conceptions of sport began to be sounded and heard with regularity. There were visions of a more participant-oriented, more democratically operated (and owned) sport; sports that were more widely and equitably accessible, and oriented toward participation rather than achievement and spectatorship, toward fitness, health, and recreation rather than winning at the highest levels. Under the influence of Jack Scott, who wrote the books that would become the "sacred texts" of the movement (1969, 1971), the equivalents of Harry Edwards's *Revolt*, there was a sustained push to emphasize the intrinsic value of pure sport and to argue for "athletics for athletes." Sport, in this vision, was "to be run in a democratic manner and all of those involved would have a say . . . Unlike today's static, authoritarian, tradition-bound athletic programs, it would allow radical change in order to serve properly each new group of athletes" (Scott 1971, p. 213).[46] Included here as well was the desire of high-performance athletes to have public lives and identities that transcended the traditional dumb-jock stereotypes, that allowed them to have interests and ideas that were neither contained by nor even connected with their participation in sport. For some, these concerns had to do mainly with politics (cf. Ashton 1972); for others—someone like Joe Namath comes to mind (Bloom 1988)—it had more to do with issues of lifestyle, self-expression, and marketability; but for many—including Steve Prefontaine, the fabulously talented and free-spirited miler from Oregon who played a key role in trying to organize alternative track-and-field competitions (Jordan 1997)—the two were indelibly linked.

Activists and organizations with related agendas, interests, and ideals began to appear in nations across the Olympic movement, as both Olga Connolly and John Sayre had alluded to in the commentaries cited above. Sayre, for example, described how the Australian rowing team (which won the silver medal in Mexico City), had defied their national organization and taken over their own training, and how athletes from Kenya, led by Kip Keino, had aired complaints about the IOC's "eligibility code." According to Sayre, athletes around the world felt that "this is the most important thing that's going to happen to the Olympics since it was started in 1896 and . . . they won't even have a chance to testify . . . to the International Olympic Committee."[47] So broad in scope and scale was this emerging movement in the United States that in the months before the 1972 Olympic Games the *Wall Street Journal* predicted that if there were demonstrations about social conditions or political causes by American athletes in Munich, it likely would not be isolated individual acts but rather "involve dozens and perhaps hundreds of U.S. athletes."[48]

The *Journal* was referring to the plans of Scott and the fledgling United Amateur Athletes that Hal and Olga Connelly had helped create. Scott claimed that "over 100 track-and-field athletes, all of them Olympic hopefuls and many of them veterans of past Olympics [had] signed up." The group said it would not dictate protest activities but would seek to "protect" any of its members who chose to use the Games as a forum for some sort of protest. According to Scott, however, the group was also considering "a couple of gestures to demonstrate the solidity—and the size—of its membership" as well as their basic desire to have more input and control over the conditions and political meanings attributed to their athletic activities. As one of the athletes, long jumper Phil Shinnick, put it, "We want control of our lives, and we don't want other people telling us what to do or what not to do." Shinnick thought the time before the Games was critical to "show them we've got the strength to protect ourselves." The athletes were especially concerned about an ongoing IOC investigation of several athletes (including Lee Evans) "for their involvement in an ill-fated movement to form a professional track venture" a few years earlier. Shinnick, who was quoted as speaking "guardedly," said the UAA would protect Evans and others "in any way we can."[49]

As multifaceted and ambitious as this other face of athletic resistance and revolt was, however, analysis of it remains frustrating. This movement has not received the historiographical attention it deserves. Aside from Scott's two books and a few isolated (and often dated) works on specific aspects of the movement (cf. Hult 1980; Spady 1976), it is almost impossible to find secondary literature on the topic.[50] But a few points are clear. One is that during the early 1970s this broad-based push for change in sport continued to pick up energy and adherents. This was in stark contrast to the resistance of black athletes, which was, as will become clearer in the following chapter, already past its peak. Second, the various constellation of interests, ideals, and groups that composed this athletic revolution played a significant (if often underestimated) role in shaping the contemporary world of sport.

To the extent that the athletic revolution is remembered today, it is probably most often associated with Jack Scott's ill-fated tenure as the athletic director at Oberlin College. In 1972 Scott took over the athletic department and instituted a series of changes designed to implement the ideals of the athletic revolution. Closely watched by activists, administrators, and sportswriters all over the country, these included hiring Tommie Smith as his track coach, having football players vote on the selection of another black coach (Cass Jackson), and expanding the women's locker room at the expense of male faculty members' space. Unfortunately, the whole "radical experiment" (as it had been dubbed by Howard Cosell when he visited the campus) came to a screeching halt when Scott allowed his contract to be bought out by the university after only two years.[51] Important and revealing as this episode may have been, the fact that so much attention was focused on it served to obscure larger and more important developments brought about by athletic unrest—ranging from the institutionalization of free agency and players' unions in professional sports and the establishment of clear and coherent standards for athletes' rights in amateur settings (McLaren 1998) to the equalization of opportunities for women and girls in sport through the enforcement of Title IX (cf. Cahn 1994; Guttmann 1991; Nelson 1991), the achievement of official representation for athletes in American Olympic organizations (de Varona 1982), and the emergence of new codes of behavior and styles of self-expression for athletes both on and off sporting fields.

The impacts of this activism and unrest may be most obvious and concrete when it came to the governance of amateur athletics. In combination with the public pressures for institutional reform that resulted from disappointments and controversies associated with the American performance in the 1972 Munich Games, as Laurence Chalip (1988) has documented in an important if little-known study, the agitation of athletes set in motion a series of reforms and transformations that culminated in the passage of the 1978 American Amateur Athletic Act. This legislation not only marked the first time the federal government intervened in American amateur athletics but also set in place the basic organizational apparatus—with the authority for "amateur" sport (as clearly delineated from free-market professional sport) being split between the NCAA and the USOC—that still governs American athletics today.

This movement's most obvious legacy may be the role it played in providing new ways of thinking about sports that athletes (and others) could use to situate and better themselves and their athletic practices, to make sense of the various grievances and discontents many had sensed but could not articulate, much less act upon. Crucial here was a whole series of works mostly by athletes and former athletes exposing the daily and often dirty details of the sports world. It is an impressive list of works, including some of the most famous, honest, and intelligent books on sport ever written: Jim Bouton's *Ball Four* (1970); Curt Flood's *The Way It Is* (1970); David Wolf's *Foul! The Connie Hawkins Story* (1972); Schollander's *Deep Water* (1971); William O. Johnson's *All That Glitters Is Not Gold: The Olympic Game* (1972); former professional football player Dave Meggyesy's *Out of Their League* (1971); Neil Amdur's *Fifth Down and the Football Revolution* (1971); Vincent Matthews's *My Race Be Won* (1974); and Linda Huey's *A Running Start: A Woman, An Athlete* (1976).

In demystifying the heretofore glamorous, glorious world of sport, these books also gave rise to entirely new, often very critical ways of writing and reporting about athletes and sport in American culture, approaches best exemplified in such well-known and influential works as Robert Lipsyte's *Sportsworld: An American Dreamland* (1975), *Rip Off the Big Game* by Canadian Paul Hoch (1972), and *Sports in America* by the populist favorite James Michener (1976). These works and others like them not only took a critical stance toward sport but seriously and systematically considered the role of athletes and sport in broader social processes. They began to break down sport's easy and self-satisfied liberalism and expose its complicity with racism, sexism, and nationalism—thus setting the stage for the development of leftist theories of sport (cf. Morgan 1994a) and for the emergence of critical feminist approaches in the 1980s. Though I can only suggest the connection here, it is no accident that the sociology of sport really took shape during this period.

Yet it is important to emphasize that the sum total of the forces that composed the movement never quite added up to the revolution activist-athletes talked so much about in its earliest days. No boycotts ever took place, no new emphasis on community-based or recreationally oriented sport ever took hold, and although the administrative structure of amateur athletics was reconfigured and athletes did gain some measure of representation and involvement (especially in professional sports with the emergence of the unions), the balance of power still remained essentially in the vision and leadership of the old regime.

The failure of the athletic revolution to make progress on its most radical goals had something to do with the inability—paralleled and reproduced in virtually all such movements of the period—of this diverse and diffuse set of actors, interests, and ideals to find either common ground or an organizational base. It also had to do with the shortcomings of its most prominent spokespersons. For example, even Jack Scott's staunchest supporters recognized that he himself often exhibited many of the worst traits he criticized in the sporting establishment: he could be authoritarian and dictatorial; he was often confrontational and aggressive; he wanted to win at almost any cost. "Scott," as his one-time student and co-collaborator Jay Weiner respectfully recalls, "had a temper, was impatient with opposition, manipulative with supporters and wanted to win as much as any straight-laced athletic director. Theory and practice didn't exactly marry very well. After two years, he was done [at Oberlin] and went in search of another place to make his controversial mark."[52]

Of course, it is essential to situate these individual shortcomings in a structural context. The forces and organizations that these activists were fighting against were far more powerful and entrenched than the insurgent ideals of a more democratically oriented sport. The list of structural constraints that stood in the way of radical change in the world of sport is extensive and imposing: the continued ascendance of market-based forces in and around sport; the nationalist political interests implicated in all of international and Olympic sport; and the dominance of rationalized, high-performance conceptions of sport. These forces were so firmly established and so much larger than the institutions of the sporting world itself that it is hard to imagine anyone—radicals, reformers, or establishment elites—waging a successful campaign against them. Recall that much of the unrest of the period had been produced by massive structural contradictions and social forces in the first place, and the athletic revolution depended on how the athletic establishment (composed of athletes, agencies, and leaders) would react to and accommodate these changes. In fact, it seems fair to suggest that the "revolution" was equally driven by the changing context and external circumstances concerning sporting events of all types and levels.

Also, the transformations of the sports world were determined as much by struggles within the existing power structure as from outside of it, on the domestic front by the ongoing battle between the NCAA and the AAU and internationally by the battles being fought over issues such as amateurism, commercialism, apartheid, doping, nationalism, and politics. As these monumental structural tensions were unfolding, the actions of the established organizations and agencies ensured, even as they fought against one another, their hold on the institutional structure and ideological control of the sporting world. This suggests a final and indeed indispensable factor in explaining why the athletic revolution ultimately fell short of many of its expressed goals and objectives: namely, the ability of the sporting establishment itself, its leaders and elites, to recognize and respond effectively to the athletic discontent in its midst.

To illustrate, it is useful to revisit the USOC board's response to John Sayre's post-1968 Olympic presentation. Much as they didn't like what they heard, the majority of the board members found themselves forced to agree with Sayre's analysis, if not necessarily its implications and his solutions. Recognizing that the "problem" went "way beyond" communication to include representation and reorganization at higher levels, for example, legal counsel Patrick Sullivan immediately set about coming up with solutions that would get to the root of the problem. Whether it was because he was genuinely sympathetic to the grievances of athletes or simply because he believed that media coverage of this discontent would constitute "a tremendous public-relations black eye" for the committee (as the AAU's Mahoney put it) is not important here. What this response reveals is that leaders of the sporting establishment understood the threat that athletic unrest posed and became committed to taking action in response—in this case, setting in motion a process that would formalize a board of athlete representatives to the USOC itself. Such responses would prove crucial to the future of the stability and continuity of the American athletic system, especially in its amateur spheres, and even more especially when it came to issues involving race.

In the Middle of It All

That race in general and African American athletes in particular remained at the center of all U.S. athletic unrest was reflected in the attention both were given in the leading texts of the movement. All core texts devoted special attention—often an entire chapter—to racial issues (many including selections from Edwards's own writings, including his 1973 textbook *Sociology of Sport*), and most singled out Smith and Carlos or Harry Edwards (or both) for special mention. The cover design of Scott's *Athletic Revolution* is—like that of Edwards's *Revolt*—composed of an angular, animated tightly clenched fist jutting upward like the rock formations in the high desert plains of the American West. A photograph in it, moreover, shows recently retired football star Dave Meggyesy hunched over a typewriter in front of a poster of Smith and Carlos on the victory stand, ostensibly working on *Out of Their League,* his exposé of professional football in the United States (see fig. 7).

Fig. 7. Dave Meggyesy working on Out of Their League, circa 1970. Photo courtesy Micki McGee Scott.

The centrality of race for John Cleve Livingston's Harvard thesis is obvious in the title of his first chapter: "Black Power on the Victory Stand."[53] Similarly, race was both the starting point and recurring point of reference for Michener's *Sports in America*. When Bud Greenspan produced and directed a video in 1980 inspired by the book, it was called "James's Michener's World: The Black Athlete" and featured exchanges between the author and Harry Edwards himself.

Suffice it to say, then, that the "revolt of the black athlete" continued to be understood not just as one dimension of the broader "athletic revolution," but as a separate and distinct movement, albeit one that was parallel to and entirely consistent with the revolution. Most seemed to think of black athletic resistance as the twin face or sister focus of movements for change in and around American sport.

And this was not just for sports activists. Few were more obsessed with the racial dimensions of athletic activism and unrest than the establishment elites and the mainstream media. Race was never far from the surface in the USOC executive board's review of the American experience in Mexico City—whether in discussions of expectations for "appropriate conduct," consideration of issues of communication and the need for better representation, or coming to realize that the habit of referring to Olympic athletes as "boys and girls" was not just patronizing but downright insulting and offensive. References to Smith and Owens and Evans—some direct, others more veiled—are scattered throughout the hundred-plus pages of meeting minutes and attached materials. In their formal proposal calling for permanent representation for athletes on the USOC's board of directors, Jesse Owens and John Sayre's "Board of Consultants" emphasized that the USOC and its affiliated sport organizations needed to include "all races, creeds and colors and especially Negro representatives."[54]

It would be the same four years later after the disappointments of the Munich Games—unimpressive results, sprinters failing to show up on time for races, behavior on the Olympic podium. Although not intentionally or all in the same fashion, all involved black athletes and were thus shot through with racial overtone, meaning, and significance (cf. Elzey 2001).

The media was similarly obsessed. At least a quarter of the groundbreaking and controversial interview with Hal and Olga Connolly that *Sport* magazine published in the wake of the Mexico City Games was devoted to Smith and Carlos and racial issues more generally. (Both Connollys, it should be noted, appeared more than willing to share their views on the subject.) And even though *Sports Illustrated*'s John Underwood went out of his way to avoid focusing on race in many of the incidents he wrote about in his landmark 1969 series on the frustrations of collegiate coaches, he couldn't help but come back to issues of race and black athletes time and again. "In matters of race," he said at one point, "there would seem to be no ground firm enough to stand on."[55] Perhaps even more remarkable and revealing, Underwood devoted a large portion of the series' final installment to an idealized portrait of the football coach at the historically black Florida A&M University, the legendary Jake Gaithers.[56] The problem of race was, as one of the graphics that accompanied Jack Olsen's famous 1968 series on the black athlete portrayed, like a dark secret bursting out of and breaking down the buttoned-up sporting establishment's very own sense of order and integrity.

There are a number of reasons race remained central to the social un-rest in and around sport. Many of them have to do with how this unrest was addressed by the athletic establishment and why this response ulti-mately proved so symbolically potent (as I will detail in the next chapter). Another factor involves direct, concrete individual and institutional con-nections. The presumed "leaders" of the two faces of athletic resistance— Edwards and Scott—were both based in the Bay Area and collaborated in writing for San Francisco–based *Ramparts* magazine. But I think that there were some other, subtler reasons in play here as well and, moreover, that examining them will usefully foreshadow the complexity and import of the institutional response to racial unrest that will occupy my attention in the next chapter.

Among the simplest and most straightforward reasons why race re-mained so central to the whole of social unrest in and around sport are those involving precedent and symbolic power: race-based activism in sport emerged before any other forms of activism, and no other issue, event, or group of athletes produced an image that even began to approx-imate the effects achieved by Smith and Carlos's victory-stand demon-stration.[57] For would-be activist-athletes, the Smith-Carlos demonstration was thus a constant source of inspiration as well as a very concrete object lesson, the empirical capital from which much of their own critical think-ing departed and derived. Leaders of the athletic establishment, the mass media, and mainstream public had little choice but to respond in kind.

This was, of course, a familiar pattern for young, white activists of the period, whether they were involved with the antipoverty movement, an-tiwar movement, or feminism. All had their social conscience and con-sciousness awakened by their participation in the racial struggle, and they learned tactics and strategies to use in confronting the authorities therein (cf. McAdam 1988; Evans, S. 1979). But it would be a mistake, in my view, to reduce the prominence of race with respect to 1960s-era athletic unrest—or any other form of sixties social unrest and political activism, for that matter—simply to a matter of historical contingency or even pow-erful symbolic iconography. Deep material and symbolic underpinnings, which were especially pronounced in the world of sport, made race cen-trally problematic in American culture.

At a very basic level, many of the worst, most blatant examples of athletic exploitation, abuse, and mistreatment in the world of sport in-volved African Americans—for example, black athletes being forced to compete against Brigham Young teams when that university continued to practice overtly discriminatory ordination policies; coaches and athletic directors who claimed they simply couldn't pronounce "Negro"; colleges that recruited and played black athletes who were not academically qualified; the racist taunting of African American athletes by majority white crowds and audiences, especially in the South. After all, the Southeastern Conference (SEC) had only begun to recruit and play African American athletes in 1966 (in the aftermath of the historic defeat of an all-white Kentucky basketball team in the NCAA championship at the hands of an all-black starting squad from Texas Western) and a great deal of resentment and counterresistance still remained. When a young black athlete named Perry Wallace broke the color line at Vanderbilt in Tennessee, for example, he endured racist insults and had Confederate flags waved in his face. "Only after I graduated and left Nashville did I realize how much was at stake emotionally and psychologically," he would remember many years later.[58] Recall also that at this time athletic clubs such as the NYAC were almost completely segregated and dozens of tennis clubs in the States wouldn't allow the 1968 U.S. Open Tennis champion, Arthur Ashe, to be a member simply because he was African American.

And even when prejudice and mistreatment could not simply or directly be traced back to race, the fact that they were often more pronounced for black athletes put sport's deepest, most entrenched problems and practices in clear relief. A good example can be found in the book *Foul!* (1972), David Wolf's acclaimed and widely read portrait of New York schoolboy superstar Connie Hawkins. Hawkins had been recruited from the streets of New York to play basketball at the University of Iowa. Although furnished with tutors, he was totally unprepared to do the academic work expected of a college freshman. One of a handful of blacks on campus and previously familiar only with life on the streets of New York, he found himself almost completely isolated when he was off the basketball court in Iowa. Then, in May 1961 when he was accused, falsely it turned out, of acting as an intermediary for New York City gamblers involved in fixing basketball games, he was forced by Coach Scheuerman and his staff to withdraw from the university. Hawkins did not hear from Iowa's athletic department again until the following summer, when they pressured him into signing and notarizing a prepared statement retracting his earlier claims that he had been paid on a monthly basis to play basketball for the university. Wolf boils the tale down to this:

> A semiliterate eighteen-year-old had been brought to a college where he had no chance of legitimate academic survival. He had been paid to perform his basketball skills—until he found himself (unjustly) in trouble. Then the school's athletic officials suddenly

> expressed dissatisfaction with his scholastic ability about which they had always known. They had abandoned him—until they needed him again, this time to lie to save their necks. (p. 125)

Wolf, notably, does not blame those who brought Hawkins to Iowa entirely. "The Iowa men," according to Wolf, "were simply acting in the only manner it was possible to act and still survive—in the big-time, profit-oriented college sports system. They had to win basketball games to keep their jobs, and to win they needed kids like Connie Hawkins. To get kids like Hawkins, they had to cheat" (p. 128). If such practices went on as regularly and systematically as Wolf suggests (and there is no reason to believe otherwise), they were rarely so exaggerated and dramatic as in cases involving African American athletes like Hawkins.

Another example appeared during the USOC Executive Committee meeting convened for the purpose of reviewing American performances at the 1968 Olympics. Referring to the generation gap between officials like himself and current Olympic athletes, USOC president Douglas Roby mentioned how his tendency to refer to athletes as "boys and girls" got him in trouble in Mexico City. "I might as well have called them—I don't know what . . ." The minutes don't say because, amid laughter, Roby asks that his comment be stricken from the record. All of these athletes, obviously, would have been implicated in this and typically offended by such comments, but no group more so than African American men. A few minutes later, when the same issue was revisited again, Roby confessed that he really became attuned to this, finally, in his interaction with three "Negroes" (undoubtedly Lee Evans and his fellow medalists in the 400 meters), who told him: "We ain't boys—we ain't boys!" Sullivan then confesses to having made a similar faux pas when talking to Smith and Carlos and their wives; Smith also told him, "Man, we ain't no boys!" Although these stories provoked (perhaps uncomfortable) laughter among the USOC's executive board, it is not difficult to imagine how they must have been experienced by the black athletes themselves. [59]

What is worth noting about this somewhat trivial and yet telling exchange is not just the different ways that being called "boys" would have registered with black athletes as compared with white ones, but also how much easier and more effective it was for black athletes to voice this complaint and force action on it—which brings us to two more reasons why race remained so central to how Americans understood athletic resistance: African American athletes were both more sensitive to and uniquely empowered to speak out and act against mistreatment than their white counterparts.

What David Halberstam (1994) has written about Curt Flood's campaign for free agency in Major League Baseball captures the unique awareness and understanding of injustice African American athletes brought to the world of sport. Treating black players with a "harsh, authoritarian hand" had even "ominous implications and was likely to produce less positive results."

> In retrospect . . . it is not surprising that the first black baseball player to draw the line on the reserve clause was black. Blacks felt far more alienated from the norms of society than did whites, and in the case of athletes, they were far more sensitive to being thought of as chattel. . . . Black players in the sports world in this new era were different. In basketball [for example] the leadership for a model professional athlete's union had already come from a generation of exceptionally thoughtful (and well educated) black athletes. Almost all had been to college and many were graduates of the nation's best schools (p. 364).

Curt Flood lacked these benefits, but he was, by all accounts, "intelligent and driven," a painter, a man who had serious thoughts and listened seriously to others—"not just to what people said," Halberstam writes, "but to what they did not say." His lawsuit against the reserve clause went all the way to the Supreme Court. Although he lost a close decision, his suit "jump-started the process that would soon bring baseball players free agency and change the face and structure of baseball negotiations" (p. 366).[60] It was the same in many professional sports and even ostensibly "amateur" ones. In alliance with white athletes through the Union of Amateur Athletes, Lee Evans and Bob Beamon, for example, played an important role in the creation of a professional track-and-field circuit in the United States.[61]

If their unique social position allowed many African American athletes to develop a particularly acute social consciousness, it also provided them a powerful position from which to act. This was especially the case in the liberal white colleges and universities that gave athletic scholarships to so many African Americans. Because much of the public controversy surrounding racial issues was located on college campuses and because leaders of these predominantly white institutions were under extreme pressure to do something about these problems, college and university presidents were prodded to respond to racial changes in and through sport. In his 1969 *Sports Illustrated* feature on collegiate coaches, John Underwood provides a perfect anecdote.

This story features a black basketball player named Bob Miller at the University of Toledo. In Underwood's account, Miller, the team's leading scorer, one day showed for a practice he wasn't supposed to be at because it conflicted with one of his classes. When his coach, Bob Nichols, insisted that he leave practice in order to go to class, Miller refused and walked off the court. Nichols suspended him the following day in what he thought would be an uncontroversial statement about the priority of education over athletics. Much to his surprise, however, Nichols almost immediately came under attack from the local Black Student Union. The BSU claimed the suspension constituted an infringement on Miller's right to determine his own educational priorities and asked for Nichols's dismissal as well as the dismissal of the football coach, athletic director and sports information director. Within days, other black players began refusing to play for Nichols, and Miller filed suit with the Ohio Civil Rights Commission on the grounds that his suspension violated the Public Accommodations Act.

Eventually Nichols won this skirmish. The commission denied the suit (on the grounds that the public accommodations law did not apply to basketball, a private, voluntary activity), the ten-person Athletic Board of Control backed Nichols (if "only faintheartedly," according to Underwood), and, after a meeting with student leaders, Toledo president William S. Carlson upheld Miller's suspension and retained Nichols as head basketball coach.[62] (Miller was never reinstated.) But the lesson of the story, in Underwood's telling, is not its outcome but the fact that it took place at all. Underwood clearly considers the incident a farce, a travesty that should have never happened. While his biases are obvious, Underwood certainly has a point. It is almost impossible to imagine such a story unfolding if its central protagonist were not African American. At its root was not just the audacity of black athletes and activists but, more important, the vulnerability of the white liberal establishment when it came to questions of race.

The athletic establishment was particularly vulnerable on this score— not just because of the racism and discrimination that it continued to perpetuate but because sport had trumpeted its previous accomplishments on racial issues so loudly that they had become central to sport's sense of itself as a progressive social force. Which brings us to perhaps the most important reason why the racial dimension of athletic unrest remained such a focal point and threat: all this attention to black athletes and racial discrimination in sport was seen as—or was by its very nature—an attack on sport itself, on everything sport stood for, everything it supposedly did best and contributed to American society.

Racial unrest not only threatened to expose the fact that sport was not the clear leader in race relations it had long purported to be, nor even that it had deep and intransigent racial problems of its own. More than this, the realization of these facts threatened to drive a wedge into the ideology, so dependent upon a color-blind vision of social justice, that sport was a special if not sacred space. And in no respect was Harry Edwards's *Revolt of the Black Athlete* a more critical and consequential historical force.

Edwards's *Revolt*

Edwards's *Revolt*, published originally in 1969 and reissued in paperback a year later, was unlike any American sports book that had come before it. At a very basic level, it was a frank and straightforward insider's account of the 1968 Olympic protest movement and of African American resistance in general—of their origins, ideals, objectives, internal processes, and so on. But it was also much more than that. The publication of *Revolt* helped to solidify the young sociology professor's role as the leading spokesperson for sports-based activism and protest. Edwards is described, in both the foreword to the paperback edition and on its back cover, as the "primary architect" of the black athletic rebellion. The author himself says the book is "not the rantings of some sideline journalist, but the documentary facts of the movement from the perspective of a man who himself was victimized by the American athletic structure, who helped plan, direct and implement the revolt and who intends to continue the fight until the goals of the revolt are achieved" (p. xxix). Edwards was quite serious about his intentions. *Revolt* was intended to be an organizing tool, a manifesto of sorts, designed to provide aspiring activists and discontented athletes a common consciousness and social understanding.

This in mind, Edwards made sure to situate the struggle against racism in sport in the historical context of the "overall black liberation movement." The black athletic protest movement, he wrote, "has its roots and draws its impetus from the resistance of black people in the dim and distant past to brutal oppression and callous exploitation. . . . And now, at long last, the black athlete has entered the arena as a warrior in the struggle for black dignity and freedom" (pp. xvii–xxix; see also pp. 38–39).[63] But the broadest and single most transformative aspect of *Revolt* as a manifesto was the new, critical way of thinking about the relationships between sport and race that Harry Edwards used to frame his account of the events of 1968.

"Recreation and athletics have traditionally been billed as essentially therapeutic measures—measures," Edwards wrote in the preface, "that cure faulty deteriorating character, that weaken prejudice and that bind men of all races and nationalities together." But the evidence, according to the sociologist, "does not support the theory." The activities of the sports world have "actually spawned [social unrest] in both the amateur and professional arenas." As for eliminating prejudice, Edwards continued, "whites may grudgingly admit a black man's prowess as an athlete, but will not acknowledge his equality as a human being. In athletics . . . a white racist does not change his attitude toward blacks; he merely alters his inclination to abuse him or discriminate against him overtly" (p. xxvi). From these preliminary observations, Edwards launched a full frontal assault:

> Recreational patterns in America widen and perpetuate racial separation. Recreation is exclusive, compounded of all sorts of considerations . . . racial and economic. There is, therefore, usually little opportunity for recreation to narrow the gap between white and black Americans. Moreover, there is absolutely nothing inherent in recreation that would change attitudes. [It simply] gives old attitudes a new start and fresh impetus. (pp. xxvi–xxvii)

"The sportsworld in America," Edwards summarized later on in the text, "has been portrayed as a citadel of racial harmony and purity. . . . The simple truth of the matter is that the sportsworld is not a rose flourishing in the middle of a wasteland. It is part and parcel of that wasteland, reeking of the same racism that corrupts other areas of our society" (p. 34).

The argument that sport was not the progressive racial force its supporters had so long claimed but in fact was connected with and thus reproduced racial stereotypes and hierarchies had far-reaching impacts and implications. For one thing, it gave rise to that whole host of sociological studies I referenced in chapter 4 to explain the emergence of African American athletic unrest that documented and confirmed racial prejudice and discrimination throughout the sporting world.[64] More than this, many critics—scholarly and otherwise—began to take the rhetoric of corruption Edwards used to characterize the racial problems of the sporting world and apply it to the entire athletic establishment. In his controversial critique of the international Olympic movement, *All that Glitters Is Not Gold* (1972), William O. Johnson, for example, drew upon *Revolt* to frame the Olympics as "an endangered species, perhaps on the brink of extinction" (p. 30). Johnson followed Edwards (whom he described as an "outspoken, articulate, iconoclastic critic") in portraying the Games as "hypocritical . . . a fountain of hypocrisy" as evidenced by "their commercialism, their built-in nationalism, their politicization, the shame of amateurism." Claiming that the Olympics had all the same mystical, materialist, and deadly elements as war itself, Johnson characterized the Games and its ideals as "passé." His conclusion was equally striking and dismissive: "The Olympics is so obviously hypocritical that even the Neanderthals watching TV know what they're seeing can't be true" (p. 31).

In a few short years, Edwards himself would turn the embryonic critique of sport he had offered up in *Revolt* into a full-fledged, formal social scientific theory of the social forms and functions of modern, American athletics. The theory appeared as a textbook titled *Sociology of Sport* (1973a). Widely used and frequently cited in academia throughout the seventies, the book drew upon the structural-functionalist theories that were then dominant in sociology to develop an extended criticism of "the American Sports Creed"—the prevailing ideology that sport was a separate and sacred social space and moral force in the United States. In sharp opposition, Edwards insisted that American sport was, like any other social sphere or institutional arena, the product of the interests and idiosyncrasies and imperfections of the human beings that made it up. Using the language and imagery prefigured in *Revolt*, Edwards insisted that sport was actually bound up with and reflective of all of the problems and injustices of the broader social world.

This text and the supporting studies that went along with it had a profound impact on both students and scholars of sport. This vision of athletics as a microcosm of all of society's imperfections quickly took hold in the fledgling field of sport sociology, as conveyed in the title and subtitle of a prominent collection that came out of the era—*Fractured Focus: Sport as a Reflection of Society* (Lapchick 1986). While a full treatment of reflectionist theories of sport is beyond the scope of the present discussion (suffice it to say, they inherited both the strengths and weaknesses of the structural-functionalist paradigm; for a discussion of the latter, see Giddens 1979), it should be emphasized that what made these reflectionist theories—originally enabled and emboldened by the specter of racial unrest in sport—so popular and compelling was that they presented a direct, core challenge to the athletic establishment's entire understanding of the social force and moral value of sport in the modern world.[65]

Some of the most pointed challenges to the traditional ideals of the sporting world came down to questions about the place of politics in the athletic realm. Indeed, a whole series of works appeared in the 1970s under the heading of "sport and politics" (Balbus 1975; Clumpner 1978; Lipsky 1978; Thirer 1978; Espy 1979; and Kanin 1981).[66] This was not necessarily a bad thing for the sporting establishment. In fact, most Americans seemed to agree with sports idealists like Avery Brundage or Jesse Owens that politics needed to be kept out of sport. This principle was one of the few that respondents to Richard Lapchick's 1973 survey on sport and race held in common. While there were clear racial cleavages in views of the Smith-Carlos demonstration, black and white Americans were in complete accord on the need to keep sport and politics separate: 77 percent of whites and 78 percent of blacks concurred that politics should have no influence whatsoever in domestic sport.[67]

In and of itself, this principle need not have served the interests of the athletic establishment. However, sports scholars failed to construct a clear or consistent definition of "politics" as contrasted with acceptable and legitimate moral engagement. Though it didn't address politics directly, Edwards's sociology of sport text is something of an example. More of a critique of the American sports creed than an elaboration (much less defense) of his alternative egalitarian vision, the book made it difficult to distinguish corrupting social influences from those that were at least acceptable if not entirely socially desirable. Without a dependable compass on moral and political issues, events as different and diverse as Hitler's use of the 1936 Olympics to glorify Nazism or the terrorist assassinations of Israeli athletes in 1972 often ended up in the same category as Smith and Carlos's 1968 victory-stand demonstration.[68]

It turns out, in fact, that the items explicitly implicated with race (such as the Smith-Carlos demonstration) were one of only two sets of issues that exhibited significant cleavages in response patterns on Lapchick's survey. This suggests that the racial cleavages resulted from the ambiguity of the term "political" as it applied (or didn't apply) to Smith and Carlos's gesture. That is, those who supported Smith and Carlos did so not because of their "racial politics" but rather because they didn't see their views on race (or at least the racial views they believed to be expressed in the demonstration) as in any way political. They were, instead, viewed as something different than politics—that is, as based in ideals and interests that were legitimate, desirable, moral, and just.

Thus the ideological challenges the sporting establishment confronted had less to do with vexing questions about sport's role in social life than with the larger social struggles about equality and justice being played out in society at large. To put it more directly to the concerns of this study, it was the politics of race rather than the politics of sport that were now in question. And on this front, the sporting establishment would have no problems working within the rights-based, integrationist standards of racial justice and progress that were dominant in American culture (and which, moreover, were at the heart of sport's historical claims to being a leader in civil rights).

It is not clear that Harry Edwards and his colleagues ever fully grasped this—or, for that matter, saw the deep ideological parallels and overlaps between sport idealism and the mainstream cultural conceptions of racial equality and fairness. But the leaders of the sporting establishment certainly did. Indeed, when it came to stabilizing and reaffirming sport's traditional power, purpose, and meaning in the modern world, these leaders found an important if unlikely opportunity in African American claims of discrimination and prejudice in sport. For the primary grievances of Edwards's *Revolt* could be remedied well within the ideological confines that constituted sport's usual ideals about itself and its place in the social world. Ironically, in other words, while racial unrest was at the root of the ideological challenge to sport—if it represented the sports world coming apart at the seams—then at the same time it was a challenge that, in comparison to all of the other criticisms and attacks sport was facing, could be dealt with directly.

Chapter 7

Resolving the Racial Crisis

So the pressure was clearly on—put on, I should reiterate, by the continued public presence of activist-athletes and the moral weight of the emerging race-based critique of sport. No longer could the various organizations and agencies of the American sporting establishment ignore or deny the crisis in their midst. They had to do or say something. But what to do? How to respond? And with what consequence or implication?

This chapter details how the American athletic establishment—represented here mainly by the organizations and elites of the United States Olympic Committee and the National Collegiate Athletic Association—went about answering these questions. It is, more specifically, an examination of how these institutional actors attempted to address and to resolve the racial challenges they faced, and how, in turn, these reactions and responses impacted the world of sport and the evolution of race-based athletic activism itself. Once they realized that the charges of racism in and around sport would not quietly go away, sport leaders and elites, acting in both deliberate and not-so-deliberate ways, went about insulating themselves and their institutions against the more radical charges. At the same time, they also took steps to reform or modify their established racial practices and policies to absorb or incorporate the more moderate and publicly legitimate aspects of African American athletic activism. In taking these steps, leaders of the American amateur athletic establishment were thus able to reestablish and eventually "re-articulate" (Omi and Winant 1994) more stable, acceptable racial arrangements in the world of sport.

Before detailing these post-1968 reactions and responses, however, it is instructive to first recall the initial impulses and reactions (or lack thereof) of sports authorities to the emergence of African American athletic resistance. These remind us not only of how reluctant the athletic establishment was to even acknowledge racial unrest, but also why it was ultimately forced to confront the reality of the institutional legitimation crisis this unrest created.

Initial Impulses, Reactions, and Responses

Given the nature of the crisis that had become full-blown in the months and years immediately following the 1968 Olympic Games, it is interesting to recall that the leaders of the American athletic organizations most directly impacted by it had not been particularly active or vigorous participants in the initial public discussions and debates about the idea of an African American Olympic boycott in the fall of 1967. Representatives from the National Collegiate Athletic Association (NCAA), for example, had been conspicuous by their absence in the condemnation of the Olympic boycott idea when it was first introduced to the American public. So, too, with leaders from the NCAA's arch rival and the other most powerful organization in American amateur athletics, the Amateur Athletic Union (AAU). To be sure, the director of the United States Olympic Committee (the next most prominent amateur athletic agency), Arthur Lentz, had told the national press that his organization "resented" being "used as an attention-getter"; and USOC president Douglas Roby suggested that the boycott initiative was "the equivalent of someone trying to burn down his own house."[1] But these responses were muted, understated, and qualified, especially in comparison to that of boycott critics such as Avery Brundage, Jesse Owens, and Ronald Reagan. They were also slow in coming. Lentz's comments, for instance, were not issued until several days after the initial cycle of reaction and reporting about the boycott had come and gone. And Roby's did not come until almost a month later, and only after his Executive Committee felt pressured to offer further elaboration and public commentary.[2]

After reopening the issue in their December meeting, USOC leadership resolved that the boycott was a decision to be left up to individual athletes and that their public statements and organizational efforts should focus simply on encouraging all athletes to try out for the team. The official statement Roby released to the press on the matter passed unanimously and with no debate, and is notable only for its timing (in mid-December, weeks after the OPHR put forward the boycott proposal) and its bland-ness:

> The United States Olympic Committee invites all qualified, American athletes to try out for the 1968 games in all Olympic sports, just as it has since the modern Olympic Games began in 1896. All those who have been on the United States teams through-out the years have received the same equal treatment in the manner of selection, housing and in feeding. The same policy will, of course, be in effect for the 1968 teams. We hope everyone who wishes to try out will do so.[3]

Taken as a whole, then, the collective public response of the three major organizations of the American amateur athletic establishment was either to downplay the challenge posed by the threat of an African American Olympic boycott or to simply ignore the matter altogether.

This low-key, lackluster response was *not* because the leading members of these organizations did not agree with the sentiments of the more out-spoken boycott critics. Quite the opposite. Not only was the American amateur athletic leadership categorically opposed to the idea of African American athletes using their participation in sport to call attention to their views on race, they had absolutely no sympathy for (much less un-derstanding of) these views in the first place. For example, in their De-cember meeting, the USOC's Executive Committee discussed how what they called the "boycott of the Olympic Games by some of our colored athletes" might impact the American basketball team in Mexico City. Dur-ing the course of the discussion (framed in such telling terms already), the boycott was described as "the most ridiculous thing that could be done" (Roby himself) and it was quite clearly the consensus of the group that the idea had come from "rabble rousers" like Harry Edwards who were inter-ested in little more than using the Olympic committee and the Olympic Games as a "vehicle for himself" and his "ill-advised cause."[4]

What then explains the initial response (or lack thereof) of these or-ganizations? There were several contributing factors here. One has to do with the nationalism, utilitarianism, and anti-intellectualism of the American athletic officials and elites. Unlike Brundage and his associates in the International Olympic Committee, leaders of the American ath-letic establishment were never very attuned to the deep and complex ideological issues embedded in their belief that sport was an inherently powerful and progressive racial force. Thus, the boycott initiative wasn't as deeply threatening for them as it was for a true sports idealist like Brundage—and certainly not to the extent that the more basic and concrete charges of racism in sport would be just a few short months later. Indeed, American sporting leaders were concerned about a boycott primarily insofar as it would impact the competitiveness and medal count of the American team in the upcoming Games, as reflected in the fact that the USOC's discussion of the proposed boycott focused almost exclusively on its potential impact on the on-court performance of the American basketball team. Nationalism, for the American leadership, far outweighed idealism—although the two were mutually supportive in this case.

To the extent they wanted to guard against an Olympic boycott, there was also a clear strategic element to the studied laissez-faire approach of American officials: they figured it was the best way to avoid further antagonizing athletes or inciting them to boycott. This approach was made clear when the USOC reopened its consideration of how to deal with the "basketball controversy" at their meeting in March 1968. The bulk of the discussion revolved around a plan put forward by the United States Basketball Committee (on the request of the USOC itself) to require potential team members to sign a pledge indicating their intent to participate in the Games before they be allowed to try out for the team. The proposed pledge stated:

> By participating in the Olympic trials, I am expressing my earnest desire to become a Member of the United States Olympic Team and to compete in the Olympic Games to be held in Mexico City, October sixth [*sic*]. I will, if selected as a candidate for the team, hold myself in readiness, keep myself in top physical condition, retain my amateur status and make myself available for training at whatever day and whatever location and altitude the Olympic Committee deems advisable.[5]

Revealingly, several members of the USOC committee opposed this proposed policy on the grounds that it could exacerbate the problem rather than resolve it. One of those was Patrick Sullivan, counselor to the board and ex-officio member. Sullivan argued that rather than putting prospective boycotters "on the spot," the pledge would give them a springboard for more publicity and attention. This was not just because of the appearance of control and distrust it would convey, but because, Sullivan believed, if athletes did refuse to compete "they would like nothing better than to violate another agreement they have made."[6]

Similar sentiments were echoed and exchanged within the NCAA's leadership circle. In a letter to executive director Walter Byers about plans for the NCAA's national track-and-field championships in the spring (a crucial qualifying meet for the Olympic trials), Hugh Hackett, chair of the Rules Committee, told Byers that he believed that some demonstrations would happen at the meet. "I could not think of a more opportune time to hold a demonstration if I were a member of a militant group," Hackett put it. He added that he also expected "verbal or physical attempts" to keep other athletes from participating. Nevertheless, Hackett warned against making any specific appeal to athletes on the grounds that "athletes will have formulated an attitude one way or the other by that time." Instead, Hackett proposed a contingency plan to identify top finishers in the various preliminary and semifinal heats to be invited to the Olympic tryouts should the finalists themselves participate in some kind of a demonstration or refuse to participate in the Games.[7]

The minutes from these meetings and records of these behind-the-scenes communications indicate something else as well: that American sports officials had absolutely no sense of the ideas and ideals (and inequities) that motivated athletes like Tommie Smith and Lee Evans to seriously consider abandoning what they had worked their entire lives to accomplish. The USOC's deliberation on the matter in March illustrates: on the one hand, the USOC brain trust figured that these athletes must be facing "tremendous pressure from the outside Negro community," including threats of punishment and physical retribution; on the other, they also speculated that the athletes were being "paid off" by someone.

Their one correct surmise was that the boycott threat was compounded by the South African "question," and the "do-gooders" in the States (led, recall, by baseball icon Jackie Robinson) who continued to harp on it. What makes their understanding of this situation—summarized by one dispirited committee member as "really vicious"—particularly interesting is that the USOC got some of its information from federal government agencies and informants. USOC executive Orth assured the committee: "The government is involved in it in various ways—and, I don't want to dwell on that here, but the investigations are being made."[8] Although he refused to elaborate further "on the record," Orth was almost certainly referring to the FBI and CIA's ongoing investigation of Smith, Edwards, and Dick Gregory (among others) during these months.[9] It is hard to imagine a better indication of the "national" interests implicated in this initiative and the lengths to which ostensibly private sport agencies in concert with the state itself would go to head it off.

But even had they wanted to take a more deliberate, proactive role, it is not clear what American amateur athletic officials could have done to head off an Olympic boycott. African American athletes couldn't be easily controlled or simply forced to compete, and the organizational structure of the American amateur athletic establishment made it difficult, it not impossible, for sports officials to craft any kind of coordinated, systematic response to the boycott proposal or, for that matter, to any other racial unrest. In fact, there was no single sport authority in the United States at that time. Indeed, to speak of a single "sporting establishment" as I have here at times is something of a misnomer (as it is still today). To the extent such a "system" or establishment existed, it was a radically localized, decentralized—some might have said disorganized—one. The day-to-day operation of sport in the United States was left mainly to separate, individual committees or federations for each of the individual sports, and many of these did little more than set national rules and regulations or perhaps hold regional or national competitions. Larger, multisport organizations such as the AAU, the NCAA, or the USOC were, in many respects, little more than administrative bodies responsible for coordination and public image making. The United States Olympic Committee's sole charge involved coordinating all the various sports agencies under the umbrella of an American Olympic team every four years. The Amateur Athletic Union did more to coordinate and organize many of the most important, highest profile sports federations in the country, but its power was limited by the fact that it was, as its name suggested, a loose confederation of organizations at best. The AAU's chief rival, the NCAA, had authority over all collegiate sport in the United States, but it too was simply an association of colleges, universities, and conferences with very little power to act on its own to change the practices and policies of its member institutions. Making coordinated action even more unlikely was the fact that the AAU and the NCAA were locked in an ongoing, all-out struggle for institutional control over amateur athletics and amateur athletes.[10] (And this isn't even to address the uneasy relationship between amateur and professional sports given Olympic eligibility requirements at the time.) Suffice it to say that no single individual or agency had the power or authority to take additional action.

Of course, such an institutional arrangement can work to the collective advantage of agencies and organizations content with the status quo, reluctant or simply unwilling to take action in the first place. And, in fact, just as this loosely organized, confederated structure made it difficult for action to be taken, it also made it relatively easy for athletic officials to either deny institutional responsibility for the racial questions they faced or delegate the task of coming up with specific, concrete responses to other, more sport-specific or locally oriented actors and agencies (or both). Such jurisdictional jockeying was suggested in the otherwise minor detail

I noted a few paragraphs earlier, in which the USOC asked the Basketball Committee to come forward with a proposal to address the problems a boycott would present for American basketball hopes. Thus we see that the USOC's initial response to the so-called basketball controversy was to place responsibility for it "in the hands of" the Executive Committee of the United States Basketball Committee.[11] Revealingly, it didn't take long for the U.S. Basketball Committee to return serve. Less than a month later, American basketball officials reported back to the USOC leadership that they did not feel it was their "place" to take this issue on. (In fact, it was the Basketball Committee's inability or unwillingness to deal with this issue on its own that alerted President Roby and his vice president Clifford Buck to the possibility that the USOC itself might need to make a further statement on the proposed boycott, if not take some kind of concrete action.) Not that the USOC came up with a better plan. I have already noted the press release that this discussion produced. Apparently the USOC's "solution" was to turn the issue back to the Basketball Committee once again—the next time they met (in March) it was only to discuss the Basketball Committee's proposed pledge. It almost seems that the reason athletic officials spent so little time and energy figuring out what they *could* do about the proposed boycott was because they spent so much time simply trying to decide *who* should *have* to do something in the first place.

Because so many of the top amateur players in the country competed for NCAA-member colleges and universities,[12] the NCAA found itself reluctantly drawn into the basketball matter as well. In fact, the NCAA was squarely at the center of the boycott controversy as far as basketball was concerned, because one of the few athletes who had spoken publicly on behalf of a boycott was Lew Alcindor, the star center of the NCAA national championship basketball team of the University of California, Los Angeles (UCLA). More than this, every indication was that Alcindor's two most talented teammates, Mike Warren and Lucius Allen, were prepared to join him in bypassing the Olympic Games. This was an unfortunate situation, as far as the NCAA was concerned, because while these were technically NCAA athletes, there was little NCAA officials could do to change their minds. Initially the NCAA president and his staff went to some lengths to communicate with the players through the UCLA athletic department. When information leaked to the press that the three would not accept the invitation to be on NCAA teams for an Olympic tryout, Byers and his staff took an unprecedented step. They released a list of some forty-eight prospective Olympians in late February (weeks before the tryouts were to begin) along with a detailed description of the selection procedures that the "NCAA Olympic Basketball Committee" would use in selecting a team to represent the United States in Mexico City:

> We think this is a tremendous squad. They represent potentially as fine a group of players as any which has ever represented the Association. We are delighted by their response. We are proud of their willingness to make significant personal sacrifices in order to go through the rigorous qualifying training period necessary to represent our nation in the Olympic games, where the United States has never lost a basketball game. They could make America proud of its basketball talent by themselves. Our country is accordingly assured of another outstanding Olympic team.[13]

Buried in the final lines of the press release, on page two, was a statement that mentioned that three UCLA players had been nominated and contacted about their availability. None, according to statement, expressed interest in the trials or said they would accept an invitation if extended; thus, the UCLA players were not invited to the tryouts. Later in March Byers would insist that "a Negro boycott of the 1968 Olympic basketball games clearly had failed." But even this strategy of downplaying what they could not control was not fully successful. The numbers and names of participants were telling. On March 17 the NCAA was forced to release a second list of "confirmed participants." Not only were there only forty-six names on this list (two fewer than before), but there were seven new names on the list—meaning that at least nine NCAA players, in addition to the three from UCLA, had, for one reason or another, decided not to try out for the team.

As little in the way of tangible reaction and response to the boycott initiative as these deliberations produced, the athletic leadership's handling of those matters reveals a remarkable racial arrogance and insensitivity. This attitude came through in the USOC's decision to devote additional time and public comment to what it had initially tried to brush off. President Roby and Vice President Buck claimed the special session was necessitated by the amount of press reporting on the proposed boycott and especially the degree of public hostility it had generated. (Roby claimed to have a "big file" of articles and clippings "both pro and con" on the subject.) What they did not refer to were the allegations about racism and discrimination in sport that were beginning to surface. This factor is easy to overlook only because the committee itself didn't talk about it much. Despite the fact that the U.S. track-and-field team, which was obviously affiliated with the USOC, had been targeted specifically by Harry Edwards, there was no explicit mention of this charge. Indeed, there were only a few vague suggestions about the fact that the committee had been criticized for its own, all-white racial composition, and only a single mention of the fact that some athletes felt there were disparities in treatment with respect to team selection, housing, and training meals.[14] In previous chapters I argued that the substance and validity of these claims was one of the driving forces behind the movement that was gaining steam at the time. But what I want to emphasize here is how the USOC dealt with—or, to be more precise, deigned not to deal with—these issues. Resistance, refusal and denial were the order of the day.

This posture was readily exemplified in the minutes of the USOC's discussion (such as it was) of the charges of discrimination against it.[15] The dialogue was clearly painful and halting, checkered with numerous hesitations, qualifications, and contradictions. Douglas Roby's attempt to lead the discussion is particularly illustrative. To begin with, he had surprising difficulty even introducing the matter to his colleagues. His attempt to respond to and refute the charges of discrimination was even more torturous. Roby insisted that "if there is a well-qualified individual whose skin is dark, but—why, we would certainly . . . as I say, why, we would certainly welcome him on this Board."[16] Realizing the implications of what he had said, the USOC president and American IOC representative then immediately backtracked to say that unfortunately it wasn't quite as simple as that. On the one hand, he said, such an individual had to be "qualified" (implying, of course, that there was a dearth of such qualified candidates). On the other, he also insisted that even a qualified candidate would have to "come in through ordinary, regular channels." Pressed to elaborate, Roby hit upon an embryonic reverse racism argument: "But, as I said before, I'd hate to see a man put on the Board just because his skin was dark."[17] In the end, despite having achieved no resolution on this matter whatsoever, Roby dropped it abruptly, cheerfully moving to a proposal to give future American Olympians some kind of "memento" (pins or rings were eventually proposed) to commemorate their participation in the Games.

The fact that the full extent of the USOC's programmatic response to prospective boycotters and the charge of institutional discrimination appears to have been the promise of token gifts would be laughable were it not taken so seriously and endorsed so enthusiastically by the board. It may be that the USOC didn't talk about the charges of racism in sport any further because they didn't believe them. Or perhaps the committee didn't discuss them because they thought these grievances and concerns would eventually go away (much as they expected for the boycott itself). This latter possibility wouldn't be surprising given the paternalistic attitude toward athletes exhibited by many of the committee members at that time and in these very meetings, good intentions notwithstanding. Here we are reminded of the various steps the USOC enacted in the weeks leading up to the Games (under direct pressure from IOC president Avery Brundage) to prevent "racial demonstrations" in Mexico City: the addition of extra athletes to the Tahoe training team, the solicitation of pledges of nondemonstration from athletes, and especially the creation of the special "Board of Consultants" headed by Jesse Owens. What is telling about all of these initiatives is that they made absolutely no attempt to deal with the racial injustices either inside or outside of sport that produced resistance and resentment among athletes in the first place; indeed, most officials steadfastly refused to even acknowledge—even in private, behind closed doors, which may well have placated some—the validity of such concerns.[18]

The NCAA was, if anything, even more adamant and deliberate about this than the USOC. Its leaders compiled only a slim, solitary folder on the racial issues in sport raised by disgruntled athletes at the time—and each one of the dozen or so pages in that folder were collected in preparation of a strategy (never enacted) to publicly discredit these claims.[19]

Clearly, then, U.S. amateur athletic officials were uninterested in any of the details about racial problems in and around sport. All they cared about was preventing demonstrations from happening. This attitude and posture betrays a serious misunderstanding or underestimation among American athletic officials of the depth and substance of the racial grievances of African American athletes against sport itself. It not only helps to explain why American athletic officials were so slow to respond to the Olympic boycott initiative but, more important, allows us to see how utterly inconceivable Harry Edwards's charges of racism in sport were for them. Regardless of what they could or couldn't do about the possibility of an Olympic boycott, the leaders of the sporting establishment simply didn't understand the extent to which racial unrest in sport stemmed directly from racism and racial discrimination that was very real. They would not be able to stay so misguided for long.

Insular and Indifferent No More

The national sporting establishment's intransigent approach to racial problems in and around sport had actually first began to fall apart in the spring of 1968 when Vice President Hubert Humphrey, chairing the newly reconstituted and expanded President's Council on Physical Fitness and Sports (PCPFS), issued his public call for more equitable African American representation in coaching and administration in sport. Humphrey's pronouncement was in large part an attempt to placate prospective Olympic boycotters, whom he strongly encouraged to "come and forward the cause" (see pp. 136–138 above).

Humphrey's nationalism, as I pointed out in chapter 5, is difficult to separate from his interest in racial equality, and it was no accident that these interests and ideals came to be linked together in sport. The vice president had a long-standing involvement with amateur sport and the Olympic movement in the United States. In the early 1960s he had chaired congressional committees overseeing American Olympic preparation and at one point even wrote a pamphlet titled "What Sport Means to Me."[20] In fact, Humphrey's initial and primary motivation for getting involved with the President's Council on Physical Fitness and expanding its focus to include "Sport" as well was to try to engineer some kind of solution to the ongoing jurisdictional disagreements and disputes between the NCAA and the AAU that threatened to compromise the performance (if not the rights) of American athletes. Humphrey was thus acutely aware of both the importance of American Olympic performances in the larger scheme of the Cold War, global politics and of the importance of African American athletes in American sport. He was also aware of the symbolic role that sport played in shaping Americans' beliefs about race relations. The vice president's personal correspondence of the period reveals, in fact, that he had been deeply concerned about the proposed Olympic boycott from its inception as well as about charges of racial inequality and discrimination in sport. He received numerous letters on the boycott itself, and in February of 1968, in fact, had personally written the NCAA to inquire about alleged charges of racial discrimination in the athletic program at the University of Southwestern Louisiana.[21] Whatever his base motives, Humphrey's statements both lent credibility to claims of racism and discrimination in sport and put pressure on national sports organizations to take action in this regard. It was, after all, difficult to hide when the vice president named names.

The USOC, in response, publicly declared itself "willing" to make such hires but claimed (in the argument Roby had rehearsed the previous December) that it had so far been unable to find "suitable applicants."[22] But the full extent of the establishment's discomfort with and resistance to the implied charge of racial bias in sport is only really captured in the debates that went on behind the scenes, out of view of the public eye, in the correspondence between the NCAA's executive director Walter Byers and the vice president.

Humphrey's public comments were formally conveyed to the NCAA by the PCPFS's director of information V. I. Nicholson in a letter to NCAA director Walter Byers dated April 17, 1968.[23] The letter indicates that Byers had not only been in contact with the vice president (or at least his office) following his public statements at the end of March but had, in these exchanges, called into question the charge of racial discrimination in sport implied in Humphrey's proposal. "(Y)ou have understood the Vice President correctly," Nicholson replied to Byers. "He does believe that there are qualified Negroes who are being denied administrative jobs in sport because of racial bias." Nicholson admitted that the vice president did not have specific "evidence" to support this claim but insisted such evidence was unnecessary, pointing out that "Negroes comprise approximately 10–12 percent of our total population" and "a somewhat larger percentage of our high school, college and professional athletes . . . yet we rarely find a Negro coach or director of athletics." These numbers were so striking, according to Nicholson, writing on Humphrey's behalf, "it hardly seems possible that so few of them could be qualified." Nicholson concluded the letter sarcastically, suggesting: "Perhaps the NCAA will want to clarify this point for us by issuing an official statement on the relative administrative abilities of its white and Negro athletes."

Byers hotly disputed these charges and implications. "During the twenty one years I have been an executive assistant or executive director of this Association," Byers wrote back, "we have never had an application from a Negro for a position on our staff." Furthermore, he went on to say, "After a random check of the major [NCAA member] conferences, I find a like situation to exist. This appears to be the case notwithstanding the fact that there are a number of Negroes who are quite active in NCAA affairs." On the other hand, Byers also pointed out, the University of Missouri and Michigan State had hired Prentice Gautt and Don Coleman, respectively, and "both are Negroes."[24]

In spite of the differences of philosophy and policy that seemingly still separated Byers and Humphrey, the vice president's spokesperson backed off considerably at this point. In mid-May, Nicholson assured Byers that neither the vice president nor the PCPFS "meant to imply that the major sports organizations are systematically excluding racial minorities from sports administration." Nicholson shifted the focus from who was at fault for the "situation" to what could be done to improve it. "All the Vice President is asking," he wrote, "is that amateur and professional sport recruit qualified Negro coaches and managers as vigorously as they do qualified Negro athletes. In other words, I think he is suggesting that we go beyond the point where there is no resistance to Negroes in coaching to a point where they are actively encouraged to seek such positions."[25]

Byers immediately accepted the olive branch. "Fair enough," he wrote back two days later. "We're glad to participate and take a leadership role on the basis of the description in the last sentence of your May 15 letter."[26]

Why did Nicholson suddenly change his tone and tactics? What had Byers said or done? It obviously had something to do with the "leadership role" to which Byers referred. Although none of these exchanges say so directly, it appears that Byers found common ground with Humphrey by promising to support one of the vice president's own pet projects: to develop a nationwide program that would open up community recreational facilities in inner-city areas that had been disrupted by rioting during the summer months the previous couple of years. (Humphrey had announced this initiative at the very same PCPFS press conference in which he leveled the charge of racial inequity in sports management.) Byers realized that this idea—which would eventually become the NCAA's "National Youth Sports Program"—was a perfect way to bring African American leadership into his organization and demonstrate a broader commitment to African Americans.

Even though this initiative was clearly a step (albeit a small one) in the right direction for Byers and his colleagues in the leadership of amateur athletic organizations in the country, it was not sufficient to head off the emerging racial crisis. The gravity of the situation finally began to hit home, it seems, in July, when the nation's leading sports weekly, *Sports Illustrated,* published its monumental five-part series "The Black Athlete: A Shameful Story." The series was both inspired by and grounded in the discontent, frustration, and downright anger of African American athletes concerning racial discrimination and inequality in the world of sport. "Almost to a man," the first installment said, Negro athletes "are dissatisfied, disgruntled and disillusioned."

> Black collegiate athletes say they are dehumanized, exploited and discarded, and some even say they were happier in the ghetto. Black professional athletes say they are underpaid, shunted into certain stereotyped positions and treated like sub-humans by Paleolithic coaches who regard them as watermelon-eating idiots.[27]

It was hard-hitting, riveting reporting—journalism that not only called attention to the grievances and discontents of African American athletes, but went out of its way to point out the stark contradictions between these problems and the popular image of sport as a leader in race relations. The first piece in the series, in fact, was called "The Cruel Deception." So powerful was the series and so intense the public response to it (Time published it as a book in a matter of months) that the leaders of the American sports world had no choice but to confront head on the issues it raised.

Given their previous reluctance to even acknowledge, much less actively engage, charges of racial inequality and discrimination in sport, it should not be surprising that sports officials were outraged by the series. A lengthy letter (seven pages single-spaced) written by the NCAA's public relations director Thomas Hansen to NCAA president Marcus Plant captures the collective attitude and response of the sporting establishment. His assessment was decisive and unyielding, a rambling diatribe against the series. He insisted that "A Shameful Story" is neither a "factual" nor "responsible" piece of journalism, and he accused both the magazine and the author of the series, Jack Olsen, of being "prejudiced and biased in their approach, choice and use of material, and editing."[28] Hansen implied, in a postscript to the letter, that *Sports Illustrated* ran the series in a desperate attempt to generate publicity and readership for itself, noting that the magazine had lost 140 pages of advertising from the previous year at the time the series went to press.[29] More substantively, Hansen claimed to have assembled enough evidence to prove his accusations of journalistic inaccuracy and distortion. In fact, the bulk of the letter was a page-by-page, interview-by-interview, incident-by-incident review and rebuttal of the series.

Hansen's self-described "lengthy epistle" was based upon his own intensive and extensive investigation. The NCAA seems to have been in contact with almost all of the institutions and many of the individuals quoted in and referred to in the series. It was in response to this article, in fact, that the NCAA began to compile documents on "racial issues."[30] For example, on August 21, Hansen wrote to James Owens, athletic director at the University of Washington (one of the schools under attack at the time), to ask for assistance, noting: "The NCAA Council discussed the Black athletic situation and will undoubtedly do so again in the future."[31] For a time, in fact, Hansen and his fellow NCAA executives gave serious consideration to making a series of public appearances to discredit the allegations and the author.[32]

But for all of this mitigating information and righteous indignation, the NCAA's smear campaign never materialized, indeed never really got off the ground at all. Even as he prepared his rebuttal for the NCAA, Hansen had his doubts as to what it would accomplish. The problem, he told President Plant, was that "no effective vehicle of reply is available."[33] It was actually more complicated than that.

For one thing, series author Jack Olsen's credentials as a journalist were impeccable, indeed beyond repute. He had been a senior editor at *Sports*

Illustrated for almost six years and had written a widely acclaimed book on Muhammad Ali in the mid-1960s (expanded from another five-part *SI* feature). More important, perhaps, and in contrast to many sportswriters, Olsen had actually cut his teeth in the journalism business outside of sports. He began his career as a newspaper reporter, working beats on crime and politics. He then spent a number of years as a correspondent for *Time* magazine (*SI*'s parent company), where he worked on at least a dozen cover stories, including one on the landmark Little Rock fight over school integration in 1957. During these years, he had also found time to write five other books (in addition to the Ali volume) on a wide variety of topics. So impressive was his record that shortly after beginning the "Black Athlete" series, Olsen was reportedly offered a prestigious and potentially profitable opportunity to write the campaign biography for one of the presidential candidates.

Olsen turned down the offer because he felt the black athlete's story was "too important to leave." He certainly found a mountain of evidence to support it. *Sports Illustrated* spent over six months researching the story, accumulating over 350,000 words of interview notes in the process. His publisher surely agreed, describing Olsen's story as "the most socially significant piece of work [his magazine] had ever published"; to this day, it remains one of *SI*'s proudest moments.[34] Olsen himself, who spent two full months writing the story, logged over half of the interview notes personally. Athletes talked with him sometimes for hours, Olsen wrote, often near tears or shaking with anger. "They would start out suspicious and in a minute or two there would suddenly come a flood of words."[35] And these words told a story, time and again, of an institution that seemed to be marked by deep racial inequalities and injustices. What this series really made clear was that the emerging resistance of African American athletes was not simply an opportunistic attempt to use sport for broader political purposes but rather—or perhaps additionally—that it was motivated and driven by prejudice, discrimination, and racism in the world of sport itself.

This was important because of what it said about the nature and significance of racial unrest in sport, and what would be required to resolve it. At a very basic level, these stories stood in stark contrast to the explanations that the sporting establishment had offered up until this point in time: namely, that the protests were driven mainly by racial extremists and sports outsiders, rabble-rousers attempting to use sport and African American athletes themselves for an agenda having nothing whatsoever to do with sport. No longer were such accounts possible. Whatever limitations and inaccuracies *Sports Illustrated*'s series on the black athlete may have suffered from, it basically got the story of African American discontent in sport right. Even Hansen, the NCAA watchdog and guardian, could not help coming to a similar conclusion. In one place Hansen actually concedes that "SI isn't totally wrong, just incredibly sloppy."[36] He summarized his conclusions to NCAA president Marcus Plant in this remarkable and revealing admission:

> None of us can say that prejudice does not exist—in athletics, on campuses, everyone in our society. We cannot defend ourselves from such a charge with our membership of 600 institutions, coaches, players, etc. Nor can we effectively answer a charge that Negro athletes have been exploited—in fact, realistically so have white athletes if "exploited" is the word one wants to use (in the context that if you make any money on anything a human does you "exploit" him). Everyone has been exploited in this context.[37]

The only way to address these very concrete problems, as well as the broader ideological and symbolic concerns I touched upon in the previous chapter, was for the amateur athletic establishment to change—to reform if not completely revamp its racial practices, policies, and attitudes. But who would assume responsibility for these changes, and how would they go about getting them done? These were questions the NCAA and other organizations of the sporting establishment would have to answer.[38]

Taking Action: Insulation, Absorption, and Rearticulation

In their well-known and influential *Racial Formation in the United States* (1994), Michael Omi and Howard Winant present a theory about the relationship between racial unrest and racial reform in the post—civil rights American era that they call an "unstable equilibrium model." In this model, racial activism and agitation present a challenge to the dominant social order, a threat that must be addressed by those in power, by the ruling racial regime, if that order is to be maintained. What is important about social movements from a racial equilibrium perspective, then, is less the revolutionary changes they promise than the more moderate reforms and rearticulations they require from those who are in power.

In Omi and Winant's formulation, it is the state that plays the role of representative, regulator, and enforcer of the established racial regime. And the state fulfills this, its essentially conservative task, through the processes Omi and Winant call absorption, insulation, and rearticulation (1994, pp. 84–88). Absorption, in Omi and Winant's description, is the state's recognition that "many movement demands are greater threats to the [established] racial order before they are accepted than after they have been adopted in suitably moderate form." Thus, the state's function is to address these demands with policy reforms that are as minimal as possible. Indeed, much of the work of absorption becomes an exercise in translating radical demands into small and mostly symbolic reform initiatives. Insulation is a closely connected process in which "the state confines demands [of the insurgent movements] to terrains that are, if not entirely symbolic, at least not crucial to the operation of the racial order." By insulating itself against the more radical demands of activists and, at the same time, adopting or incorporating the more moderate, symbolic elements of their activist programs, the state works to reestablish the once-threatened racial equilibrium. Thus, at any given time and place, the relative racial equilibrium is "the product of the interaction of racially based social movements and the [state-based] institutions that represent and regulate the established social order" (p. 87).

What is most striking and original about Omi and Winant's scheme (and what therefore justifies their idiosyncratic terminology over the more familiar paradigm of "cooptation") is not the institutional compromise the state strikes with movement activists, interests, and ideals; rather it is the ideological context and consequence of this bargain. For what is at stake in this deal, as Omi and Winant understand it, is not just control over institutions and resources but actually the ideological function these arrangements serve by making it seem as if racial progress has been made. In other words, a reestablished racial equilibrium involves not just a new institutional balance of power but an acceptance of the legitimacy of this new arrangement. This goes to their whole understanding of racial orders as fundamentally unstable, inherently prone to breakdown and thus re-quiring repair. Indeed, one of the most interesting and often overlooked aspects of Omi and Winant's framework is their understanding that racial regimes require constant institutional innovation and ideological reaffirmation to remain vibrant and functioning.

Omi and Winant's general model can be applied to the actions under-taken by the various organizations and elites of the athletic establishment in response to the challenge of activism and unrest among African American athletes as represented powerfully in Smith and Carlos's victory-stand demonstration. Even before they were fully aware of the crisis (and probably even without being fully conscious of what they were doing), the various institutions and elites of the American amateur athletic establishment had begun to follow the logic of Omi and Winant's racial equilibrium model, to set up the conflict in terms they would be able to deal with directly. For example, they tried to insulate themselves against the more radical demands of African American athletic activists by painting Harry Edwards as an extremist and an opportunist, while creating possibilities for absorption and rearticulation by giving generous attention to "moderate" athletes like Ralph Boston. The fact that USOC president Douglas Roby and others moderately defended Evans and his teammates (and even took a bit of responsibility for their gesture themselves) against the perceived militancy of Smith and Carlos is surely part of this dynamic as well, especially when set against the USOC leak of shoe payments to Smith and Carlos, which was obviously intended to discredit them and their cause further (if not also to allow the IOC to strip them of their medals).[39] Even erstwhile moderates and progressives participated in this process. For example, in presenting the findings of the Board of Consultants, John Sayre felt compelled to say that there were a "few" athletes, a "minority . . . causing certain kinds of trouble," who were "loud-mouthed and rude and arrogant and took no responsibility for representing their team or their country and had a 'what's-in-it-for-me' attitude."[40]

Time and again, the media used the reference point of the 1968 Olympic demonstration as the standard against which reasonable, rational demands were separated from radical, unreasonable ones. A *Denver Post* commentary on the protests of a group of black football players at the University of Wyoming is exemplary: "The most disturbing thing about it all, however, is that the 14 Negro players involved are not making up their own minds but being used as cat-paw by the same kind of movement that would use the athletic field as a sociological laboratory." The implicit reference to the young scholar Harry Edwards was obviously not incidental. The article concluded by editorializing: "The whole mess smacks of the kind of meddling advocated by Harry Edwards who masterminded the disgraceful black-glove incident by John Carlos and Tommie Smith in the last Olympic Games."[41]

Perhaps because it had no other jurisdictional power or authority, the national office of the NCAA under the direction of Walter Byers seems to have been the most adamant and aggressive about trying to marginalize, isolate, and exclude the more radical, demanding elements of African American athletic resistance from the mainstream sporting scene in the aftermath of 1968. The national office took a hard line against protest aimed at athletic programs and encouraged its member institutions to do likewise. On the one hand, the NCAA's national leadership refused official public acknowledgment of any practices, policies, or systematic patterns of racial discrimination in its purview and even went so far as to provide advice and assistance to university officials at member institutions trying to deal with such charges and accusations. (This was apparent in the protests against schools such as Wyoming who competed against the racially discriminatory Brigham Young University: the national office followed the situation closely, compiling a small file of media reports and staying in close, albeit secret and largely undocumented, contact with officials at schools so targeted.)

The NCAA also targeted protesters and the schools at which they were enrolled. In its most dramatic (and ill considered) such action, the NCAA even suspended San Jose State from competition in 1964, thus denying them the right to defend the national championship they had won the previous year. San Jose State officials believed this was because John Carlos competed on their team. The NCAA vigorously denied this, emphasizing jurisdictional disputes, but the racial subtext was so obvious that even the usually conservative *Sports Illustrated* editoralists found the denial difficult to believe.[42] At the root of the magazine's doubt was a "special news feature" the NCAA released—via its newly created publication, the *NCAA News*—in the fall of 1969. The "report" warned against "an organized, outside pressure campaign" that had connections and direct communications with "Communist-oriented, revolutionary . . . groups" (among them, the NCAA included Students for a Democratic Society, the Black Panther Party, the Student Non-Violent Coordinating Committee, the Black Student Union, and the Peace and Freedom Party) that was trying to recruit athletes at various NCAA member institutions. According to the NCAA,

> Intercollegiate athletics is a prime target and vehicle for them because of the publicity value inherent in sports and the fact that the Negro or black athlete involved in a mild disorder will be a subject of newsprint from coast to coast whereas the acts of a less-publicized [incident] may only be reported in the campus newspaper.

The NCAA named Harry Edwards as one of the leaders of these "hard line insurrectionists" who employed tactics of "violence and force" with the ultimate aim of "polarize[ing] the races" in the United States. The title of the story said it all: "Militant Groups Doing Great Disservice to Black College Athletes."[43] It is difficult to imagine a more obvious attempt to isolate and insulate against racial resistance.

Such an absolutist, uncompromising position obviously made it impossible for the NCAA's national leadership to carry out the activities of absorption and rearticulation in Omi and Winant's model. But this is where the decentralized, confederate structure of the NCAA and the amateur athletic world in general worked to the collective advantage of a sporting establishment that needed to take constructive action. It allowed the leaders of the largest national organizations to avoid having to assume actual, day-to-day responsibility for the racial crisis, leaving the task instead to their member agencies, organizations, and affiliates. This is supported by David K. Wiggins's (1991, 1997) careful historical case studies of how predominantly white, NCAA-member colleges and universities responded to racial unrest on their campuses. According to Wiggins, the institutions were, for better or for worse, left to their own devices. In fact, he concludes that there was "no coordinated effort by any athletic conference (or agency) to identify common grievances of black athletes and find solutions to disturbances occurring on university campuses" (Wiggins 1997). Such coordination was, from the point of view of the national office of the NCAA itself, neither necessary nor (more important) desirable as it would have admitted culpability.

Despite a lack of concerted, coordinated effort, however, the similarity of the responses of these academic institutions is remarkable. In each of the three cases of revolt that Wiggins examines in detail—at the University of California, Berkeley; Syracuse University; and Oregon State University—he finds that the highest-ranking institutional officer (Chancellor Heyns, Chancellor Corbally, and President Jensen respectively) accepted the legitimacy of African American grievances. Each set up fact-finding committees (or their equivalents) to determine the situation regarding the charges and to recommend policy changes if and where they were necessary. And, in contrast to many such university commissions, Wiggins claims that the recommendations made by these committees often led to important, substantive reforms in university policies for and serving African American athletes.[44]

In the context of these individualized, institutional responses, it is worth noting that the response of some of the coaches of these athletes—the best coaches of their period, people like Bud Winters and John Wooden—focused on sport and let these athletes hold and express political opinions they may not have agreed with. These were not particularly political men but understood and accepted the politics and personal concerns of their athletes often, one has to believe, over and above the objections of their own administrations, athletic departments, and local media. Tommy Smith calls Winter a "humanitarian" to this day. "This white, middle-aged gentleman coached Lee Evans, John Carlos, Ronnie Ray Smith and me at a time when we were all quivering with the beginnings of the politics of the black athlete and he never said a word to us about any of that. He simply coached us and left us free to live our lives creatively."[45] Kareem Abdul-Jabaar has expressed similar sentiments about his UCLA coach John Wooden as well. Wooden's mutual admiration for Abdul-Jabaar was expressed in his own autobiography (1988),

> I can say without equivocation that in the four years Lewis Al-cindor played for me at UCLA, his mere presence created problems that shouldn't have existed, but the young man himself personi-fied cooperation as exemplified by his greatness on the basketball floor. . . . [He] was, in my opinion, the finest truly big man ever to play basketball up to his time. He could do everything you asked of him, and do it almost to perfection. His tremendous physical ability, however, could not have been nearly so effective had it not been for his intelligence and exceptional emotional control. (pp. 145–146)

Harry Parker, coach of the Harvard rowing team, and U.S. men's swim-ming coach George Haines were two coaches who had similar reputations of tolerance and respect for politically active white athletes.

If it had the luxury of allowing member institutions and individual coaches to do the actual dirty work of dealing with the most blatant and publicly damaging forms of racial discrimination and exploitation, the NCAA's national office did not sit idly by. It couldn't afford to. The NCAA not only had its own reputation to protect, it had also made a commit-ment to Vice President Humphrey and the President's Council on Physical Fitness and Sport to take a leadership role in bringing African Americans into the administration ranks of amateur athletics. It was a pledge the NCAA, led by executive Walter Byers, took seriously and hoped to make good on with an innovative, inner-city-based youth outreach program.

I have already mentioned how Hubert Humphrey, at the very same press conference in which he questioned the sporting establishment's commitment to racial integration, had issued a call for the nation's may-ors and school officials to keep school facilities open throughout the sum-mer of 1968. Humphrey's idea was that athletes, coaches, and teachers be mobilized to serve as supervisors, leaders, and instructors for the effort, and additionally announced the formation of a privately staffed and fi-nanced National Sports Committee for Youth to assist local officials and practitioners in the effort. In concert with this proposal, PCPFS staff mem-bers began working with Mayor's Councils on Youth Opportunity to or-ganize functioning sports and recreation committees in fifty of the largest cities in the country.[46] This was just the opportunity the NCAA leadership was looking for. In 1967 the NCAA's Executive Committee had granted initial approval for the organization to become involved in a youth de-velopment program that looked a great deal like the initiative outlined by the vice president.[47] Based upon the archival evidence currently available, it is difficult to establish whether these two proposals were connected in any way in their initial conceptions. But what the NCAA's archival records indicate clearly is that sometime shortly after Humphrey's formal public announcement, the NCAA's Byers embarked upon an aggressive and ultimately successful campaign to link up with the federal government in order to coordinate such a program.

The first organizational meeting between the NCAA and the PCPFS was held in Chicago in November 1968. The committee, which included representatives from Humphrey's office and the NCAA's top officials (including Byers), reviewed existing summer sports programs and a draft program paper titled "Summer Youth Sports Program." Apparently the collaboration went well. In February 1969 the NCAA convened a meeting of a newly formed administrative committee to formalize timetables and guidelines for the National Summer Youth Sports Program (NSYSP).

In the next couple of weeks, maps and application forms received by the NCAA from PCPFS were mailed out to "invited participating institutions," together with the established guidelines and budget forms. The deadline for schools to return completed applications was March 31, and on April 3–4 the committee held a meeting to review and approve the applications for the one hundred original programs. The minimum program was to run at least five weeks between June 1 and September 1, four days per week (six were recommended), with at least two hours of activity. Participants were to be between twelve and eighteen years old. Required components included education, a meal, and medical examination.[48] The official NSYSP press release described the program in the following manner:

> NCAA member colleges and other institutions of higher education are joining together to conduct a youth sports program on an unprecedented scale. Probably the NCAA's most challenging project, this program will provide sports training, health instruction and competition for poverty-area youngsters from 12 to 18 years of age. In cooperation with the President's Council on Physical Fitness and Sports, backed by Federal government financial support, this inaugural program involving approximately 150 colleges is based on the conviction that sound sports instruction and sports participation in an educational atmosphere will help young people learn good health habits and sound competitive principles.[49]

On April 7, 1969, the federal Office of Economic Opportunity assigned funds to the Department of Health, Education, and Welfare (HEW) to support the NSYSP effort, and all systems were "go."

In its first full year of operation, the NSYSP program operated at one hundred institutions serving fifty-four different metropolitan areas. It enrolled 33,475 participants at an overall cost of approximately $5 million ($3 million from federal sources; $1.8 million from participating institutions; and the remainder from the NCAA national office) for a per-participant, per-day cost of $3.79.[50]

A variety of interests were served by this collaborative project.[51] For one, it afforded the federal government the opportunity to do something (even if it was simply symbolic) in and for the inner-city communities that had been plagued recently by violence and rioting. The theme of the press release dispatched from Washington, D.C. detailing Vice President Spiro Agnew's (the Democrats lost control of the program when Humphrey lost the presidential election in 1968) unveiling of the program was "Long, Hot Summer Made Cooler"—an obvious and intentional reference to the urban racial disturbances of the previous year. The NSYSP also allowed individual colleges and universities, especially those located in many of the urban areas most impacted by problems of the previous summer, to demonstrate their commitment to the neighborhoods and communities in which they were situated. The NSYSP initiative must also be understood as one dimension of a much larger, ongoing effort on the part of the NCAA to cement their relationship with federal authorities and lawmakers in their dispute with the AAU.[52] Perhaps most of all, as far as the NCAA and the American sporting establishment was concerned, the NSYSP program served to renew and reestablish a basic commitment to racial equality and African American advancement.

As with all agencies and programs that adhere to a color-blind, meritocratic ideology, this final point is easier to assert than to demonstrate. In both public forums and private communications, Walter Byers explicitly and vociferously denied that the program had any racial or even sociological agendas. An example can be found in a letter he wrote to public relations director Thomas Hansen regarding the production of a video that followed Vice President Spiro Agnew in describing the program as a way to "cool off" racial agitators. According to Byers, this concept did not express the real reason the NCAA was involved in this undertaking. With obvious annoyance, he explained:

> The reason that I have encouraged and urged the NCAA to play this sometimes stimulating, sometimes frustrating game with the Federal Government is because of a deeply-felt belief in what sports can do for young people. Although you have heard it and read it before, I will repeat it here: "We know what sports can do for the

young—in building good habits, in directing the competitive urge toward constructive ends, in stimulating the imagination toward new goals and in satisfying the human desire to belong and participate." . . . I would much prefer to see that approach taken in explaining the objective and concept of the program as opposed to the NSYSP program being a device to cool off the agitators.[53]

Byers was obviously reiterating old individualist themes of sports idealists here. But what stands out about this letter are some of the things it didn't include.

For one thing, Byers did not explicitly deny that the program would impact racial unrest in cities or even that NSYSP participants might be those who would pose problems for urban areas (or for the NCAA member school situated in urban areas). Also, despite the annoyance about it he expressed to Agnew, Byers had himself used the ghetto crime and violence theme to "sell" the NSYSP project to the President's Council in the first place. For example, Byers sent a letter to one prominent member of the President's Council, V. I. Nicholson in which he recommended (and attached) an article from the February 1969 issue of *The Modern Gymnast* that articulated these exact themes. Furthermore, in publicizing and promoting the program in his own organization, the NCAA executive rarely failed to highlight the racial demographics of the populations it targeted, and photographs and descriptions of program participants never left their racial identity in question.

At the root of Byers's objections, then, was not whether race was an issue but rather how to talk about race and what to do about it. In a view that resonated deeply with that of IOC president Avery Brundage, the NSYSP was intended not to regulate and control black communities but rather to guide and direct the individuals who composed these communities. As an overtly nonracial policy that nevertheless had deliberate racial overtones and consequences, the NSYSP allowed Byers to deny problems of race in his sporting purview and, at the same time, to claim that his institution was one ultimately committed to racial justice and harmony. The contradictions of Byers's position also come out in a letter to Bud Wilkinson, the former chair of the President's Council on Physical Fitness, who was at that time serving as a special consultant to President Nixon on sport. Byers claimed that the NCAA had invested considerable resources to the NSYSP effort not to improve its "ledger sheets" but rather "because of our deeply-felt conviction that this program has unrealized potential for advancing the welfare and ultimate strength of the youth in this country." Byers went on to explain how his organization hoped to expand the program in future years and yet was "willing and prepared to take the blame for its failures if and when they occur." Yet despite all these promises and responsibilities, Byers returned again to the opening theme of his communication to stress that he "did not see" how the program could "be a benefit to the NCAA" because of its anticipated annual cost ($50,000) and the fact that it would "add work at the busiest time of the year." Byers insisted that the NCAA's involvement was completely altruistic: "We're in it simply because we believe in it," was the last line he wrote.[54]

It doesn't appear that the other major organizations of the American amateur athletic establishment, the AAU and the USOC, were as active and adamant about isolating leaders of African American athletic protests and insulating themselves against racial activism and unrest as was the NCAA. But they confronted the challenge of racial unrest in and around sport in their own ways, usually along the lines of incorporating the more moderate, symbolic elements of the movement. As I have alluded to above, USOC officials clearly recognized the extent of the racial crisis brought out by the events in Mexico City. Speaking for the group, Orth acknowledged that the problem had "almost turned out to be a full-blown donny-brook" and insisted, "We have—we are facing—some very serious questions, maybe a serious dilemma as to what we should do."[55] On the one hand, USOC officials agreed that the boycott problem should have been dealt with better, should have been foreseen and headed off, and they extensively discussed how to ensure that this wasn't repeated in the future. They also took several important steps, perhaps the most important of which was the creation of a permanent board of athletic consultants. While this initiative obviously addressed a whole range of athletic discontents and concerns, at least two African American representatives joined the board and were featured prominently in USOC publicity and promotion (see fig. 8).

Rearticulation: Jesse Owens and the Idealist Defense of Sport

While the various institutions and agencies of the American sports regime were preoccupied with acts of insulation and absorption, others in the sporting world took it upon themselves to defend sport's racial form, function, and historical record. One of the most famous of those was Jesse Owens. Although he was far from an intellectual, Owens had a keen sense of the broad ideas and ideals at stake in all of this, one that paralleled the views of the Olympic establishment and Avery Brundage himself. But while Brundage, working mostly on the international scene out

Fig. 8. USOC Athletes Advisory Panel, 1970. © IOC/Olympic Museum, archives. Photograph: Ardmore Studio, Miami.

of IOC headquarters in Lausanne, Switzerland, was able to dismiss the Smith-Carlos demonstration and black athletic resistance more generally as a matter of "politics," Owens knew that Edwards's attack on the sports world as fundamentally racist could not be so easily dismissed. Edwards's use of the Smith-Carlos demonstration and black athletic resistance more generally as a means of elaborating a thoroughgoing critique of sport's progressive, idealist ideology was just the impression Owens feared the "sick headlines" from Mexico City would leave on the American public (Baker 1986, pp. 211–215). Owens, of course, had opposed the boycott stringently and did everything in his power in Mexico City to minimize the impacts of Smith and Carlos's demonstration once it occurred. (For this, Owens was, incredibly, described in one USOC executive board meeting as "one of the bright spots" of the 1968 Games and praised for having "done a remarkable and constructive job" in dealing with the racial problems in Mexico City.)[56] When he returned home to the States, Owens focused all his righteous indignation on a manuscript designed to provide a definitive critique of African American athletic resistance in all its forms. The product of these labors was the awkwardly titled *Blackthink: My Life as a Black Man and White Man* (1970), ghostwritten with Paul Neimark.

Blackthink was, at its core, a rebuttal to Harry Edwards, Tommie Smith, and John Carlos, and everything they stood for both literally and symbolically: from their race-based critique of sport to their racial politics more generally. For these reasons, this remarkable, unguarded volume reveals a great deal about both the ideological dimensions of the legitimation crisis brought on by Smith, Carlos, and Edwards in the world of sport and the lengths to which sports idealists would go to defend their institution and the values it was believed to represent. At a very basic level, Owens believed that what he called these "Olympic incidents" had damaged the image of "the Negro athlete in America" as well as the reputation of sport itself, an institution Owens described as "vitally important" in American life. Owens summarizes the main thrust of his argument against them on the final page of the book's opening chapter: "The Negro can never catch his precious quicksilver by making his hand into a fist" (p. 27).

It almost goes without saying that the Smith and Carlos demonstration, which Owens calls a "black power salute" (p. 78) and compared to the gestures of Nazi soldiers (p. 79), is the crucial point of departure for the entire analysis. Owens's account of these events is presented in a chapter titled "Negroes Have Human Hangups?" He begins with a startling, implausible, and yet revealing claim: that the "happenings in Mexico City" were, for Americans, "past history," and "not even a dim memory for most" (p. 80). More than this, he insists that in Mexico City, the whole incident was a "black herring" with "as many overtones . . . as two grammar school kids trying to create a tidal wave by skipping stones in the Pacific Ocean." The proof, he argues (again, in stark denial of all other evidence) is that not one of the more than seven thousand other athletes in the Village "went along with Smith and Carlos," not even, he claims, "the Africans." Cutting against all of this is the fact that Owens himself felt the need to write an entire book in response.

In any case, after having "set the record straight" about 1968, the former Olympian and American icon sketches the outlines of his vision about sport and its social value in America:

> . . . more than anything else to the kid who starts off poor or underfoot, sports represent the American dream. If a boy can't grow up and make it there, he can't make it anywhere. Well, a Negro kid can make it there, especially there. It's no accident that there's a higher percentage of colored major league baseball players than

in the population at large. Or that almost half the pro basketball players are black. . . . It's because we're making it. (p. 80)

Owens's claims about sport being a positive racial force are not limited to its role as an avenue for African American mobility. They also involve the traditional notion that as an arena of social interaction, sport fosters harmonious relations between the two races.

Owens elaborates these points (as he did with so many of the arguments in this explicitly autobiographical treatment) with anecdotes and examples from his own personal experience. Indeed, the climactic chapter of *Blackthink* (pp. 167–193) is an extended and embellished thirty-page account of his famous 1936 Berlin Olympic story: of his four Olympic gold medals, of the intense personal friendship he struck up with the German Luz Long in the course of their spectacular competition in the long jump, and, of course, the apocryphal account of how Hitler snubbed him after his first Olympic championship on Aryan soil. These stories are, for Owens, enduring testaments to the power of sport as a site for promoting interracial harmony and understanding, an interpretation that contradicted the conclusions Harry Edwards had drawn from the Smith-Carlos incident just a year earlier. The former Olympic champion concludes this extended anecdote and implicit argument with an appeal to none other than Harry Edwards himself. Owens exhorts the young sociologist to look back to his own athletic experiences and follow the model of his elders in order to contribute to "the true cause."[57]

At the heart of Owens's faith in sport, then, was obviously his understanding of this "true cause" itself. For Owens this cause spoke to his complete and unconditional commitment to the ideals of individualist meritocracy, the notion that the best, most just society was one that had fair rules that applied equally to all individuals regardless of race, class, creed, or other social distinction; as long as these rules were equally and fairly enforced, individuals would be granted the freedom and autonomy to interact and compete freely in the public sphere of social life. Sport was, for Owens as for many sports idealists, a symbol of and model for this ideal, its perfect embodiment.

Of course, one of the most fundamental claims issued by African American activists in this post–civil rights period was that this ideal of color-blind, individualistic meritocracy was not equal to the task of solving the challenges faced by black Americans in the United States. In this view, the problem for African Americans was no longer one of prejudice and the lack of individual rights and freedom, or even of unequally applied formal laws (as Owens understood racism), but rather of persistent structural inequalities that made it difficult for African Americans to realize any kind of meaningful, substantively equal participation in American society. As I have shown, it was precisely this fundamentally sociological, post–civil rights orientation that persuaded OPHR activists to use their involvement in sport in a more direct and deliberate fashion than African American athletes had ever envisioned before. (Any less would have rendered these athletes pawns of the dominant racial order because their prominence would have served to legitimate the openness and success of the racial status quo.) And this is to say nothing of the uncomfortable tension between Owens's expressed universalism and his unquestioned American nationalism.

Unswerving in his commitment to the individualist-meritocratic ideology he believed sport so thoroughly embodied, Owens would have none of this. To think in any other terms—that is, to delve into sociological consideration of external structures and collectivist concerns—was itself a perversion of social justice. This, in fact, was the very essence of what Owens called "blackthink." Indeed, in a chapter called the "Anatomy of a Black Militant," Owens compares the collectivist, separatist rhetoric of post–civil rights activists like Edwards with that of Adolf Hitler's *Mein Kampf.* Overdrawn and out of touch as this analogy may have been, its inspiration and implication was clear: that race-thinking of any kind or collective action of any sort was akin to Nazism and fascism, a form of "tyranny" as Owens puts it (p. 107). Much as it did for Brundage before him, Owens's idealized defense of this individualistic ethos led him to argue that the problems of race in the United States had, for all intents and purposes, been solved by the accomplishments of the civil rights movement. The title of the third chapter of his book, in fact, boldly proclaims: "Equality Is Here." The chapter goes on to recount his father's experiences with segregation in the South and his own segregated childhood, building up to the conclusion that "the torture is over."

> The memory may still be painful . . . But, by god, it's only a memory . . . Believe it or not, most black men today start just about equal with the white. We may not begin with as well-off a set of parents and we may have to fight harder to make that equality work. But we can make it work. Because now we have the one all-important gift of opportunity. . . . If the Negro doesn't succeed in today's America, it is because he has chosen to fail.[58]

Though rarely as unguarded and controversial as this passage (which raised the ire of countless African American readers), such characterizations permeate the text. Owens concludes the book by quoting an unnamed professor from Northwestern University's Center for Urban Affairs who predicted that the riots among inner-city blacks would be "going out of the picture." Owens endorses the prediction wholeheartedly, explaining it according to his own particular worldview: "the Negro is so well off and getting more well off with each new day. Yes, the Negro has problems—sometimes terrible problems. But they are almost always human problems now, and who in the hell doesn't have those?" (p. 84).

Owens's views of race relations obviously collapsed into delusion and self-deception because of the color-blind, individualist ideals he associated with sport. What is most interesting and revealing about this American icon is that he mounted his defense of these ideals primarily by defending the honor of sport itself.

In this respect, Owens diverges from his only possible equal as an icon and representative on these issues: Jackie Robinson. Robinson, too, was an individualistic idealist—indeed, perhaps more so than Owens. Having taken a leave of absence from his column at the *New York Post* to work on the Nixon presidential campaign in 1960, Robinson eventually went to work for Republican governor of New York Nelson A. Rockefeller.[59] Unapologetically individualist and free-market oriented (indeed, in many ways a black conservative ahead of his time), Robinson was nevertheless fully attentive to the inequalities African American faced even in the aftermath of the civil rights movement, and indeed he was something of an activist on these issues even in the sports arena. While this obviously requires more study, it is clear that Robinson, unlike Owens, did not idealize his participation in sport. A fierce, individualist personality, Robinson found it difficult to contain his anger and resentment upon first breaking into the big leagues—and this was something he never quite got over or forgot. After his retirement, the former baseball star came to see that sport was no panacea, no dream world where race didn't matter. Instead, Robinson realized sport as a battleground, an arena in which to push the struggle for fully realized freedom and equality. This is probably why he was one of the OPHR's supporters and why he was so active in the apartheid sports boycotts of South Africa.

Robinson unveiled his unique sensibilities in the autobiography he completed just before his early death in 1972: *I Never Had It Made*. Robinson held no illusions about the sports world, and in fact had a pretty well-developed understanding of both its possibilities and its limitations for the promotion of racial justice. If Robinson died broken and bitter, it was not because of his disappointments with sport (that he was realistic about); rather, it stemmed from his belief that American society had failed to live up to its liberal democratic ideals of freedom and equality for all.

Against this backdrop, what is most surprising and revealing about Owens's *Blackthink* is how seriously it was taken in the mainstream American press and how positively it was received. According to Owens's biographer, in fact, mainstream reviewers praised the book "almost without exception" (Baker 1986, pp. 214–215). As problematic and idealized as Owens's vision was, in other words, it was just more indication of the constellation of ideologies and interests that stood in the way of Edwards's attempt to initiate even the most basic of racial critiques in and through the world of sport.[60]

And it was probably the various individuals and organizations that composed the sporting establishment that gave Owens his most enthusiastic response. Owens made an unscheduled, impromptu presentation in front of the USOC three months after the 1968 Games, where he rehearsed many of the themes that became the core of his book. Owens's appearance in the room was greeted by "laughter and applause," and the meeting's presiding officer promised that his remarks would "add a little color to the meeting." His remarks received a standing ovation from everyone in attendance and were followed by very friendly, personal exchanges and some rather off-color jokes and innuendos.[61] Six months later, Owens made a more formal and consequential appearance at the Ninth Olympic Academy in Olympia, Greece, August 29–September 17.[62]

The purpose of such academies, which had been convened by Brundage since 1961, were clearly stated: "[T]o maintain the Olympic Spirit, to disseminate the principles of the Olympic Movement, to study and apply the educational and social principles of the Games and, finally, to establish the philosophy of the Olympic idea, according to the principles laid down by the ancient Greeks and those who revived the modern Olympic Movement through the initiative of Baron Pierre de Coubertin." The speakers, panelists, and participants of the Academy devoted most of their time to the usual tributes to Olympic ideals, presentations on the philosophical and historical aspects of the Games, technical reports on coaching, training, and officiating techniques, and the immediate bureaucratic questions about eligibility and the status of the Winter Games. But it was Owens, speaking on the seemingly mundane topic "A Pedagogical Evaluation of the Olympic Games from the Point of View of Athletes," who stole the show.[63]

Owens's presentation was so well received, according to official conference notes, that the audience asked that the former Olympic champion be granted additional time to field questions and comments after his talk. When even this wasn't enough to satisfy the audience, it was arranged for Owens to make a special, informal appearance the following day.

This unscheduled discussion itself generated additional "laughter and ap-plause" among the conference participants as well as a good deal more question and comment. So compelling and important was Owens's pre-sentation that 30 of the 240 pages of the final conference report (far more than were devoted to any other lecture or presentation) were reserved for a complete transcription of all of his responses to various questions and comments over the course of his public appearances at the Academy.[64]

Reading over these pages today there is little Owens said or did that would seem to have warranted such excitement and attention. Relying heavily on stories and parables drawn from his already well-known expe-riences, Owens did little more than reiterate basic Olympic truisms—such as "sport is a universal human language" or "goodwill and understand-ing are promoted through the competition between individuals"—these listeners held near and dear to their hearts, rehearsing the themes that would become *Blackthink* itself.[65] But when situated in the aftermath of the 1968 Olympic Games, Owens's remarks—even his mere appearance—take on much more significant symbolic and ideological dimensions. Specifically, they function to reinforce and legitimate the claims of Brun-dage and his colleagues in the international movement that Olympic sport was not only racially unbiased but that it was a leader in the move-ment toward racial justice in the United States and all around the world. Though they often pretended to ignore it, Olympic authorities well un-derstood the challenge Smith and Carlos and their colleagues had put to these ideals. Having Owens come to Olympia served as a counter to any doubts they may have had. And Owens himself was more than a willing participant in this process of ideological reaffirmation and consolidation; indeed, it was precisely the task he had set for himself.

Near the end of his remarks, he described what he called the "Smith-Carlos incident" as a strictly "American problem" and contrasted that per-formance with Bob Beamon's almost unfathomable world-record-setting long jump. Owens attributed Beamon's performance entirely to his "pa-triotism."[66] Moreover, the Olympic legend assured his admirers that he had heard absolutely no discussions about "political ideologies" during his stay in Mexico City. Owens understood the acute ideological chal-lenge of racial unrest in American sport, and his words were exactly what Olympic authorities and officials wanted—and needed—to hear. Thus, it is not surprising that portions of Jesse Owens's address were reprinted in the official publications of both the IOC and the USOC.[67]

If Owens's *Blackthink* was among the most visible and important exam-ples of how a coherent racial ideology was being rearticulated in the world of sport, this rearticulation process involved other approaches as well.

One of them was pursued by a journalist named Martin Kane, who wrote a famously controversial article for *Sports Illustrated* attributing the success of African American athletes to their inherent physical superiority.[68]

A great deal of ink has been spilled over this piece, as seems to be the case every time such racialist arguments are recited.[69] I won't attempt to review or recapitulate all of that here except to make a couple of very basic points about the tone, tenor, and social functions of Kane's story. While this piece obviously must be read as a direct response to the racial unrest of the period, it was a different kind of response than that of Owens's and indeed responded to an altogether different aspect of the racial crisis. More specifically, Kane's point was to refute the arguments—now conventional for sociologists of sport (cf. Eitzen and Sage 1978, p. 300; Coakley 1986, pp. 146–150; Sailes 1991) but then only beginning to be fashioned—that African American athletic success was the ironic result of deep structural inequalities in American society that made athletic success a socially viable option in the black community. A racialist response such as Kane's served to minimize or even deny the larger racial inequalities and injustices in the society as a whole. Notably, one of Kane's primary protagonists in this debate was Harry Edwards, who used the opportunity to formulate—in venues as varied as *The Black Scholar* (1971), *Intellectual Digest* (1972), and *Psychology Today* (1973a)—some of his most powerful important arguments about the social context within which African American athletic success could be explained. But also important is the unexpected impacts this formulation had for popular ideologies about sport. For if implicit in Kane's analysis was, as Patrick Miller (1998) has put it, "an attempt to isolate black achievements to the arena where natural physical abilities supposedly accounted for their triumphs," it also had the simultaneous effect of undermining the social significance of sport as idealists like Jesse Owens understood it.

Somewhere in between Kane's racialism and Owens's color-blind optimism was an attempt to downplay the existence of racial problems in sport on the grounds that racial problems in general were simply unavoidable in American society. This thesis was forwarded in a book penned by Bill Glass and William Pinson (with a foreword by Dallas Cowboys quarterback Roger Staubach) instructively titled *Don't Blame the Game: A Look at What's Right with Sports* (1972). The book was actually a response to the whole social upheaval among athletes in American sports—what I called in the previous chapter the "athletic revolution." Its authors claimed that those who represented this movement (in addition to those I cited in the previous chapter, Glass and Pinson singled out Joe Namath's *I Can't Wait Until Tomorrow; Bump and Run* by Marty Dames; and Bernie Parrish's *They*

Call It a Game) used "partial truths to arrive at corrupt conclusions." "This book," Glass and Pinson proclaim, "is a response to what men such as these are saying" (1972, p. 11). In short punchy chapters, Glass and Pinson then defend competition, Christianity, sportsmanship, and private ownership of sports teams. Like Owens, the authors saw sport as one of the last lines of defense against the "radical views . . . representative of a growing lifestyle in America" (p. 9). But race obviously posed a particular problem for them, and their approach to dealing with it is revealing.

First, they tried to downplay the existence of racism in sport, saying (a) that sport had done a great deal in the fight against racism in society and (b) that the problems of racial prejudice in sport were "getting better." Interestingly, they cite an interview with O.J. Simpson to make the case. "Five years ago," Simpson is quoted as saying, "you might find a guy in the Southeastern Conference who came into pro ball and had never played with or against a white ball player. You see, that is going on quite a bit now because they are integrating the conference. They are playing schools with black athletes and it's changing" (p. 37). Later they return to the Simpson interview to insist not only that things were getting better but to reiterate the old, traditional line that sport was actually a progressive racial force in society, an avenue of upward mobility. "In athletics, the black-white relationship explains itself. When you're on a team, you don't care if there is a black or white guard, just as long as he can block. . . . You're looking at a person by his ability not his color, creed or whatever. . . . In other words, you judge a person for what he is and can do, instead of his color, etc." (p. 41).

In spite of all this, the authors could not deny that racial problems still remained in sport. All they could do was insist that "the black athletes' problems rest more outside the team than within it. Even if a black athlete is treated fairly by the coaches, he still has to live in a prejudiced society. . . . It must be hard to take—accepted as a black athlete but rejected as a black human being. Black athletes have legitimate gripes. There is no doubt about that" (p. 44). But whatever gripes they may have recognized, the authors were insistent that their source remained completely outside of the sports arena. "[P]ro sports," they concluded, "reflect the prejudice of American life, but they don't contribute to it." Indeed, they "deserve some credit for all the improvements in race relations over the last few years. . . . [A]ny racism in pro sports is the product of a sickness in our society and in mankind in general." But "don't," the authors plead in the line that became the book's title, "blame the game." Uninspiring as it was and unacceptable as it would have been to folks like Owens and Brundage, that line speaks volumes about the complexity and contradictions of the racial rearticulation process the world of sport was working through.

End of an Era

For all his bravado about its intensification in the years following Smith and Carlos's victory-stand demonstration, the movement Harry Edwards christened "the revolt of the Black athlete" did not sustain the energy, intensity, and purpose it had in the late 1960s in the seventies. The "Federation of Black Athletes" that Edwards had boldly promised to organize never materialized, and the number of actual grassroots protests and demonstrations declined dramatically. In 1973 Edwards himself was forced to concede that black athletic rebellions had receded from a high water mark of 180 during the 1968–69 school year to less than 30 in 1971–72. Both figures are almost certainly inflated but the general downward trend was unmistakable and telling. And one searches the historical record in vain to find any mention of race-based athletic protests in the years that followed. The revolt, in short, was no more.

Confronted with these realities in March 1972, Edwards himself admitted as much (although he put it somewhat differently, saying that activism was "moving to another level" of activity, shifting from "protest" to "political analysis"—foreshadowing his move into the academy and scholarly writing).[70] Any remaining doubts about the decline and disappearance of a meaningful African American protest movement in and around sport were laid to rest with an incident that occurred at the 1972 Olympic Games in Munich. Its outlines were familiar—its outcomes were not.

Upon placing first and second respectively in the 400-meter dash in Munich, Vincent Matthews and Wayne Collett, Olympic teammates of Smith and Carlos in 1968, mounted the awards podium with memories of their former teammates and what they represented. They were painfully aware of how little had changed and how unlikely additional change seemed. That Matthews, a former Olympian, had had to pay his own way to the U.S. trials only compounded the frustration and alienation these athletes felt. Thus, like Smith and Carlos before them, Matthews and Collett refused to follow the established conventions of the Olympic victory ceremony. However, the performance enacted by Matthews and Collett was somewhat different from that of their predecessors. They stood casually, even somewhat sloppily, during the anthem, at one point twirling their medals on their fingers. If their specific intentions were not entirely clear, their general disdain and disrespect was, and most critics and commentators took these athletes to task for not taking the ritual seriously enough.[71]

Once again, the USOC brought in Jesse Owens (on his request) to meet with Matthews, Collett, and other athletes on the morning after the incident. Owens wanted the demonstrators to apologize and asked that they let him represent them before the IOC. If they would only say that they weren't aware of what they were doing, Owens promised, he would secure post-Olympic jobs for them in large (unnamed) American corporations. Not surprisingly, the athletes refused. The insensitivity, misunderstanding, and downright stupidity of the American Olympic authorities in allowing Owens—who had absolutely no repartee with the young black athletes to begin with, and who himself privately described Matthews and Collett as "the Munich culprits"—to try to serve as a mediator is apparent in retrospect. (In his account, in fact, Matthews directed the bulk of his criticism and bitterness toward Owens.) But at a deeper level it is worth considering the extent to which this demonstration—or, to be more precise, this absence of a demonstration—was the product of these athletes' refusal to participate even in the most basic elements and assumptions about nationalism, patriotism, and race displayed in the ceremony. They viewed the ritual so seriously that they could not participate in it in good conscience—or, as the case may have been, consciousness. This is an interpretation that John MacAloon has formulated quite convincingly (MacAloon, forthcoming); it is also supported by the historical evidence. As Matthews himself observed to a reporter immediately following his expulsion: "If we did have any ideas about a demonstration, we could have done a better job than that."[72]

With respect to the collapse of the athletic protest movement, however, what Matthews and Collett meant and whether this was seen as appropriate or not is less important than how Matthews and Collett's postperformance experience differed from that of Smith and Carlos. On the one hand, they received a more immediate and less ceremonious dismissal from the Olympic Games (and the Olympic movement itself) than Smith and Carlos. This was, perhaps, to be expected. But the modest support they found among athletes and public audiences was probably a surprise. Some black newspapers (the *Chicago Defender,* the *Pittsburgh Courier,* and the *Amsterdam Press* among them) did, according to Chris Elzey's recent research (2001), editorialize on behalf of the two athletes but there was little other public outcry or even awareness to be found. Unlike the reception Smith and Carlos received, Matthews and Collett were mostly ignored, almost immediately and conveniently forgotten.

That African American athletic activism had become passé is underscored when we consider Matthews's own immediate post-Olympic career. With the assistance of noted sportswriter Neil Amdur, Matthews produced what in my view is one of the finest, most revealing and deeply probing sports autobiographies ever written, a memoir called *My Race Be Won* (1974). Unlike most such books, this one is deeply provocative and reflective—not just about sport and not just about Matthews own experiences in sport but also about race and its relation to sport, and about sport's place in contemporary culture broadly conceived. It is also a detailed insider's account of many of the events and incidents that are the substance of the present study. Indeed, the book provides a good deal of historical information that I have used in previous chapters. Nevertheless, the book received surprisingly little attention when it was released and is virtually unknown today. It is almost impossible to imagine better evidence that the African American athletic protest movement was not only over, it was all-but-forgotten.

Other events at the 1972 Games make the point as well. One of the most revealing involves a couple of the African American members of the U.S. basketball team, Mike Bantam and Tommy Burleson. Upon entering the tournament, these young black athletes had postured as racial renegades or rebels of a sort. They were very critical of the Games (which they saw as hypocritical) and of the treatment of black athletes in sport. Clearly influenced and informed by the ideas of Harry Edwards and Jack Scott, they would talk only about playing ball for themselves. But during the course of Olympic competition their attitudes changed dramatically. This, remember, was the Olympic Games where the Soviet Union won the gold medal the Americans believed they had already won on the basis of a highly questionable decision by a member of the international basketball federation. In the face of this perceived injustice, Bantam and Burleson dropped their racial pretext and suddenly were transformed into patriotic, anticommunist Americans. Such a dramatic turnabout seems unlikely if there had been any kind of a meaningful movement to fall back on (Elzey 2001).

A number of factors help account for the decline of race-based resistance in and around sport. One was the deterioration and collapse of the broader culture of racial radicalism itself. The broader civil rights and black power movements had been the key to the alternative understandings of racial justice that inspired and drove athletic activism in the first place. Moreover, they had provided the concrete political institutions, resources, and social networks that encouraged and sustained political commitment from athletes who were not constitutionally inclined toward and were actively discouraged from political consciousness and activity. Once these supports were gone, athletes, somewhat new to political consciousness and activism to begin with, had few opportunities to be or become political.

The usual problems of grassroots organizing and mobilizing also had a good deal to do with the decline of the movement. The "revolt of the black athlete" had never been unified and clearly focused in the first place, making it impossible for Harry Edwards (or anyone else for that matter) to consolidate, channel, and direct the energies unleashed in each of these various arenas and instances toward any consistent, coherent set of goals. As I suggested in my analysis of the collapse of the OPHR's original boycott proposal (chapter 4), there were surely problems with the movement-building strategies Edwards and his colleagues employed. Many of these repeated themselves in his failed Federation of Black Amateur Athletes project: its stance was almost certainly too adversarial for most athletes, going far beyond the elimination of basic, overt racial injustices and inequalities. It was also essentially a top-down organization, lacking grassroots legitimacy and not deeply embedded in the experiences of African American athletes and the actual problems of their sporting milieu. Finally, it was insensitive to the complexities of the sports world and variations among different sports and athletes. There were, in fact, already some indications of these problems in *Revolt*. For example, the vagueness of its plans and the difficulty of finding an appropriate agency to serve as the legal and financial arm of the federation are obvious in retrospect.[73] Already at this point Edwards was saying: "If the federation does nothing more than preserve the dignity of one black athlete . . . it will have been worthwhile. The days of the Negro Uncle Tom athlete are numbered. For from this point on, their kind shall be harder and harder to come by" (1969, p. 114).

To the extent such organizations began to emerge, athletic unions on the professional level are the only tangible, sustained result. Elsewhere athletes have never been able to see the need or find the resources for a mutual support organization. Here also it seems likely that black athletic resistance may have remained too focused on race itself—unable to capitalize on or connect with the other frustrations and alternative ideals that composed the so-called athletic revolution. And even for African American athletes and activists there were unresolved tensions between those who were motivated by their desire to enable and enact traditional, civil rights–type reforms within the world of sport, and those who wanted to move toward a more collectivist-structuralist critique of racial policies and practices in sport and in American culture in general.

This brings me to the third and perhaps most significant factor hastening the decline and eventual collapse of African American athletic protest: the reforms undertaken by the various agencies and authorities of the sporting establishment.

Racial Equilibrium Reestablished

I have already mentioned a number of the small, symbolic steps taken by leaders of the sporting establishment to address their racial crisis— ensuring the representation of African American athletes, hiring black coaches, championing race-targeted programs such as the National Youth Sport Program, and so on. But what I want to highlight here are some of the more concrete, institutional reforms these organizations under- took. One of the leading actors in this respect was the NCAA's Big Ten Conference, which in 1972, as David K. Wiggins (1991) has documented, appointed an advisory commission to "identify complaints of black ath- letes in the conference and to recommend solutions to racial disturbances plaguing most league schools" (p. 174). The commission comprised for- mer black athletes from conference schools, chaired by the dean of the College of Urban Development at Michigan State, and reported directly to the Big Ten Joint Committee. Interviews conducted by the advisory commission supported many of the charges made by African American activists and, as Wiggins puts it, uncovered "rampant academic abuses and exploitation." In order to remedy these problems, detailed in a report called "The Status of Blacks in the Big Ten Athletic Conference: Issues and Concerns," the commission suggested a whole host of measures, among them the establishment of an office of athletic-academic counseling for all member institutions; the guarantee of a fifth year of financial support to athletes to ensure their graduation; educational seminars to improve the coaches' ability to communicate with black athletes; the inclusion of minorities on coaching search committees; and the addition of minority candidates in conference searches for athletic administrators.

According to Wiggins, the Big Ten Joint Committee "strongly endorsed the advisory commission's report and almost immediately began imple- menting its suggestions" (p. 175). Conference leaders set up an athletic- academic counseling program at each conference school and dictated that these programs be managed by a faculty athletic representative (rather than coaches or athletic directors) responsible for counseling athletes on curriculum content and academic progress toward collegiate degrees. The Joint Committee also granted a fifth year of financial aid to athletes who had not yet finished their degrees, strongly encouraged the implemen- tation of the proposed coaches' educational seminars, and began devel- oping a list of African Americans who could be employed as coaches, trainers, officials, administrators, and other athletic personnel. Last, the committee announced plans to appoint a black assistant commissioner to oversee the implementation of these policies; in June 1974 C. D. Henry was hired to fill the position. It amounted to what one knowledgeable observer described as a full-fledged "affirmative action" policy (Behee 1975).

The significance of these self-imposed reforms, and the myriad others like them that appear to have occurred all throughout the world of amateur athletics (though not in any concerted fashion; see also Wiggins 1988), extends far beyond the fact that they eliminated many of the most personal and most socially legitimate reasons for African American athletic activism. Indeed, such reform initiatives were often initiated, sustained, and expanded long after the collapse of the protests that had demanded them in the first place. Ironically, in other words, the mid-1970s simultaneously marked both the last gasps of the African American athletic protest movement and the heyday of the racial reform movement in athletics.[74] More important, such institutional reforms helped to usher in (and now form key institutional components of) a new era of sport and race relations in American culture, an era and new cultural and institutional order where direct racial protest has all but disappeared and where the worst, most blatant forms of racial prejudice and discrimination appear only in extraordinary individual instances from which all other parties can quickly distance themselves. At the same time, serious structural issues of academic preparation, social isolation, and discrimination outside of sport, and representation of racial minorities in terms of coaching, officiating, and administrative leadership have not been solved, and the cultural meaning and symbolic import of African American athletes is more powerful, multifaceted, and misunderstood than ever.

I will have more to say about this new racial order in sport—an order whose basic cultural and institutional components remain very much with us still today—in the next chapter, especially with respect to its broader symbolic meanings and implications in contemporary American culture. But what should be clear by now are the responses of the American amateur athletic establishment to African American athletic unrest that allowed this new order to take shape. Although these actions were not necessarily premeditated or even carefully and consciously coordinated, together they combined to formally disavow and drastically reduce the most blatant forms of racial prejudice and discrimination in the world of sport; create new organizational practices, policies, and procedures for dealing with persistent problems of race; and began to reestablish sport's reputation as a leader in the advancement of African Americans.

There are many ways to document the success of the racial reform and rearticulation project as it unfolded in sport in the 1970s. Perhaps the most compelling and concrete such indicator came in 1978. Few Americans—sports aficionados or otherwise—are aware of it, but 1978 marked a watershed year for the institutional organization of sport in the United States. With the Amateur Sports Act of 1978 (PL 95–606) Congress designated the United States Olympic Committee (the USOC) as the public agent authorized and empowered to oversee the structure, organization, and development of amateur sport in the country. For the first time in the history of the American republic, in other words, the U.S. government formally acknowledged that sport was a matter of national, public interest and that federal policy was required to ensure that these interests were properly served (Chalip and Johnson 1996).

Many things can be said (many of them quite critical) about this exceptional and quintessentially American piece of policymaking: that it delegates public authority to a private agency while retaining few powers of oversight or modes of accountability; that it subordinates grassroots, participatory sports access and development to the interest of producing top-flight, internationally competitive athletes; that scholastic and collegiate sport remain strictly private, in the hands of the autonomous and essentially unregulated National Collegiate Athletic Association (NCAA) and National High School Federation (NSHF); that by failing to address the corporate, market-based structure of so-called professional sports and their relation to "amateur athletics," the greedy processes of capitalism and commodification are left unchecked, able to reach their tentacles into sport at every level and community in America (cf. Chalip 1988, 1991).[75] But the most striking aspect of this seminal and consequential legislation—at least in the context of this present study—is that race was not explicitly mentioned in it. There are numerous references to and indeed extensive provisions for gender equity, athlete's rights, sports development, and so on—that is, all the major social issues of the athletic resistance and unrest of the 1970s—except race, the issue that was first contested and was arguably the most prominent and problematic in the public mind. The Amateur Athletic Act of 1978 is, in a very real sense, color-blind or race-neutral. There may be no surer indication of the fact that the racial equilibrium in sport, disrupted by the unrest of the previous decade, had been, for all intents and purposes, reestablished.

CONCLUSION

When cultural studies scholarship started, critics often questioned
whether it made sense to call cultural practices and preferences
political. They wondered whether the music people play or the
products they purchase have any real impact on public struggles
for everyday life and politics; they failed to see the significance
of how popular culture creates its own micro-politics of
organization, location, identity and affiliation. But in the era of
de-industrialization, de-Stalinization, and post-coloniality, we
might better wonder whether politics can ever be political,
whether political discourse will ever again amount to anything
other than a cultural performance designed to divert attention
from who actually has power and what they have done with it.

—George Lipsitz, *Dangerous Crossroads* (1994)

Chapter 8

The Cultural Politics of Sport and Race in the Postprotest Era

To argue, as I have, that the racial crisis in American amateur athletics had been effectively resolved by the end of the 1970s is not to imply that resistance—racial or otherwise—dropped out of the athletic arena altogether, much less that everything was better or that things simply went back the way they had been before racial unrest erupted onto the scene in the fall of 1967. Such suggestions would not only be based in a utopian vision of history (one that misunderstands the complicated, uncertain, and piecemeal processes in and through which meaningful social change are forged), they would be impossible to square with the historical record. Instead, it is to insist that a relative racial order had emerged out of the struggles between activists and elites of the late 1960s and early 1970s, an "order" that was in some ways better and in some ways worse but for the most part both institutionally stable and ideologically legitimate. By the end of this decade of disruption, in other words, a coherent and believable racial ideology had been rearticulated and a relative racial equilibrium reestablished.[1]

In this final chapter I will sketch the outlines of this new racial equilibrium in sport whose core institutional and cultural components remain, for better or for worse, essentially in place today. Even more ambitiously, I want to suggest that the establishment of this postactivist racial order allowed sport to reemerge in American popular culture in the 1980s as a public symbol of and model for race relations. It was a development that fit well within the ostensibly universal but actually culturally specific visions of citizenship, patriotism, and nationalism that took shape in American popular and political culture during this period (cf. Jeffords 1989, 1994; Lipsitz 1998). Its racial form and function thus transformed, the idea of sport as a conflicted and contested racial terrain (Hartmann 2000) takes on new historical salience and significance, centering more than ever on the representations and performances of (especially male) African American athletes.

Obviously I will not be able to document these ideas about the racial form and symbolic function of sport in the postprotest era as fully and systematically as I might like in the space of a single, concluding chapter. What I will do instead is try to illustrate and elaborate the provisional theoretical framework they give rise to by focusing on the 1984 Los Angeles Olympic Games. The L.A. Olympics are useful for my purposes both because of the ways in which issues of race were dealt with by the Organizing Committee (LAOOC) as well as because of the way in which racial images and ideologies were presented in Olympic symbology and media coverage, especially as mobilized by President Ronald Reagan in constructing and legitimizing his idealized vision of American culture, identity, and citizenship. This is a case, in other words, that is both representative and uniquely revealing. It also brings this study, finally but not incidentally, full circle—back to Tommie Smith and John Carlos and their dramatic victory-stand demonstration.

The New and Improved Sport

Perhaps the first point about sport's "new" racial order to reiterate and underscore is that it was not as if racial problems in the world of sport had finally been solved by the close of the 1970s. Quite the contrary: though many of the worst abuses were severely curtailed, deeper structural inequalities persisted and the fledgling sociology of sport carved a niche for itself by documenting them. Sociologists demonstrated the miniscule odds of African American mobility through sport, explained how white-dominated athletic organizations colonized and exploited black bodies and labor, and isolated persistent discriminatory practices such as "stacking" players of color at the same positions (see Margolis and Piliavin 1999). In a review of scholarly studies of the period, James H. Frey and D. Stanley Eitzen (1991) summarize some of the disturbing racial patterns that remained.

> American sport sociologists have devoted considerable attention
> to the examination of racial discrimination in sport. The major con-
> clusion of this work . . . is that just as racial discrimination exists in
> society, [so also] it exists in sport. Blacks do not have equal oppor-
> tunity; they do not receive similar rewards for equal performance
> when compared to whites; and their prospects for a lucrative career
> beyond sport participation are dismal. (p. 513)[2]

Racial disparities and very limited opportunities were particularly pronounced in ownership and management (cf. Brooks, Althouse, and Tucker
1997; Lapchick with Matthews 1997) and with respect to access and opportunity to recreational and fitness-oriented sport (Shivers and Halper
1981; Chalip 1988). Real racial problems, in short, remained.[3]

Nor should it be implied that racial resistance disappeared from the
sporting scene altogether. I am thinking here, for example, of the emergence of progressive African American leadership in elite institutions of
sport (by the end of the 1980s the three major positions of the American
amateur athletic establishment were occupied by African Americans—the
president of the USOC was LeRoy Walker, America's IOC representative
was Anita DeFrantz, and the cochair of the Atlanta Organizing Committee
was Andrew Young) and even of the consolidation of a race-based critique
of sport among academics and some public intellectuals. Regular, everyday folks also contrived to push for racial change in, around, and through
local, community-based sport, as Kenny Moore described (without further
comment) in his 1991 *Sports Illustrated* story on Smith and the Olympic
cohort of 1968. Almost all the members of the 1968 American team (including Smith and Carlos) gravitated to community service or teaching
based around or drawing upon their own personal experiences in sport.[4]
And nowhere was racial resistance more on display than with respect to
the cultural and aesthetic transformation of sport itself.

Connected with the transformation of sport into a mass-market commodity form (Gruppe 1991), African American individuals (Muhammad
Ali and Dr. J, for example) and styles like daring, base-stealing baseball;
sack dances and end zone celebrations in football; and, most of all, fast-
paced, flamboyant fast-break, slam-dunk basketball (see George 1992)
emerged as one of the most prominent and defining features of the American sporting landscape. With this genuine black aesthetic (see, especially,
George 1992), sport became an ever more important source of collective
identification for the African American community and site for the "new
cultural politics of difference" (West 1990) that emerged in the United
States in the post–civil rights era.

These points established, the key feature of this new, postprotest racial order in sport, then, was not that struggles over the racial substance and function of sport had disappeared but rather that they had assumed new, subtler, and more institutionalized forms where the organizations of the sporting establishment, including the sports media, took a far more proactive (if not entirely progressive) approach to dealing with race. Race was not gone but it was no longer a problem that threatened to undermine the entire sporting world. And no organization may better have grasped and enacted the postprotest racial order in sport than the Los Angeles Olympic Organizing Committee (LAOOC).

At first glance, it is not obvious that the 1984 Olympic Games were preoccupied and shot through with racial issues. There were no major protests, problems, or eruptions either during the Games or in the years of preparation leading up to them. And racial issues were rarely raised in the extensive *Los Angeles Times* coverage of the organization of the Games, and post hoc writings—journalist Kenneth Reich's (1986) insider's account the most notable among them—contain very few racial references or discussions. Indeed, Reich himself notes that the absence of racial turmoil and contention was "one of the most impressive accomplishments" of the LAOOC. But Reich's language of accomplishment here is revealing, for it was no accident that race was not much of an issue or at least not a problem for the 1984 Olympic Games and its organizing committee.[5]

Racial and ethnic issues were very much on the minds of the Los Angeles Olympic organizers when they set about their work in 1978 (the same year, of course, that Congress legislated its reform of American amateur athletics). Indeed, the possibility of racial and ethnic protests ranked high among the problems the LAOOC identified early in the organizational process (other concerns included terrorism, price gouging, and a Soviet boycott).[6] Race was considered a potential problem for two very obvious reasons: Southern California was home to large minority populations, and several crucial events venues were located in relatively poor, largely minority neighborhoods (notably, the Coliseum in South Central Los Angeles, home to the Opening and Closing Ceremonies as well as all the track-and-field events). And, at various times, some problems did emerge. For example, there were early concerns about licensing for minority-owned businesses. There was talk of widespread protests by communities of color partially in connection with the dismissal of a key LAOOC aide on "minority affairs," and the organizing committee also faced complaints from Native American groups over the poor treatment and low status of Jim Thorpe in the Olympic movement.[7] Yet through it all, racial protest and unrest never erupted as a major public issue in the organizing of the Games, much less derailed or disrupted the staging of any competitions or ceremonies.

A closer reading of the archival records and conversations with those close to the Olympic effort shows how this racial quiescence was actually accomplished. Despite its adherence to a color-blind, race-neutral discourse, race was in fact one of the crucial items on the LAOOC agenda from the very beginning. One of the LAOOC Board of Directors' first orders of business (undertaken during their first official meeting) was to adopt and implement a policy of "equal opportunity and affirmative action" that guided its every act of decision making, hiring, contracting, and subcontracting.[8] In addition, the almost exclusively white LAOOC made a point of bringing African American and other minority leaders into the planning process and administrative structure at almost every opportunity. This included, most notably, Los Angeles mayor Tom Bradley, who came to see the Olympic effort as one of the most important legacies of his entire administration, as well as Anita DeFrantz, the current American IOC representative. She was put in charge of Olympic housing villages after gaining prominence as a leader of the athletes who sued the Carter administration for its 1980 Moscow Games boycott (on the grounds that it violated their rights as athletes).[9]

Another aspect of the LAOOC's racial strategy was its rapid response to any and all threats of racial unrest or disturbances of any sort. When controversies arose about the dedication of possible revenues from the Games, the LAOOC was quick to pledge that any surplus it generated would go to youth sport, especially in communities of need. Here, the committee used images of African American youth in the advertising campaign to convey this message.[10] Another important public indication of this emphasis came when LAOOC president Peter Ueberroth hired John Carlos (who had been running the "John Carlos Youth Development Program" he founded in Los Angeles in the late 1970s) as a special consultant on minority affairs.[11] While the tangible, community-level impact of Carlos's appointment on minority relations is hard to document conclusively, the move was an unquestioned public relations success. At least one reporter—the OPHR's old friend, Pete Axthelm—listed the hiring of Carlos as one of the three keys to the success of the 1984 Los Angeles Olympics. As Axthelm (1987) put it: "Ueberroth's deputy for community relations on the streets of Los Angeles was none other than the formerly ostracized Olympian John Carlos. This can be viewed as a mere cosmetic touch, appealing to sentimental veterans like this one. But Carlos and others like him . . . seemed to have a genuine impact. . . . People feared wild overcharging, hostility, even rip-offs of cars. What they got was a community almost universally eager to please and share in the festivities" (p. 109). Perhaps even more remarkably, when the threat of community protests arose at one point and Harry Edwards emerged as a potential leader, Ueberroth sought out the former OPHR organizer personally. After a secret, weekend meeting, Edwards eventually gave Ueberroth and the organizing committee his blessing, allowing the organization effort to proceed without racial protest.[12]

Arts were also an important part of the LAOOC's strategies for circumventing potential race problems. The Olympic Arts Festival had numerous exhibitions and performances reserved for various racial and ethnic communities (though these were, according to critics, uneven and problematic), and a former All-Pro NFL lineman, an African American named Ernie Barnes, was named the official sports artist of the Games.[13] In the wider culture, the recently deceased Olympic hero Jesse Owens made another comeback of sorts, his biography featured just prior to the Games in July in a nationally telecast four-hour biographical drama, *The Jesse Owens Story*.[14] Then there were the Games themselves. Not only were several of the biggest stars and celebrities of the Games African American—athletes like Jackie Joyner-Kersee, the members of the gold-medal-winning basketball squad, and especially Carl Lewis, who was trying to duplicate Jesse Owens's historic four-gold medal performance—but Olympic events such as the Torch Relay and the Opening Ceremonies made a point of featuring athletes of color. In one of its most public decisions, the LAOOC went so far as to enlist Gina Hemphill, the granddaughter of Jesse Owens, to run the final leg of the torch relay, handing off to 1960 Olympic champion and L.A. native Rafer Johnson (who himself had played a minor role in the events of 1968) to climb to the top of the Coliseum and finally light the torch (see fig. 9).

The LAOOC had learned the lessons of the previous decade very well. They were very much aware of and attentive to any perception of racial inequality or injustice, both inside and outside of sport, and took active, aggressive measures to head off potential protest and unrest. Indeed, the LAOOC can be seen as a perfect example of the postprotest American sports regime, a regime that had learned to avoid racial resistance and unrest by incorporating relatively moderate but symbolically powerful racial actors and progressive ideals into its practice and official policies.

Sport and Racial Rearticulation in Reagan's America

The various racial practices, policies, and procedures the LAOCC adopted in order to absorb and assimilate "race" stand as an excellent microcosm

Fig. 9. Rafer Johnson anchoring the torch relay, Los Angeles Olympic Games, 1984. Photograph used with permission of AAF/LPI.

of the social landscape of sport and race in 1980s American society. But it is also and perhaps more important to consider how such actions affected sport as a public symbol for race in America—that is, what racial meanings and implications the postprotest regime in sport now conveyed in the larger public culture. Here it is essential to reiterate that despite its attentiveness to race and its success in creating a racially harmonious

Olympics, the LAOOC almost never discussed racial issues or ideas explicitly, concretely or openly. Quite the contrary, in both its public dealings and official documents the LAOOC consistently portrayed its handling of racial issues in race-neutral, color-blind language. The permanent records of the Organizing Committee and the Committee's official final report contain only scant references to issues of race, buried primarily under the labels of "community relations" or "human resources."[15] Even the myriad pictures of African American and other minority athletes that appear in official reports and signage are presented without specific textual references to race, as if it is only their individual effort and identity that matters. The collective impact of this official framing and practice is striking. Without the benefit of context and additional outside perspectives such as those I have collected above, one might well conclude that racial problems in and around sport in the United States had, in fact, been overcome.

My sense is that leaders of sporting organizations like the LAOOC assumed this stance because it was consistent with the long-held and deeply felt color-blind, individualist, and integrationist ideals I have described throughout this project as part of the deep cultural structure of race and sport relations in the United States. What is even more important, however, are the ways in which this ostensibly race-neutral discourse and practice has overlapped with and supported the abstract, universalist ideals about racial justice, social harmony, and national identity that have been ascendant in American culture in this post–civil rights era. Indeed, what appears to have happened is that the LAOOC's color-blind, race-neutral discourse was picked up and extended in mass media coverage of the Games. That is, the media adopted a way of reporting on racial issues and African American athletes that not only replicated the larger pattern but seemed to celebrate the athletic version as a model for the rest of American society. A systematic reading of the *Los Angeles Times* and *Sports Illustrated,* the paper of record for the Games and the nation's most widely read sports periodical, shows their favored storylines celebrated successful African American athletes as examples of the openness of American society and color-blind ideals.

The special supplements the *Times* published in the days leading up to the Games illustrate and encapsulate the effect. An extensive profile of Carl Lewis, certainly the most publicized athlete of the Games, discussed the star sprinter's private life in detail and his quest to equal Jesse Owens's unprecedented four-gold-medal performance at the 1936 Games—all without once mentioning Lewis's race.[16] Perhaps even more revealing was a profile on Jackie and Al Joyner, described as the "first family" of American track and field. On the one hand, the story made no specific mention of the Joyners' being African American; on the other, the piece made a point of saying that despite "growing up in the ghettos of East St. Louis" (Harry Edwards's notorious hometown) the Joyners were "without chips on their shoulders."[17] Though ostensibly blind to racial difference, such comments obviously relied upon and only made sense in the context of comparisons to racialized others. Black athletes were imagined as somehow exceptional (or at least potentially different), having overcome problems of race that plagued others like them. And it was all because of their participation in athletics. Sport, the implication seems clear, was a model the rest of Americans could aspire to, a symbol for dominant liberal individualist ideals about meritocratic color blindness, racial integration, and cultural assimilation.[18]

How powerful and pervasive were such symbolic messages in the culture at large? And how might this have been impacted by the transformations of the previous decade? Given that that these are questions about a single historical case without obvious historical precedent or comparison, they are difficult to answer with absolute, empirical certainty. Nevertheless, a small, preliminary study that I recently conducted speaks to the second.

With the help of a research assistant, I collected a sample of articles and commentaries drawn from three mainstream, national magazines—US News and World Report, Newsweek, and Time—focused on issues of race and racism for two separate five-year periods, 1973–1978 and 1979–1984.[19] The magazine sample was chosen to represent mainstream, American culture; the two periods to correspond with the years in which there was significant racial unrest and institutional turmoil in and around sport, and those years in the aftermath of this period of crisis (in short, sport's protest and postprotest phases). Drawing on lists of widely recognized sports terms and metaphors, we then coded and recorded the number of sports metaphors used in each article in each time span. Our hypothesis was that articles on race in the era of unrest would have far fewer sport-based metaphors and references than those in the postprotest period. And, in fact, this is exactly what we discovered.

Our findings, reported here for the first time, were quite clearly consistent with the argument. For the initial period of racial unrest and reform (1973–1978), there were 1.2 sporting terms or metaphors used in each article (12 in the 10 articles in the sample). For the postprotest period (1979–1984), in comparison, this increased dramatically to 3.53 sports-oriented references per article (53 in the 15 articles). In other words, mainstream national magazine articles devoted specifically to racial issues were almost three times more likely to use sport-oriented metaphors or references in the postprotest period than they were during the years of racial unrest.

These admittedly preliminary findings are only partial evidence to support the argument that once sport had "resolved" its own, internal racial problems, it was far more likely to be used as a metaphor for or symbol of race relations in the United States. But they certainly help make sense of another, relatively minor and ad hoc piece of contemporary American history: President Ronald Reagan's prolific use of sports metaphors, anecdotes, images, and stories. Widely recognized and frequently commented upon, Reagan's deployment of sports-based tropes is often minimized or dismissed as an eccentric if effective personal-communicative quirk. Sport scholars, however, have insisted that that the former president's fascination with sport is best understood as the result of the deep structural connections between Reagan's political ideologies and the ideals that animate and organize so much of American sport.[20] Building upon these insights, I want to emphasize how race fit into this ideological constellation—which brings us to the striking manner in which the former president used the Olympic Games during his (successful) 1984 reelection campaign.

Reagan's appearances with American Olympic champions in the aftermath of the most dominating (if Soviet-less) American performances in Olympic history were certainly part of what I am gesturing toward here. But the Olympics were mobilized much more extensively in his acceptance speech to the Republican nominating convention.[21] The president began his speech in typical individualist fashion by characterizing his vision of government as one that "serves all of the people of America as individuals." He spent the bulk of his time then explaining how his administration had stabilized domestic affairs and reestablished America's international dominance without sacrificing but actually by maximizing individual rights and freedoms. He summed it all up with the poetic phrases that became the centerpiece of his fall campaign: that he was leading a "national crusade" to "make America great again"; that this "springtime in America" was, in fact, a time of everyone "coming together." To give concrete expressions to this powerful, emotive language, the president used the image of the torch relay that had crisscrossed America in preparation of the 1984 Los Angeles Games.[22]

Reagan talked of how in traveling some nine thousand miles across the country, carried by some four thousand runners, the relay "crossed a portrait of our nation." It was, in his words, "a celebration of America," in which each and every American was a full participant. This way of framing the relay was very much about his vision of individuals uniting around a common cause. "Each story," according to Reagan, "was typical." In a now familiar style, the president named American citizens to make his point: "There was Ansel Stubbs, a youngster of 99 who passed the torch in Kansas to 4-year-old Katie Johnson." He described how the torch was greeted by churchgoers singing "God Bless America" and spectators holding candle-lit midnight vigils. But what was most interesting and revealing in the context of our present discussion is how Reagan closed the speech. In seemingly uncharacteristic fashion, the president talked not about individuals but about those who represented different groups. In what were perhaps the speech's most dramatic and stirring flourishes, Reagan recounts visions of the torch relay:

> And then in San Francisco, a Vietnamese immigrant, his little son held on his shoulders, dogged photographers and police motorcycles to cheer a 19-year-old black man pushing an 88-year-old white woman in a wheelchair as she carried the torch.

"My friends," Reagan concluded (and even in the written text one senses Reagan's skillful, theatrical pause), "that's America."

It was a powerful, evocative, and revealing moment—not just because of Reagan's personal charisma or his considerable rhetorical skill, nor even because of the way the president tipped his hat to the remarkable social diversity of America. What was remarkable about this speech, which was surely one of the most important of his campaign and career (as such speeches are for any presidential candidate), was that the president devoted almost a full third of it—the final third and most dramatic of all of his remarks—to the Olympic torch relay that had winded its way through the country in the weeks and months leading up to the Olympic Games. "In 16 paragraphs of stunning brilliance," as John MacAloon (1987) has written in what to my knowledge is the only extended treatment of the speech,[23] "the president presented the Los Angeles torch relay as empirical, evangelical proof of America reborn during his administration" (p. 127). This sporting anecdote thus served Reagan not only as a metaphor and a model for American race relations but as the literal embodiment of melting pot America.[24] It is difficult to imagine a single more compelling piece of evidence of the broad symbolic import and power of the newly reconstituted sporting world when it came to the matter of race.

New Kinds of Contestation

If Reagan used the 1984 Olympic torch relay as the centerpiece of his vision of America as coming together, it is essential to consider what social problems or even social groups may have been left out of or marginalized in Reagan's idealized portrait. In a certain sense this is obvious: Reagan's individualist, market-based conception of citizenship and belonging allowed no way to think about the historic inequalities and injustices that have accompanied social distinctions such as race and class and gender. In Reagan's individualist vision, such problems either didn't exist or simply couldn't be addressed in any meaningful collective way. Focusing on the traditional heteronormative family forms endorsed in his presidential rhetoric, cultural studies scholars such as Susan Jeffords (1989, 1994) and George Lipsitz (1998, chapter 4) have shown that Reagan's seemingly inclusive conceptions of patriotism actually privileged white, middle-class practices and values. Even stronger than this, the argument implied in Reagan's melting-pot vision was that attending to such social categories and groupings could only divide and separate Americans one from another. The need for America to overcome such social divisions and the social unrest of the previous generation came out in the portions of the speech where Reagan contrasted his understanding of national identity and his party with the Democrats, whom he described as the party of "special interests," "pessimism," and "fear and division" that he believed perpetuated the troubled legacy of the 1960s.

The particularities of Reagan's conception of patriotism and citizenship are revealed when juxtaposed against the images Democratic presidential hopeful Jesse Jackson used to animate his "rainbow coalition" campaign some four years later. Jackson began his speech to the Democratic convention not by talking about abstract American ideals but by recalling his own childhood growing up black and poor in South Carolina. He recalled, in particular, his grandmother, who was so poor she could not afford to buy the blanket she so desperately needed. Forced to make one, she gathered up all the pieces of leftover and discarded fabric she could find around the house and sewed them together into a quilt. The social problems of poverty and inequality were, of course, called to mind by Jackson's story, but Jackson used it to tell a somewhat different tale. The quilt, according to Jackson, was a good metaphor for American society—or at least what American society could be. Like scattered scraps of cloth, Jackson portrayed the many groups of people who made up the fabric of the American nation as limited and fragmented on their own. But sewn together, they could be strong, stable, and secure. "Just as his grandmother had pieced together a quilt from different patches," Lipsitz (1990) has summarized, "Jackson urged workers, women, blacks, Chicanos, Native Americans, Asian Americans, homosexuals and lesbians, senior citizens, and the handicapped to piece together a coalition that could encompass them all" (p. 33).[25] My purpose in referencing Jackson's story is, first of all, to highlight a compelling alternative to Reagan's melting-pot, individualist vision of citizenship and belonging. But I also want to suggest how difficult it would have been for Jackson to use sport—especially Olympic sport—to serve his political purposes. With its abstract individualism, its masculinized belief in the virtue of meritocracy, and its thoroughly naturalized nationalism, sport—particularly sport as practiced and idealized in the 1984 Los Angeles Olympics—became the perfect model for and near literal embodiment of Reagan's vision of social good and racial justice.

What also should be emphasized here is the central import and significance of individual and mostly male African American athletes themselves. This is an important point because it goes to C. L. Cole's seminal work (1996; Cole and King 1998) on the ways in which sport in general and black athletes in particular have functioned in constructing images and ideals of race in contemporary American culture. Set against the backdrop of the perceived breakdown of the traditional African American family, Cole's work has been posited on the notion that sport represents the socially desirable set of behaviors for young African American men, and gangs the deviant and dysfunctional alternative. But precisely because sport is believed to be a viable and desirable alternative, African American athletes, especially African American male athletes, have become more culturally dangerous and potentially problematic than ever before. Indeed, as Cole (Cole and Andrews 1996; Cole and Denny 1994) and others (cf. Boyd 1997; V. Andrews 1996; Hawkins 1995; Page 1997; Palm 2002) have made clear, the sporting industry in the 1980s adopted, both consciously and unconsciously, new practices for containing and controlling black male athletes, ensuring that they present images and engage in behaviors that serve to maintain rather than disrupt established racial images, ideologies, and hierarchies. What unites all these works is that they are speaking about the domestification and assimilation of not only racial difference but of racial deviance and defiance through sport, where athletes are closely watched and essentially stripped of agency and radical intent because of their place in the imagined sport-gang racial dyad.

Seeing how and why the black male athlete has become such a central figure in the culture of contemporary American citizenship and race relations calls to mind the large, theoretical questions about sport's historically evolving role as a racial symbol. This argument begins from the same point as this study: namely, that prior to 1968, sport was an undisputed institutional leader for and symbol of progressive race relations in the United States and that the emergence of racial unrest in sport in the late 1960s both presented a "crisis" for sporting institutions and elites (as the previous chapters demonstrated) and undermined sport's historic cultural role as a public symbol of and model for race relations in the United States. The specter of racial unrest in and around sport in the late 1960s made the indisputably powerful public presence and prowess of African American athletes in the American popular culture suddenly problematic. What did these athletes now represent? Were they still symbols of racial progress? Or were they now to be seen as the results of a thoroughly racialized if not simply racist social structure? Certainly it was difficult to claim the former, if these athletes themselves were arguing the latter. How, in short, could an institution plagued by racial unrest of its own possibly serve as a model of race relations in the United States? Once the concrete racial organization of sport was called into question, it was no longer natural and inevitable that African American athletes and sport itself necessarily stood as an exemplar of racial progress.

In the preface, I borrowed from Stuart Hall (1981, 1996) to describe sport as a contested racial terrain. The most obvious and immediate implication of this description was to suggest that sport exhibits both progressive and conservative racial forms and forces, that it is best understood as an empty cultural form (MacAloon 1995), a social site where racial images, ideologies, and inequalities are constructed, transformed, and constantly struggled over rather than a place with specific and determined racial politics or ideals. But there is more to my argument about seeing sport as a "contested terrain" that should now be evident. I have also addressed the broader, more public symbolic significance of sport and the racial struggles that occur in, through, and around it. Here I am referring especially to how unusually prominent and important all of these sport-centered struggles are in the public culture. Any number of examples of the broad, symbolic significance of this story and of sport itself for race relations broadly conceived could be given: the widespread media attention (and condemnation) generated by the mere idea of an African American Olympic boycott; the public figures who felt compelled to weigh in on one side or the other of the debate; the covert governmental investigation of African American athletic activists; or, the formal, federal governmental involvement in the racial reforms of the postprotest period (whether Humphrey's work through the President's Council on Physical Fitness or Nixon's interest in the NCAA's NSYSP program). But the common and overriding point is that sport has a particularly privileged and prominent role in American culture when it comes to matters of race, meaning that the racial structure, dynamics, and struggles of the sporting world dramatize race in a larger sense for all of us.

And now in this chapter, with the emergent institutional and cultural structures of the 1980s, we are introduced to a new and even more com-plicated way to think about the racial form and function of sport. Sport, in this era, can still be thought of as contested and conflicted, but these contests are much subtler and more institutionalized than before, center-ing around the meaning and implication of star African American athletes as portrayed by the sporting establishment and in the mass media, and interpreted—often without full consciousness of the racial images and ideologies being constructed—by the general public. All this comes out in relief when we consider the way in which the image of Tommie Smith and John Carlos on the victory stand in Mexico City was reinterpreted and rehabilitated under this new racial order.

Revealing Transformations

When we left (in chapter 6) Smith and Carlos and the image that has been synonymous with them in the public imagination, all three were objects of mainstream American scorn and derision, symbols of a public deeply divided on a whole host of issues, race paramount among them. In the 1980s, as we glimpsed earlier in this chapter, this had begun to change. Americans suddenly began to associate a whole new set of mem-ories and meanings with the athletes once described to them as "racist, black-skinned storm troopers" and the image they had equated with ur-ban violence and rioting not even a quarter of a century earlier. The first public indication of this change revealed itself during the organizational period leading up to the 1984 Los Angeles Olympic Games, when LAOOC president Peter Ueberroth hired Carlos as a special consultant on minority affairs (as I discussed above). Some sources have intimated that Smith was offered a similar position, and it was reported that he helped the LAOOC as an "Olympic site coordinator." Smith was also one of the two hundred people Peter Ueberroth singles out for special recognition in his autobio-graphical account of the LAOOC.[26] Suddenly, the erstwhile racial radicals of 1968 had become the darlings of the Los Angeles Olympic Organizing Committee.

Even more powerful and concrete evidence of this nascent transforma-tion can be found in a presentation titled "The Black Olympians, 1904–1984," produced by the California Afro-American Museum for its inaugu-ral exhibition held in conjunction with the Olympic Arts Festival spon-sored by the LAOOC. Here I discovered, for the first time in a mainstream public document, Smith and Carlos's demonstration portrayed not as taboo, but instead as worthy of celebration and tribute.[27] "[W]hat the Mexico City demonstrations served to do," according to this exhibition (which was actually composed of four mini-exhibits and was later shown in at least two other formats), "was to call attention—in ways that had never been done before—to the actual athletic servitude in which [black athletes] had often found themselves." And as a result, the curators conclude, "after the Mexico City Olympiad, the entire premise of sports as the black man's expressway out of ghetto poverty and inequality lay suspect before the world."[28]

This was only the beginning of the revisionist history. Drawing largely from Edwards's original account of the OPHR, Arthur Ashe, in *A Hard Road to Glory* (his popular, three-volume history of the African American athlete in the United States [1988]), described the 1968 Olympic protest movement as "a logical extension of the Civil Rights movement,"[29] and Olympic historical guru David Wallechinsky (1984) does the same. Even such conventional, sports idealists as Carlson and Fogarty grudgingly conceded in *Tales of Gold* (1987) that "Smith and Carlos's black power salute was a genuine, even dignified gesture of protest" (p. 384). But the fullest and most revealing version of this rehabilitation came in the summer of 1991 (August 5 and 12) when *Sports Illustrated*—the same magazine that twenty-three years earlier had treated the demonstration with utter contempt—devoted a special two-part story to the episode it now called "A Courageous Stand."

The story was part of a mammoth cover story and multipart series on the status of "the black athlete" in the United States. The series was purportedly designed to review and update the question posed by Jack Olsen's famous five-part series "The Black Athlete—A Shameful Story" published by *SI* in the summer of 1968: "Was [the world of sport] really the model of racial tolerance and equality it prided itself on being, or were black athletes slaves by another name?"

The story was researched and written by Kenny Moore, who (as the editors made sure to point out) finished fourteenth in the 1968 Olympic marathon and was one of Smith's roommates in the Olympic Village in Mexico City. In the story itself Moore claims that he told Smith that civil rights history itself remained "incomplete" without his "dramatic two cents worth." Smith replied, " 'What I did grew directly out of my education as an American. So I guess I can't refuse to contribute to others' " (p. 63). It appears that some kind of compensation deal may have played a role as well. In any case, Smith's story, according to Moore's recollections, came out "freshly afire"; like the stories, Moore told me, of those Vietnam veterans who hadn't been able to talk for years about their experiences but then, suddenly, twenty years later found themselves not only able to talk but with a great deal to say.[30]

As far as the connections between the story and the series, little was left to chance or imagination. The magazine's cover read, "The Black Athlete: In the 23 years since *SI*'s groundbreaking examination of blacks in sports, things have changed. But how much?"[31] Even though Smith's story was not mentioned by name, the lower right-hand corner of the otherwise dark-toned cover portrays a black-gloved fist against a stark white background. Furthermore, in his foreword to the series the managing editor of the magazine begins not by discussing Olsen's piece but by talking about Smith and Carlos's demonstration. "In the history of sport, few images have been as riveting as that of Tommie Smith and John Carlos on the award platform. . . . Their heads bowed and the black-gloved fists raised in silent protest, the two black sprinters hoped to remind America that all was not well, that the country's lofty promise of equality rang hollow in the black community" (p. 4). This reading was in fact confirmed by Roy S. Johnson, one of the two senior editors who assembled the series: they saw Smith's story as an unparalleled opportunity to revisit the issues posed back in 1968.[32]

The story itself was both expansive and revealing (and in fact provides a number of the details that supplement and inform the account I have offered in the preceding chapters). Moore's account not only accepted but dramatically extended the reading of the demonstration proposed in the 1984 California exhibition, making Smith into a great American hero in the process. Moore's sentimental conclusion in the second installment of the piece is definitive. In "everything" Smith and Carlos have done and said since, Moore wrote, "they became their gesture. . . . And now, perhaps, their gesture becomes them. When freedom called, they stood up. They still stand" (1991b, pp. 71–72). Underscoring this reinterpretation in conspicuous visual form is a photograph of Smith that takes up roughly two-thirds of the final page of the story. Against a backdrop of dark curtains, a somber, mature Tommie Smith stands once again on some sort of podium. This time, however, the stand is draped by a dark cloth and Smith himself is wearing a full-bodied leopard-skinned cloak. His hands are folded and his eyes are focused, it would seem, on the horizon. "For Smith," the caption reads, "the resolute stand he took at the '68 Olympics will always be, like his life, cloaked in pride and dignity" (p. 73). Incredibly, then, what was once derided as "an embarrassment visited upon the country" had become an act of tremendous personal courage and heroism and, as well, a matter of national pride. The athletes themselves were transformed from dangerous, irrational radicals into courageous and dignified American heroes.[33]

Within two years, such romanticized readings and recollections would become the norm—so typical and taken for granted that, to the extent the image has a history in the public imagination, this is it. On the twenty-fifth anniversary of the demonstration in 1993 (two years after the *Sports Illustrated* story), newspapers, magazines, and television stations around the country commemorated the occasion with various tributes, testimonials, and remembrances. The *New York Times,* to take one notable example, ran a full page of stories, photographs, and quotes devoted exclusively to the Mexico City event now presented as a positive and progressive episode in the history of race and sport in the United States.[34] This is how it has been ever since—most recently in the television histories produced by HBO (*Fists of Freedom,* 1999) and TNT as part of the *15 Seconds of Fame* series.

Part of the explanation for this dramatic transformation goes back to the dynamics of cultural remembering and rehabilitation I mentioned in the first chapter: the cultural processes by which "radical" images, objects, and practices such as those associated with the 1960s are appropriated and transformed into commodities available for mass-market consumption in ways that dilute or subvert their original meanings and intentions. Another factor has to do with the racial reforms and transformations in sport in the 1970s that I described in chapter 7. Without such changes in place, Smith and Carlos's demonstration would have remained potent and controversial in the athletic arena and thus "inappropriate" for mainstream public celebration and mass consumption. With them, however, the radical impulses and controversial ideals could, to use the language I also used in that chapter, be absorbed and insulated, thus relegated to the sports world's past and rendered impotent with respect to its future. Also important was the progress (however limited) of the post–civil rights American racial landscape, broad social and cultural transformations that help explain how a whole host of racial activists of the period—Martin Luther King Jr. most notable among them—have come to be reevaluated and valorized in mainstream American culture. But let us not forget what is lost in these rehabilitative processes.

Though many readers unfamiliar with the history were probably not aware of it (and most of my own interviews and conversations suggest that they were not), Kenny Moore's portrait of Tommie Smith was actually quite particular, even somewhat selective. Smith, Moore writes, was "hardly a campus radical," highlighting the fact that he was in the Army ROTC at the time and "[made] it a point to follow the rules" (1991a, p. 65). Smith himself is quoted as recalling that he did not even want to go to the inaugural Olympic Project for Human Rights workshop, and did so reluctantly and only after his teammate and friend Lee Evans convinced him that he had a deeper "obligation." "If I didn't use the influence I'd gained from being a world-class athlete," Smith says he realized, "I wouldn't be doing my part in society" (p. 68). Moore elaborates on this: "[Smith] knew that no social improvement has ever arrived without disproportionate sacrifice by a few human beings. He knew that sacrifice can get out of hand. He knew that if he joined this movement, he would move into the unknown." Not that Smith was a mere pawn or a radical, of course. Here Moore paints Smith as thoughtful and reasonable ("I could read the Constitution and compare the contradictions in American society"[p. 66]), passionate and yet controlled ("Smith repeatedly said that he loved his country and simply wanted it to be better," according to the story, which then quotes a 1968 comment: "It was not a gesture of hate. It was a gesture of frustration" [1991b, p. 60]). In short, Smith is shown as a civil rights hero much along the lines of how Martin Luther King Jr. is represented in current popular culture and collective memory. Remarkably, in fact, the first picture contained within the text of the story is the scene of King's assassination at a Memphis motel in 1968.[35]

But King's rehabilitation, as numerous historians and cultural critics have correctly reminded us, has come at a cost. As he has been turned into a national icon and his birthday celebrated as a national holiday, the more challenging, subversive aspects of his activism—his early and entirely unpopular opposition to the Vietnam War, for example, or the multiethnic Poor People's Campaign—have been blunted, blurred, or forgotten altogether. And so, too, with the more militant edges of Smith and Carlos's demonstration (many of which are contained only in the history itself): the structuralist racial critique; the aggressive use of sport as a political forum; the willingness to put their identity as African Americans above that of their identity as Americans—the actual experiences and grievances and radical intent that prompted their demonstration have been neglected or ignored in favor of their individual courage and an abstracted commitment to equality, dignity, and justice. And I believe that the cost of this "mainstreaming" may be quite a bit greater in the world of race and sport than it has been in the realm of racial politics more generally. In the latter, King's moderated image is nevertheless still complemented by or contrasted with the more radical racial image of Malcolm X (cf. Wood 1992; Dyson 1995), while in the former Smith and Carlos is about as radical as it gets, thus leaving athletes and activists in sport without a more progressive template or exemplar and imposing yet another barrier against making social change in and through sport. This is, perhaps, the perfect, if tragic, example of how easily and effortlessly sport can be turned in service of the racial status quo in the absence of legitimate, public protest, unrest, or critique of the sporting establishment on racial grounds; under the conditions, in other words, of the postprotest racial regime in the world of American sport.

Of course, old ambiguities, political possibilities, and historical complexities have not been completely forgotten. Writing in the *New York Times* on the twenty-fifth anniversary of their protest, William Rhoden, for example, recalled the "militance [of the gesture]" and how "it allowed me to expand the definition of myself as an athlete."[36] No longer did he feel he had to keep his identities of "student" and "athlete" separate and apart. "Smith and Carlos made me understand that athletes were not removed from the fray; in fact, their visibility and contact with the public allows a certain opportunity to speak loudly." Where "Jesse Owens and Jackie Robinson had been forced to react to racism; Smith and Carlos had gone on the attack . . ." For Rhoden, the protest becomes "more heroic" each year he replays it in his mind. Rhoden concludes with a story he heard about the high school graduation of Carlos's son. "As he walked across the stage, some of his classmates raised clenched fists and thrust them over their head [*sic*], a salute to the gesture Smith and Carlos had made before many of them were born" and, it is implied, to a more critical, alternative understanding of the realities of both race and sport in contemporary American culture. Unfortunately, according to Rhoden, Carlos never saw this gesture, for, like any proud father, he was busy snapping pictures of his own son. Carlos, Rhoden concludes with a flourish of his own, deserves to "know they were there."

If, as Rhoden suggests, Carlos deserves to know of such gestures, I am convinced that a full understanding of the social and historical complexity of sport and race relations in American culture requires us not only to know of them, but to better understand their meaning and significance—to know why such images remain powerful, what they tell us about the role of sport in the culture of American race relations and the possibilities for resistance and change that are present therein. Just as important, we need to realize the crucial ways in which power and privilege—both the power residing in control over resources and institutions as well as the power of ideals of color-blind, individualist meritocracy that are so pervasive in the culture as a whole—will structure and determine the struggles they invoke and hope to reinvigorate. In addition to an understanding of the racial power and complexity of that peculiar popular cultural form we know as sport, what is to be gained is a better appreciation of how race itself is produced, reproduced, and struggled over in contemporary American culture. Thus the drama of African American athletic revolt plays on.

Epilogue: Atlanta, 1996

In the middle of the long process of research and writing that went into making this book, I went to Atlanta, Georgia, for the Centennial Olympic Games. I expected to see Tommie Smith and John Carlos— or at least the image they produced back in 1968—in certain significant places, if not one or two more sacred spaces. After all, Atlanta had won the right to host the Games largely because the International Olympic Committee believed it would display for the peoples of the world a model of racial harmony, progress, and prosperity. It was to be the Olympics of civil rights and African American pride, and I knew that organizers were doing their best to make these connections as clear as possible in the Arts Festivals, the Torch Relay, and especially the Opening Ceremonies— in the latter case, by celebrating African American performers like Jessye Norman and musical legacies such as gospel and jazz. The presumed connections between sport and racial progress were drawn most forcefully in the pre-Olympic stump speeches of Andrew Young, the former mayor of Atlanta and the cochair of the Atlanta Organizing Committee. Around the world, Young—who first came to prominence working as the executive director of Martin Luther King Jr.'s Southern Christian Leadership Council—touted the Olympic movement as the secular, global realization of his friend and mentor's dream for a truly color-blind society. Surely the recently rehabilitated image of Smith and Carlos and all that it implied about the 1960s and the civil rights movement in particular had a role to play in this Olympics.

But for all of this attention to race, my expectations were not met. I found the image of Smith and Carlos on the victory stand, to be sure. It was on a bootlegged poster in an Afrocentric bookstore in the neighborhood of Atlanta's famed cluster of black colleges; on a few T-shirts being sold by street vendors on the street; in a radical pamphlet distributed by homeless people; in a couple of clips run by NBC. But these appearances were few and far between, in isolated and out-of-the-way places. I learned from vendors that the Smith-Carlos T-shirts were selling poorly, and the homeless article was actually a small piece I myself had been asked to contribute after attending a workshop on Olympic organizing earlier in the year. From impotent to irrelevant, it seemed.

In another setting I might have been disappointed, if not because of my political orientation than simply because of my research interests. I was essentially left without a concrete object of study. Surprisingly, however, what I experienced during those couple of weeks in Atlanta was less along the lines of disappointment than of indifference. This was, after all, the Olympic Games, my first. There were so many other things to see and do, many of which satisfied not only my thirst for excitement but also my quest for social and political significance. I quickly turned my attention to other things, among them what was surely the single most dramatic and widely celebrated moment of an otherwise rather unspectacular (for the Olympics) Games—this, of course, was Muhammad Ali appearing out of the darkness of the night at the climax of the Opening Ceremonies, struggling with all his might and dignity against the muscular tremors of Parkinson's disease to raise the Olympic flame—a flame that had come from thousands of miles around the world and across the country—to the cauldron it would illuminate for the seventeen days of the Games.

I witnessed the lighting live on the huge video screens set up in the Centennial Olympic Park along with thousands of others, including a dozen or so new (if fleeting) African friends of mine who were moved beyond speech when they realized who was doing the lighting. But so were many of us. The fragility of the human body; the dangers of boxing itself; the triumph of the will; dignity in the face of disease: Ali, as the writers told us, represented the triumphs and tragedies of the human condition.[1] Who could not help feeling for—and with—this man who was once one of the most gifted athletes in the world, once (perhaps even still) the most famous person on the face of the earth?

But Ali also represented much more than that, at least for me and certainly for the ceremony producers that had chosen him.[2] For Muhammad Ali also had an Olympic story, one that just so happened to overlap, in many concrete and direct ways, the story that I was by this time so deeply immersed in. As I touched upon in several places in the narrative above, Ali, when he was still Cassius Clay, had won a gold medal in boxing as a light-heavy weight in 1960 in Rome. He had beaten a Russian. He had proclaimed to the world his pride in being an American, in having represented his country well against the communists, and in his desire to live out the American dream. But when he returned to the States he found that his Olympic triumph had not changed the color of his skin—the social fact that mattered most to many of his countrymen. It was, as Ali explained many times, a terrible, crushing discovery, one that led to his conversion to Islam, his black political radicalism, and his opposition to the draft and the Vietnam War. And this was not even to mention the apocryphal story (contained in his early autobiography) of how on one cold Kentucky day, Ali with tears in his eyes had thrown his Olympic gold medal—together with the red, white, and blue ribbon with which he had tied it around his neck during his triumphant return home—into the deep waters of the Ohio River.[3] Yet these elements of Ali's past were, as they had been for Smith and Carlos before him, downplayed or disregarded in most of what I read and those I interviewed.

So here was the story I had come expecting to find, I told myself and anyone who was willing to listen. Ali—the man who had been called, by none other than Harry Edwards himself, the "patron saint" of the revolt of the black athlete—was the Atlanta version of my story, the story of sixties sport radicalism celebrated and rearticulated and rehabilitated by the postprotest sporting establishment. I began to grasp once again the extraordinary difficulties of confronting and really engaging racism in and through the history of sport in the United States. What I understood in Atlanta was that Smith and Carlos were already forgotten and discarded, long before I had even begun to pull together my analysis of the implications their performance still posed for the established racial order today. And now Ali? How could one hope to keep up, in a culture and cultural arena given over to the immediacy and intensity of emotional experience and the celebration of individual athletes and accomplishments?

If they were potentially depressing for me, such questions simply confirmed the worst suspicions about sport in general and the Olympics in particular of the crowd with whom I spent a good deal of time during the Games. This "crowd" was a rather motley constellation of radical activists and organizations of one sort or another who actually didn't know much about sport or the Games but who were using this forum to promote welfare rights and to protest homelessness, economic exploitation, and racial segregation. It would have been easy to fall into their skepticism except for two other things I discovered in being in Atlanta.

The first had to do with my African acquaintances' sheer optimism about sport and the Olympics in general as tools for racial progress, especially those associated with Nelson Mandela and the ill-fated South African bid committee (cf. Mbaye 1995). They really and truly believed athletics was a positive racial force in the modern world. While somewhat refreshing, what was really eye-opening about this discovery for me was that my friends in the Atlanta activist circles would have none of it. They simply refused to believe that impoverished and disempowered Africans could see anything socially redeeming in sport, least of all their beloved Mandela. (In fact, on one occasion when I described speeches the South African leader had made about the power and progressive social force of sport, I was dismissed as being either misinformed or a liar.) Here

I was reminded, once again, of the incredible complexity of the sport-race nexus, and especially of the possibilities and promise that can stand alongside all of its persistent problems; I was also alerted to the need to examine these questions of race and sport in global and comparative contexts where athletic representation has unique meaning and importance.[4]

The second experience I had in Atlanta also spoke to the ironies and complexities of thinking about the racial functions of contemporary sport. It had to do with some "alternative bus tours" of the city my activist friends had set up in order to show foreign journalists the underside of the Atlanta Olympics and of Atlanta itself. The culmination of these tours was supposed to have been a series of interactions with residents of the poor, mostly African American neighborhoods immediately surrounding the downtown Olympic Stadium venues. The idea was to allow these residents, who received few of the benefits of the Games and bore many of the expenses (including having access to their own streets and sidewalks cut off by security fencing), to express their displeasure and frustration with the Games. Unfortunately for the tour organizers, this did not happen. Instead, when the journalists were put into contact with residents in these communities of color, they heard testimonials of how great the Games were for the City of Atlanta; they heard how, despite all of the inconveniences, these Olympics were the best thing that had ever happened to them or their community; they heard how passionately these folks, all of them African American, loved sport in all its forms. Here, once again, were opportunities and genuine optimism under the radar of conventional popular imagery and mass media presentations of race.

Experiences like these don't change everything—the racial form and function of sport is still largely determined by persistent structural inequalities, mediated through color-blind discourses and ideals that minimize their impact. Nevertheless, they remind us of the complexity and possibility of the racial terrain that is sport. If sport is to be a truly progressive racial force in years to come, it is likely realities like these will be the vehicle for that change.

Notes

Preface

1. The telephone poll surveyed a random national sample of one thousand people. It was conducted in May 1996 by the Tarrance Groups, Lake Research and KRC (TARR).

2. For a review that captured the state of the field at that time, see Frey and Eitzen 1991.

3. The term "contested racial terrain" is obviously closely related to the Gramscian notion of "contested ideological terrain" used by Vernon Andrews (1996) and feminist sport scholars such as Messner (1988) or Kane and Disch (1993). For more on hegemony theory in sport scholarship, see William Morgan's (1994b) insightful review.

4. I discuss these points more fully in my treatment of C. L. R. James's *Beyond a Boundary* (1963/1993) (see Hartmann 2003a). For a piece that applies such insights to the Canadian case, see Kidd 1987.

5. Amy Bass's *Not the Triumph But the Struggle* (2002) appeared only after this manuscript was completed and entering into production. While a close reading was not possible, my initial impression is that Bass's account focuses primarily on African American athletes (why they protested and how these protests impacted those who came in their wake), while my own tendency is to use the case to analyze the symbolic role that sport plays in contemporary American culture when it comes to matters of race. My account is also intended to sketch out the reforms that came about as a result of this movement—reforms that became the concrete, institutional conditions under which African American athletes now participate in athletics and that largely determine sport's broader racial meaning and significance. In any case, my hope is that such work will bring renewed attention to and discussion of this important historical era and event.

6. Garrow 1986, p. 589. This striking omission stands in contrast to many of the most recent sport-oriented accounts of the Olympic boycott movement. They not only cite King's support but characterize it as crucial to the legitimacy of the movement (cf. Moore 1991a; for an earlier exception, see Cashmore 1982, pp. 11–22). In other words, what is now seen as a major moment in one context is barely remembered in another. This probably says less about King's biographers than about the place of sport in American culture. Until recently, in fact, sport has been left out of most civil rights narratives in the United States (and scholarship more broadly) altogether, and even now it remains underdeveloped. One well-known and otherwise admirable chronicle of the civil rights movement that makes this point nicely (if painfully) is Robert Weisbrot's *Freedom Bound* (1990). To its credit, this book mentions the Smith-Carlos protest in a discussion of how black role models in the 1960s refused to continue to play the roles white society had assigned them. Unfortunately this two-sentence reference is marred by at least three factual mistakes and one very questionable

interpretive claim: "In the 1968 Olympics, Tommie Smith and John Carlos finished first and second [1] in the 100-meter dash [2], then raised their fists in a Black Power salute during the hoisting of the American flag. The U.S. Olympic Committee confiscated their medals [3] as punishment" (pp. 226–227). For a more factually accurate account (albeit one that characterizes the protest in simplistic black power terms), see Gerstle 2001, pp. 303–306.

7. For representative compilations, see McAdam and Snow 1997; Morris and Mueller 1992.

8. The notion of culture as structure, which received its classic formulation in the work of the French anthropologist Lévi-Strauss, stands as an alternative to the subjectivist conceptions of culture that typically circulate in sociology. Obviously, these ideas have been subsequently updated and revised in recent years by various poststructural and postmodernist theorists. For recent discussions and reviews that have informed this metatheoretical frame, see Sewell 1999; Hays 1994; and Wuthnow 1987.

9. This general critical orientation is shared by many feminists working in and around sport (cf. Theberge 1985; Bryson 1987; Birrell and Cole 1994), though the connections between race and gender are only beginning to be worked out. I try to touch on the intersections of race with gender in a number of places throughout the text—especially those that relate to race, masculinity, and individualism—but the connections are highlighted in the last chapter of the book, drawing on the leading work of C. L. Cole.

10. What this project represents in this respect is a theoretically derived case study in which the case is chosen precisely to reveal underlying and otherwise unseen social and cultural structures at work. In the context of ethnography, Michael Burawoy has referred to the "extended case method" (1998, 1991), but there are fewer sociological works that use movements and theory in this fashion than one might imagine. One of the most well known may be Frances Fox Piven and Richard A. Cloward's study *Poor People's Movements* (1977). A work that served as something of a model for me in this project was Lawrence Goodwyn's *The Populist Moment: A Short History of Agrarian Revolt in America* (1978). Goodwyn's study combines description and analysis, enabling his readers to discover social and cultural forces and structures in the course of a historical narrative full of dramatic events, colorful personalities, and exciting, uncertain political struggles. For more recent work in sociology rethinking the relationship between cases, theory, and narrative, see Sewell 1996b; Abbot 2001, chapters 4 and 6; and Ragin and Becker 1992.

11. The research archives I utilized and those individuals I interviewed are listed in the acknowledgments. I have not been able to officially interview any of the principals—Harry Edwards, John Carlos, or Tommie Smith. Edwards simply did not respond to either my written requests or phone calls. Smith and Carlos, however, are more complicated cases. I had several telephone conversations and exchanges with Smith but he declined, on the advice of his lawyer, to respond on the record to my questions and inquiries. Fortunately, Smith has spoken on the record several times in recent years (including for *Sports Illustrated* and HBO) and I have used these interviews to clarify and support my reading of events. I had also had a lengthy and detailed conversation with the reporter (Kenny Moore) who did the interview and wrote the two-part story for *Sports Illustrated*. Carlos

was an even more complicated case. For several years after the 1984 Olympics, he eluded the media. He only offered a few remarks to Moore in 1991. Since then, to my knowledge, he has refused to comment publicly. However, in 1996 he did consent to a lengthy and detailed interview with an undergraduate student of mine, Dani Dennenberg, who had attended high school in the Palm Springs area where he currently works. Dennenberg and I spent several weeks prepping for the interview, and though many of Carlos's accounts and ideas are dubious and unbelievable, the transcript—which is more than twenty-five pages long—serves as a remarkable statement of his present frame of mind and his own constructed version of these events, their significance, and their impact upon his life in the years since 1968.

12. Notable exceptions exist, of course (Gamson 1990; Tarrow 1998; Giugni 1998; and most recently K. Andrews 1997, 2001), but it is nonetheless widely acknowledged that the collective action literature has been dominated for the past two decades by issues concerning the emergence and evolution of movements on their own terms and in their particular social environments—recruitment, political opportunity structures, resources and mobilization, grievances and justice frames, and so on—to the neglect of their larger impacts, outcomes, and accomplishments.

13. Much of this work comes out of humanities departments—and thus begins from different questions, has a particular vocabulary and rhetorical style, and uses alternative analytical tools and techniques. I believe, however, that a deeper, more significant part of the disconnect of critical race scholarship from conventional social scientific approaches stems from the materialist and rationalist presuppositions of the latter. More specifically, I suggest that dominant social theories and political ideologies are hard pressed to grasp *either* the challenge that collectivist identities such as race pose *or* the power and import of culture as the site on which such racial formations are constructed, reproduced, challenged, and transformed.

Chapter 1

1. *Chicago Tribune,* September 5, 1968; Wallenchinsky 1984, p. 15.

2. "Mexico 1968," official report of the Mexican Organizing Committee to the International Olympic Committee.

3. *Sports Illustrated,* October 28, 1968, p. 22.

4. This quote and a number of the details from the previous paragraphs come from Kenny Moore's 1991 *Sports Illustrated* interview and two-part cover story. In addition to Moore's indispensable account, I have drawn extensively from a variety of primary and secondary sources dealing with the episode, including existing videotape footage, recent television documentaries, oral history transcripts, and interviews I personally conducted (including one with Moore, who was a teammate of Smith and Carlos's in Mexico City).

5. Edwards 1969, p. 104.

6. For examples, see Unger and Unger 1988, pp. 213–214; Caute 1988, pp. 408–410; Collier and Horowitz 1989, p. 290; and Koning 1987, pp. 193–194.

7. William Rhoden in the *New York Times,* October 23, 1993.

8. "In the Game? Sport, Race and Politics, "*Race and Class* 36, no. 4 (April–June 1995): special issue; *TV Guide,* June 29–July 5, 1996.

9. Interview with Patty Van Wolvelaere, San Diego, CA, April 12, 1994. For other examples, see *New York Times,* October 25, 1993.

10. Moore 1991b, p. 66.

11. When I alerted my young friends to this strange gap in their knowledge about this image, many of them were quite taken aback and suddenly began to take a genuine interest in this wild-haired, wide-eyed young white boy and his little research project. The experience was so successful that, for a while, I used it as a model for breaking the ice with other students I worked with.

12. For work on "the sixties" in this vein, see the essays contained in the volumes edited by Reed (1986) and Farber (1994). See also Piccone 1988.

13. *New York Times,* October 20, 1968.

14. *Chicago Tribune,* October 19, 1968.

15. *Chicago American,* October 19, 1968.

16. For an excellent example of putting visual texts in historical contexts, see Wendy Kozol's 1994 *Life* magazine study of representations of 1950s American family life.

17. *New York Times,* October 17, 1993.

18. *Ebony,* December 1968, pp. 160–161.

19. In the early twentieth century, the raised clenched fist was initially a symbol that carried labor or even communist overtones, at least in the American context. Then in the 1960s it began to be used by those who considered themselves a part of the New Left. The earliest known group portrait of Students for a Democratic Society (SDS) taken in September 1963 during a national council meeting in Bloomington, Indiana, captures the delegates with fists— mostly right-handed ones—in the air. (See the cover illustration of James Miller's *Democracy Is in the Streets* (1987.) From what I have been able to determine, the first time this clenched-fist gesture was used explicitly in connection with black power was on June 17, 1966, when Stokely Carmichael, fresh out of jail, famously introduced the slogan (Sitkoff 1981, p. 215; Weisbrot 1990, p. 222). Just how quickly the gesture took on the connotations of black power itself, I am not entirely certain.

20. Bourdieu 1988 [1982], p. 159. This anecdote comes from Bourdieu's "Program for a Sociology of Sport," which—especially when read in concert with an article like "Sport and Social Class" (1991 [1978])—has become almost paradigmatic for the sociological investigation of sport and all manner of popular culture. Bourdieu's empirical work on the relationship between sport (and culture more generally) and the social stratification of French society is predicated on notions of taste distinctions as constituted in stratified and stratifying practices. In sport, for example, he is concerned with mapping the preferences or dispositions conditioned by the social groups to which one belongs (or aspires to belong) as well as by the bodily relations (and their deeply embedded "ways of being") each group favors, requires, or excludes. Bourdieu's formulations of the logic of taste distinctions as they operate in and through sport have obviously been path-breaking. Nevertheless, I believe that the analytical model Bourdieu articulates would seriously misread sport's social "flavor" in the United States. In general terms, I am persuaded by John MacAloon's (1988a) suggestion that such relations would not work out so neatly in this country as they do in Bourdieu's hierarchical and unathletic France, and because a great deal of the social signif-

icance of sport in the United States is connected with its status as mass, spectator sport—that is, as a form of what has been called "public culture" (see also Brownell 1995, pp. 67–98; Appadurai and Breckenridge 1988). Another, more specific limitation of Bourdieu's approach to sport is that he does not adapt his class-based model to the racial and ethnic dynamics at the heart of the American experience. (For a body of work that does, see Wacquant 1995, 1992.) Still, the notions of field, practice, symbolic power, and hegemony within and around which Bourdieu situates his understanding of sport inform the larger theoretical sensibilities that undergird this analysis.

21. See MacAloon 1981, 1984, 1988b, 1990, forthcoming. MacAloon's work on Olympic ceremony and ritual is an extension from and directly in dialogue with Victor Turner's pioneering analyzes of ritual and ceremony (1967, 1969). Sociologists will associate Turner's studies with the work on symbols, presentations, and performances that Joseph Gusfield (1989) and Robert Wuthnow (1987) describe as "dramaturgical." Pioneering analysts in this genre include Erving Goffman, Kenneth Burke, and Clifford Geertz; Durkheim's classic *Elementary Forms of Religious Life* (1965 [1915]) is perhaps the foundational text. (See also Gusfield and Michalowicz 1994; Gusfield 1987.) A dramaturgical approach to high-performance international sport such as MacAloon's stands in stark contrast to the theoretical framework offered by sociologist-historian Allen Guttmann in *From Ritual to Record* (1978), in that it conceives of sport as intimately and dialectically connected with social structure rather than emphasizing how increasing specialization and rationalization transforms the quest for excellence in sport into an end in and of itself.

22. Social theorists may detect a "Durkheimian" logic at work here. This is explicit and not accidental. As MacAloon detailed in his full-length biographical study (1981), Pierre de Coubertin, the founder of the modern Olympic movement, was directly influenced by his contemporary, the great French sociologist Emile Durkheim.

23. This "flop," which, as MacAloon (1988b, p. 288) points out, had been considered both physically impossible and aesthetically unconscionable, was taken by Europeans at the time as "an archetypal expression of the American character: achievement through innovation whatever the cost to dignity and decorum." In one of the ironies of capital, culture, and nationalism that permeate studies like this one, the IBM Corporation featured Fosbury's flop in national advertising campaigns connected with the 1996 Olympic Games as a symbol of innovation and ingenuity that this very American organization is supposed to embody. The retrospective dark side of this appropriation will be apparent in a few paragraphs.

24. *New York Times*, October 23, 1993.

25. *L.A. Weekly*, October, 1993. See also *Los Angeles Times*, February 5, 1980.

26. On this same point, Jeffrey Sammons (1995, p. 162) notes how the fact Smith and Carlos were forced to share a single pair of gloves reveals both the "drama" and the "lack of organization" of the gesture. Recollections from both Smith and the second-place finisher, Australian Peter Norman, contained in recent documentaries (one installment in the *Fifteen Minutes of Fame* series, TNT 2002; *Fists of Freedom*, HBO 1999) also confirm these claims.

27. My concept of understanding here is informed by Martin Heidegger's

distinction between "primordial" and "discursive" understanding, as well as by Gadamer's attempt to "understand understanding." These concepts are intended to animate and encourage ways of thinking about knowledge and rationality that diverge from the materialist, consciousness-centered theory and practice that dominates contemporary social science. That such an alternative theoretical tradition comes to the fore in the context of cultural practices and symbol meanings associated with sport is no accident. Sport, play, and bodily activity have all provided the intellectual capital from which such theoretical explications have departed and been derived. Hubert Dreyfus's use of the metaphor of swimming in explicating Heidegger's notions in "Holism and Hermeneutics" (1980) is illustrative:

> Practical understanding [Heidegger's primordial understanding] is holistic in an entirely different way from theoretical [discursive] understanding. Although practical understanding—everyday coping with things and people—involves explicit beliefs and hypotheses, these can only be meaningful in specific contexts and against a background of shared practices. And just as we learn to swim without consciously acquiring a theory of swimming, we acquire our social practices by being trained in them, not by forming beliefs and following rules. . . . Such skills embody a whole cultural interpretation of what it means to be a human being and what counts as real. (p. 7)

The study of sport and, more specifically, of the knowledge and understanding necessary to successfully play a sport, provides one of the most important cultural spaces by which we can begin to "understand understanding" as something more than a strictly conscious, deliberate, and willful act, as a complex process of bodies and minds interacting in the world. It is no accident, I believe, that some of the most important theoretical expressions of this style of thought in recent years (such as Anthony Giddens's notion of structuration, Bourdieu's understandings of practice, or Norbert Ellias's "figurational sociology") come from social theorists who were at one time sportsmen and developed their concepts, to one degree or another, out of these experiences.

28. These differences, downplayed in Moore's 1991 *Sports Illustrated* story, are accentuated in a 1984 *Los Angeles Times* write-up (February 12).

29. John Carlos interview (with Dani Dennenberg), June 10, 1996. A few years earlier, Carlos had told Kenny Moore that he had "made up his mind" to "give Smith a gift" after Smith agreed to go along with his prerace suggestion that they "do something on the stand." Carlos goes so far as to claim that after coming out of the turn during the race itself, he actually "pulled back on the reins" and shouted for Smith to pass him. While not conclusive, existing videotape of the race does not lend any support to Carlos's claim. If anything, in this footage Carlos appears startled to see Smith passing him on the turn. Of Carlos's account, Smith simply says, "If Carlos wants to say that, I applaud him for his benevolence"(Moore 1991a, p. 75).

30. Edwards reported this claim and dismissed it summarily in *Revolt*. Carlos, to this day, repeats the explanation he had suggested more than twenty years

earlier in a *Sport* magazine interview (Moore 1991b, p. 62; *Sport,* August 1969): namely that his arm was bent because he wanted to be ready to react if he were shot at. In repeating this account to my research assistant in 1996, Carlos also added that his bent arm ensured the gesture would not bear any resemblance to a "[heil] Hitler" salute.

31. I report and discuss Carlos's public statements—which tended to be much harsher—in detail in chapter 5.

32. Interestingly, analysts from outside the world of sport scholarship are less likely to say much about Edwards and more likely to focus on the athletes themselves.

33. For fuller, more formal statements, see Hartmann 2000, 2003.

Chapter 2

1. Edwards 1969, p. 55; *Los Angeles Times,* November 24, 25, 1967. See also *Sports Illustrated,* December 4, 1967; and *Track and Field News,* December 1967.

2. *U.S. News and World Report,* August 7; *New York Times,* July 23, 24, 1967.

3. Fekrou Kidane interview, July 1994, Los Angeles, CA; see also Mbaye 1995; Archer and Baullion 1982; Lapchick 1975.

4. Gregory with Lipsyte 1964, pp. 192–193.

5. For examples, see Dudziak 1988; Layton 1995; Plummer 1996; Skrentny 1998; McAdam 1998; Von Eschen 1997.

6. *Ebony,* March 1964, pp. 95–100.

7. *Track and Field News,* December 1967, p. 12. Basketball—Alcindor's sport—and boxing were the two other Olympic sports in which a Negro boycott would have made a significant impact.

8. A full history of the role that the Olympic Games played in American foreign policy during the Cold War remains to be written, even though scholars began to be aware of the full extent of State Department usage of international sport in the mid- to late 1970s (cf. Espy 1979; Clumpner 1978; and Kanin 1981). John MacAloon (1986) has produced a study of spies in American sport that is an excellent start.

9. "A Bold Proposal for American Sport," *Sports Illustrated,* July 27, 1964, p. 13. See also *New York Times,* May 5, 1964. In typical fashion, Orth laid all the blame for the "politization" of sport at the feet of the Soviets: "[Olympic caliber sport] is part of the policy of the Kremlin in the unrelenting battle to win men's minds."

10. *Track and Field News,* August 1967, p. 23. Boston's comments were particularly significant because of his age and maturity and because he had reportedly led an aborted (and little-known) rebellion by black athletes at two meets the previous summer (*Chicago Daily News,* September 23, 1967).

11. The wire services quoted Smith as saying "there was considerable sentiment among black athletes favoring a boycott of the Olympic Games in order to protest racial injustice"; however, according to *Track and Field News* (November 1967, pp. 3, 22–23), this was not an accurate report: as their reporter on the scene describes the exchange, Smith was asked about the possibility of a boycott only *after* he had discussed with Japanese reporters how blacks in the United States were not treated equally. Following this exchange, he was then asked about a boycott and gave this simple and straightforward reply: "Depending upon the

situation, you cannot rule out the possibility that we Negro athletes might boycott the Olympics."

12. A large sampling of these letters was published in *Track and Field News,* December 1967.

13. *San Francisco Chronicle,* November 27, 1967. Dick Drake's reporting in *Track and Field News* was widely quoted on these matters (*T&FN,* December 1967, p. 12).

14. *Track and Field News,* November 1967, pp. 22–23.

15. Moore 1991a.

16. Levine focuses on Louis's role in the black community, where the boxer was both hero and role model, a living example of how a poor and uneducated black man from the South could literally fight his way out of the ghettos of the North (Detroit, in Louis's case). In my view, however, Louis's role in the civil rights movement was more complicated than this. As Chris Mead's (1985) biography of the champion makes clear, Louis also represented—or quite literally embodied—a black identity, a "blackness" that white America could also embrace and hold up as a model for racial integration. Louis was what white people called "a good Negro," "a credit to this race." In a probing review of Mead's biography, Gerald Early (1989) argues that Louis's heroism has been misunderstood by a public—both black and white—that insisted he was a victim of his origins, of American social or political structures, the "prototypical pawn in the white man's game." According to Early, this characterization is a "horribly misguided reduction of the man and the divinity of his stature," revealing "more about our collective unease about prizefighting and the meaning of black male heroism in popular culture." Early contends that Louis was not "used" any more than any social hero ever is and suggests instead that the boxer should be seen as "the greatest, the most expansive and mythical blues hero in twentieth-century America, nothing less" (1989, p. 177). None of this, in my view, undermines the fundamental point that Louis fulfilled all these functions simply by being an athlete.

17. For historical discussions focused especially on colleges and universities, see Wiggins 1993; Spivey 1983. See also Spivey 1988 for an episode that deviates from this general assimilationist script.

18. *Sport,* August 1967, p. 76.

19. *Track and Field News,* November 1967, pp. 3, 22–23.

20. Ibid.

21. When early in my research I came upon the title of this article, "Tommie Smith and His Brief Bursts of Violence," I was certain it would lay out Smith's radical politics, his defiant personality, and the background leading up to his speculative endorsements of an Olympic boycott. Ironically, however, the title referred only to his explosive foot speed—and the article portrayed Smith as strictly positive and upbeat, intent on athletic brilliance and fame.

22. For useful introductions and overviews to the volumes that have been written on Ali, see Marqusee 1999 and the collections edited by Early (1998) and Gorn (1995). Ali, it is worth noting, made a good symbolic figure for an Olympic boycott because he also had his own story of Olympic discontent: according to his ghostwritten autobiography (Ali with Durham 1975), when Ali returned to Louisville after winning an Olympic gold medal in boxing at the 1960 Rome

Olympics, he became so disgusted with the treatment he received as a black man in his hometown that he threw his gold medal into the Ohio River.

23. *New York Times,* August 24, 1967.

24. *Sport,* March 1968, p. 42.

25. Edwards 1969, pp. xxvii, 38.

26. *Track and Field News,* November 1967, pp. 3, 22–23.

27. The sociohistorical sketch I am presenting here is informed by a large body of literature. Some of the works that have been most useful for me include Payne 1995; Mercer 1994; and Singh 1998. See also Weisbrot 1990; Branch 1988; Marable 1984; Matusow 1984; McAdam 1982; Morris 1984; Chafe 1986, 1988; Sitkoff 1981; and Piven and Cloward 1977. For more particular treatments of organizations, Fairclough 1987; Garrow 1986; Oates 1982 (on SCLC); and Carson 1981 (on SNCC).

28. Russell 1966, pp. 200–211.

29. Moore 1991a, p. 66.

30. None of this should be taken to suggest that Smith and Evans didn't have problems with how they were treated in the sports world—either as athletes or as African Americans. In July 1967, Smith had objected to being required by American track authorities to compete in the U.S.-British Commonwealth Games in Los Angeles despite being simultaneously involved in Army ROTC training in Fort Lewis, Washington (*San Francisco Chronicle,* July 10, 1967). And in later chapters I will show that such treatment would be a motivating factor for many athletes, white and black, to get involved in athletic activism. At this time, however, Smith and Evans chose not to dwell upon problems in the world of sport itself.

31. *Track and Field News,* November 1967, pp. 3, 22–23.

32. Ibid., p. 22.

33. The details of this account come mainly from the San Jose State College paper, the *Spartan Daily* (especially September 18, 20, 22, 25, 27, 1967); *The Nation* (November 6, 1967, pp. 465–466); the *Los Angeles Times;* the *San Jose Mercury-News;* and Edwards's own accounts (1969, pp. 42–44; 1971).

34. *Spartan Daily,* September 20, 1967. According to the campus paper, Edwards had "vaguely warned" that the UBSA would not be able to control these protesters and that if, for example, they were met with a barrage of bottles or garbage, they were likely to "retaliate in kind."

35. *The Nation,* November 6, 1967, p. 465.

36. Ibid.

37. Edwards 1969, pp. 44, 47.

38. *Spartan Daily,* September 22, 25, 1967. Edwards himself issued only vague and strangely passive statements regarding the protest, while President Clark later attributed the protest and the threat of violence that surrounded it strictly to "off-campus persons and groups."

39. Edwards 1969, pp. 41, 47.

40. *Track and Field News,* November 1967, p. 22.

41. *Chicago Daily News,* September 23, 1967 (story compiled from the AP).

42. Moore 1991a, p. 66.

43. Edwards 1969, p. 41. The precise nature of the link between the consideration of a boycott in the fall of 1968 and Gregory's Black Power Conference

resolution earlier that summer is somewhat unclear. Although Edwards mentions Gregory's original attempts to organize boycotts of international sporting events in *Revolt*, he does not refer to the 1967 Black Power Conference revolution or Mal Whitfield's earlier proposal. In the fall of 1967, in fact, Edwards had told the press, "The idea is mine, totally and completely" (*New York Times*, November 27). Smith claimed he had not begun to consider the "possibility" of a boycott until the moment the Japanese reporter actually put it before him in Tokyo; however, he never actually denied having heard, thought, or even talked about the idea previously. Evans, in fact, confirmed that Ali's treatment and Gregory's boycott resolution had "affected their thinking," though he reiterated that they were driven to consider an Olympic boycott simply because they, like "many Negroes," were "becoming aware of what's happening" in the United States and "didn't dig . . . these things at all" (*Track and Field News*, November 1967). At one point, Evans claimed to have first considered the idea of an Olympic boycott the previous year when he learned that a white South African had been invited to compete in the Compton Relays (*Sports Illustrated*, December 4, 1967, p. 31; see also Lapchick 1975).

44. Edwards 1969, pp. 44, 49.

45. *Sports Illustrated*, November 3, 1969, p. 35.

46. Ibid., pp. 37–38. These same themes are reiterated and elaborated in Phil Pepe's 1970 biography *Stand Tall: The Lew Alcindor Story;* see also Abdul-Jabaar 1983.

47. Edwards 1969, pp. 49–51.

48. In *Revolt*, Edwards clearly distinguishes the OCHR, the organizing group or what the social movement scholars (McCarthy and Zald 1977; see also Tarrow 1998) would have called the "social movement organization (SOM)," from the OPHR, the larger movement that the committee was attempting to coordinate and direct. I have tried to follow his usage in these chapters in order to keep the motives, understandings, and contributions of the social movement organization distinct from actors in the movement and the movement taken as a whole as discussed in the first chapter. Nonetheless, it is difficult to say exactly who was in this organization, as Edwards never explicitly identifies the third member to whom he alludes in *Revolt*. If the individual came from among those who attended the inaugural October 7 meeting (as Edwards suggests), it was probably Tommie Smith. He was, after all, the most prominent and forceful athlete who spoke on behalf of the boycott. However, in the fall of 1967 and throughout 1968 Smith consistently denied that he was actively organizing; in recent years he has even claimed that Lee Evans had to persuade him to attend the November OPHR workshop in Los Angeles (Moore 1991a). Evans, then, seems the more likely candidate. Why, then, didn't Edwards say so specifically? This, I suspect, is probably a function of Edwards's own disappointment and disapproval of Evans's actions in Mexico City and the period immediately thereafter when *Revolt* was being written. In any case, it seems clear that the various public relations and organizational responsibilities regarding the Olympic boycott were shared primarily among these four men.

49. Edwards 1969, p. 52.

50. *Track and Field News*, November 1967.

51. Ibid., p. 23.

52. *San Francisco Chronicle,* November 10, 1967.

53. Edwards 1969, p. 51. Edwards attributed this failure to the financial difficulties of printing and mailing, as well as the fact that coaches in "white-dominated athletic departments" censured or destroyed letters addressed to athletes in care of the athletic department.

54. *Track and Field News,* November 1967, p. 22.

55. Edwards 1969, pp. 51–57. I have supplemented and confirmed Edwards's account, as much as possible, with details culled from newspapers and other sources. One of the best of these is Johnathan Rodgers, *Sports Illustrated,* December 4, 1967, pp. 30–31. Rodgers, an African American, was one of the few sportswriters allowed to observe the proceedings. See also *Newsweek,* December 4, 1967.

56. Edwards 1969, p. 53.

57. Ibid.

58. *Los Angeles Times,* November 24, 1967.

59. Ibid., November 25, 1967.

60. *Chicago's American,* November 25, 1967.

61. *Track and Field News,* December 1967, p. 15.

62. *Los Angeles Times,* November 24, 1967. It is, however, important to note that only a month or two later Smith published a lengthy statement in *Sport* magazine (March 1968) confirming that he both "agree[d] with and voted for" the "Black Youth Conference Resolution" to boycott the 1968 Olympic Games.

63. Edwards 1969, pp. 54–56. See also the *San Francisco Chronicle Sporting Green; Los Angeles Times,* November 25, 1967; and *Sports Illustrated,* December 4, 1967.

Chapter 3

1. *Los Angeles Times,* November 24, 1967.

2. *San Francisco Chronicle,* November 24, 1967.

3. *Los Angeles Times,* November 24, 1967.

4. *Track and Field News,* December 1967, pp. 12, 16; *San Francisco Chronicle,* November 26, 27, 1967. At the time Boston was the reigning world champion in the long jump and Greene a six-time national sprint champion. Hines would win the 100-meter dash in Mexico City in world-record time.

5. Associated Press, November 30, 1967.

6. *Chicago Tribune,* November 25, 1967.

7. *Track and Field News,* December 1967, p. 15.

8. *San Francisco Chronicle Sporting Green,* November 25, 1967.

9. *Track and Field News,* December 1967, pp. 15, 16.

10. *Chicago Tribune,* November 25, 1967.

11. *Santa Barbara News-Press,* November 25, 1967.

12. *New York Times,* November 28, 1967; *Chicago Tribune,* November 25, 1967.

13. *Chicago Tribune,* November 25, 1967.

14. See William Baker's full-length biography (1986). Despite Baker's well-researched and accessible revisionist account, Hitler's snub of Owens still circulates widely in American popular culture and collective memory. Baker char-

acterizes Owens's reaction to the boycott announcement as "cautious," citing a quote from the *Chicago Defender:* "We have been conscious of racial problems for many years, but it is no good dropping out of the Olympics. We have to be there, we have to be everywhere it counts." As Baker describes it, Owens (along with people like Metcalfe and Johnson) was sympathetic to the motives but rejected the method of protest. I agree with this characterization but, based upon how he was quoted in the national media, would reject Baker's claim that Owens was cautious in formulating his position. Baker, for his part, claims that Owens did not "take the offensive" in the matter until February, when the IOC readmitted South Africa. It was at this point, according to Baker, that Owens unambiguously condemned the boycott, arguing that the "South African question" was "peripheral to American arenas" (p. 207).

15. *Chicago Tribune,* November 25, 1967.

16. Dave Eisenberg, "Conversations in Sports," Hearst Headline Special Service; the USOC's *Amateur Athlete,* May 1968, p. 17.

17. *Chicago Tribune,* November 25, 27, 1967.

18. *Chicago Tribune,* November 25, 1967.

19. *Track and Field News,* December 1967. Of the nine said to be considering a boycott, four (Smith, Evans, Bill Gaines, and John Carlos) said they would support it if asked to by "unspecified" black leaders; three (Charles Craig, Steve Brown, and Jerry Proctor) said they would go along with the majority decision; and two (Henry Jackson and Willie Davenport) were simply undecided. The eighteen who planned to compete no matter what included Otis Burrell and Ron Copeland (both of whom were at the OPHR workshop), Dave Smith, Clarence Ray, Ralph Boston, Charlie Green, Orin Richburg, Larry Livers, Darnell Mitchell, Ed Caruthers, Jim Freeman, Steve Carson, Thurman Boggess, Art Walker, John Thomas, Willie Turner, Gayle Hopkins, and Bob Beamon.

20. *Chicago Tribune,* November 25, 1967.

21. *Chicago Defender,* November 30, 1967. Although there is a good deal of scholarship on the reactions and role of the black sports press regarding the African American experience in sport in the first half of the century (see, for examples, Wiggins 1983a, 1983b; Tygiel 1983; Simons 1985), I have found no published works that address this episode specifically. Nevertheless, while Young's comments are rhetorically excessive, I believe they are representative of the views of many African American elites. I base this claim on an analysis conducted by a Minneapolis-based reporter named Phil Johnston (n.d.) when still an undergraduate journalism studies major, as well as on evidence such as *Ebony's* ambivalent, conflicted reactions to Smith and Carlos's victory-stand demonstration and the fact that Mal Whitfield felt obligated to describe his earlier boycott suggestion as "a shocking proposal."

22. I am quoting here from Singh 1998, although I have not been able to find these exact formulations in Hall et al. 1978. (Variations appear on pp. 240–247.)

23. *Los Angeles Times,* November 26, 1967. In a sense, of course, Maher would be proven absolutely correct in claiming that the Olympics could be an "effective line of communication" by the victory-stand gesture less than a year later.

24. *Human Events,* December 9, 1967.

25. Chamberlain's only evidence for this assertion is that one out of seven U.S. athletes who took part in the 1964 Olympic Games were black, compared with the fact that blacks numbered only one out of ten Americans in the general

population.

26. *Ebony,* March 1968, p. 116.

27. Associated Press, November 30, 1967.

28. *Track and Field News,* December 1967, p. 17.

29. *Spartan Daily,* September 22, 1967; see also *The Nation,* November 6, 1967, pp. 465–466.

30. *Spartan Daily,* September 22, 1967.

31. Interestingly, Reagan's initial fury seems to have been occasioned primarily by an egregious misprint (or misreport) in the *Los Angeles Times* stating that fifty-six of the fifty-nine members had voted against the settlement with the university, when in fact the vote represented those in favor of the settlement.

32. *Chicago Tribune* Press Service, November 29, 1967.

33. *New York Times Magazine,* May 12, 1968.

34. Rafferty would soon emerge as a vocal critic of all manner of activism and social unrest in interscholastic athletics. He is perhaps best remembered in this capacity for a speech he delivered to the 1969 California State Conference of Athletic Directors because Jack Scott reprinted the address in his activist volume *The Athletic Revolution* (1971). According to Scott, the address, titled "Interscholastic Athletics: The Gathering Storm," was an example of "the dominant philosophy in American athletics" (p. 13). See also *Salt Lake Tribune,* December 14, 1969.

35. This provoked a great deal of anger against Reagan and his colleagues, whom various student and faculty groups accused of trying to make President Clark into the scapegoat Clark Kerr had been at Berkeley. See, especially, *Spartan Daily,* October 5, 11, 12, 16, 1967. (The faculty union, the AFT, was particularly involved in Clark's defense and also the target of conservative rebuke.) The accusations escalated and played out predictably. Senator Bradley came to campus on October 11 to argue that tutorials for minority students were a "waste of cash," charging that Clark was adopting "Kerr type policies" that were "aiding and abetting the enemies of our country," while Clark himself accepted an invitation to be the keynote speaker for the Fourth National Conference of Student Governments the following month (*Spartan Daily,* November 21, 1967).

36. *Track and Field News,* November 1967.

37. *Chicago Sun-Times,* December 18, 1967.

38. *San Francisco Chronicle,* November 26, 1967.

39. *Life,* December 8, 1967.

40. Young 1963, p. 14.

41. *Chicago Tribune,* June 3, 1968.

42. For reviews of historiography on the topic, see Sammons 1994; Wiggins 1986.

43. Guttman 1984, p. x. The tensions in the Olympic Charter I am referring to here are also paralleled in modern social thought. It was the French social theorist Emile Durkheim who introduced the concept of the sacred into social thought in *The Elementary Forms of the Religious Life* (1915). As he understood it, the sacred was the realm of ultimate concern, distinct from the profane— the ordinary or mundane. In her subsequent work on ritual and order, Mary Douglas (1966) argued differently. In Douglas's view the sacred was never quite so strictly separated or set apart from routine, daily life as Durkheim's formulations imagined or implied. Instead, she drew a distinction between purity and danger as a more direct and true-to-life way of ordering the world through a

sanctified category of practice. For Douglas what is important is that the laws governing taboo and danger conform to some logic for the people that follow them and that these boundaries reinforce deeper social relationships and identities.

44. It is, according to MacAloon, the closest thing to an operating principle as is now in place in the international Olympic movement.

45. Guttmann 1984, pp. 115–116. Italics added.

46. Another example of the power of the connections between sport culture and color-blind social justice was the fierce and ultimately impenetrable opposition that liberal Democrats like Lyndon Baines Johnson ran up against when trying to craft social policies and programs to advance the African American cause beyond formal, procedural ideals (e.g., simple freedoms, basic civil rights) in the middle of the 1960s. Johnson's is a particularly interesting case in this regard because, like King, he attempted to mobilize the metaphor of the footrace to justify this shift. In his now-famous speech ("To Fulfill These Rights") to Howard University graduates honoring the university's hundredth anniversary on June 6, 1965, Johnson redirected the metaphor of the footrace away from equality of opportunity toward equality of outcomes. This attempt to merge liberal meritocracy with collectivist equality (e.g., affirmative-action programs) obviously has a more complicated, controversial history than I can detail here. For a treatment, see Walk 1995.

47. *New York Times,* July 23, 24, 1967.

48. Guttmann 1984, p. 129.

49. Guttmann (1984, p. 244) argues that Brundage was not a racist as defined by prejudice because he decidedly opposed overt forms of racism in competition and certain forms of segregation. Guttmann quotes Brundage as having said: "The Southerners who won't register a Negro [to vote] do not realize how ridiculous they have made themselves." In concluding that Brundage simply stood for the "egalitarian principles implicit in the nature of modern sports and explicit in the Olympic rules," Guttmann may have neglected other, fragmentary evidence from Brundage's files that might prompt us to consider the entire matter more closely, including references to Smith and Carlos as "colored boys" (personal letter dated November 11, 1968; Avery Brundage Collection). Guttmann does mention that Brundage replied to a virulently racist letter with his own criticism of *Brown vs. Board of Education.*

50. *Track and Field News,* November 1967, p. 22.

51. *New York Times,* December 14, 1967.

52. For more on Robinson, see Tygiel 1998.

53. *San Francisco Chronicle,* December 13, 1967.

54. Edwards 1969, appendix E, pp. 183–192.

55. *San Francisco Chronicle,* December 13, 1967.

56. For useful recent treatments, see Mercer 1994; Carby 1998; and Kelley 1996, pp. 23–25, 112–115. Their ideas, as each of these authors acknowledge, owe a great deal to the work of feminists of color in the 1970s (cf. Combahee River Collective 1997 [1977]).

57. Sport scholars have often followed Robert Connell (1990, 1995) in characterizing sport as an arena of "hegemonic masculinity" (Trujillo 1991), rightly insisting that its cultural qualities are deeply connected with its domination by men, serving as a kind of "male preserve" (Dunning 1986). For works that

grapple with these issues, see Bryson 1987, Willis 1982, and Whitson 1994—all three of which are contained in an excellent collection edited by Birrell and Cole (1994). In the context of his larger critique of masculinity in sport, Michael Messner's work (1990, 1992) has probably been as helpful as any in helping scholars begin to think about the relationships between race and gender in sport. Some of his main points are encapsulated in a quote from (nonsport specialist) Kobena Mercer: "As a major public arena, sport is a key site of white male ambivalence, fear and fantasy. The spectacle of black bodies triumphant in rituals of masculine competition reinforces the fixed idea that black men are 'all brawn and no brains,' and yet, because the white man is beaten at his own game—football, boxing, cricket, athletics—the Other is idolized to the point of envy. . . . The ambivalence cuts deep into the recess of the white male imaginary" (1994, pp. 178–179).

58. *New York Times*, November 25, December 15, 1967.

59. See also Oriard 1995 and Riccella 1991. Sammons's previous work on boxing (1988) anticipates this point as well, as do Gerald Early's masterful essays on similar topics (cf. 1989). See also Marqusee 1999; Hamm 2000; and Nelson George's treatment (1992) of the black basketball aesthetic in contemporary American culture.

60. This analysis drew on a large literature on social movements and popular culture. For influential works from each camp, see Gitlin 1980 and Lipsitz 1994. In addition to Harvey 1990, a useful account of the structural underpinnings that made such cultural politics prominent at this particular historical moment can be found in the introduction to Lowe and Lloyd 1997. See also Gray 1995, chapter 1.

61. *New York Times Magazine*, May 13, 1968, p. 50.

62. *New York Times*, December 14, 1967.

63. *Chicago's American*, December 2, 1967. Interestingly, after the 1968 Olympic Games another journalist would report that Whitfield had been "deeply offended by the Black Power demonstrations on the podia of Mexico City" and quote Whitfield saying, "It's untenable to use sport for political ends. I appreciated their civic interest, but they could've withdrawn from the U.S. team or kept their promises to participate graciously" (Avery Brundage Collection; *Olympic Newsletter*, spring 1969). Whitfield still clearly understood the foreign policy possibilities inherent in Olympic sport better than ever; in this report, Whitfield claims that his "after-track fulfillment" would come not from battling the social problems of black America at home but in confronting "prejudice against high plateau Africans." He also says, "African countries are focusing their attention on sport as one of the forms of nation-building. [It is] identification and unification—getting the tribes together to compete—and then sending the best of them out to represent their country, that sort of thing." Whitfield's curious path to Africa would be followed by Jesse Owens and, of all people, Muhammad Ali (Wenn and Wenn 1993) in the decade that followed.

64. *International Tribune*, December 18, 1967.

Chapter 4

1. Edwards 1969, pp. 183–192; appendix E, "OPHR Information Booklet Excerpts."

2. *International Tribune*, December 18, 1967.

3. *Sports Illustrated,* January 29, 1968, pp. 56–59. See also the *Los Angeles Times* and the *Los Angeles Herald-Examiner.* Indeed, Smith's comments suggest that he and his colleagues were actually coming to understand, accept, and even celebrate criticism as a symbol of their success, a kind of badge of racial courage and honor.

4. Edwards 1969, pp. 57–58. In a November column the Bay Area sportswriter Art Rosenbaum described a debate between Edwards and Lomax at San Jose State as "a rare confrontation between Negro leaders of the violent vs. non-violent schools" (*San Francisco Chronicle,* November 27, 1967). Lomax again appeared with Edwards on the San Jose campus in early December for the presentation of a secretly filmed debate between Lomax and Malcolm X. In the discussion that followed, Lomax claimed Malcolm had drastically changed his opinion of whites before his assassination, while Edwards argued that he had only shifted his view on white racism from a biological to a sociological foundation (*Spartan Daily,* December 5, 1967).

5. Edwards 1969, pp. 58–59; see also *Chicago Tribune,* December 15, 1967. Several publications described them—inaccurately as far as I can tell—as "resolutions" that had been passed at the workshop in Los Angeles.

6. Headline quote in *Chicago Sun-Times,* December 16, 1967.

7. SCLC papers, boxes 132 and 133. See also the document marked "MARTIN LUTHER KING FILM PROJECT," dated 12–14–67, from ABC Television.

8. The troubled place of King and his SCLC in the fragmented civil rights coalition has been well documented (Fairclough 1987, pp. 309–384; Garrow 1986, pp. 575–624; and Oates 1982, pp. 433–458). What is worth adding here is that King's main reason for being in New York at the time of the OPHR press conference was to conduct reorganizational meetings with his SCLC staff (Fairclough 1987, pp. 361–362). This administrative shuffling resulted in Andrew Young's promotion to executive vice president, a post from which he also assumed responsibility for both the Olympic boycott initiative and King's long-envisioned "Poor People's Campaign." (Press release, December 13, 1967, 122, 8, SCLC papers.)

9. Edwards 1969, p. 187.

10. *International Tribune,* December 18, 1967.

11. *New York Times,* December 14, 1967.

12. *Sports Illustrated,* March 18, 1968.

13. Matthews 1974, p. 162.

14. Edwards 1969, p. 65.

15. For a work that captures some of this context, albeit from an entirely different perspective, see Considine and Jarvis 1969.

16. *Newsweek,* February 19, 1968, p. 85.

17. *Sports Illustrated,* February 26, 1968, p. 25.

18. Ibid. Johnson and Roediger (2000) supply a more recent discussion of Simpson's role in the black athletic protests of the era. Several of the essays in Morrison and Brodsky's edited collection (1997) made similar points. Toni Morrison, for example, notes that Simpson was not a "vocal, high-profile activist." And, as Andrew Ross puts it in that same volume, "Despite his initial fame as a 'black athlete,' it was widely perceived that the O.J. Simpson was less socially black than almost any other black man in America" (p. 262).

19. *New York Times,* January 30, 1968.

20. *Chicago Daily News,* February 18, 1968.

21. *Track and Field News,* February 1968.

22. *Newsweek,* February 19, 1968, p. 85.

23. Ibid., p. 83. Eventually, the NYAC "quashed" a subpoena of its records by the New York City Commission on Human Rights when a judge ruled that the commission could not force a private organization to open its membership records (*Track and Field News,* June 1968).

24. *San Jose Mercury-News,* February 23, 1968.

25. *New York Times,* February 14, 1968.

26. Edwards 1969, pp. 65–69; *New York Times,* February 16, 1968.

27. Edwards 1969, p. 67.

28. *Sports Illustrated,* February 26, 1968, p. 25.

29. *Newsweek,* February 26, 1968, pp. 82–83.

30. *San Jose Mercury-News,* February 23, 1968. See also *Sport,* March 1968, pp. 42–43.

31. *Sports Illustrated,* February 26, 1968, pp. 24–27. Among the African American athletes in attendance were Bob Beamon and four teammates from the University of Texas, El Paso, Jamaican sprinter Lennox Miller, and another high jumper from Los Angeles named Franzetta Parham. Beamon, Miller, and Parham all won their respective events (Parham, obviously, in the women's division).

32. *Sports Illustrated,* February 26, 1968.

33. Film footage, California Afro-American Museum; *The Black Olympians* (videotape, 1984).

34. *Sports Illustrated,* February 26, 1968.

35. Edwards 1969, pp. 68, 69.

36. *Sports Illustrated,* February 26, 1968, p. 24.

37. The South African boycott movement has been given substantial treatment from Olympic historians. See Keech 2000; Booth 1998; Guttmann 1992, pp. 124–140; Guttmann 1984, pp. 223–255; Mbaye 1995; Gafner and Muller 1995; Schantz 1995; Roberts 1991; Kidd 1990. See also Lapchick 1975; Archer and Baullion 1982.

38. *New York Times,* May 8, 1967. Numbered among those Americans listed who supported the ACOA position were Arthur Ashe, Roy Campanella, Oscar Robertson, Floyd McKissick, Bayard Rustin, Stokely Carmichael, Langston Hughes, and Reinhold Niebuhr.

39. King papers, box 2, folders 20, 21.

40. *Sports Illustrated,* February 26, 1968, p. 25.

41. IOC Archives, Circulaires 1967–1968 folder, heading: "Lausanne, March 18th 1968" (reference no. M/406).

42. *Sports Illustrated,* February 26, March 11, 1968.

43. *Olympic Newsletter,* April 1968, p. 117.

44. This situation persists in many ways to this day. The official history of the IOC commissioned by President Samaranch for the organization's centennial, for example, only briefly refers to the African American Olympic protest movement, hidden in a chapter on apartheid in South Africa. See also Killanin's autobiographical comments (1983).

45. *Sports Illustrated,* February 26, 1968, p. 25.

46. *Newsweek*, February 26, 1968, pp. 82–83.

47. *New York Times*, February 18, 1968; Edwards 1969, p. 66.

48. *Sports Illustrated*, February 26, 1968.

49. *Sport*, March 1968, p. 43.

50. *Ebony*, March 1968, pp. 112–115.

51. *Newsweek*, February 19, 1968, p. 85.

52. Axthelm 1968, p. 58.

53. *New York Times*, March 3, 1968. Lincoln Lynch, a spokesman from the United Black Front who was also affiliated with the OCHR, explained: "To us and millions of other blacks at home and throughout the world, Ali is still the champion."

54. *Sports Illustrated*, July 1, 1968, publisher's page.

55. For additional treatments, see Ashe 1988; Spivey 1984, pp. 239–262; Baker 1982, pp. 289–295; and Grundman 1979. For contemporaneous accounts, see Matthews 1974; Scott 1971, pp. 80–88; Edwards 1969; 1970, pp. 144–155); Olsen 1968.

56. Grundman 1979, p. 78.

57. Several sports reporters also penned important stories, which bore closely related titles, on these developments: Jack Olsen's five-part series, "The Black Athlete: A Shameful Story" (*Sports Illustrated*, July 1968); Pete Axthelm's "The Angry Black Athlete" (*Newsweek*, July 15, 1968); and Dick Schaap's "The Revolt of the Black Athletes" (*Look*, August 6, 1968).

58. Bob Wheeler, assistant superintendent of Kansas City schools, quoted in Olsen 1968, p. 22.

59. Axthelm 1968, p. 57D. According to Axthelm, Murphy's comments came from an interview he conducted with *Newsweek* assistant editor Johnathan Rodgers. When asked how things could be improved for him, Murphy's answer was emphatic: "The first way is for them to stop calling me boy! The guys in the dorms—even the priests—call me this and don't realize what they are saying. To me it's worse than being called nigger."

60. For applications of Du Bois's famous double-consciousness formulation in sport, see Wiggins 1994; Harrison 2000. The experience of New York schoolboy superstar Connie Hawkins is another, more well-known case in point. See Wolf 1972, especially pp. 65–93. I will return to this case in chapter 7.

61. Edwards 1970, p. 145.

62. Edwards 1969, pp. xvii–xviii.

63. See Edwards 1969; 1970, pp. 144–155. Edwards and the entire sociology of sport would forge their academic reputations in the following decade with studies and statistics confirming these racial practices and policies. See, for representative examples, Edwards 1973b; Loy and McElvogue 1970; Scully 1974; Eitzen and Sanford 1975; McPherson 1975; J. S. Evans 1979; McClendon and Eitzen 1975; and Phillips 1976.

64. For more on the pre-1960s frustrations of African American athletes, see Harris 2000; Ross 1999; and Ashe 1988.

65. Axthelm 1968, p. 58.

66. *Look*, August 6, 1968, pp. 72–80. An obvious and well-known example of the kind of athlete this story refers to is O.J. Simpson, star football running back and sprinter at USC. See Ashe 1988, p. 192; Hutchinson 1996, pp. 140, 149; and Johnson and Roediger 2000.

67. Matthews 1974, p. 161. According to Matthews, the discussion was presented "in broad terms, stressing the need for unity and the importance of black athletes banding together."

68. Ibid., p. 162.

69. Interview, April 5, 1989, Chicago, IL.

70. Olsen 1968, pp. 73–74. Italics in original.

71. See Wiggins 1988, p. 308, and compare to Edwards 1969, pp. 80–81.

72. Interview, April 5, 1989, Chicago, IL.

73. *Track and Field News,* November 1967.

74. *Sport,* March 1968, pp. 42–43, 68–69. This article comprised two position papers, Tommie Smith's "Why Negroes Should Boycott the Olympics," and Boston's retort, "Why They Should Not." Although they are fairly lengthy and hash over many of the themes I have already laid out, they provide a fabulous, firsthand view of the Olympic boycott controversy from the prospective black Olympians themselves. The pieces are notable in two other respects. One has to do with the tortured rhetorical machinations each athlete goes through. The other involves the fact that despite being presented as a matter of stark, unambiguous "opposing points of view," the feature actually suggests that these two African American athletes agree on almost every point except the question of whether a boycott was the best way to achieve their goals.

75. Moore 1991a.

76. Even Harry Edwards himself acknowledges this now: "We also didn't do the job we should have done in terms of women. Even with all of those black women athletes in the Olympics, we never really approached them. In today's language that means we were sexist, an indictment that could be extended to the whole civil rights movement" (Edwards quoted in Leonard 1998, p. 21).

77. *Newsweek,* July 15, 1968, pp. 59–60.

78. *International Tribune,* December 16, 1967. Hazel Carby's 1998 gender-based critique of C. L. R. James informs my reading of Edwards's rhetoric and style.

79. *Saturday Evening Post Magazine,* March 9, 1968.

80. Hano 1968, pp. 32–50; see also *Life,* March 15, 1968, pp. 20–23 ("The Olympic Jolt: 'Hell No, Don't Go!'" None of this is to suggest that this radical rhetoric represented Edwards's and the OPHR's ultimate moral convictions. Hano, I think, had a pretty good reading of Edwards's style. For all his rhetoric and separatism, Hano pointed out, Edwards had a very good relationship with both his white and black students. "Somewhere short of what he says is what he means," Hano wrote. "The trick is to find it. . . . He is a moderate and a militant, separatist and integrationist." He may say "stay out!" but he secretly means "come in." Whatever its intent, however, this approach was several steps beyond the comprehension or legitimation of most participants in sport-based protests.

81. *Sport,* September 1969, p. 72.

82. *Sports Illustrated,* April 15, 1968, p. 91; *Basketball Weekly,* March 11, 1968, p. 9.

83. Walter Byers papers, vol. 57. Press release dated February 27, 1968.

84. *Sport,* November 1968, pp. 26–27.

85. Pepe 1970, p. 115.

86. Moore 1991a, p. 66.

87. *Sports Illustrated,* April 15, 1968, p. 21. See also *Los Angeles Herald-*

Examiner, June 27, 1968.

88. Moore 1991a.

89. *Chicago Defender,* May 18, 1968.

90. *New York Times,* April 24, 1968.

91. Matthews 1974, p. 165.

Chapter 5

1. Axthelm 1968, p. 56.

2. Matthews 1974, p. 165. I use Matthews's recollections (ghostwritten by Neil Admur) here, even though they seem to be based upon the *International Tribune* interview Harry Edwards gave to Robert Lipsyte in December 1967.

3. Axthelm 1968, p. 56.

4. Matthews 1974, pp. 168–169.

5. Axthelm 1968, p. 60.

6. *Sports Illustrated,* July 8, 1968, p. 13.

7. Axthelm 1968, p. 60. The two athletes were Jim Hines and Army Captain Mel Pender.

8. Edwards 1969, p. 98.

9. Axthelm 1968, p. 57D; Edwards 1969, p. xx; Matthews 1974, p. 188.

10. Matthews 1974, p. 169. Nevertheless, Matthews does credit the OCHR with "planting the first seeds of social awareness in my head. It gave me a sense of relating events in my life that I had taken for granted to the plight of the black man in America" (p. 173). These seeds would bear fruit four years later in Munich.

11. Ibid., pp. 169–173.

12. Moore 1991a, p. 72.

13. *New York Times,* March 30, 1968.

14. Letter dated April 8, 1968. NCAA Archives, Walter Byers papers, NSYSP 1967–3/69 folder. See also HHH Papers, VP Files, 1965–68, 150.E.18.3(f), Box 966.

15. *New York Times,* May 23, 1966.

16. Ibid., March 30, 1968.

17. Ibid., March 29, 1968.

18. *San Jose Mercury-News,* February 25, 1968.

19. Brown's BEU was apparently a short-lived venture. Years later, Brown claimed that, under the motto "PRODUCE, ACHIEVE, PROSPER," the BEU "touched" more than four hundred businesses in April 1968 alone and had elaborate plans to fund the college educations of black high school students in various cities across the country. Apparently, there is not much else to say. According to Brown, "It's only a drop because what's happened is, there has been no follow-through with black athletes today" (*Sports Illustrated,* August 16, 1994, p. 60).

20. *New York Times,* March 30, 1968; see also Baker 1986.

21. *Amateur Athlete,* July 1968, p. 11.

22. At least fifteen other athletes were seeded automatically into the "final" trials scheduled for South Lake Tahoe. These included Billy Mills, Willie Davenport, Richard Flowers, Paul Wilson, Willie Turner, Oliver Ford, Neil Steinhauer, Ken Moore, Jere Van Dyke, Aaron Hopkins, Ron Kutschinsky, Dave Thoreson, and Larry Walker (*Los Angeles Times,* June 27, 1968).

23. Roby letter to Brundage, August 8, 1968, Brundage files, box 62, Roby

folder.

24. Axthelm 1968, p. 57D.
25. Ibid., p. 60.
26. *Chicago Tribune,* July 1, 1968.
27. Axthelm 1968, p. 57D.
28. Ibid., p. 60.
29. Ibid., p. 56.
30. Time-Life Books published a compilation of these articles under the same title that year (Olsen 1968). Even in 1991, *Sports Illustrated* writers and editors still remembered Olsen's series as the most successful, famous, and highly praised in magazine history. In fact, as I pointed out in the introduction, the series on the black athlete they ran that year was explicitly framed and depicted as an "update" of Olsen's classic piece.
31. *Newsweek,* July 15, 1968, p. 3.
32. *London Times,* July 13, 1968.
33. *Los Angeles Herald-Examiner,* June 27, 1968.
34. *Newsweek,* July 15, 1968, p. 3.
35. *Chicago Tribune,* July 24, 1968.
36. *New York Times,* July 30, 1968.
37. Quoted from the AP wire in the *Chicago Sunday Tribune,* August 4, 1968.
38. *Chicago Tribune,* July 5, 1968.
39. *New York Times,* July 4, 1968.
40. *New York Times,* July 23, 1968.
41. In comments that were not broadcast, Alcindor gave another reason for his decision to forgo the Games: that he would have lost a whole academic quarter (because of the October scheduling) and would not have been able to graduate in June as he had planned (*New York Times,* July 23, 1968).
42. *New York Times,* August 1, 1968. A lengthier version of this text, containing several specific references to the Olympic Project for Human Rights, is reprinted in *Revolt* (Edwards 1969, pp. 108–110).
43. USOC Archives, Rowing files, August 1968.
44. *New York Times,* August 1, 1968.
45. Ibid., September 1, 1968 (dateline August 31). For what Edwards calls the "full text of the statement released at the conference," see *Revolt,* pp. 178–182.
46. I am not certain when this press conference happened. It had to follow the Black Power Conference statement of August 31, but Edwards also claims that they released a statement dated August 15 supporting a group of students in Mexico City protesting the Olympic Games. It may simply be that the statement was written at that time and not released to the press until September. The statement read, in part: "We, the colonialized and oppressed Black people of racist American, support one-thousand percent all and any efforts on your parts to obtain redress of your grievances against the Uncle Tom puppet government of Mexico. It seems ridiculous to us also to see a government spend 150 million dollars on an imperialistic spectacle while millions of its citizens live at sub-human levels of existence. . . . The anti-human governments of the world must be made to understand BY ANY MEANS NECESSARY, that the rising tide of youth will use any means necessary to stop the generation to generation flow of inhumanity . . . Viva la Revolucion del Mundo!" (Edwards 1969, p. 101).
47. Because the OCHR seems to have been little more than Edwards's per-

sonal ghost organization, what this implies is questionable. It may be that it indicates that Edwards himself moved out of the picture. On the other hand, Spivey (1984, p. 248) has claimed that during the final days before the Games, Edwards "could be found working out of the back of a rented van near the Olympic Village" urging prospective spectators not to attend.

48. Matthews 1974, p. 187.

49. Moore 1991a, p. 72.

50. Matthews 1974, p. 188.

51. Edwards 1969, p. 102.

52. *Los Angeles Times,* June 26, 1968.

53. *Wall Street Journal,* June 19, 1968.

54. For one account, see Quezada 1998.

55. *Sport,* August 1968. This quote comes from a story about the former professional baseball player Jim Bouton's trip to Mexico City with a contingent of antiapartheid activists from Jackie Robinson's American Committee on Africa. Bouton, who would write the controversial sports exposé *Ball Four* (1970), and his entourage were rudely received, accused by American officials of being "commies, crackpots and trouble-makers."

56. *New York Times,* October 12, 1968. A few weeks earlier, the newly crowned U.S. Open tennis champion Arthur Ashe had appeared on CBS's Sunday morning *Face the Nation* (the first athlete ever to do so). His experience stood in stark contrast to Lew Alcindor's national television experience that summer. Ashe told a national audience that "Negro athletes should back Negro causes." Ashe also said he was "adamantly opposed to separatism" but suggested that it was possible for black power to be used effectively (*New York Times,* September 16, 1968).

57. Moore 1991b. Hines explained at the time: "We made no formal request. We asked them who was going to present the medal and they replied Brundage. We didn't say anything. Neither did we smile. They apparently got the message" (*New York Times,* October 15, 1968). The move had been foreshadowed by a number of other African American athletes, including Ralph Boston and Tommie Smith, who had discussed possible 100-meter event protests (such as all-black outfits or no U.S. insignias) with Neil Allen of the London *Times* (October 17, 1968).

58. *Newsweek,* October 21, 1968, p. 65.

59. *New York Times,* October 16, 1968.

60. When ABC's expert track technicians played a slow-motion tape of Carlos's 200-meter qualifying trial, they discovered "that the US's John Carlos who won the heat had plainly stepped over the chalk line separating his lane from the next—an automatic disqualification [under the rules]. Since the judges had missed the infraction [Roone] Arledge [ABC's executive Olympic director and producer] had to decide whether to re-televise the tape—this time pointing out the foul—and thus taking the sheen off a possible Carlos victory in the finals" (*Newsweek,* October 28, 1968, pp. 71–72). This comes from an article by television-radio editor Harry F. Walters on ABC's Olympic coverage.

61. *Black Olympians* (videotape), California Afro-American Museum.

62. Cosell, 1973, p. 58.

63. Ibid., pp. 47–55; on the pioneering role the 1968 Games played in media

coverage, see Wenn 1993.

64. Cosell himself would be strongly criticized by some Americans for interviewing Smith and then Evans (see below) and thus "deliberately introducing controversy into the Olympics" (though he also received a week in residence at Yale University as a Hoyt Fellow for his work in Mexico City).

65. *New York Times*, October 24, 1968.

66. *Life*, November 1968, p. 64C.

67. Ibid. Name from anonymous reviewer.

68. *Spartan Daily*, October 22, 23, 1968.

69. See photograph in 1991 *Sports Illustrated* reprisal (Moore 1991a).

70. *Sport*, September 1969, pp. 70–71.

71. Brundage Olympic journal entry, October 16, 1967. Avery Brundage Collection, Mexico City files.

72. See also USOC Minutes (hand-titled "Black Power Scandel, 1968"), Thursday, October 17, 1968.

73. *New York Times* and *Chicago Tribune*, October 18, 1968.

74. USOC Minutes, October 17, 1968.

75. "Statement of the US Olympic Committee—17.10.1968," in Avery Brundage Collection. See *New York Times*, September 18, 2000 for Norman's story.

76. Smith 1982, p. 38; quoted in *Time*, October 25, 1968. See also *Wall Street Journal*, October 20, 1968.

77. *The News*, 1968 Olympic Edition.

78. *Newsweek* simply noted that a "murmur rippled through the stadium." Several days after the fact, the *New York Times* (perhaps to account for its own initially inadequate coverage) claimed that the incident "actually passed without much general notice in the packed Olympic stadium." "Over some applause," according to Kenny Moore (1991b, p. 60), "there were boos, catcalls." *Time* magazine reported that "a wave of boos rippled through the spectators" as the pair left the field and that Smith and Carlos responded by "making some interesting gestures at the stands." My own reading of Mexican newspaper headlines suggests that the Mexican press was far more interested with what Smith and Carlos had meant to say about American society than with assessing any insult to their own; and the Mexican authorities were for their part, as MacAloon has documented, much more concerned simply with trying to get through the rest of the Olympiad—unsettled by construction delays, student riots, and threats of violence—without a hitch. The only caution to this reading I have discovered so far comes from a San Jose State reporter who was sitting in the press booth when Smith and Carlos accepted their medals. In his *Spartan* column, Mike Elvitsky says that "Mexican officials and press people were screaming so loudly you'd thought the curse of Montezuma had returned" while "American officials sat silent and dumbfounded wondering what the fist gestures meant." There is some confusion in his report, however, as he initially attributes these reactions to the Mexican government itself and later can only point to one unnamed Mexican official who actually declared the demonstration a disgrace to all of Mexico (*Spartan Daily*, October 25, 1968).

79. Art of Murray DePillars; see cover to Jewell 1993.

80. *The News*, 1968 Olympic Edition; see also Associated Press story dated October 16: "Black-Fist Display Gets Varied Reaction in Olympic Village."

81. MacAloon forthcoming, p. 31.

82. *World Sports,* December 1968, p. 13.

83. *New York Times,* October 20, 1968.

84. Moore 1991b, p. 61.

85. *Spartan Daily,* "Guest Room" statement by Robert D. Clark, October 24, 1968. First reported in the October 21 edition, the statement presumably was issued at least a day before. There were others who supported Smith and Carlos's gesture as well. For example, nationally syndicated columnist Red Smith wrote: "The simple little demonstration by Smith and Carlos had been a protest of the sort every black man in the United States had a right to make. It was intended to call attention to the inequalities the Negro suffers" (Smith 1982, p. 38). Also in a story about the events surrounding Smith, Carlos, and Evans, *Life* magazine claimed, "They're not separatists. They do not believe in violence. They are dedicated to ending what they see as exploitation of black athletes, and, in the process, gaining dignity and equality for all black people." They are "competitors and individualists by nature and political activists only sporadically" (*Life,* November 1968). Sandy Pawde, now a senior editor at *Sports Illustrated,* recalls writing in support of Smith and Carlos as a columnist for the *Philadelphia Inquirer* back in 1968. Nevertheless, there is no doubt that those attempting to legitimate the protest in any fashion were in the minority as far as the national media was concerned.

86. *Sports Illustrated,* October 28, 1968, p. 27. A few years later in his book *Highlights of the Olympics,* John Durant (1973, pp. 181–185) would juxtapose pictures of Smith and Carlos and Foreman under the caption: "In contrast to the blacks shown on the opposite page ["one of the most unpleasant scenes in Olympic history"], George Foreman, an American Negro, proudly waves his country's flag in the ring."

87. *New York Times,* October 20, 1968.

88. Lapchick 1975, p. 132.

89. Avery Brundage Collection, 1968 Olympic diary, October 26 entry. It has never been clear how much of this was intended by Foreman himself and how much was crafted by his coach, Pappy Gault, who supplied the flag Foreman waved in the ring. Gault himself had bragged that his boxers were not interested in any form of racial protest in the days leading up to the Games and then again after the Smith-Carlos incident. In an October 23 story titled "US Boxers Spurn Racial Fights," for example, the *New York Times* quotes Gault: "None of my fighters have been involved in any of this demonstration stuff. We came here to fight. We're proud to be fighting for the United States. This is our country. We're all brothers, aren't we?" After the Games, Gault took a job with the International Seafarer's Union, which was later revealed to be funneling campaign funds to Nixon.

90. *Newsweek,* October 28, 1968, p. 3 (table of contents page).

91. Matthews 1974, pp. 196–200.

92. *Life,* November 1, 1968, p. 64C, D. According to Hoffman, "What the Olympic Committee has done here is to enforce its own opinions as to what is and is not proper. And by law and by their own congressional charter, they cannot do this. Our lawyers tell us that what they did to Smith and Carlos violates the First Amendment."

93. USOC Minutes, December 1968.

94. Moore 1991b, p. 64.

95. *The Black Olympians* (videotape, 1984), California Afro-American Museum. See also Edwards 1969, photo gallery.

96. *The News*, "Olympic Trouble Threat Eases," October 19, 1968.

97. Matthews 1974, p. 200.

98. Edwards 1969, pp. 105–106.

99. Matthews 1974, p. 200.

100. *Sports Illustrated*, 1974, p. 38.

101. Moore 1991a.

102. Matthews 1974, p. 199. IOC officials like Brundage and Lord Killanin, in fact, would always recall that there were three African American athletes that gave clenched-fist salutes during the victory ceremony in 1968 (Killanin 1983, p. 55). That Brundage himself was upset with Evans and his relay teammates (as well as Smith and Carlos) is even clearer. In his personal files he kept a postcard showing the four athletes with raised fists on the victory stand immediately after the ceremony, along with a collection of angry letters from persons condemning their actions (Avery Brundage Collection, Miscellaneous file 1968).

103. *Sports Illustrated*, February 18, 1974, p. 41.

104. Matthews 1974, p. 200.

105. Moore 1991b, p. 64.

Chapter 6

1. Moore 1991b.

2. *Sports Illustrated*, August 1969, p. 57; see also *Sport*, September 1969, pp. 70–72, 98.

3. President Johnson recognized the team in a statement released from the White House. It said that the athletes had "reawakened our national pride and renewed our faith in the future . . . In victory and defeat you brought new honor to your country. America is in your debt." The wire duly noted that the president did not "mention any athletes by name, nor did he make reference to the controversy" concerning Smith and Carlos (UPI wire story, October 1968). The USOC's February 1969 newsletter reports that two American gold medalists were received by LBJ in Washington "shortly after the Games." They were George Foreman (accompanied by "Pappy" Gault) and Bill Toomey. They reportedly attended a state dinner at the White House with the premier of Iran (*USOC Newsletter*, vol. 4, no. 7, p. 14).

4. Moore 1991b.

5. Guttmann 1992, pp. 131–132.

6. Avery Brundage Collection, Film Archives. See also USOC Newsletter, vol. 4, no. 6 (December 1968).

7. Guttmann 1984, pp. 243–244. For a minor example: Brundage's IOC colleague and close friend Lord Burghley's proposed 1969 revisions to official protocol in the Olympic Charter was to "encourage" organizing committees to hold victory ceremonies on-site and immediately following championship events, and to allow victorious athletes to wear "only" his/her uniforms (IOC Archives, Burghley, David George Correspondence, 1933–1969, Regels Olympiques 1969 folder).

8. *Sport,* September 1969, pp. 70–72, 98; Sendler 1969.

9. Edwards 1969, pp. 107–108.

10. See photograph in *Revolt.* These reenactments appear to have taken place especially in the context of collegiate athletic events involving Brigham Young University because of its discriminatory racial policies and practices. At Eastern Washington State College, for example, black student-athletes sought a restraining order against their athletic department from enforcing an athletic code that supposedly prohibited "the use of clenched-fist salutes at athletic events." The Utah assistant attorney general denied the injunction, saying that the code was "necessary to prevent athletes from using the athletic arena for political expression because it causes team disunity" (*Salt Lake Tribune,* November 25, 1969).

11. "Two Black Fists and the Olympics," *The Daily Aggie,* October 24, 1968.

12. Michael Palm (2002) argues that the portrayal of race relations in Hollywood films of the period was deeply affected by the imagery of Smith and Carlos's demonstration as well. Perhaps most notable in this regard was James Earl Jones's Oscar-nominated portrayal of Jack Johnson in the 1970 film *The Great White Hope.* In a crucial scene, Jones as Johnson delivers this line to erstwhile supporters: "I ain't nothing to you but a black ugly fist!"

13. Lapchick 1975, p. 215. The poll surveyed 233 people in New York, Philadelphia, Washington, Norfolk, Denver, and Los Angeles on a series of questions regarding the relationships between sport and politics. Respondents were broken down by race, gender, and age: 77 were black (34 percent), 155 white (66 percent); 87 were women (37 percent), 146 men (63 percent); and 42 percent of respondents were younger than thirty. Responses were reported only by race, however, and personal correspondence with the author confirms that the data cannot be broken down further.

14. Later in the film, the friendship and mutual respect that supposedly emerged between black and white teammates during the course of the tumultuous but ultimately successful season is captured when one of the white antagonists in the opening scene raises a clenched first to his black teammate and newfound friend. Needless to say, this incident is probably not representative of historical dynamics.

15. For examples, see Katsiaficas 1987, p. 82; Caute 1988, pp. 408–410.

16. Telephone interview, October 27, 1993.

17. IOC Archives, Mexico 1968 folders, clippings files. See also Caute 1988; Coote 1968; Phillips 1968; and the British Olympic Committee's Official Report on the 1968 Games. For a German variation, see Ueberhort 1976. Like many Europeans, Coote, who covered the Games for the *Daily Telegraph,* was also critical of the sponsorship ties Smith and Carlos had to Puma. He argues that their use of shoes in the demonstration was "not a racialistic gesture but commercialism" (p. 30). Although he also notes that it was "unfair" to single out these two individuals when "leading athletes in almost every country" also accept such payments, Coote complains that Carlos charged the BBC $2,000 a head for interviews in the immediate aftermath of his dismissal. (The British journalist does not say whether or not his colleagues acquiesced to these demands.)

18. Lapchick 1984, p. 150.

19. *New York Times,* October 23, 1993.

20. Edwards 1969, pp. 178–182. See also *New York Times,* September 1, 1968.

21. It was not until 1973 that Ashe was granted a visa to compete in South Africa. See also Archer and Bouillon 1982, p. 273; Lapchick 1975.

22. See Hartmann and Staff 2002; see also Chalip 1988.

23. *Sports Illustrated,* August 25, 1969.

24. See photographs in Scott 1971. Many of the athletes pictured in Scott's famous text are shown with beards and mustaches, Afros and long hair. It would be easy to write this off as a product of the era, but at that time these fashions constituted a real political statement and were a crucial part of the emerging athletic revolution. Scott includes one picture (p. 6) of Hayward State College (California) NCAA wrestler Sylvester Hodges, who was banned from the national championship tournament for sporting a mustache that was almost invisible to the naked eye. Scott writes: "Your eyes are not failing you; [the] mustache really was that minuscule."

25. I have borrowed this phrase from Michael Burawoy, who used it in a written review of this study.

26. *Sports Illustrated,* August 25, 1969, p. 74.

27. Ibid., pp. 70–71.

28. Ibid.

29. Ibid., p. 76.

30. Although it served as the title for Jack Scott's 1971 manifesto, "athletic revolution" seems to have been what anthropologists might call a "native term" for the movement—that is, athletes themselves used it to describe the ideas, interests, and activities that unified this otherwise disparate constellation of grievances, protests, and organizing activities.

31. "Proceedings: Minutes of the Executive Committee of the United States Olympic Committee, December 1, 1968," in USOC Archives, "Minutes of Meetings Held March 23, 1968—December 1, 1968," vol. 19, no. 8, p. 79.

32. *Sports Illustrated,* August 25, 1969, pp. 73, 75.

33. USOC Newsletter vol. 4, no. 8 (April), 1969.

34. USOC Archives, Rowing File letter dated September 2, 1968.

35. USOC Archives, Rowing File letter dated September 17, 1968. That the "demonstration" emerged as a central concern is interesting. Clearly, these athletes were motivated and inspired by the problems of racial inequality they believed their prospective teammates were trying to "dramatize." They saw their involvement as "another effort at communication, communication from concerned athletes to the rest of society," to "dramatize the plight of the masses of Negroes in this society."

36. *New York Times,* June 7, 1970.

37. *Sport,* March 1969, pp. 46–47, 76–79.

38. "Proceedings: Minutes of the Executive Committee of the United States Olympic Committee, December 1, 1968," USOC Archives, "Minutes of Meetings Held March 23, 1968-December 1, 1968," vol. 19, no. 8, p. 77.

39. Ibid., pp. 69–72.

40. Ibid., p. 86.

41. Ibid., p. 75.

42. Ibid., p. 74.

43. Ibid., pp. 99–100.

44. "Report from the Board of Consultants to the United States Olympic Committee Board of Directors." Addendum to Official USOC Meeting Minutes, December 1, 1968.

45. USOC Meeting Minutes, December 1968, p. 92.

46. See also Scott 1973. Some of Scott's ideas were initially fleshed out in the pages of the *Track and Field News* in the spring of 1968 as a critique of prevailing attitudes and approaches to coaching. The subsequent April edition contained a number of (often hostile) rejoinders from coaches that clearly foreshadowed the conflicts that Jack Underwood brought to national attention some fifteen months later. *Ramparts* magazine provided another medium through which Scott's radical critique was circulated. The October 1971 issue (vol. 10, no. 4), for example, focused on steroid use in sport; the November and December issues (nos. 4 and 5) contained selections from Meggyesy's *Out of Their League.* The following January and February had contributions from Scott on sport and masculinity, and sport and the oppression of women.

47. USOC Meeting Minutes, December 1968, pp. 81–82. See also Guttmann 1992 and volume 2 of the IOC's official history. The full force of activism within the international movement is conveyed by the fact that the 1976 International Olympic Academy chose for its topic "The New Generation and Olympism."

48. Undated newspaper clipping, Avery Brundage Collection, Munich Games files.

49. Ibid. Among the others named were John Smith (quarter mile), John Dobroth (high jumper), Russ Hodge (decathlon), Gary Power (hurdler), Milan Tiff (triple jump), and John Pennel (pole vault).

50. Many libraries do not even have the documents and books that give evidence of any broad-based athletic activism. While working on this chapter at the Olympic Studies Center in Lausanne, Switzerland, for example, I could locate no copies of Jack Scott's famous books. Indeed, his name did not even appear in the catalog. In contrast, the Center had virtually all of Harry Edwards's books and everyone on staff knew of him. In addition to the kinds of primary sources cited in the text, a full history of this aspect of 1960s sports activism will require extensive interviews and oral histories. Formal (and in several cases multiple) interviews with John MacAloon, Patty (Johnson) Van Wovlvelaere, John Dobroth, Willie Whyte, Bill Toomey, and Art Shinberg have helped inform and fill out the account I am providing here. Conversations with sports journalists Kenny Moore and Jay Weiner, former "rebel athletes," also proved stimulating and helpful.

51. Again, the history of Scott's radical experiment at Oberlin remains to be written. Some of these details came out in the tributes written at the time of Scott's death in late 1999. See, for examples, pieces in the *New York Times,* November 7, 1999 (Jay Weiner), and the *Buffalo News,* February 27, 2000 (Ross T. Funfola).

52. *Minneapolis Star Tribune,* February 13, 2000. See also Ingham 1976. Scott's post-Oberlin life was just as radical and varied. For a time he served as mentor and business adviser to countercultural NBA star Bill Walton. In 1975, in an action that brought him attention and notoriety far beyond the world of sport, Scott admitted to a grand jury in Harrisburg, Pennsylvania, that he had harbored radical heiress Patty Hearst. In the 1980s and 1990s, he worked as a physiotherapist for world-class track athletes including Joan Benoit Samuelson, Carl Lewis,

and Jackie Joyner-Kersee.

53. *New York Times,* June 7, 1970.

54. "Report from the Board of Consultants to the United States Olympic Committee Board of Directors." Addendum to Official USOC Meeting Minutes, December 1, 1968. See also "Report of the Olympic Games, Mexico City, 1968: Recommendations for Future Games" (dated November 25, 1968; prepared by Everett Barnes, acting executive director).

55. *Sports Illustrated,* August 25, 1969, p. 73.

56. Ibid., September 8, 1969, pp. 37–38.

57. Perhaps the closest that the movement came was the celebrity of the free-spirited Oregon miler Steve Prefontaine, whose life and tragic death in a car wreck were romanticized in two different Hollywood films in the mid-1990s, and those who continued his legacy in creating the Nike global athletic conglomerate (see Jordan 1997).

58. *Sports Illustrated,* "Culture Shock in Dixieland." August 12, 1991, p. 54.

59. Minutes of the Executive Committee of the United States Olympic Committee, vol. 19, no. 8 (December 8), pp. 94–95, 96.

60. When Curt Flood took the stand that eventually brought about free agency in Major League Baseball, he acted not only on behalf of black baseball players but for white ones as well. Halberstam writes that when Marvin Miller brought Flood to a meeting of all the players' reps at the time, Tom Haller of the Dodgers asked him point-blank how much of what drove him was racial. Flood acknowledged that blacks had it worse. However, he insisted that what he was doing was for all baseball players, regardless of color. Though he knew that taking this stand would effectively end his career in baseball, Flood told the union representatives that "no other profession in the country left talented men so little control over their own destiny and deprived them of [their] true market value." "I want to go out like a man," Flood told Miller in a rhetoric that echoed the language Edwards used in promoting the Olympic boycott (Halberstam 1994, pp. 365–366).

61. Interview with John Dubroth, Santa Barbara, CA, Spring 1994.

62. *Sports Illustrated,* August 25, 1969, pp. 72–74.

63. Edwards had more in mind here than the continued attention black athletic protests were bringing to the problems of race in post–civil rights period that I have emphasized in previous chapters. He was also talking about the direct role that African American athletes were assuming in other, nonsport initiatives. In the provocative if now-forgotten study *Black Students* (1970), Edwards produced compelling evidence that student athletes were at the center of the black student movement on colleges and universities around the country, especially in their demands for black studies courses and programs.

64. Edwards produced several of these studies himself, including an influential analysis of how the white power structure exploited African American athletes (1973b).

65. Sports authorities were not the only ones troubled by the ideological repercussions of this conception of sport; some of those most deeply sympathetic to what Smith and Carlos stood for on the victory stand also worried about its unintended consequences—albeit for much different reasons. John MacAloon (whose ritual analyses I relied on so heavily in the first chapter of this book), who had previously written that the "courageous choices" made by

these African American athletes were among the experiences that "compelled" him into his professional career and lifelong obsession (1981, p. x), elaborated on this when I interviewed him in the spring of 1989:

> Even though it didn't touch us directly, for some of us [the demonstration] absolutely tore our hearts out. My whole vocation as somebody who studies the Olympics was born in what Tommie Smith and John Carlos did on the victory stand. Because even as college kids, as a college student, [there was] that horrible tension between accepting and sharing all of the reasons they did what they did and realizing that if, if political protest became frequent or common in the Olympics, that would be the end of the Olympics as we know them. (April 5, 1989, Chicago, Illinois)

If "everything had changed" with Smith and Carlos's victory-stand gesture (as Lapchick had said), MacAloon and others like him were not at all convinced that the change would be for the better.

66. Edwards himself didn't write much explicitly about politics in his *Sociology of Sport* volume, but the subject matter was never far from the surface. For example, he reprinted an essay from Sandy Pawde of the *Philadelphia Inquirer* called "Sports and Politics Must Be Separate—At Least Some Politics That Is" (Edwards 1973a, p. 94), dealt with nationalism and the Vietnam War in several places in the text (this was the concrete focus of the Pawde commentary as well), and detailed the ways in which Richard Nixon (and other politicians) mobilized sport for political effect (pp. 96–98). There is more on Nixon's engagement with sports in the following chapter.

67. Another area in which Lapchick's respondents were in substantial agreement with one another (but differed with sports idealists like Brundage) had to do with international issues. Only one-third (33 percent) of Lapchick's respondents (again, black and white alike) believed that politics had no role to play in international, Olympic-style athletic events. It is hard to know exactly how to interpret this finding. On the one hand, it could be that the average American saw issues of nationality and international relations as so political and so clearly implicated in the Olympic that he or she, unlike someone like Avery Brundage, believed it either impossible or undesirable to maintain the sport/politics boundary in this instance; on the other hand, it could be that Americans didn't see issues of international relations and national identity as "political." In any case, Lapchick's own scholarship and activism on sport and apartheid in South Africa (1976), which explicitly drew these two problematic areas of race and nation directly together, deserves to be reexamined in light of the argument I am presenting here.

68. This helps to explain why Richard Espy, despite putting Smith and Carlos on the cover of *The Politics of the Olympic Games* (1979), had so little to say about them. Espy mentions their demonstration in only two places, and all that comes through in these statements is his ambivalence and confusion about them: "The victory stand protest and the African success at the Games may have indicated changing political relationships, but that process was far from complete" (p. 121). If all politics and protests were equal, it was hard to justify any of them—they all seemed problematic and corrupting. Another, later

example can be found in a piece written by sportswriter Pete Axthelm in 1987 on "international politics and Olympic crises." This may be best illustrated, as John MacAloon (1987) points out, by the photographs selected to accompany this article. On consecutive page turns Axthelm shows Hitler's propaganda Olympics (p. 103), the Smith-Carlos demonstration (p. 105), and the 1972 Arab terrorist attack in Munich (p. 107).

Chapter 7

1. *New York Times,* November 28; December 18, 1967.
2. USOC Meeting Minutes, vol. 19, no. 7 (December 16–17, 1967), pp. 6–10.
3. Ibid., p. 319.
4. Ibid., pp. 6–10.
5. Actually, this proposal was intended to speak to two issues. One was the boycott itself, what the committee called a "hidden threat." The other was the threat of prospective Olympians signing professional contracts that would revoke their Olympic status. USOC Meeting Minutes, vol. 19, no. 8 (March 23, 1968), p. 188.
6. USOC Meeting Minutes (December 16–17, 1967), p. 190.
7. Byers files, Track and Field folder, 1/68–11/68. Letter dated April 23, 1968.
8. USOC Meeting Minutes (March 23, 1968), p. 152.
9. Freedom of Information requests filed with the CIA in 1995 revealed that at least twenty-two documents on or relating to Tommie Smith, John Carlos, and Dick Gregory were collected by the CIA. FBI documents, long rumored among OPHR participants, would almost certainly reveal much more intensive investigations on the domestic side. Unfortunately, further searches were not possible because they require the full name, date and place of birth, nationality, and citizenship status as well as a signed, notarized statement from each individual authorizing the release of personal information— obviously a major stumbling block given that none of the principals agreed to be interviewed by me on the record.
10. The NCAA and the AAU were the major (if adversarial) powers in the American amateur athletic establishment in the late 1960s, as they have been throughout the course of the twentieth century (Flath 1964). However, over the period of the next several years and, as we will see, in direct connection with the events and issues under consideration in the present chapters, the AAU would lose much of its authority and control to the NCAA and, especially, the USOC, which stood as an organizing, institutional umbrella over the various sports federations and authorities that had previously been directly organized and coordinated in and through the AAU. The AAU's rapid decline in organizational resources and power led to the unfortunate dispersal, disorganization, and inaccessibility of its records and archives to sports organizations (either because records were seized by newly empowered sports federations or because there were no resources to properly organize, sort, and store them). The AAU archives, now located in Florida, are currently not available for historical research, which explains why the AAU plays so little part in the history I am documenting. (Telephone conversation with AAU librarian and archivist, Spring 1999.)
11. USOC Meeting Minutes, vol. 19, no. 7 (December 16–17, 1967), pp. 6–10.
12. Indeed, the tryout system itself was organized around and dominated by

the NCAA, which was responsible for bringing at least half of the prospective Olympians to the camp and assembled four of the eight teams in the qualifying tournament. Other teams were provided by, among others, the AAU and the military academies. But the final team was composed of the top individual competitors in the tournament—who tended to be almost exclusively from the NCAA contingents.

13. Byers papers, vol. 57, Olympic Basketball folder. Press releases, February 27 and March 15, 1968.

14. USOC Meeting Minutes, vol. 19, no. 8, (December 16–17, 1967), pp. 6–10.

15. Ibid., no. 8, March 23, 1968.

16. Ibid., pp. 6–7.

17. Ibid., p.10.

18. This attitude is also apparent in the exchanges among the USOC, the U.S. Rowing Federation, and the Harvard crew that would row the American eight-man boat (mentioned in the previous chapter). In response to the letter they had written trying to lay out the motivation for their involvement with the OPHR, the Harvard team received a letter on USOC stationery signed by four representatives of U.S. Olympic Rowing. It stated that while American Olympic officials were "in sympathy with the problems of the black man in America . . . you are being sent to Mexico to row for your country and not to engage in activities of this sort." The letter went on to state that they were "required" to sign a statement indicating their promise not to participate in "any demonstration of support for any disadvantaged people in the United States." That same day, the chairman of the Rowing Committee sent a letter to the USOC's acting executive director assuring him that measures were being put in place that would allow the board to "ship [the boys] back to the United States" should anything along the lines of a demonstration transpire (USOC Archives, Rowing file, letters dated September 17, 22, and 30, 1968).

19. Byers papers, 1968, Racial Issues folder.

20. HHH Archives, Minnesota Historical Society, St. Paul, MN.

21. HHH Papers, VP Files 144 E18-6 F. Three African American athletes were suspended for allegedly receiving improper outside funds. The NCAA's response, which was signed by the University of Michigan's Marcus Plant, the president of the organization, appealed to both the "educational integrity" of its member institutions as well as to their institutional autonomy, thus setting aside the racial nature of the incident altogether.

22. USOC Archives, "Correspondence 1968."

23. Byers papers, NSYSP 1967–3/69. (Vol. XXXIX).

24. Ibid., letter from Byers to Nicholson dated May 10, 1968.

25. Ibid., letter from Nicholson to Byers dated May 15, 1968.

26. Ibid., letter dated May 17, 1968.

27. *Sports Illustrated,* July 5, 1968, p. 15.

28. NCAA Archives, Racial Issues folder, letter dated August 13, 1968, pp. 1 and 2.

29. Ibid., p. 7.

30. NCAA Archives, Racial Issues folder.

31. Ibid., letter dated August 21, 1968.

32. In an August 29 reply to Hansen, Plant, for example, speaks of his intention to make a public statement "outlining the deficiencies in this article and holding it up as an horrible example of irresponsible journalism."

33. NCAA Archives, Racial Issues folder, August 21, 1968, p. 1.

34. *Sports Illustrated,* July 5, 1968, publisher's page; see also August 5, 1991, publisher's page.

35. *Sports Illustrated,* July 1, 1968, publisher's page.

36. NCAA Archives, Racial Issues folder, August 13, 1968, p. 5.

37. Ibid., p. 1.

38. Note how the institutional roles were shifting here: in the fall of 1967, the IOC had taken the public lead; in the aftermath of the *Sports Illustrated* story, however, it was the NCAA and other American organizations who were placed on the defensive. Part of this, of course, was that the terrain of the debate and the nature of the grievances had changed from racial injustice in general to racial inequality in the world of sport. This required a more immediate institutional response but was much less threatening to the broader moral and political ideals and ideologies that the elites of the international Olympic movement felt obligated to protect.

39. *New York Times,* December 16, 1968. After all, nothing in the Olympic Charter at that point explicitly prohibited the kind of gesture Smith and Carlos made on the victory stand, but there were strict and specific prohibitions in place then against any kind of commercial endorsements. The old "amateurism" issue was itself, as we have seen, beginning to come under fire from athletes and others.

40. USOC Archives, "Minutes of Meetings, March 23, 1968—December 1, 1968," vol. 19, no. 8: "Proceedings: Minutes of the Executive Committee of the United States Olympic Committee, December 1, 1968," pp. 69–70.

41. *Denver Post,* October 22, 1969.

42. *Sports Illustrated,* January 26, 1970, p. 6.

43. *NCAA News,* December 1969, pp. 2–3.

44. Although the records at my disposal are extremely limited (see note 10 above), it seems as though the AAU (which also had a decentralized bureaucratic structure) followed a similar line. An example of this would be the New York Athletic Club Track meet in February of 1968 (discussed in chapter 5). Despite the long tradition and ties that bound the track club to the AAU, the AAU seems to have left NYAC officials pretty much on their own in dealing with the boycott directed against them.

45. Moore 1991b, p. 64.

46. *New York Times,* March 30, 1968.

47. NCAA Archive, NSYSP folder 1967–9, promotional press release dated March 4, 1969.

48. NSYSP guidelines required that the program include employment opportunities for residents in target areas, classify 90 percent of its participants as "disadvantaged," maintain contact with mayors' offices, and mandate medical examinations and daily food service. Some of the description here is drawn from a 1995 NYSP internal document titled "Historical Overview." This overview was compiled and composed by the current NYSP staff based upon their survey of the NYSP documents and materials contained in the Walter Byers

papers.

49. Byers papers, NYSP folders, press release dated March 4, 1969.

50. Byers papers, NYSP folders.

51. Many of these continue to be served today. The program, one of the NCAA's longest running and most celebrated, continues service today.

52. The NCAA was positioning itself in relation to other sporting agencies and organizations, establishing an institutional niche in American public policy (funding, for example, came from the Office of Economic Development, transferred through the Department of Health, Education, and Welfare), as well as the informal political networks and alliances that came with such institutional linkages. Thus, the program met with strong opposition from the Amateur Athletic Union and the National Recreation and Parks Association. These institutional transformations set the stage for the reforms of the 1978 Amateur Sports Act detailed by Chalip (1988).

53. Byers papers, NYSP folders. Byers also notes that this formulation came from Jim Wilkinson and was used in an *NCAA News* story to describe the project.

54. W. Byers to C.B. Wilkinson, April 17, 1970 (box 1). For more on President Nixon's engagement with sports, see Sarantakes 1997.

55. USOC Minutes, December 1, 1968, p. 27.

56. Ibid., pp. 62–65.

57. Much of Owens's defense of sport and counterattack is aimed directly at Harry Edwards and is surprisingly personal. The epigraph to the first chapter of Owens's book is this quote from Edwards: "Jesse Owens is a bootlicking Uncle Tom!" Owens also singles out the young sociologist no fewer than ten times in the first ninety pages of the text. One of the most remarkable of these passages reads as follows:

> Today a young Negro like Harry Edwards can climb out of the ghetto and go to a tuition-free university, become an articulate leader, and then use his articulation against those who taught him the words. Still, if it was nothing compared to what it took my father to get out of the South fifty years ago, Harry Edwards and those like him didn't just leap out of their poverty and ignorance in one easy vault. You didn't wish yourself out of the East St. Louis jails where the Harry Edwardses finally landed because they couldn't stand drinking drainage ditch water and eating from white garbage cans. . . . It took grit, the same kind of grit that was at work when Harry later threw the discus almost two hundred feet for his school's record. But when he shouts in one breath that every white man on earth is no good and in the next tacks up a picture of me on the wall with the words "Traitor of the Week," Harry Edwards is saying that the jails and alleys have claimed some important part of him. (pp. 14–15)

In conclusion, Owens addresses Edwards directly. "Harry Edwards, my name has never been Tom. But I am old enough to be your uncle. I know the trouble you've seen. How can I make you—and everyone—see that it's nothing, absolutely nothing next to the trouble you and your *blackthink* are about to make?" (p. 27).

58. Owens 1970, pp. 43–44.

59. Tygiel 1983; see also Sarantakes 1997, pp. 199–200.

60. This does not mean that Owens's romantic vision of race and sport in the United States carried the day among all Americans. Owens received hundreds of letters from African Americans all over the country damning his insensitivity to racism and the intolerable social conditions they faced in their own daily lives as well as taking him to task for not appreciating the courage and legitimacy of social demonstrations like that of Smith and Carlos in Mexico City. So powerful and compelling were these criticisms that Owens found it necessary to write a second book—titled, instructively, *I Have Changed* (1972)—acknowledging the legitimacy of social protest and admitting that opportunities for African Americans were still severely restricted. But even though Owens offered these concessions and toned down his rhetoric overall, the book nevertheless, as his biographer (Baker 1986, p. 215) puts it, "retained the mindset of another era, another ideology." Baker points out that the views Owens expressed in all of his addresses and interviews of the period remained essentially consistent with those of his earlier writings.

61. USOC Minutes, February 22, 1969, vol. 19, no. 11, pp. 72–81.

62. International Olympic Academy 1970, "Report of the Ninth Session of the International Olympic Academy," Olympia, Greece, 29 August—17 September, 1969, p. 7. This particular meeting had 132 participants (including 13 IOC members) from thirty different countries. It included ten talks/lectures, eleven seminars, and five language groups. It also featured the opening of a new library on the Olympic grounds.

63. IOA (1970), pp. 174–205.

64. Ibid., p. 181.

65. Ibid., especially pp. 190–191, 199.

66. Ibid., pp. 193–194; see also p. 188.

67. USOC Newsletter, vol. 5, no. 3, November 1969, p. 4; "Report of the Ninth Session of the International Olympic Academy."

68. *Sports Illustrated*, "An Assessment of 'Black Is Best.'" January 18, 1971.

69. For some of the most useful scholarly treatments, see Miller (1998); Wiggins (1989); Hoberman (1997); and Davis (1990).

70. *New York Herald Tribune*, March 15, 1972.

71. In addition to general media coverage and commentary, this account is drawn from Baker (1986) and Matthews (1974).

72. *New York Times*, September 8, 1972.

73. In the main text Edwards notes that their search for an agency "took one funny turn" that involved an unnamed Washington, DC–based organization misrepresenting itself as a civil rights organization, when its actual mission was "to quell civil rights agitation brought about by the active factions of the movement."

74. This curious continuation and expansion of reform in the absence of actual unrest and protest pressure can be partially explained as an institutional lag, with organizational policies and practices only belatedly addressing the concerns that originally required them. But I think such reforms also show how deeply the sporting establishment had been impacted by this decade of racial disruption and how far they were willing to go both to live up to

some of their lofty claims about sport being a truly equal, color-blind institution and to reestablish sport's historic reputation as a leader in American race relations.

75. Laurence Chalip has been one of the strongest scholarly critics of the President's Commission on Olympic Sports and its legislation. His criticisms rest largely on the grounds that it "subsum[ed] development under administration rationalization, [by] failing to specify mechanisms to assure provision of resources to grassroots sports development and [by] failing to give adequate attention to the sports interests of minorities, the poor and rural and inner-city residents" (1988, p. 213). Importantly, Chalip's original dissertation study shows that these shortcomings were not the result of a lack of information or awareness of these issues. In fact, Chalip documents, all these concerns—many of which came directly out of the interests and ideals of the athletic revolution discussed in the previous chapter—were raised repeatedly during the testimony, surveys, interviews, and focus-group follow-ups with athletes and others the commission undertook in preparation for its recommendations. I will have to leave it to others to document more fully the links between racial unrest and these other forms of activism and insurgency in shaping national sport policy.

Chapter 8

1. "Order" here is not a stable and inert state but rather a dynamic social system, predicated on movement, transformation, and change. As with Omi and Winant's concepts of rearticulation and equilibrium, this conception draws its inspiration most directly from Antonio Gramsci's (1971) classic conception of hegemony (see also Hall 1996; Lipsitz 1988). What Gramsci means by hegemony is famously complicated and a matter of more discussion and debate among social scientists than I can go into here. Several aspects of his usage, however, are crucial to my discussion. The first is his understanding of hegemony as the product of ongoing social struggle. This is an important point in general theoretical terms because it implies that order is not something established once and for all or simply imposed upon a society from the top down. Rather, social order must be understood as an ongoing process, an achievement that is and must be continually renewed and renegotiated by the various (and variously empowered) groups and interests that make up an identifiable society or social system. This multifaceted understanding of order produces a historical orientation that is both more sustaining and more attentive to historical contingencies than is often the case in sociological analysis. It also puts a premium on the continued influence of seemingly excluded, marginalized, or vanquished social movements and interests and the way that the dominant social parties deal with them.

And then there is the aspect of hegemony for which Gramsci is perhaps best known: the importance of ideology and cultural legitimation in this struggle for order. Any attempt to maintain hegemony on the part of the ruling party is, in Gramsci's view, as much ideological as it is institutional; that is, a matter of establishing the legitimacy and even necessity of its regime in the eyes of the subordinated or aggrieved populations and movements as it is of controlling concrete resources, policies, and institutions. This, in fact, is the point of his famous distinction between the war of maneuver and the war of position. The war of maneuver, according to Gramsci, has to do with control over resources, policies, and institutions, the usual mechanisms by which the ruling regime exercises its power and maintains "order"; the war of position, in contrast, involves the ongoing struggle to make resource distribution, institutions, and current social relationships—inherently inequitable as they might seem to be—legitimate and desirable in the eyes of those on the short end of the struggle. The ideological dimensions of Gramsci's understanding of hegemony are relevant to my present concerns in at least two respects: first, because I am arguing that athletic protest presented an institutional legitimation crisis for the American athletic establishment (given that it based so much of its moral posturing on the claim to being a leader in the fight for African American advancement); second, with respect to the symbolic role that sport itself played (and continues to play) in American culture as a model of and for race relations, social justice, and American citizenship and national identity. It is with this second emphasis on the popular cultural form of sport that the present work is intended to contribute to Omi and Winant's understanding of the complexity of racial rearticulation processes in contemporary American culture.

2. See also Berghorn, Yetman, and Hanna 1988; Yetman and Eitzen 1984; Paul, McGhee, and Fant 1984.

3. For more, see the studies collected in Brooks and Althouse 1993 and Sailes 1998.

4. In a mass media, large-scale society such as the United States, such lives and forms of work are rarely seen as activism or, for that matter, in any way "political"; they are seen, instead, as simply outside of politics. But as radical as the critiques produced by Harry Edwards and his community of sport scholars and critics may have been, these teaching and coaching positions certainly had potentially important impacts on the communities where they were working. In no other setting have African American athletic activists—whether working in the academy, the public sphere, or actual neighborhoods and communities— achieved the public attention and political teeth that allowed them to imagine themselves bringing about a revolution in 1968. I remember meeting in the late 1980s one educator-coach who, upon being handed a very early draft of the history of the Olympic protest movement that constituted some of the first chapters of this book, told me: "This is my story, what I have been trying to work on and carry out for all of these years" (interview with Larry Hawkins, May 1989; see also Hartmann 2003b).

5. John MacAloon's (1990) analysis of the Dubin inquiry into Ben Johnson's steroid use in Canada called my attention to the language and institutional apparatus of "accomplishment."

6. Reich 1986; Ueberroth 1985.

7. *Los Angeles Times*, January 21, 1982; March 4, 13, 16, 1984; July 20, 1984.

8. August 15, 1979. LAOOC "Policy Manual" (section 1, chapter 13), LAOOC papers, box 106, f4.

9. Sonenshein 1993; *Los Angeles Times*, July 16, 1984. It is almost impossible not to notice the irony of a progressive African American athlete opposing a boycott in the postprotest era. But what should be pointed out here is that this boycott was promoted by the U.S. government against the objections of both individual athletes and the International Olympic Committee.

10. The photo archives at the International Olympic Studies Center contain fascinating LAOOC Olympic signage and advertising that prominently features dark-skinned young athletes as the faces of the Games, festivals, and fundraising.

11. *Los Angeles Sentinel,* January 28, 1982; *Los Angeles Times,* February 12, 1984.

12. Telephone interview with Kenneth Reich, May 1994. Not long after the Games, when Ueberroth, in his new position Major League Baseball commissioner, was forced to deal with the fallout from Al Campanis's comments about black athletes, he famously appointed Edwards to oversee the "integration" of Major League Baseball's front offices and administrations. Edwards, in turn, spoke up for Ueberroth when he was being criticized for his handling of the Rebuilt Los Angeles (RLA) initiative that emerged in the aftermath of the 1992 L.A. riots (*Los Angeles Times,* June 14, 1992).

13. Levitt 1990; *Los Angeles Times,* June 18 and 25, 1984.

14. *Chicago Tribune TV Week,* July 8–14, 1984; *Los Angeles Times,* July 12, 1984.

15. Los Angeles Olympic Organizing Committee Records, 1978–1984, collection 1403, Department of Special Collections, University Research Library, University of California, Los Angeles.

16. *Los Angeles Times,* July 22, 1984.

17. Ibid., July 26, 1984.

18. The Olympic historian Otto Schantz offers an alternative reading that foreshadows the points I will come to shortly: "The fact that the flag bearer for the United States . . . was Rafer Johnson, an Afro-American, could be interpreted as an emancipative symbol but bearing in mind the racial discrimination around at the time, the symbol was something of an illusion" (1996, p. 138).

19. To be included in our sample, an article or commentary had to be listed in the *Reader's Guide to Periodical Literature* under one of the following headings: race, racism, race relations, race problems, racial discrimination, and American race relations. A search of these terms yielded some thirty-three articles, twenty-five of which were included in the final sample. (Several were eliminated because they did not focus specifically on race; for an article to be defined in this way, a majority of the piece—at least half of the paragraphs—had to deal specifically with race.) This left us with ten articles from the period 1973–1978, and fifteen from 1979–1985.

We coded these articles for twenty-one sports terms and metaphors, compiled from those used in previous studies (Palmatier and Ray 1989 and Considine 1982). These included: *run, defeat, tackle, fight, play, gain, challenge, fall behind, win, score, lose, defend, achieve, oppose, beat, goal, play together, teamwork, compete, throw, chase, make strides, sulk on the sidelines, outlast (your opponents), jab, hurl, new round, leapfrog, late start, run headlong into, outperform, one for all and all for one,* and *raise the arm.* The only term we did not find in any of the articles was *teamwork.*

20. See, for examples, Walk 1995; Oriard 1991; and Muir 1988.

21. "Text of Reagan Speech Accepting Nomination for New Term," *New York Times,* August 23, 1984.

22. According to John MacAloon (1987), Reagan likely used the torch relay rather than the athletic competitions themselves due to American conventions

regarding the separation of sport and politics.

23. Goldman and Fuller (1985) mention the 1984 Games only as a "tide of nationalism" Reagan was riding in his campaign (p. 247). Similarly, several of the contributors to Pomper (1985) recognize the importance of the Olympics as metaphor, but none as an actual mechanism impacting the outcome.

24. None of this would have been possible if the institutions of sport were still plagued by accusations of discrimination and mistreatment, racial and otherwise. Only because the sporting world itself had been reformed and effectively depoliticized could sporting metaphors be used in this capacity.

25. For a treatment that connects Jackson's Rainbow Coalition to the Gramscian theory underlying this study, see Radhakrishnan 1996.

26. *Los Angeles Times,* February 12, 1984; Ueberroth 1985, p. 352.

27. It is interesting, for example, to see that the official pre-Olympic book published by the USOC had not yet caught up, still treating Smith and Carlos as outsiders to the American Olympic movement (Eller 1984). The same might be said of the *Chicago Tribune,* which used a picture of Smith and Carlos's 1968 protest to illustrate a story on the Soviet boycott of the 1984 Games titled "Controversy No Stranger to the Games" (May 9, 1984).

28. Bunch and Robinson 1984, pp. 44–46.

29. In our 1989 conversation, Ashe repeated this phrase several times and, it seemed to me, took great consolation in it. Ashe himself is a perfect representative of this liberal humanist mode of thinking (see his 1993 memoir, written with Princeton professor Arnold Rampersad not long before Ashe died from AIDS complications).

30. Telephone conversation with Kenny Moore, fall 1993.

31. Interestingly, the magazine found itself trying to reconcile the empirical realities of these claims with its long-established tradition of touting the positive racial force of sport. Series editors Sandy Padwe and Roy S. Johnson were "struck by how many of the questions asked in the [1968] series still needed to be addressed today." On balance, according to Johnson (who himself is African American), "black athletes still feel they're on the outside looking in." "They're gladiators," he put it, "highly paid gladiators, I'll allow, but they are still denied access to power." When asked whether he believed things had gotten better, Padwe (who is white) was noncommittal, saying only that he finds race "one of the most perplexing questions about American sport." The text of the article framing the series concluded by saying: "Glacial as it may be, there has been progress over the decades. The young black men rising now to big league sports have it far, far better than they may know because of other athletes who have gone before" (*Sports Illustrated,* August 5, 1991, p. 4). The magazine's confused, ambivalent response to the questions of the racial form and function of sport stands as an excellent example of the basic theoretical questions that inspired this project. But perhaps the important point to make here is that these reflections were timed to coincide with, and probably only made possible by, the "breaking" of the Tommie Smith story based upon first public comments on the demonstration since the fall of 1968.

32. Telephone interview, October 14, 1993.

33. Carlos had played an even more active role in reconstituting images of himself and his protest back in 1984, when he told the *Los Angeles Times* that although he is always remembered as "John Carlos, the protestor, the radical,"

he preferred to think of himself as "a humanist who was merely protesting the state of the human condition in the best way he knew how." While one cannot discount the fact that he was working for the LAOOC at the time, his language is nonetheless powerful and revealing: "They say I was a Black Panther, a terrorist, a this or a that. I was nothing but a young American who believes [*sic*] in the ideals of America, freedom and justice for all, the land of the free." Near the end of the story, looking back at what he did in 1968, Carlos remarked: "I'd still do something today . . . but I wouldn't do what I did in 1968. . . . I think I have a better idea of how to get things done" (February 12, 1984).

34. *New York Times*, October 23, 1993. Having run the two-part special story on Smith and Carlos only two years earlier, *Sports Illustrated* was not really in a position to do a full report; nevertheless, it commemorated the occasion with an item in its "Scorecard" column on the "forgotten third man" in the picture, the Australian Peter Norman. According to the report, Smith and Norman had remained in touch over the years (despite the physical limitations restricting Norman's travel outside Australia), and Norman had even stayed with Smith in California when an Australian television station flew him to Los Angeles for a commemorative on the 1968 Games. Norman was described as being "proud of his small role in history but despairing of its lasting impact." "There is still a lot of hatred of people who are different because of their color or religion," he said. "What we did appears to have been to little avail." Norman's role in the events of 1968 was recalled once again in the media in connection with the 2000 Games in Sydney—see, for example, *New York Times*, September 16, 2000.

35. The same can be said of the HBO and TNT historical documentaries mentioned earlier. While admirable for their attempt to situate the demonstration in an appropriate historical context (especially the HBO piece), both of these treatments nevertheless conclude with rehabilitative strokes that render the demonstration a mainstream, civil rights statement stripped of radical intent and import.

36. *New York Times*, October 23, 1993.

Epilogue

1. See, for example, *New York Times*, July 21, 1996: "Choosing Ali Elevated These Games."

2. Ali served many other symbolic roles as well, which is partly why he was such an ideal candidate. For his own part, as I understand it, Ali (who is perfectly cognizant despite his deteriorating physical condition) decided to light the torch because of what he thought it would symbolize about and for the Muslims of the world.

3. See chapter 3, note 22.

4. The Africans, for their part, had no real appreciation of the problematic side of the cultural politics of race and sport focused as they were on access and representation, which African Americans had achieved decades earlier.

References

Abbot, Andrew. 2001. *Time Matters: On Theory and Method*. Chicago: University of Chicago Press.

Abdul-Jabaar, Kareem, with Peter Knobler. 1983. *Giant Steps*. New York: Bantam Books.

Amdur, Neil. 1971. *The Fifth Down: Democracy and the Football Revolution*. New York: Coward, McCann and Geoghegan.

Ali, Muhammad, with Richard Durham. 1975. *The Greatest: My Own Story*. New York: Random House.

Andrews, Kenneth T. 1997. "The Impacts of Social Movements on the Political Process: A Study of the Civil Rights Movement and Black Electoral Politics in Mississippi." *American Sociological Review* 62: 800–819.

———. 2001. "Social Movements and Policy Implementation: The Mississippi Civil Rights Movement and the War on Poverty, 1965–1971." *American Sociological Review* 66 (February): 71–95.

Andrews, Vernon. 1996. "Black Bodies—White Control: The Contested Terrain of Sportsmanlike Conduct." *Journal of African American Men* 2 (1): 33–59.

Appadurai, Arjun, and Carol B. Breckenridge. 1988. "Why Public Culture?" *Public Culture Bulletin* 1 (1): 5–9.

Archer, Robert, and Antoine Baullion. 1982. *The South African Game: Sport and Racism*. London: Zed Press.

Ashe, Arthur R., Jr., with the assistance of Kip Branch, Ocania Chalk, and Francis Harris. 1988. *A Hard Road to Glory: A History of the African American Athlete Since 1946*. New York: Warner Books.

Ashe, Arthur, with Arnold Rampersad. 1993. *Days of Grace: A Memoir*. New York: Knopf.

Ashton, Steve. 1972. "The Athlete's Changing Perspective: A Student View." *Journal of Health, Physical Education and Recreation* 43 (4): 46.

Axthelm, Pete. 1968. "The Angry Black Athlete." *Newsweek*, July 15, 56–60.

———. 1987. "Deceiving Stories: International Politics and Olympic Crises." *Gannet Center Journal* 1 (2): 99–110.

Baker, William J. 1982. *Sports in the Western World*. Urbana: University of Illinois Press.

———. 1986. *Jesse Owens: An American Life*. New York: Free Press.

Bass, Amy. 2002. *Not the Triumph But the Struggle: The 1968 Olympics and the Making of the Black Athlete*. Minneapolis: University of Minnesota Press.

Behee, John. 1975. "Race Militancy and Affirmative Action in the Big Ten Conference." *Physical Educator* 32–33 (March): 3–8.

Bellah, Robert N., Richard Madsen, William M. Sullivan, Ann Swidler, and Steven M. Tipton. 1985. *Habits of the Heart: Individualism and Commitment in American Life*. Berkeley and Los Angeles: University of California Press.

Berendt, John. 1994. *Midnight in the Garden of Good and Evil*. New York: Random House.

Berghorn, Forrest J., and Norman R. Yetman, with William E. Hanna. 1988. "Racial Participation and Integration in Men's and Women's Intercollegiate Basketball: Continuity and Change, 1958–1985." *Sociology of Sport Journal* 5: 107–124.

Birrell, Susan. 1989. "Race Relations Theories and Sport: Suggestions for a More Critical Analysis." *Sociology of Sport Journal* 6: 221–227.

Birrell, Susan, and Cheryl L. Cole, eds. 1994. *Women, Sport, and Culture*. Champaign, IL: Human Kinetics.

Bloom, J. D. 1988. "Joe Namath and Super Bowl III: An Interpretation of Style." *Journal of Sport History* 15 (1): 64–74.

Booth, Douglas. 1998. *The Race Game: Sport and Politics in South Africa*. London and Portland: Frank Cass.

Bourdieu, Pierre. 1977. *Outline of a Theory of Practice*. Cambridge: Cambridge University Press.

———. 1988 [1982]. "Program for a Sociology of Sport." *Sociology of Sport Journal* 5: 153–161.

———. 1991 [1978]. "Sport and Social Class." Pp. 357–73 in *Rethinking Popular Culture*, edited by Chandra Mukerji and Michael Schudson. Berkeley and Los Angeles: University of California Press.

Bourdieu, Pierre, and Loïc J. D. Wacquant. 1992. *An Invitation to Reflexive Sociology*. Chicago: University of Chicago Press.

Bouton, Jim. 1970. *Ball Four*. New York: World Publishing.

Boyd, Todd. 1997. " . . . The Day the Niggaz Took Over: Basketball, Commodity Culture, and Black Masculinity." Pp. 123–142 in *Out of Bounds: Sports, Media, and the Politics of Identity*, edited by Aaron Baker and Todd Boyd. Bloomington: Indiana University Press.

Branch, Taylor. 1988. *Parting the Waters: America in the King Years, 1954–1963*. Ann Arbor: University of Michigan Press.

Briley, Ron. 1989. "It Was 20 Years Ago Today: Baseball Responds to the Unrest of 1968." Pp. 81–94 in *Baseball History: An Annual of Original Baseball Research*, edited by Peter Levine. Westport, CT: Mecklen.

Brooks, Dana, and Ronald Althouse, eds. 1993. *Racism in College Athletics: The African-American Athlete's Experience*. Morgantown, WV: Fitness Information Technology.

Brooks, Dana, Ronald Althouse, and Delano Tucker. 1997. "African American Male Head Coaches: In the 'Red Zone,' But Can They Score?" *Journal of African American Men* 2: 93–112.

Brownell, Susan. 1995. *Training the Body for China: Sports in the Moral Order of the People's Republic*. Chicago: University of Chicago Press.

Bryson, Lois. 1987. "Sport and the Maintenance of Masculine Hegemony." *Women's Studies International Forum* 10 (4): 349–360.

Bunch, Lonnie G., III, and Louie Robinson. 1984. "The Black Olympians, 1904–1984." Exhibit guide. Los Angeles: California Afro-American Museum.

Burawoy, Michael. 1991. "The Extended Case Method." Pp. 271–290 in *Ethnography Unbound: Power and Resistance in the Modern Metropolis*. Berkeley and Los Angeles: University of California Press.

————. 1998. "The Extended Case Method." *Sociological Theory* 16(1): 63–92.

Cahn, Susan K. 1994. *Coming on Strong: Gender and Sexuality in Twentieth-Century Women's Sport*. New York: Free Press.

Carby, Hazel. 1998. *Race Men*. Cambridge: Harvard University Press.

Carlson, Lewis H., and John J. Fogarty. 1987. *Tales of Gold*. Chicago: Contemporary Books.

Carmichael, Stokely, and Charles V. Hamilton. 1967. *Black Power: The Politics of Liberation in America*. New York: Vintage.

Carrington, Ben. 1998. "Sport, Masculinity and Black Cultural Resistance." *Journal of Sport and Social Issues* 22 (3): 275–298.

Carson, Clayborne. 1981. *In Struggle: SNCC and the Black Awakening of the 1960s*. Cambridge: Harvard University Press.

Cashmore, Ernest. 1982. *Black Sportsmen*. London: Routledge and Keegan Paul.

Caute, David. 1988. *The Year of the Barricades: A Journey through 1968*. New York: Harper and Row.

Chafe, William. 1986. "The End of One Struggle, the Beginning of Another." In *The Civil Rights Movement in America*, edited by Charles W. Eagles. Jackson: University Press of Mississippi.

————. 1988. *Civilities and Civil Rights: Greensboro, North Carolina and the Black Struggle for Freedom*. New York: Oxford University Press.

Chalip, Laurence H. 1988. "The Framing of Policy: Explaining the Transformation of American Sport." Ph.D. dissertation, Committee of Public Policy Studies, University of Chicago, Chicago, IL.

————. 1991. "Sport and the State: The Case of the United States of America." Pp. 243–250 in *Sport . . . The Third Millennium: Proceedings of the International Symposium*, edited by Fernand Landry, Marc Landry, and Magdeleine Yerles. Sainte-Foy: Les Presses de l'Universite Laval.

Chalip, Laurence, and Arthur Johnson. 1996. "Sports Policy in the United States." In *National Sports Policies: An International Handbook*, edited by Chalip, Johnson, and Lisa Stachura. Westport, CT: Greenwood Press.

Cleaver, Eldidge. 1968. *Soul on Ice*. New York: Delta.

Clumpner, Roy A. 1978. "American Foreign Policy and Sport: The Impact of the 1965 State Department Study." Pp. 331–339 in *Sociology of Sport* (9). Miami, FL: Symposia Specialists FNC.

Coakley, Jay. 1986. *Sport in Society: Issues and Controversies*. St. Louis: Times Mirror/Mosby College Publishers.

Cole, Cheryl L. 1994. "Resisting the Canon: Feminist Cultural Studies, Sport, and Technologies of the Body." Pp. 5–30 in *Women, Sport, and Culture*, edited by Susan Birrell and Cheryl L. Cole. Champaign, IL: Human Kinetics.

————. 1996. "American Jordan: P.L.A.Y., Consensus and Punishment." *Sociology of Sport Journal* 13: 366–397.

Cole, Cheryl L., and David L. Andrews. 1996. "Look—It's NBA Showtime! Visions of Race in the Popular Imagery." *Cultural Studies Annual* 1: 141–181.

Cole, Cheryl L., and Harry Denny III. 1994. "Visualizing Deviance in Post-Reagan America: Magic Johnson, AIDS and the Promiscuous World of Professional Sport." *Critical Sociology* 20 (3): 123–147.

Cole, Cheryl L., and Samantha King. 1998. "Representing Black Masculinity and Urban Possibilities: Racism, Realism and *Hoop Dreams.*" Pp. 49–86 in *Sport and Postmodern Times*, edited by Genevieve Rail. Albany: SUNY Press.

Cole, Cheryl L., and Melissa A. Orlie. 1995. "Hybrid Athletes, Monstrous Addicts, and Cyborg Natures." *Journal of Sport History* 22 (3): 228–239.

Collier, Peter, and David Horowitz. 1989. *Destructive Generation: Second Thought About the Sixties.* New York: Summit Books.

Combahee River Collective. 1997 [1977]. "A Black Feminist Statement." Pp. 63–70 in *The Second Wave: A Reader in Feminist Theory,* edited by Linda Nicholson. New York: Routledge.

Connell, Robert W. 1990. "An Iron Man: The Body and Some Contradictions of Hegemonic Masculinity." Pp. 83–95 in *Sport, Men and the Gender Order,* edited by Michael Messner and Donald Sabo. Champaign, IL: Human Kinetics.

————. 1995. *Masculinities.* Berkeley and Los Angeles: University of California Press.

Considine, Bob, and Fred Jarvis. 1969. *The First Hundred Years: A Portrait of the NYAC.* Toronto: Macmillan.

Considine, Tim, with introduction by Jim McKay. 1982. *The Language of Sport.* New York: Facts on File.

Coote, James. 1968. *Olympic Report 1968: Mexico and Grenoble.* London: Robert Hale.

Cosell, Howard. 1973. *Cosell.* Chicago: Playboy Press.

Cruse, Harold. 1967. *The Crisis of the Negro Intellectual: A Historical Analysis of the Failure of Black Leadership.* New York: Quill.

Davis, Angela. 1997. "Reflections on Race, Class and Gender in the U.S: Interview with Lisa Lowe." Pp. 303–323 in *The Politics of Culture in the Shadow of Capital,* edited by Lisa Lowe and David Lloyd. Durham, NC: Duke University Press.

Davis, Laurel R. 1990. "The Articulation of Difference: White Preoccupation with the Question of Racially Linked Genetic Differences Among Blacks." *Sociology of Sport Journal* 7 (June): 179–187.

de Varona, Donna. 1982. "Partnership Between the Athletes and Organization of the Olympic Movement." International Olympic Academy, Twenty-second Session (July 11–25). Lausanne: International Olympic Committee.

Doane, Ashley W., Jr. 1997. "Dominant Group Ethnic Identity in the United States: The Role of 'Hidden' Ethnicity in Intergroup Relations." *Sociological Quarterly* 38 (3): 375–397.

Douglas, Mary. 1966. *Purity and Danger: An Analysis of the Concepts of Pollution and Taboo.* New York: Praeger.

Doyle, Andrew. 1994. " 'Causes Won, Not Lost': College Football and the Modernization of the American South." *The International Journal of the History of Sport* 11 (2): 231–251.

Dreyfus, Hubert. 1980. "Holism and Hermeneutics." *Review of Metaphysics* 34 (1): 3–23.

Dudziak, Mary L. 1988. "Desegregation as a Cold War Imperative." *Stanford Law Review* 41: 61–120.

Dunning, Eric. 1986. "Sport as a Male Preserve: Notes on the Social Sources of Masculine Identity and Its Transformations." *Theory, Culture and Society* 3 (1): 79–90.

Durant, John. 1973. *Highlights of the Olympics from Ancient Times to the Present.* New York: Hastings House.

Durkheim, Emile. 1965 [1915]. *The Elementary Forms of Religious Life.* New York: The Free Press.

Dyreson, Mark. 1998. *Making the Olympic Team: Sport, Culture and the Olympic Experience.* Champaign: University of Illinois Press.

Dyson, Michael Eric. 1995. *Making Malcolm: The Myth and Meaning of Malcolm X.* New York: Oxford University Press.

Early, Gerald. 1989. *Tuxedo Junction: Essays on American Culture.* Hopewell, NJ: Ecco Press.

————. 1998. "Performance and Reality: Race, Sports and the Modern World." *The Nation,* August 10–17: 11–20.

————, ed. 1998. *The Muhammad Ali Reader.* Hopewell, NJ: Ecco Press.

Edwards, Harry. 1969. *The Revolt of the Black Athlete.* New York: Free Press.

————. 1970. *Black Students.* New York: Free Press.

————. 1971. "The Sources of Black Athletic Superiority." *The Black Scholar* 3 (November): 32–41.

————. 1972. "The Myth of the Racially Superior Athlete." *Intellectual Digest* 2 (March): 58–60.

————. 1973a. "20th Century Gladiators for White America." *Psychology Today* 7 (November): 43–52.

————. 1973b. *Sociology of Sport.* Homewood, IL: Dorsey Press.

————. 1979. "The Olympic Project for Human Rights: An Assessment Ten Years Later." *The Black Scholar* 10: 2–8.

————. 1980. *The Struggle That Must Be: An Autobiography.* New York: Macmillan.

————. 1984. "The Black 'Dumb Jock': An American Sports Tragedy." *The College Board Review* 131: 8–13.

Eitzen, D. Stanley, and George Sage. 1978. *Sociology of American Sport.* Dubuque, IA: WC Brown Company.

Eitzen, D. Stanley, and D. C. Sanford. 1975. "The Segregation of Blacks by Playing Position in Football: Accident or Design?" *Social Science Quarterly* 55: 948–959.

Eller, Buddy. 1984. *USA and the Olympics 1984.* Atlanta, GA: Philmay Enterprises/USOC.

Elzey, Chris. 2001. "The Shot Heard Round the World: The 1972 US-USSR Gold Medal Basketball Game." Unpublished MS. University of Purdue, Department of History.

Espy, Richard. 1979. *The Politics of the Olympic Games.* Berkeley and Los Angeles: University of California Press.

Essed, Philomena, and David Theo Goldberg, eds. 2002. *Race Critical Theories: Text and Context.* Malden, MA: Blackwell.

Evans, J. S. 1979. "Differences in the Recruitment of Black and White Football Players at a Big Eight University." *Journal of Sport and Social Issues* 3: 1–9.

Evans, Sara. 1979. *Personal Politics: The Roots of Women's Liberation in the Civil Rights Movement and the New Left*. New York: Vintage.

Fairclough, Adam. 1987. *To Redeem the Soul of America: The Southern Christian Leadership Conference and Martin Luther King, Jr*. Athens: University of Georgia Press.

Fanon, Franz. 1986. *Black Skin, White Masks*. London: Pluto.

Farber, Daniel, ed. 1994. *The Sixties: From Memory to History*. Chapel Hill: University of North Carolina Press.

Flath, Arnold W. 1964. *A History of Relations between the National Collegiate Athletic Association and the Amateur Athletic Union of the United States (1905–1963)*. Champaign, IL: Stipes.

Flood, Curt, with Richard Carter. 1971. *The Way It Is*. New York: Trident Press.

Foster, J., and D. Long. 1970. *Protest! Student Activism in America*. New York: William Morrow.

Frankenberg, Ruth. 1993. *White Women, Race Matters: The Social Construction of Whiteness*. Minneapolis: University of Minnesota Press.

Frey, James H., and D. Stanley Eitzen. 1991. "Sport and Society." *Annual Review of Sociology* 17: 503–522.

Gafner, Raymond, and Norbert Muller, eds. 1995. *The International Olympic Committee—One Hundred Years: The Ideas, the Presidents, the Achievements*. 3 vols. Lausanne: International Olympic Committee.

Gamson, William. 1990. *The Strategy of Protest*. 2nd ed. Belmont, CA: Wadsworth.

Garrow, David J. 1986. *Bearing the Cross: Martin Luther King, Jr. and the Southern Christian Leadership Conference*. New York: W. Morrow.

Geertz, Clifford. 1973. "Deep Play: Notes on the Balinese Cockfight." Pp. 412–454 in *The Interpretation of Cultures*. New York: Basic Books.

George, Nelson. 1992. *Elevating the Game: Black Men and Basketball*. New York: HarperCollins.

Gerstle, Gary. 2001. *American Crucible: Race and Nation in the Twentieth Century*. Princeton, NJ: Princeton University Press.

Giddens, Anthony. 1979. *Central Problems in Social Theory: Action, Structure, and Contradiction in Social Analysis*. Berkeley and Los Angeles: University of California Press.

Gilligan, Carol. 1982. *In a Different Voice*. Cambridge: Harvard University Press.

Gitlin, Todd. 1980. *The Whole World Is Watching: Mass Media in the Making and Unmaking of the New Left*. Berkeley and Los Angeles: University of California Press.

———. 1987. *The Sixties: Years of Hope, Days of Rage*. New York: Bantam.

Giugni, Marco. 1998. "Was It Worth the Effort? The Outcomes and Consequences of Social Movements." *Annual Review of Sociology* 24: 371–393.

Glass, Bill, and William M. Pinson Jr. 1972. *Don't Blame the Game: A Look at What's Right with Sports*. Waco, TX: Word Books.

Goldberg, David Theo. 1993. *Racist Culture: Philosophy and the Politics of Meaning*. Cambridge, MA: Blackwell.

Goldman, Peter, and Tony Fuller. 1985. *The Quest for the Presidency 1984*. New York: Bantam Books.

Goodwyn, Lawrence. 1978. *The Populist Moment: A Short History of the Agrarian Revolt in America*. New York: Oxford University Press.

Gorn, Elliot J., ed. 1995. *Muhammad Ali: The People's Champ*. Urbana: University of Illinois Press.

Gramsci, Antonio. 1971. *Selections from the Prison Notebooks*. Edited by Quintin Hoare and Geoffrey Nowell Smith. New York: International Publishers.

Gray, Herman. 1995. *Watching Race: Television and the Struggle for "Blackness."* Minneapolis: University of Minnesota Press.

Gregory, Dick, with Robert *Lipsyte*. 1964. *Nigger*. New York: Washington Square Press.

Griswold, Wendy. 1994. *Cultures and Societies in a Changing World*. Thousand Oaks, CA: Pine Forge Press.

Grundman, Adolph H. 1979. "Image of Collegiate Protest and the Civil Rights Movement: A Historian's View." *Arena Review* (October): 17–24.

Gruppe, Ommo. 1991. "The Sport Culture and the Sportization of Culture: Identity, Legitimacy, Sense and Nonsense of Modern Sport as Cultural Phenomenon." Pp. 135–145 in *Sport . . . The Third Millennium: Proceedings of the International Symposium,* edited by Fernand Landry, Marc Landry, and Magdeline Yerles. Sainte-Foy: Les Presses de l'Universite Laval.

Gusfield, Joseph. 1987. "Sports as Story: Form and Content in Agonistic Games." Conference proceedings, The First International Conference on the Olympics and East/West and South/North Cultural Exchange in the World System, Seoul, Korea.

———. 1989. Introduction to *On Symbols and Society,* selections by Kenneth Burke. Chicago: University of Chicago Press.

Gusfield, Joseph, and Jerry Michalowicz. 1984. "Secular Symbolism: Studies of Ritual, Ceremony, and the Symbolic Order of Modern Life." *Annual Review of Sociology* 19: 417–435.

Guttmann, Allen. 1978. *From Ritual to Record: The Nature of Modern Sports.* New York: Columbia University Press.

———. 1984. *The Games Must Go On: Avery Brundage and the Olympic Movement.* New York: Columbia University Press.

———. 1991. *Women's Sport: A History.* New York: Columbia University Press.

———. 1992. *The Olympics: A History of the Modern Games*. Urbana: University of Illinois Press.

Haines, Herbert H. 1988. *Black Radicals and the Civil Rights Mainstream, 1954–1970*. Knoxville: University of Tennessee Press.

Halberstam, David. 1994. *October 1964*. New York: Villard Books.

Hall, Stuart. 1981. "Notes on Deconstructing 'the Popular.' " Pp. 227–40 in *People's History and Socialist Theory,* edited by R. Samuel. London: Routledge and Keegan Paul.

———. 1996. "Gramsci's Relevance for the Study of Race and Ethnicity." Pp. 411–440 in *Stuart Hall: Critical Dialogues in Cultural Studies,* edited by David Marley and Kuan-Hsing Chen. London: Routledge.

Hall, Stuart, Chas Critcher, Tony Jefferson, John Clarke, and Brian Roberts. 1978. *Policing the Crisis: Mugging, the State and Law and Order.* New York: Holmes and Meier.

Hamm, Theodore. 2000. "Bill Versus Wilt: A Tale of Two Centers, 1955–1965." Paper presented at the American Studies Association annual meeting, Detroit, MI (October).

Hano, Arnold. 1968. "The Black Rebel Who 'Whitelists' the Olympics." *New York Times Magazine*, May 12, 32–50.

Harris, Othello. 1995. "Muhammad Ali and the Revolt of the Black Athlete." Pp. 54–69 in *Muhammad Ali: The People's Champ*, edited by Elliot J. Gorn. Urbana: University of Illinois Press.

———. 2000. "The Rise of Black Athletes in the U.S.A." Pp. 150–176 in *The International Politics of Olympic Sport in the 20th Century*, edited by Jim Roirdan and Arnd Kruger. London: E & FM Spon (Routledge).

Harrison, C. Keith. 1998. "The Assassination of the Black Male Image in Sport." *Journal of African American Men* 3 (3): 45–56.

———. 2000. "Racing with Race at the Olympics: From Negro to Black to African American Athlete." Pp. 63–71 in *The Olympics at the Millennium: Power, Politics and the Games*, edited by Kay Schaffer and Sidonie Smith.

Hartmann, Douglas. 1996. "The Politics of Race and Sport: Resistance and Domination in the 1968 African American Olympic Protest Movement." *Ethnic and Racial Studies* 19 (3): 548–566.

———. 2000. "Rethinking the Relationships between Race and Sport in American Culture: Golden Ghettos and Contested Terrain." *Sociology of Sport Journal* 17: 229–253.

———. 2003a. "What Can We Learn from Sport If We Take Sport Seriously as a Racial Force? Lessons from C. L. R. James's *Beyond a Boundary*." *Ethnic and Racial Studies* 26 (3): 451–483.

———. 2003b. "Theorizing Sport as Social Intervention: A View from the Grassroots." *Quest* 55: 118–140.

Hartmann, Douglas, and Jeremy Staff. 2002. "Sport's Contribution to the 'War on Poverty': The Story Behind the NCAA's National Youth Sports Program." Unpublished MS. Department of Sociology, University of Minnesota.

Harvey, David. 1990. *The Condition of Postmodernity*. Cambridge, MA: Blackwell.

Hawkins, Billy. 1995. "The Black Student Athlete: The Colonized Black Body." *Journal of African American Men* 1 (3): 23–25.

Hays, Sharon. 1994. "Structure and Agency and the Sticky Problem of Culture." *Sociological Theory* 12 (1): 57–72.

Hebdige, Dick. 1979. *Subculture: The Meaning of Style*. New York: Methuen.

Hoberman, John. 1984. *Sport and Political Ideology*. Austin: University of Texas Press.

———. 1986. *The Olympic Crisis: Sport, Politics, and the Moral Order*. New Rochelle, NY: Aristide D. Caratzas.

———. 1997. *Darwin's Athletes: How Sport Has Damaged Black America and Preserved the Myth of Race*. Boston: Houghton Mifflin.

Hoch, Paul. 1972. *Rip Off the Big Game: The Exploitation of Sports by the Power Elite*. New York: Doubleday Anchor.

Huey, Lynda. 1976. *A Running Start: An Athlete, A Woman*. New York: Quadrangle.

Hult, Joan. 1980. "The Philosophical Differences in Men's and Women's Collegiate Athletics." *Quest* 32: 77–94.

Hutchinson, Earl. 1996. *Beyond O.J.: Race, Sex and Class Lesson for America.* New York: Black Rose Books.

Ingham, Alan G. 1976. "Sport and the New Left: Some Reflections Upon Opposition Without Praxis." Pp. 238–248 in *Social Problems in Athletics: Essays on the Sociology of Sport,* edited by D. M. Landers. Urbana: University of Illinois Press.

International Olympic Academy. 1970. *Report of the Ninth Session of the International Olympic Academy at Olympia.* Athens, Greece: Hellenic Olympic Committee.

James, C. L. R. 1993 [1963]. *Beyond a Boundary.* Durham: Duke University Press.

Jeffords, Susan. 1989. *The Remasculinization of America: Gender and the Vietnam War.* Bloomington: Indiana University Press.

———. 1994. *Hard Bodies: Hollywood Masculinity in the Reagan Era.* New Brunswick, NJ: Rutgers University Press.

Jewell, Sue K. 1993. *From Mammy to Miss America and Beyond: Cultural Images and the Shaping of US Social Policy.* New York: Routledge.

Johnson, Leola, and David Roediger. 2000. "Hertz, Don't It? Becoming Colorless and Staying Black in the Crossover of O. J. Simpson." Pp. 40–73 in *Reading Sport,* edited by Susan Birrell and Mary G. McDonald. Boston: Northeastern University Press.

Johnson, Lyndon. 1966. *"To Fulfill These Rights."* Commencement address, Howard University, June 4, 1965. Pp. 635–640 in Public Papers of the President's Office of the United States, Lyndon Johnson, 1965. Washington, DC: U.S. Government Printing Office.

Johnson, William O., Jr. 1972. *All That Glitters Is Not Gold: The Olympic Game.* New York: Putnam.

Johnston, Phil. N.d. "The OPHR Protest in the Black Press." Unpublished MS, in author's possession.

Jones, Wally, and Jim Washington. 1972. *Black Champions Challenge American Sports.* New York: David McKay Company.

Jordan, Tom. 1997. *Pre: The Story of America's Greatest Running Legend, Steve Prefontaine.* 2nd ed. Emmaus, PA: Rodale Press.

Kane, Mary Jo, and Lisa Disch. 1993. "Sexual Violence and the Reproduction of Male Power in the Locker Room: The 'Lisa Olsen Incident.'" *Sociology of Sport Journal* 10:331–352.

Kanin, David B. 1981. *My Olympic Years.* London: Seeker and Warburg.

Katsiaficas, George 1987. *The Imagination of the New Left: A Global Analysis of 1968.* Boston: South End Press.

Keech, Marc. 2000. "At the Centre of the Web: The Role of Sam Ramsamy in South Africa's Readmission to International Sport." *Culture, Sport, Society* 3 (3): 41–62.

Kelley, Robin D. G. 1992. "The Riddle of the Zoot: Malcolm Little and Black Cultural Politics During World War II." In *Malcolm X: In Our Own Image,* edited by Joe Wood. New York: St. Martin's.

———. 1996. *Race Rebels: Culture, Politics and the Black Working Class.* New York: Free Press.

Kellner, Douglas. 1996. "Sports, Media, Culture, and Race—Some Reflections on Michael Jordan." *Sociology of Sport Journal* 13:458–467.

Kidd, Bruce. 1987. "The Philosophy of Excellence: Olympic Performances, Class Power and the Canadian State." Pp. 343–371 in *The Olympics and Cultural Exchange*, edited by Kang, MacAloon, and DaMatta. Seoul: Hanyang University Institute for Ethnological Studies.

———. 1990. "From Quarantine to Cure: The New Phase of Struggle Against Apartheid in Sport." Pp. 35–55 in *Challenges Facing South African Sport*, edited by C. Roberts. Cape Town: Township Publishing Corporation.

———. 1995. *The Struggle for Canadian Sport*. Toronto: University of Toronto Press.

Killanin, Michael Morris "Baron." 1983. *My Olympic Years*. New York: W. Morrow.

King, Martin Luther, Jr. 1986. *I Have a Dream: Writings and Speeches That Changed the World*. New York: HarperCollins.

Kirshenbaum, Jerry. 1974. "Generating Eclectic Power." *Sports Illustrated*, February 18, 32.

Koning, H. 1987. *Nineteen Sixty Eight: A Personal Report*. New York: W. W. Norton.

Kozol, Wendy. 1994. *Life's America: Family and Nation in Postwar Photojournalism*. Philadelphia: Temple University Press.

Lapchick, Richard E. 1975. *The Politics of Race and International Sport: The Case of South Africa*. Westport, CT: Greenwood Press.

———. 1984. *Broken Promises: Racism in American Sports*. New York: St. Martin's.

———. 1986. *Fractured Focus: Sport as a Reflection of Society*. New York: Lexington Books.

Lapchick, Richard E., with Kevin J. Matthews. 1997. *The 1997 Racial Report Card*. Northeastern University's Center for the Study of Sport in Society.

Layton, Azza Salama. 1995. "The International Context of the U.S. Civil Rights Movement: The Dynamics Between Racial Politics and International Politics, 1941–1960." Ph.D. dissertation, Department of Government, The University of Texas at Austin.

Leonard, D. 1998. "What Happened to the Revolt of the Black Athlete? A Look Back Thirty Years Later: An Interview with Harry Edwards." *Color Lines* 1: 1.

Levine, Lawrence W. 1977. *Black Culture and Black Consciousness: Afro-American Folk Thought from Slavery to Freedom*. Oxford: Oxford University Press.

Levitt, Susanna Halpert. 1990. "The 1984 Olympic Arts Festival." Ph.D. diss., Theatre Department, University of California, Davis.

Linden, Glenn M., Dean C. Brink; and Richard H Huntington. 1986. *Legacy of Freedom: U.S. History Since Reconstruction*, vol. 2. River Forest, IL: Laidlaw Brothers.

Lipsitz, George. 1988. "The Struggle for Hegemony." *Journal of American History* 75 (1): 146–150.

———. 1994. "Who'll Stop the Rain? Youth Culture, Rock 'n' Roll, and Social Crises." Pp. 206–234 in *The Sixties*, edited by David Farber. Chapel Hill: University of North Carolina Press.

————. 1990. *Time Passages: Collective Memory and American Popular Culture.* Minneapolis: University of Minnesota Press.

————. 1998. *The Possessive Investment in Whiteness: How White People Profit from Identity Politics.* Philadelphia: Temple University Press.

Lipsky, Richard. 1978. "Toward a Political Theory of American Sports Symbolism." *American Behavioral Scientist* 21: 345–360.

Lipsyte, Robert. 1975. *SportsWorld: An American Dreamland.* New York: Quadrangle.

Lowe, Lisa, and David Lloyd, eds. 1997. *The Politics of Culture in the Shadow of Capital.* Durham, NC: Duke University Press.

Loy, J. W., and J. F. McElvogue. 1970. "Racial Segregation in American Sport." *International Review of Sport Sociology* 5: 5–24.

MacAloon, John J. 1981. *The Great Symbol: Pierre de Coubertin and the Origins of the Modern Olympic Games.* Chicago: University of Chicago Press.

————. 1984. "Olympic Games and the Theory of Spectacle in Modern Societies." Pp. 241–280 in *Rite, Drama, Festival, Spectacle: Rehearsals Toward a Theory of Cultural Performance,* edited by MacAloon. Philadelphia: Institute for the Study of Human Issues Press.

————. 1986. "You Don't Say: Why There Are No Spies in American Sport." Unpublished MS, Division of the Social Sciences, The University of Chicago, Chicago, IL.

————. 1987. "Missing Stories: American Politics and Olympic Discourse." *Garnett Center Journal* 1 (2): 111–142.

————. 1988a. "Double Visions: Olympic Games and American Culture." Pp. 279–294 in *The Olympic Games in Transition,* edited by Jeffrey O. Segrave and Donald Chu. Champaign, IL: Human Kinetics Books.

————. 1988b. "A Prefatory Note to Pierre Bourdieu's 'Program for a Sociology of Sport.'" *Sociology of Sport Journal* 5 (2): 150–152.

————. 1990. "Steroids and the State: Dubin, Melodrama and the Accomplishment of Innocence." *Public Culture* 2 (2): 41–64.

————. 1995. "Interval Training." Pp. 32–53 in *Choreographing History,* edited by Susan Leigh Foster. Bloomington: Indiana University Press.

————. Forthcoming. *Brides of Victory: Nationalism and Gender in Olympic Ritual.* London: Bery.

Majors, Richard. 1998. "Cool Pose: Black Masculinity and Sports." Pp. 15–22 in *African Americans in Sport,* edited by Gary Sailes. New Brunswick, NJ: Transaction.

Marable, Manning. 1984. *Race, Reform and Rebellion: The Second Reconstruction in Black America, 1945–1982.* Jackson: University Press of Mississippi.

Margolis, Bradley, and Jane Piliavin. 1999. "'Stacking' in Major League Baseball: A Multivariate Analysis." *Sociology of Sport Journal* 16: 16–34.

Marqusee, Mike. 1999. *Redemption Song.* New York: R. R. Donnelley & Sons.

Matthews, Vincent, with Neil Amdur. 1974. *My Race Be Won.* New York: Charter House.

Matusow, Allen. 1984. *The Unraveling of America: A History of Liberalism in the 1960s.* New York: Harper and Row.

Mbaye, Keba. 1995. *The International Olympic Committee and South Africa: Analysis and Illustration of a Humanist Sports Policy.* Lausanne, Switzerland: International Olympic Committee.

McAdam, Doug. 1982. *Political Process in the Development of Black Insurgency, 1930–1970*. Chicago: University of Chicago Press.

———. 1983. "Tactical Innovation and the Pace of Insurgency." *American Sociological Review* 48: 735–754.

———. 1988. *Freedom Summer*. Oxford: Oxford University Press.

———. 1998. "On the International Origins of Domestic Political Opportunities." Pp. 251–267 in *Social Movements and American Political Institution*, edited by Anne N. Constain and Andrew S. McFarland. Lanham, MD: Rowman & Littlefield.

McAdam, Doug, and David A. Snow. 1997. *Social Movements: Readings on their Emergence, Moblization, and Dynamics*. Los Angeles: Roxbury.

McCarthy, John D., and Mayer N. Zald. 1977. "Resource Mobilization and Social Movements: A Partial Theory." *American Journal of Sociology* 32: 1212–1241.

McClendon, J. J., and D. S. Eitzen. 1975. "Interracial Contact on Collegiate Basketball Teams: A Test of Sherif's Theory of Superordinate Goals." *Social Science Quarterly* 55: 926–938.

McKay, Jim. 1995. "Just Do It: Corporate Sports Slogans and the Political Economy of 'Enlightened Racism.'" *Discourse: Studies in the Cultural Politics of Education*, 16 (2): 191–201.

McLaren, Richard. 1998. "A New Order: Athletes' Rights and the Court of Aribration at the Olympic Games." *Olympika* 7: 1–24.

McPherson, B. D. 1975. "The Segregation by Playing Position Hypothesis in Sport: An Alternative Hypothesis." *Social Science Quarterly* 55: 960–966.

Mead, Christopher. 1985. *Champion Joe Louis: Black Hero in White America*. New York: Scribner's.

Meggyesy, Dave. 1971. *Out of Their League*. New York: Ramparts Press.

Mercer, Kobena. 1994. *Welcome to the Jungle: New Positions in Black Cultural Studies*. London: Routledge.

Messner, Michael. 1988. "Sports and Male Domination: The Female Athlete as Contested Ideological Terrain." *Sociology of Sport Journal* 5: 197–211.

———. 1990. "Men Studying Masculinity: Some Epistemological Issues in Sport Sociology." *Sociology of Sport Journal* 7: 136–153.

———. 1992. *Power at Play: Sports and the Problem of Masculinity*. Boston: Beacon.

Michener, James A. 1976. *Sports in America*. New York: Random House.

Miller, James. 1987. *Democracy Is in the Streets: From Port Huron to the Siege of Chicago*. New York: Simon and Schuster.

Miller, Patrick B. 1998. "The Anatomy of Scientific Racism: Racialist Responses to Black Athletic Achievement." *Journal of Sport History* 25 (1): 119–151.

Moore, Kenny. 1991a. "A Courageous Stand." *Sports Illustrated*, August 5, 61–77.

———. 1991b. "The Eye of the Storm." *Sports Illustrated*, August 12, 60–73.

Morgan, William J. 1994a. *Leftist Theories of Sport: A Critique and Reconstruction*. Urbana: University of Illinois Press.

———. 1994b. "Hegemony Theory, Social Domination, and Sport: The MacAloon and Hargreaves-Tomlinson Debate Revisited." *Sociology of Sport Journal* 11: 309–29.

Morris, Aldon D. 1984. *The Origins of the Civil Rights Movement: Black Communities Organizing for Change.* New York: Free Press.

Morris, Aldon D., and Carol McClurg Mueller, eds. 1992. *Frontiers in Social Movement Theory.* New Haven, CT: Yale University Press.

Morrison, Toni. 1992. *Playing in the Dark: Whiteness and the Literary Imagination.* Cambridge: Harvard University Press.

Morrison, Toni, and Claudia Brodsky, eds. 1997. *Birth of a Nation'hood: Gaze, Script, and Spectacle in the O.J. Simpson Case.* New York: Pantheon.

Muir, William K., Jr. 1988. "The Primacy of Rhetoric." Pp. 260–295 in *Leadership in the Modern Presidency.* Edited by Fred I. Greenstein. Cambridge: Harvard University Press.

Muller, Norbert. 1998. *International Olympic Academy: Thirty-Eight Years of Lectures, 1961–1998.* Lausanne, Switzerland: International Olympic Committee.

Nelson, Mariah Burton. 1991. *Are We Winning Yet? How Women Are Changing Sports and Sports Are Changing Women.* New York: Random House.

Oates, Stephen B. 1982. *Let the Trumpet Sound: The Life of Martin Luther King, Jr.* New York: Nal Penguin.

Olsen, Jack. 1968. *The Black Athlete: A Shameful Story.* New York: Time-Life Books.

Olson, Mancur, Jr. 1965. *The Logic of Collective Action: Public Goods and the Theory of Groups.* New York: Shocken Books.

Omi, Michael, and Howard Winant. 1994. *Racial Formation in the United States: From the 1960s to the 1990s.* 2nd ed. New York: Routledge.

O'Neil, William L. 1978. *Coming Apart: An Informal History of America in the 1960's.* New York: Quadrangle.

Oriard, Michael. 1991. *Sporting with the Gods: The Rhetoric of Play and Game in American Culture.* Cambridge: Cambridge University Press.

———. 1995. "Muhammad Ali: The Hero in the Age of Mass Media." Pp. 5–23 In *Muhammad Ali: The People's Champ,* edited by Elliot Gorn. Urbana: University of Illinois Press.

Orr, Jack. 1969. *The Black Athlete: His Story in American History.* New York: Publishers Company.

Owens, Jesse, with Paul G. Neimark. 1970. *Blackthink: My Life as a Black Man and a White Man.* New York: Morrow.

———. 1972. *I Have Changed.* New York: Morrow.

Page, Helen. 1997. " 'Black Male' Imagery and Media Containment of African American Men." *American Anthropologist* 99 (1): 99–111.

Palm, Michael. 2002. "Free Agent Justice and the Promotion of Policing: Race, Rights and Remediation in US Professional Sports." Unpublished seminar paper, New York University, American Studies Program.

Palmatier, Robert Allen, and Harold L. Ray. 1989. *Sports Talk: A Dictionary of Sports Metaphors.* New York: Greenwood Press.

Paul, Joan, Richard V. McGhee, and Helen Fant. 1984. "The Arrival and Ascendance of Black Athletes in the Southeastern Conference, 1966–1980." *Phylon* 45: 284–297.

Payne, Charles M. 1995. *I've Got the Light of Freedom: The Organizing Tradition and the Mississippi Freedom Struggle.* Berkeley and Los Angeles: University of California Press.

Pepe, Phil. 1970. *Stand Tall: The Lew Alcindor Story.* New York: Grosset and Dunlap.

Phillips, Bob, ed. 1968. *Official Report of the Olympic Games, 1968: The British Olympic Association.* Manchester, UK: World Sports.

Phillips, J. C. 1976. "Toward an Explanation of Racial Variations in the Top-Level Sports Participation." *International Review of Sport Sociology* 11: 39–55.

Piccone, Paul. 1988. "Reinterpreting 1968: Mythology of the Make." *Telos* 76: 7–43

Piven, Frances Fox, and Richard Cloward. 1977. *Poor People's Movements: Why They Succeed, How They Fail.* New York: Pantheon.

Plummer, Brenda Gayle. 1996. *A Rising Wind: Black Americans and U.S. Foreign Affairs, 1933–1960.* Chapel Hill: University of North Carolina Press.

Pomper, Gerald. 1985. *The Election of 1984: Reports and Interpretations.* Chatham, NJ: Chatham House.

Quezada, Sergio Aguayo. 1998. *1968: Los Archivos de la Violencia.* Grijalbo: Reforma.

Radhakrishnan, R. 1996. "Toward an Effective Intellectual: Foucault or Gramsci?" Pp. 27–61 in *Diasporic Meditations: Between Home and Location.* Minneapolis: University of Minnesota Press.

Ragin, Charles C., and Howard S. Becker. 1992. *What Is a Case? Exploring the Foundations of Social Inquiry.* New York: Cambridge University Press.

Reed, Adolph Jr., ed. 1986. *Race, Politics and Culture.* New York: Greenwood Press.

Reich, Kenneth. 1986. *Making It Happen: Peter Ueberroth and the 1984 Olympics.* Santa Barbara: Capra Press.

Riccella, Christopher. 1991. *Muhammad Ali.* Los Angeles: Melrose Square.

Riordan, Jim, and Arnd Kruger. 1999. *The International Politics of Sport in the 20th Century.* London: E & FM Spon (Routledge).

Roberts, C. 1991. *South Africa's Struggle for Olympic Legitimacy.* Cape Town: Township Publishing.

Robinson, Jackie, with Alfred Duckett. 1972. *I Never Had It Made.* New York: Putnam.

Roediger, David R. 1995 [1991]. *The Wages of Whiteness: Race and the Making of the American Working Class.* New York: Verso.

———. 2002. *Colored White: Transcending the Racial Past.* Berkeley and Los Angeles: University of California Press.

Ross, Charles K. 1999. *Outside the Lines: African Americans and the Integration of the National Football League.* New York: New York University Press.

Russell, Bill (as told to William McSweeny). 1966. *Go Up for Glory.* New York: Coward-McCann.

Sahlins, Marshall. 1985. *Islands of History.* Chicago: University of Chicago Press.

Sailes, Gary. 1991. "The Myth of Black Sports Supremacy." *Journal of Black Studies* 21 (June): 480–487.

———, ed. 1998. *African Americans in Sport.* New Brunswick, NJ: Transaction.

Sammons, Jeffrey T. 1988. *Beyond the Ring: The Role of Boxing in American Society.* Urbana: University of Illinois Press.

————. 1994. " 'Race' and Sport: A Critical, Historical Examination." *Journal of Sport History* 21 (3): 203–278.

————. 1995. "Rebel with a Cause: Muhammad Ali as Sixties Protest Symbol." Pp. 154–180 in *Muhammad Ali: The People's Champ*, edited by Elliot J. Gorn. Urbana: University of Illinois Press.

Sarantakes, Nicholas Evan. 1997. "Richard Nixon, Sportswriter: The President, His Historical All-Star Baseball Team, and the Election of 1972." *Journal of Sport History* 24 (2): 192–202.

Schaap, Dick. 1968. "The Revolt of the Black Athletes." *Look* 32 (August 6): 72–77.

Schantz, Otto. 1995. "The Presidency of Avery Brundage." Pp. 77–200 in *The International Olympic Committee—One Hundred Years: The Ideas, the Presidents, the Achievements*, vol. 2, edited by Raymond Gafner and Norbert Muller. Lausanne: International Olympic Committee.

————. 1996. "From Rome (1960) to Montreal (1976)." Pp. 131–139 in *Olympic Ceremonies: Historical Continuity and Cultural Exchange*, edited by Miguel de Moragas, John MacAloon, and Montserrat Llines. Lausanne: International Olympic Committee.

Schollander, Don, and Duke Savage. 1971. *Deep Water*. New York: Crown.

Scott, Jack. 1969. *Athletics for Athletes*. Berkeley and Hayward, CA: Otherways.

————. 1971. *The Athletic Revolution*. New York: Free Press.

————. 1973. "Sport and the Radical Ethic" *Quest* (winter): 71–77.

Scully, G. 1974. "Discrimination: The Case of Baseball." Pp. 221–274 in *Government and the Sports Business*, edited by Roger G. Noll. Washington, DC: Brookings Institute.

Sendler, D. 1969. "The Black Athlete—1968." In *In Black America, 1968: The Year of Awakening*, edited by P. W. Romeio. New York: Publishers Company.

Sewell, William H., Jr. 1996a. "Historical Events as Transformation of Structures." *Theory and Society* 25: 841–881.

————. 1996b. "Three Temporalities." Pp. 245–280 in *The Historic Turn in the Human Sciences*, edited by Terrance McDonald. Ann Arbor: University of Michigan Press.

————. 1999. "The Concept(s) of Culture." Pp. 35–61 in *Beyond the Cultural Turn*, edited by Victoria Bonnell and Lynn Hunt. Berkeley and Los Angeles: University of California Press.

Shivers, Jay S., and Joseph W. Halper. 1981. *The Crisis in Urban Recreational Services*. Madison, WI: Associated University Presses.

Simons, William. 1985. "Jackie Robinson and the American Mind: Journalistic Perceptions of the Reintegration of Baseball." *Journal of Sport History* 12 (spring): 39–64.

Singh, Nikhil Pal. 1998. "The Black Panthers and the 'Undeveloped Country' of the Left." Pp. 57–105 in *The Black Panther Party [Reconsidered]*, edited by Charles E. Jones. Baltimore: Black Classic Press.

Sitkoff, Harvard. 1981. *The Struggle for Black Equality, 1954–1980*. New York: Hill and Wang.

Skrentny, John David. 1998. "The Effect of the Cold War on African-American

Civil Rights: America and the World Audience, 1945–1968." *Theory and Society* 27: 237–285.

Smith, Red. 1982. *To Absent Friends, From Red Smith*. New York: Atheneum.

Sonenshein, Raphael J. 1993. *Politics in Black and White: Race and Power in Los Angeles*. Princeton, NJ: Princeton University Press.

Spady, William G. 1976. "Commentary on Sport and the New Left." Pp. 212–223 in *Social Problems in Athletics: Essays on the Sociology of Sport,* edited by D. M. Landers. Urbana: University of Illinois Press.

Spivey, Donald. 1983. "The Black Athlete in Big-Time Intercollegiate Sport, 1941–1968." *Phylon* 44 (June): 116–125.

———. 1984. "Black Consciousness and Olympic Protest Movement." Pp. 239–262 in *Sport in America: New Historical Perspectives,* edited by Donald Spivey. Westpoint, CT: Greenwood Press.

———. 1988. "End Jim Crow in Sports: The Protest at New York University, 1940–1941." *Journal of Sport History* 15 (winter): 282–303.

Stinchcombe, Arthur L. 1982. "The Deep Structure of Moral Categories: Eighteenth-Century French Stratification and the Revolution." Pp. 66–95 in *Structural Sociology,* edited by Ino Rossi. New York: Cambridge University Press.

Tarrow, Sidney. 1998. *Power in Movement*. 2nd ed. Cambridge: Cambridge University Press.

Theberge, Nancy. 1985. "Toward a Feminist Alternative to Sport as a Male Preserve." *Quest* 37 (2): 193–202.

Thelen, David P. 1999. "The Nation and Beyond: Transnational Perspectives on United States History." *Journal of American History* 86: 965–975.

Thirer, Joel. 1978. "Politics and Protest at the Olympic Games." Pp. 153–159 in *Sport and International Relations,* edited by Benjamin Lowe, David B. Kanin, and Andrew Strenk. Champaign, IL: Stipes.

Trujillo, Nick. 1991. "Hegemonic Masculinity on the Mound: Media Representations of Nolan Ryan and American Sports Culture." *Critical Studies in Mass Communication* 8: 290–308.

Turner, Victor. 1967. *Forest of Symbols*. Ithaca, NY: Cornell University Press.

———. 1969. *The Ritual Process: Structure and Anti-Structure*. Ithaca, NY: Cornell University Press.

Tygiel, Jules. 1983. *Baseball's Great Experiment: Jackie Robinson and His Legacy*. New York: Vintage.

———, ed. 1998. *The Jackie Robinson Reader: Perspectives on an American Hero*. New York: Plume.

Ueberhort, Horst. 1976. "The New Generation and Olympism in West Germany." *International Olympic Academy,* 16th Session (July). Lausanne, Switzerland: International Olympic Committee.

Ueberroth, Peter, with Richard Levin and Amy Quinn. 1985. *Made in America: His Own Story*. New York: Fawcett Cress.

Unger, Irwin, and Debi Unger. 1988. *Turning Point: 1968*. New York: Charles Scribner's Sons.

Van Deburg, William L. 1992. *New Day in Babylon: The Black Power Movement and American Culture, 1965–1975*. Chicago: University of Chicago Press.

———.1997. *Black Camelot: African-American Culture Heroes in Their Times, 1960–1980*. Chicago: University of Chicago Press.

Von Eschen, Penny. 1997. *Race Against Empire: Black Americans and Anticolonialism, 1937–1957*. Ithaca, NY: Cornell University Press.

Wacquant, Loïc J.D. 1992. "The Social Logic of Boxing in Black Chicago: Toward a Sociology of Pugilism." *Sociology of Sport Journal* 9: 221–254.

———. 1995. "The Pugilistic Point of View: How Boxers Think and Feel About Their Trade." *Theory and Society* 24: 489–535.

Walk, Stephan. 1995. "The Footrace Metaphor in American Presidential Rhetoric." *Sociology of Sport Journal* 12: 36–55.

Wallace, Michele. 1978. *Black Macho and the Myth of the Superwoman*. New York: Dial Press.

Wallechinsky, David. 1984. *The Complete Book of the Olympics*. New York: Penguin.

Weisbrot, Robert. 1990. *Freedom Bound: A History of America's Civil Rights Movement*. New York: Plume.

Wenn, Stephen R. 1993. "A History of the International Olympic Committee and Television, 1936–1980." Ph.D. dissertation, Pennsylvania State University, Department of Exercise and Sport Science.

Wenn, Stephen R., and Jeffrey P. Wenn. 1993. "Muhammad Ali and the Convergence of Olympic Sport and U. S. Diplomacy in the 1980s: A Reassessment from Behind the Scenes at the U. S. State Department." *Olympika* 2: 45–66.

West, Cornell. 1990. "The New Cultural Politics of Difference." In *Out There: Marginalization and Contemporary Cultures,* edited by Russell Ferguson, Martha Gever, Trinh T. Minha, and Cornell West. New York and Cambridge: New Museum of Contemporary Art and the Massachusetts Institute of Technology Press.

Whitson, David. 1994. "The Embodiment of Gender: Discipline, Domination and Empowerment." Pp. 353–372 in *Women, Sport and Culture,* edited by Susan Birrell and Cheryl L. Cole. Champaign, IL: Human Kinetics.

Wiggins, David K. 1983a. "The 1936 Olympic Games in Berlin: The Response of America's Black Press." *Research Quarterly for Exercise and Sport* 54: 278–292.

———. 1983b. "Wendell Smith, the *Pittsburgh Courier-Journal* and the Campaign to Include Blacks in Organized Baseball, 1933–1945." *Journal of Sport History* 10 (summer): 5–29.

———. 1986. "From Plantation to Playing Field: Historical Writings on the Black Athlete in American Sport." *Research Quarterly for Exercise and Sport* 57 (2): 101–116.

———. 1988. "The Future of College Athletics Is at Stake: Black Athletes and Racial Turmoil on Three Predominately White University Campuses, 1968–1972." *Journal of Sport History* 15 (winter): 304–333.

———. 1989. "Great Speed But Little Stamina: The Historical Debate Over Black Athletic Superiority." *Journal of Sport History* 16: 158–185.

———. 1991. "Prized Performers, by Frequently Overlooked Students: The Involvement of Black Athletes in Intercollegiate Sports on Predominately White University Campuses, 1890–1972." *Research Quarterly for Exercise and Sport* 62 (June): 164–177.

———. 1993. "Critical Events Affecting Racism in Athletics." Pp. 23–49 in *Racism in College Athletics: The African-American Athlete's Experience,* edited by Dana Brooks and Ronald Althouse. Morgantown, WV: Fitness Information Technology.

———. 1994. "The Notion of Double-Consciousness and the Involvement of Black Athletes in American Sport." Pp. 133–55 in *Ethnicity and Sport in North American History and Culture,* edited by George Eisen and David K. Wiggins. Westport, CT: Greenwood Press.

———. 1997. *Glory Bound: Black Athletes in White America.* Syracuse, NY: Syracuse University Press.

Willis, Paul. 1982. "Women in Sport in Ideology." Pp. 117–135 in *Sport, Culture and Ideology,* edited by Jennifer Hargreaves. London: Routledge and Keegan Paul.

Wolf, David. 1972. *Foul! The Connie Hawkins Story.* New York: Holt, Rinehart and Winston.

Wood, Joe, ed. 1992. *Malcolm X: In Our Own Image.* New York: St. Martin's Press.

Wooden, John, with Jack Tobin. 1988. *They Call Me Coach.* Chicago: Contemporary Books.

Wuthnow, Robert. 1987. *Meaning and Moral Order: Explorations in Cultural Analysis.* Berkeley and Los Angeles: University of California Press.

Yetman, Norman, and D. Stanley Eitzen. 1984. "Racial Dynamics in American Sport: Continuity and Change." Pp. 324–345 in *Sport in Contemporary Society,* edited by D. Stanley Eitzen. New York: St. Martin's.

Young, A. S. 1963. *Negro Firsts in Sports.* Chicago: Johnson Publishing.

Yu, Henry. 2000. "How Tiger Woods Lost His Stripes: Post-National American Studies as a History of Race, Migration, and the Commodification of Culture." In *Post-Nationalist American Studies,* edited by John C. Rowe. Berkeley and Los Angeles: University of California Press.

Index

activism, post–civil rights: athletes complacent to progressive shift, 46; misleading characterizations of, 41–42; structural vs. traditional racial justice, 42, 43, 99, 234–35, 244

affirmative action, 246, 255

Agnew, Spiro (vice president), 229, 230

Ahmad, Omar, 103

Alcindor, Lew: admiration for Wooden, John, 226–27; comments at Thanksgiving Day Workshop, 56; disinterest in 1968 Olympic tryout invitation, 128, 213; explanation of tryout disinterest, 129; Islamic name, 177; NBC *Today* appearance, 145, 295n. 41; Operation Sports Rescue Program, 145, 177; OPHR participation, 29; progressive motivation, 51–52; refusal to commit to boycott, 57

Ali, Muhammad: appearance at Atlanta Olympic Games, 272; athletic accomplishments, 272; despised figure, 33; historiography of, 282n. 22; mainstream icon, 10; masculinity, 86, 87–88; model for athletes, 40, 177, 273; National Black Power Conference, 30; Olsen's book on, 221; support of Olympic boycott, 62

Allen, Lucius, 51, 128, 213

Allen, Neil, 143

alternative bus tours, 274

Amateur Athletic Union (AAU), 30; administrative structure, 212; counterresistance, 231; muted response to victory stand demonstration, 208; rivalry with NCAA, 193–94, 217, 229, 305n. 10

Amateur Sports Act of 1978, xxi, 191, 246–47

Amdur, Neil, 192, 242

American Committee on Africa. *See* Robinson, Jackie, American Committee on Africa

American Communist Party, 57, 61

American Jewish Council, 102, 111

American Sports Creed, 204, 205. *See also* Edwards, Harry

Andros, Dee, 181

Arledge, Roone, 154, 296n. 60

Ashe, Arthur, 41, 176, 198, 266, 291n. 38, 296n. 56, 313n. 29

athletes' rights, xxi, 189, 191

athletic revolution, 181; democratic view of sport, 189; human rights stance, 184; impacts, 191–92; institutional response, 194; literature on, 192, 239; native term, 301n. 30; parallels with black athletic revolution, 185; shortcomings of, 192–94

Atlanta Olympic Games, 1996, 271–74

Autobiography of Malcolm X, The, 52

Axthelm, Pete, 304n. 68; backlash against Smith, Tommie, 94; "The Black Athlete," 143; boycott coverage, 106, 144, 152; description of NYAC boycott, 105; and Carlos and Smith, 20; Carlos, as consultant to, 255; OPHR, attention given, 141; and Smith, Denise, 125

Bantam, Mike, 243

Barnes, Ernie, 256

Barnes, Everett, 147, 163–64

Bass, Amy, 275n. 5

Beamon, Bob: black sock protest, 162; creation of professional track circuit, 200; kicked off University of Texas at El Paso team, 112, 177; NYAC participation, 291n. 31; record-setting jump, 238; response to boycott, 286n. 19

Beaumont, Compte de, 107

Beddos, Dick, 155